Der Einfluss neuer Technologien auf die Ausbildung von Translatoren / The Influence of New Technologies on Translator and Interpreter Education

FORUM TRANSLATIONSWISSENSCHAFT

Herausgegeben von / Edited by
Lew N. Zybatow, Alena Petrova, Astrid Schmidhofer und / and
Michael Ustaszewski

BD./VOL. 25

Alena Petrova, Bianca Prandi & Astrid Schmidhofer (Hrsg./eds.)

Der Einfluss neuer Technologien auf die Ausbildung von Translatoren / The Influence of New Technologies on Translator and Interpreter Education

PETER LANG
Berlin · Bruxelles · Chennai · Lausanne · New York · Oxford

Bibliografische Information der Deutschen Nationalbibliothek
Die Deutsche Nationalbibliothek verzeichnet diese Publikation in der Deutschen Nationalbibliografie; detaillierte bibliografische Daten sind im Internet über http://dnb.d-nb.de abrufbar.

Library of Congress Cataloging-in-Publication Data
Names: Petrova, Alena editor | Prandi, Bianca, 1990- editor | Schmidhofer, Astrid editor
Title: Der Einfluss neuer Technologien auf die Ausbildung von Translatoren = the influence of new technologies on translator and interpreter education / Alena Petrova, Bianca Prandi, Astrid Schmidhofer (Hrsg./eds.).
Other titles: Influence of new technologies on translator and interpreter education
Description: Berlin ; New York : Peter Lang, 2026. | Series: Forum Translationswissenschaft, 1610-286X ; Bd./vol. 25 | Includes bibliographical references and index. | Includes 10 English and 4 German contributions
Identifiers: LCCN 2025047854 (print) | LCCN 2025047855 (ebook) | ISBN 9783631917756 hardback | ISBN 9783631917763 pdf | ISBN 9783631917770 epub
Subjects: LCSH: Translating and interpreting--Study and teaching--Technological innovations | Translators--Training of | Translating and interpreting--Technological innovations | Artificial intelligence--Educational applications | Translators--Effect of technological innovations on | LCGFT: Essays
Classification: LCC P306.5 .E46 2026 (print) | LCC P306.5 (ebook)
LC record available at https://lccn.loc.gov/2025047854
LC ebook record available at https://lccn.loc.gov/2025047855

Abbildung auf dem Umschlag:
Tempel: Arbeit von Schüler/inne/n der 2.a des GRG
Ettenreichgasse, gemeinsam mit Mag. Franz Dvoracek.
Abdruck mit freundlicher Genehmigung des
Österreichischen Bundesministeriums für Unterricht und
kulturelle Angelegenheiten. Abt. 1/4 Alfred Fischl.

Herausgeberinnen und Verlag danken dem Vizerektorat für Forschung der Universität Innsbruck für die Förderung der Publikation. / Gratefully acknowledging financial support by the Vice Rectorate for Research at the University of Innsbruck.

ISSN 1610-286X
ISBN 978-3-631-91775-6 (Print)
ISBN 978-3-631-91776-3 (ePDF)
ISBN 978-3-631-91777-0 (ePUB)
DOI 10.3726/b21748

Verlegt durch Peter Lang GmbH, Berlin, Deutschland

info@peterlang.com

www.peterlang.com

Kontaktadresse nach EU-Produktsicherheitsverordnung: gpsr@peterlang.com

Inhaltsverzeichnis/Contents

Preface

In recent years, technological developments primarily fuelled by advances in artificial intelligence (AI) have led to rapid, almost revolutionary changes in the translation industry and, to a lesser extent, the interpreting industry. This presents educational institutions with the challenge of adapting their programmes to meet the employability requirements set out in the key pillars of the European Higher Education Area. At the same time, such adjustments are often aimed at presenting training programmes as market-relevant and future-proof and thus counteracting declining enrolment rates.

Against this backdrop, the present volume strives to contribute to mapping AI-induced developments in translation studies training programmes. With this aim in mind, we have sought to include both general perspectives and texts focused on specific phases of training. The chapters were contributed by authors from 12 universities in seven European countries, thus providing a diverse picture of developments in translation studies programmes in the European area.

The first part of this volume deals with general questions concerning the use of generative AI tools. Accordingly, the first two contributions focus on the concept of *AI literacy*, which is currently being discussed – not only in translation studies, but also in other disciplines – as an important goal of modern university education. The importance of familiarity with this concept is examined by Sonja Trzin Berta (University of Innsbruck). In her chapter, she highlights the risks of digitalisation and presents various models of AI literacy that should enable students to overcome the challenges associated therewith. The chapter by Ralph Krüger (TH Köln - University of Applied Sciences) introduces a definitive proposal for the field of translator and interpreter training; therein, the author presents a domain-specific framework of AI literacy for translation, interpreting and specialised communication with various levels of competence that also takes into account automation trends in the language-services industry. The contribution by Jim Ureel (University of Antwerp), Enrique Cerezo Herrero (University of Valencia), Astrid Schmidhofer (University of Innsbruck) and Melita Koletnik (University of Maribor and University of Vienna) explores how and for what purposes students of translation studies programmes use generative AI-based tools.

The subsequent part of the volume is dedicated to the use of AI tools in translator training. The chapter by Belén Lozano Sañudo (University of Valencia) illustrates how machine translation (MT) can be used at an early stage to raise awareness of the potential and limitations of MT and to boost motivation, taking the translation of advertising texts as an example. Borislava Eraković (University of Novi Sad) presents a study on research skills and post-editing using MT and generative AI in the early stages of translator training and emphasises the need for targeted training of these skills. Maria Elisa Fina (Ca' Foscari University of Venice) offers specific suggestions on how students can be introduced to post-editing and develop the necessary competences required.

The following three contributions focus on specific areas of translator training. Juan Antonio Albaladejo Martínez (University of Alicante) uses the example of a short literary text to outline a teaching unit in which students use MT and AI-generated translations to compare and analyse different solutions to previously identified translation problems. The chapter by Katharina Walter (University of Innsbruck) explores the effects of using MT and generative AI on students' creativity when translating a poem and how these tools can nevertheless be used effectively in the translation of poetry. In his chapter, Marco Agnetta (University of Innsbruck) looks at the automation of individual steps in the subtitling of videos and discusses how students evaluate the process when working in different language combinations.

The penultimate section of this volume brings together contributions from other areas of translator training. It begins with a chapter by Rossella Resi (University of Innsbruck) and Christian Lang (Kaleidoscope GmbH), who analyse in detail the challenges posed by AI to terminology and its teaching in university courses. Irene Fuentes-Pérez (University of Alcalá de

Henares) and Cristina Plaza-Lara (University of Málaga) discuss the impact of AI on project management and the skills required for the new era based on an exploratory interview study. The section is rounded off by a chapter on interpreter training by Bianca Prandi, Ira Torresi and Nicoletta Spinolo (University of Bologna), who present the new Interpreting and Technologies for Communication (InTeCo) curriculum in the master's degree programme in Interpreting, which has been offered at the University of Bologna since the winter semester of 2024/25.

The final section of the volume includes two contributions on translation-oriented language training. Eva Seidl (University of Graz) discusses which skills should be prioritised in this training in the age of AI tools. The usefulness of such tools as a tutor and proofreading resource in this context is examined by Saverio Carpentieri, Natalie Mair and Astrid Schmidhofer (University of Innsbruck) with reference to the language pairs German/Italian and German/Spanish.

All of the contributions to this volume could be submitted in either German or English. In the German-language contributions, authors were free to select their preferred default form regarding gender-inclusive language.

We would like to thank Stefanie Pörnbacher and Matthias Schaffrath, who contributed to the editing of the texts, as well as our colleagues who assisted us in the peer review process.

The editors
Innsbruck, February 2026

Vorwort

In den letzten Jahren haben technologische Entwicklungen, die vor allem auf Fortschritten im Bereich der KI basieren, zu rasanten, fast revolutionären Veränderungen in der Übersetzungsindustrie und, in etwas geringerem Ausmaß, der Dolmetschbranche geführt. Dies stellt Ausbildungsstätten vor die Herausforderung, ihre Programme so umzustellen, dass diese der in den Grundpfeilern des Europäischen Hochschulraums geforderten Employabilität gerecht werden. Gleichzeitig zielen solche Anpassungen oft auch darauf ab, Ausbildungsprogramme als marktrelevant und zukunftsfähig zu präsentieren und damit rückläufigen Studierendenzahlen entgegenzuwirken.

Vor diesem Hintergrund möchte der vorliegende Band einen Beitrag dazu leisten, die KI-induzierten Entwicklungen in translationswissenschaftlichen Ausbildungsprogrammen abzubilden. Dabei war es uns ein Anliegen, sowohl allgemeine als auch auf bestimmte Phasen der Ausbildung fokussierte Perspektiven zu berücksichtigen. Die Texte wurden von Beitragenden aus 12 Universitäten in 7 europäischen Ländern verfasst und bieten daher ein vielfältiges Bild der Entwicklungen in der translationswissenschaftlichen Ausbildung im europäischen Raum.

Der erste Block beschäftigt sich mit allgemeinen Fragen der Nutzung von generativen KI-Tools. Die ersten beiden Beiträge thematisieren das Konzept der *KI literacy*, das derzeit – nicht nur in der Translationswissenschaft, sondern auch in vielen anderen Disziplinen – als wichtige Zielsetzung moderner universitärer Ausbildung diskutiert wird. Deren Bedeutung zeigt Sonja Trzin Berta (Universität Innsbruck) auf. Sie beleuchtet in ihrem Kapitel Risiken der Digitalisierung und stellt verschiedene Modelle der *KI literacy* vor, die dazu befähigen sollen, die mit der Digitalisierung verbundenen Herausforderungen zu bewältigen. Einen konkreten Vorschlag für das Feld der translationswissenschaftlichen Ausbildung bietet der Beitrag von Ralph Krüger (TH Köln); darin stellt der Autor ein domänenspezifisches Framework der *KI literacy* für das Übersetzen, das Dolmetschen und die Fachkommunikation mit verschiedenen Kompetenzniveaus vor, das auch auf Automatisierungstendenzen in der Sprachdienstleistungsindustrie eingeht. Wie und wofür Studierende translationswissenschaftlicher Studiengänge auf generativer KI basierende Tools konkret nutzen, wird im Beitrag von Jim Ureel (Universität Antwerpen), Enrique Cerezo Herrero (Universität Valencia), Astrid Schmidhofer (Universität Innsbruck) und Melita Koletnik (Universität Maribor und Universität Wien) untersucht.

Der nächste Teil ist dem Einsatz von KI-Tools in der Übersetzungsdidaktik gewidmet. Das Kapitel von Belén Lozano Sañudo (Universität Valencia) zeigt anhand von Werbetexten, wie maschinelle Übersetzung bereits im frühen Stadium zur Sensibilisierung für die Möglichkeiten und Grenzen der MÜ und Steigerung der Motivation eingesetzt werden kann. Borislava Eraković (Universität Novi Sad) stellt eine Studie zu Recherchekompetenz und Post-Edition mithilfe von MÜ und generativer KI in der Frühphase der Übersetzungsausbildung vor und weist auf die Notwendigkeit hin, diese Kompetenzen gezielt zu trainieren. Konkrete Vorschläge dazu bietet der Beitrag von Maria Elisa Fina (Ca' Foscari Universität Venedig), der beschreibt, wie Studierende an das Posteditieren herangeführt werden und die dafür erforderlichen Kompetenzen entwickeln können.

Die nächsten drei Beiträge thematisieren spezifische Bereiche der Übersetzungsdidaktik. Juan Antonio Albaladejo Martínez (Universität Alicante) skizziert am Beispiel eines kurzen literarischen Texts eine Unterrichtseinheit, in der Studierende anhand von MÜ und KI-generierten Übersetzungen verschiedene Lösungen zu zuvor identifizierten Übersetzungsproblemen vergleichen und analysieren. Die Arbeit von Katharina Walter (Universität Innsbruck) untersucht mithilfe eines Gedichts, welche Auswirkungen der Einsatz von MÜ und generativer KI auf die Kreativität der Studierenden beim Übersetzen haben und wie diese Tools dennoch sinnvoll in der Lyrikübersetzung eingesetzt werden können. Der Text von Marco Agnetta (Universität Innsbruck) beschäftigt sich mit der Automatisierung einzelner

Schritte bei der Untertitelung von Videos und wie Studierende diese für die Arbeit in unterschiedlichen Sprachkombinationen bewerten.

Der vorletzte Block vereint Beiträge aus anderen Bereichen der translationswissenschaftlichen Ausbildung. Er beginnt mit dem Kapitel von Rossella Resi (Universität Innsbruck) und Christian Lang (Kaleidoscope GmbH), die die Herausforderungen, vor die KI die Terminologie und deren Vermittlung in der universitären Lehre stellt, ausführlich analysieren. Die Auswirkungen von KI auf das Projektmanagement und die für die neue Ära notwendigen Kompetenzen wurden von Irene Fuentes-Pérez (Universität Alcalá de Henares) und Cristina Plaza-Lara (Universität Málaga) in einer explorativen Interviewstudie untersucht. Abgerundet wird dieser Block durch ein Kapitel zur Dolmetschausbildung: Bianca Prandi, Ira Torresi und Nicoletta Spinolo (alle Universität Bologna) stellen den neuen Studienplan *Interpreting and Technologies for Communication* (InTeCo) im Master Dolmetschen vor, der seit dem Wintersemester 2024/25 an der Universität von Bologna angeboten wird.

Die abschließende Sektion umfasst zwei Beiträge zur translationsorientierten Sprachausbildung. Eva Seidl (Universität Graz) diskutiert, welche Kompetenzen in Zeiten von KI-Tools in der translationsorientierten Sprachausbildung besonders stark gefördert werden sollten. Die Nutzbarkeit solcher Tools als Tutor und Korrekturwerkzeug in diesem Kontext wird von Saverio Carpentieri, Natalie Mair und Astrid Schmidhofer (alle Universität Innsbruck) anhand der Sprachenpaare Deutsch/Italienisch und Deutsch/Spanisch untersucht.

Die Beiträge konnten wahlweise auf Deutsch oder Englisch verfasst werden. In deutschsprachigen Beiträgen entschieden die Verfassenden selbst, in welcher Form sie gendergerechte Sprache nutzen.

Wir bedanken uns auch herzlich bei Stefanie Pörnbacher und Matthias Schaffrath, die an der redaktionellen Bearbeitung der Texte mitgewirkt haben, sowie bei allen, die uns beim Peer-Review unterstützt haben.

Die Herausgeberinnen
Innsbruck, im Februar 2026

Digital literacy: what is it, and do translators and interpreters need it?

Sonja Trzin Berta
University of Innsbruck

ABSTRACT
The world has become increasingly digital, affecting media consumption habits and lifestyles. Excessive use of online media and the widespread use of generative artificial intelligence (GenAI) bring many challenges – political polarisation, fake news, attention problems, overreliance on technology, deterioration of language skills and less engagement in democratic and civic activities. It is believed that digital literacy could help mitigate these issues. Digital literacy is a multifaceted concept, with several different frameworks in use. These frameworks were put forward by organisations such as the OECD, UNESCO, and the European Commission for the development of policies, achievement and measurement of goals such as the SDGs. In translation and interpreting, digital literacy has mostly been applied in the context of machine translation and GenAI, while topics such as media literacy and balanced use of technology have not been prominently featured. As translators and interpreters rely heavily on the use of media in many aspects of their work, it is important for digital literacy to comprise media literacy and other literacies which allow for effective use of modern technology.

Keywords: digital literacy, media consumption, social media, internet, AI

1. Introduction

It is no understatement that rapid technological development has radically transformed how we live and learn and, with that, how we work. Reading newspapers or watching TV to get the latest news is history, as are the days when the internet or a hand-held device were novel. Social media and AI seem to rule the world of younger generations.

This, in turn, leads to the following question: What could this new way of media and technology consumption do to translation and interpreting students? Many potential problems arise from using the latest technology, most notably AI and social media: fake news and disinformation, shorter attention span, overreliance on the new technology, the perpetuation of different biases, information overload, lack of critical thinking skills, mental health issues and even media addiction (Chan/Colloton 2024, pp. 57–58).

Digital literacy is perceived as an antidote to many of these dangers (International Panel on the Information Environment 2024). However, digital literacy is a complex concept with no single definition or model used to explain it. Is it a skill that can be taught and learned, or is there no need for it because it is something that digital natives are born with? One way to adapt teaching to the aforementioned changes is to understand what we are up against and what this umbrella term might mean.

This paper is divided into four main sections. Section 2 examines the definition of digital literacy, while section 3 looks at different digital literacy frameworks and proposed competencies. It also takes a closer look at how the concept of digital literacy has been evolving in translation and interpreting studies and the state of the current debate. Section 4 examines media consumption habits and risks in the context of digital literacy, and section 5 highlights their relevance for translators and interpreters. The goal of this paper is twofold. The first is to warn about the dangers that the lack of digital literacy, especially through a prism of media consumption habits, poses to (trainee) translators and interpreters as this has not been reflected enough in the current debate on digital literacy in translation and interpreting. The second goal is to offer ideas on how digital literacy might be incorporated into teaching.

2. Definition of digital literacy

Although literacy has for decades been at the forefront of many a public discussion, most notably concerning education and teaching, before the 1970s, the term referred exclusively to reading, or rather, not being able to read, i.e., being illiterate (Lankshear/Knobel 2007, p. 7). From the 1970s until the present time, depending on the science whose primary focus it was as well as socio-historical and technological developments, different kinds of literacies emerged: computer literacy, media literacy, web literacy, information literacy (Nichols/Stornaiuolo 2019, pp. 14–17). Nowadays, the omnipresence of AI in every segment of society has put much focus on AI literacy, defined as "a set of competencies that enables individuals to critically evaluate AI technologies; communicate and collaborate effectively with AI; and use AI as a tool online, at home, and in the workplace" (Long/Magerko 2020, p. 2). In a way, these definitions imply that one can communicate and discern meaning. However, they also imply that, to be effective, one needs to approach the media, computers or information critically and knowledgeably (Lankshear/Knobel 2007, p. 20).

Contrary to what one might think, digital literacy is a term that dates back to the 1990s. Although not the first person to have used the phrase, Gilster was the first to propose its definition in the broad form, and the phrase has since been in widespread use (Bawden 2008, pp. 18–21; Belshaw 2012, pp. 83–84; Buckingham 2008, p. 76; Nichols/Stornaiuolo 2019, pp. 17–18). For Gilster, digital literacy is: "[…] the ability to understand and use information in multiple formats from a wide range of sources when it is presented via computers" (1997, p. 1). Building on Gilster's definition, Bawden suggests that digital literacy is "a framework for integrating various other literacies and skill-sets […]" pointing out that it is not "sensible to try to reduce it to a finite number of linear stages," and warning that digital literacy is an evolving concept depending on the individual's and societal changes (Bawden 2008, p. 28). Other authors also strongly highlight that digital literacy is an ever-changing concept dependent on the context that needs to be adaptable to suit educational needs (Belshaw 2012, p. 204; Chetty et al. 2017, p. 4). There is criticism that the proliferation of the term *literacy* has rendered it void of its broader meaning, reducing it to merely a competence or skill, instead of entailing the notion of education (Buckingham 2010, p. 60). Furthermore, some believe that media literacy or media competence – defined as a competence that would enable one to distinguish between true and false information, primarily in the context of combating fake news, to know how to find information and how to assess it – does not exist as it is impossible to differentiate between true and false without previous knowledge or a network thereof (Spitzer 2020, pp. 77–79).

As it might be expected, more recent attempts to define digital literacy reflect rapid technological progress. Still, these definitions are similar to the previous notions of digital literacy, focusing on digital technology and its importance in helping individuals become successful participants and contributors in a world dominated by the digital information landscape (Baron 2019) or critical use of technology, with emphasis on communication and problem-solving skills (UNESCO, n.d.). In some definitions, digital literacy is described as the "critical enabler of economic transformation as it promotes employment opportunities through the ability to access digital content and online services" (Chetty et al. 2017, p. 5).

Table 1: Four pillars of digital literacy research (Tinmaz et al. 2022)

4 pillars of digital literacy research			
1. Literacies	**2. Competencies**	**3. Skills**	**4. Thinking**
Computer literacy **Media literacy** **Cultural literacy**	Problem solving Safety Information processing Content creation Communication	Communication skills Ethics Social intelligence	Critical thinking Computational thinking Analytical thinking
Intertwined with personal and professional life, technological progress, networking, academia, citizenship, and education.			

Although digital literacy is not a straightforward concept, research, shows that four recurrent themes dominate the academic landscape on this topic (Table 1): 1) literacies (such as computer literacy, media literacy, cultural literacy, etc.), 2) competencies (problem solving, safety, information processing, content creation, communication, etc.), 3) skills (communication skills, ethics, social intelligence, etc.) and 4) thinking (critical thinking, computational thinking, analytical thinking, etc.). These elements are intertwined with the application of digital literacy in personal and professional life, technological progress, networking, academia, citizenship, education, and many others (Tinmaz et al. 2022).

3. Digital literacy models and their main characteristics

It is not easy to single out one digital literacy model as there are many and they focus on different skills. Over the course of the last decade, many scholars, practitioners, and international organisations have conducted research on the topic of digital literacy. The following models were chosen based on their level of detail and the different aspects they consider; however, they do not represent an exhaustive list. It must also be emphasised that most of the models have been developed by organisations and institutions such as UNESCO, the OECD, the European Commission, and the Institute of Electrical and Electronics Engineers (IEEE), arguably driven by the need to have a framework that would be a starting point for obtaining desired digital skillsets needed in the twenty-first century.

The translation and interpreting community has seen the importance of digital and AI literacy and has offered didactic approaches to it (elaborated in section 3.5). The following sub-sections offer an overview of the most recent digital literacy models used for the general population and those introduced in translation and interpreting.

3.1 European Commission's Digital Competence Framework for Citizens (DigComp)

The European Commission's digital literacy model, called Digital Competence (DigComp) Framework for Citizens, was first introduced in 2013 and has undergone several reviews since then. The most recent one occurred in 2022, when DigComp 2.2 was published. DigComp has been serving as a foundation for the various social policies and policy programmes in the field of digital skills and employment of the European Commission and other organisations. The framework comprises five major competence areas: 1) Information and data literacy, 2) Communication and collaboration, 3) Digital content creation, 4) Safety and 5) Problem Solving, each of them being divided into specific sub-competencies. Each of the main competencies branches out into further competencies, 21 in total (see Table 2). In addition to the description of competencies and levels of proficiency, ranging from foundation to highly specialised, the updated version from 2022 contains concrete examples of how each competence translates into reality with necessary knowledge, skills and attitudes described in great detail (Vuorikari/Kluzer/Punie 2022, pp. 1–4).

Table 2: DigComp 2.2 (European Commission)

Information and data literacy	Browsing, searching and filtering data, information and digital content Evaluating data, information and digital content Managing data, information and digital content
Communication and collaboration	Interacting through digital technologies Sharing information and content through digital technologies Engaging in citizenship through digital technologies Collaboration through digital technologies Netiquette Managing digital identity

(Continued)

Table 2: (*Continued*)

Digital content creation	Developing digital content Integrating and re-elaborating digital content Copyright and licences Programming
Safety	Protecting devices Protecting personal data and privacy Protecting health and well-being Protecting the environment
Problem solving	Solving technical problems Identifying needs and technological responses Creatively using digital technologies Identifying competence gaps

3.2 UNESCO's Digital Literacy Global Framework

Published in 2018, UNESCO's Digital Literacy Global Framework was developed to support the measurement of the Sustainable Development Goal (SDG) thematic Indicator 4.4.2: "Percentage of youth/adults who have achieved at least a minimum level of proficiency in digital literacy skills," and is based on the previously described European Commission's Digital Competence Framework for Citizens (DigComp 2.0) from 2018 (Law et al. 2018, p. 5).

UNESCO's panel of experts thoroughly analysed DigComp 2.0 by conducting four empirical studies, including public consultation. The experts expanded the original model (Table 2) by adding two competence areas and one competence numbered as follows: 0. Devices and software operations, 5.5 Computational thinking and 6. Career-related competencies that they found were lacking in the original model. Perhaps the main difference between the Digital Literacy Global Framework and DigComp 2.0 lies in its geographic focus. While the Commission focuses on the EU member states, which are technologically developed high-income countries, UNESCO has a more holistic approach and includes developing countries in their exercise (Law et al. 2018).

3.3 Digital Intelligence (DQ) Framework

The Digital Intelligence Framework or DQ Framework was developed in 2018 by the Coalition for Digital Intelligence (CDI), a joint project of the

DQ Institute, the OECD, the World Economic Forum and IEEE ("DQ (Digital Intelligence)," n.d.). The DQ aims to help foster the development of digital literacy and help individuals become "future-ready" in terms of digital skills. In addition to that, when listing skills, the DQ Framework also considers well-being and sustainable development goals. The framework is a matrix of 32 different digital skills across the eight key areas of digital life (identity, use, safety, security, emotional intelligence, literacy, communication and rights) and four different levels, relevant to each society: citizenship, creativity, connectivity and competitiveness ("DQ Institute," n.d.). In 2020, the DQ Framework became the IEEE Global Standard, the first standard worldwide to deal with digital skills and literacy, enabling governments and industries to build on these findings and prepare for the digital future (IEEE SA, n.d.).

3.4 Assemblage approach to digital literacy

Unlike the previously described frameworks, Nichols and Stornaiuolo examine the history of the concept of digital literacy in their research, proposing that we see digital literacy not as a "bounded concept," but rather "as an assemblage – a layering together of historical meanings and practices that have congealed, for the moment, into a useable discourse" (Nichols/Stornaiuolo 2019, p. 17). Their assemblage model does not list skills and competencies that a person should have in order to be digitally literate, but emphasises instead the importance of the interplay of the socio-technical, socio-economic and socio-historical elements. This model's biggest value lies in its looking at digital literacy from many different angles, such as users, technology, content, business models, ownership, and governance. It also points out that defining digital literacy merely as a catalogue of necessary skills brings about the danger of turning a blind eye to some of the most pressing issues of today, like "surveillance, algorithmic bias, commercial profit motives … " (Nichols/Stornaiuolo 2019, p. 22).

3.5 Digital literacy and AI literacy in translation and interpreting

Digital literacy has been a subject of scientific interest in translation and interpreting for many years. Drechsel emphasised the importance of two types of literacies crucial for translation and interpreting professionals: information literacy, which means finding and using the right information online, and technology literacy, which means familiarising oneself with the technology needed for work and keeping up with the developments in the field of AI, bearing in mind its potential to disrupt the profession (Drechsel 2019, p. 261, 266).

O'Brien and Ehrensberger-Dow (2020) elaborated on the concept of MT literacy as part of digital literacy. MT literacy encompasses several abilities, starting from understanding how MT processes text to the types of texts that lend themselves to MT, to how post-editing works. This type of literacy is of paramount importance both for the public and for language professionals to dispel the myth that machines are equal to or better than humans, prevent damage to the reputation of the translation profession and avoid commercial losses as well as reduce the fear of translators becoming redundant (O'Brien/Ehrensberger-Dow 2020, pp. 145–147, 160).

The DataLit^{MT} project, which was implemented from 2021 until 2023 at the Cologne University of Applied Sciences, offers a didactic approach to teaching MT literacy. The project's target groups were BA and MA students of translation and communication studies who were taught MT literacy within a framework based on five key elements: technical MT literacy, linguistic MT literacy, economic MT literacy, societal MT literacy and cognitive MT literacy (Krüger/Hackenbuchner 2022, pp. 384–387).

The ever-increasing automation of translation and the use of neural machine translation have motivated scholars to grapple with the concept of AI literacy, particularly concerning the use of ChatGPT-4 and other LLMs in the translation process (Krüger 2023). Krüger (2024) posited that the interplay of three literacies is crucial for the translation industry, which today is highly digitalised and data-driven: MT literacy, data literacy and artificial intelligence literacy (AI literacy). He also proposed an AI literacy framework, building on the work of Long and Magerko (2020), which will serve as a foundation for didactic resources to come. The framework spans five different dimensions – technical foundations, domain-specific performance, interaction, implementation and ethical/societal aspects – envisaging three different levels of competence ranging from informed prosumers (producers and consumers), and skilled users to expert creators (Krüger 2024, pp. 14–15, 21; Krüger in this volume).

Giustini and Dastyar (2024) offers an interesting view on AI literacy in interpreting or, as Giustini calls it, critical AI literacy (CAIL). She advocates abandoning the dualistic human vs machine approach and the competition of who does what better, which tends to dominate the debate. According to her, language professionals would be wiser to embrace the synergistic, assemblage approach to AI (see section 3.4) which could result in a "hybrid intelligence." Implementing CAIL might help human interpreters to incorporate AI tools into the interpreting process more successfully while at the same time taking into consideration various ethical aspects of AI (Giustini/Dastyar 2024, pp. 197–199, 201).

Regarding data literacy and what translators and interpreters expect from data literacy training, a study conducted in Japan in 2021 shows that respondents believe they are good at finding, using and creating the information they need online but lack specific knowledge on using computer-assisted interpreting (CAI) and CAT tools (Djafri/Wahidati 2022, p. 94). Another study conducted in Korea in 2023 shows that translators and interpreters want data literacy training on concrete skills and tools (CAI and CAT) they can utilise in everyday work (Jin/Lee/Lee 2024, p. 223). It should be noted here that the term "digital literacy" is used very narrowly to refer to the technology used for and at work, thus disregarding the larger picture presented in the models and frameworks discussed above.

The frameworks discussed in the previous sections can be seen as a blueprint of essential competencies for the modern-day workforce and adapted to a specific profession's needs. The frameworks used in translation and interpreting are useful because they focus on specialised skills such as MT and AI in the translation and interpreting process. Given the state of play in the language industry, which is becoming digital and AI dominated, these skills are much needed. Still, digital literacy in the context of translation and interpreting could benefit from additional skills such as media and information literacy and balanced use of technology, which seem to have been sidelined from the current discussion on the topic. This is why the following sections look at media consumption habits, especially with regard to the challenges they bring and how this relates to translation and interpreting.

4. Media landscape and the challenges it brings to the interplay of media consumption and digital literacy

Central to the issue of digital literacy in all of the mentioned models is how we consume digital information and data, how we interact with others, and how we engage in citizenship by using digital technologies.

Translators and interpreters have been relying on traditional and online media to get the knowledge and current news relevant to their work, which is an important part of their assignment preparation (Stoll 2009, p. 89; Setton/Dawrant 2016, pp. 340–341). The internet, social media and YouTube have offered unprecedented possibilities for research, language learning, translation and interpreting practice (Kalina 2014, p. 21). Translators and interpreters can use the internet not only to read the news or research the topic of their interest, but they can now use social media to follow the speakers they will have to interpret to prepare in advance, use YouTube to find and/or upload practice material, or resort to GenAI tools such as Copilot, Gemini and ChatGPT to get a quick glossary or a summary of the document they need. Many resort to social media to advertise their services and act as content creators, posting content about language and/or the profession online.

Against this backdrop, being aware of the online media consumption habits (i.e., social media) and the risks (infotainment, echo chambers, fake news, news softening, netspeak, attentional overload, etc.) is an important part of digital literacy relevant for future generations of translators and interpreters, as is elaborated on in the following sections.

4.1 Modern-day media consumption trends

The following Eurobarometer survey on media habits in the EU in 2023 refers to the general population, but it can be assumed that there are no significant differences regarding translation and interpreting students and professionals. Data show that TV remains the main source of information for 2/3 of respondents, followed by online media outlets, social media platforms such as Facebook and Instagram and radio. This, however, is not the case for the younger generation, where 60 % of those aged 15 to 24 use social media and video platforms (YouTube) as their primary source of information. Regarding the news topics of interest, local news and national politics are the most interesting, followed by EU and international affairs. Again, this holds true only for the older generation. Younger respondents are mostly interested in hobbies and lifestyle, celebrities, crime and accidents ("Media & News Survey 2023," n.d.).

Statistics on the consumption of online media from 2023 show that young people (14–29) spend 257 minutes daily consuming video, audio and text online, not considering the time spent on activities such as communication (chatting, liking, commenting), playing games, internet shopping, using online maps, etc. Furthermore, there is a decrease in the consumption of text online which is attributed to the fact that people, especially young people, are tired of the news, and the fact that online newspapers rarely offer free-of-charge content (Beisch/Koch 2023). More than 58 % of people aged 16–29 cannot imagine their lives without social media any longer and 55 % claim they would not be informed about the world events, were it not for social media (Rohleder 2023).

In terms of the most recent development – the use of generative AI – a recent survey conducted in Germany (n > 3,000) (Schlude et al. 2023) shows that 81 % of all internet users in the country are familiar with generative AI and what they can do with it (text creation, proofreading of texts, code creation, etc.). However, only one-third of all respondents have used some generative AI and one-quarter of the employed respondents used AI in their work. Regarding the perceptions of opportunities and risks, almost half of all online users in Germany believe that there are as many opportunities as there are risks. Younger people (16–29) perceive AI quite cautiously as only 20 % of the respondents think that it brings opportunities, while 80 % believe that it brings risks. Almost half of the respondents believe that there is an imminent risk of losing control over AI and fear they might become redundant due to the use of AI, especially highly educated ones working in administration. More than 50 % of all respondents advocate strict regulation of the use of AI.

4.2 The characteristics of online and social media

Objective and credible news has always been regarded as the foundation of democracy. In the modern-day media landscape, whose main characteristic is hybridity – a mixture of news and entertainment known as infotainment – it has been getting more and more difficult to distinguish between what news is and what it is not, especially for younger generations who have been born into “a media environment of high choice and hybridity” (Edgerly/Vraga 2020). Journalists have reported being caught between a rock and a hard place in today’s media environment. They have lost their gatekeeping function and can no longer exclusively decide what gets published, but at the same time they are no longer impartial observers on social media as they are incentivised to post and comment to drive more traffic to their media outlets (Salaverría

2019, pp. 7–8; Degen/Olgemöller/Zabel 2024, pp. 406–408; Ross Arguedas et al. 2022, p. 1829).

On the one hand, journalism has profited from platforms such as Facebook which generates a lot of website traffic. On the other, this has been done at the expense of journalistic practices vital for the trust in the media (impartiality, verification before publishing information, controlling caustic comments online, appealing and shocking headlines i.e., clickbait headlines). Furthermore, one of their main concerns is the "echo chambers" – content and advertising tailored to one's preferences – on social media, which seems to exacerbate polarisation as well as not being able to control the life of a news story after being published (Ross Arguedas et al. 2022, p. 1828; pp. 1832–1835). In terms of content, news softening seems to be the usual practice. This practice entails publishing less content dealing with politics, business or foreign affairs, especially on social media, to attract the audience. In addition to that, journalism adapts to social media (Twitter, Facebook) by changing its traditional communication style, which is now more conversational, concise and often resorting to humour to be more appealing (Degen/Olgemöller/Zabel 2024, p. 410).

Research conducted in Australia shows that a new genre of journalism – social news – has emerged. Social news is a specific blend of pop culture and politics with elements of social media, relying on native marketing (advertising imitating journalistic content) for funding. Thanks to its innovative approach, transparency, and clear positioning, social news could play a role in the strengthening of democracy (Hurcombe/Burgess/Harrington 2021). On the other hand, fake news fuels polarisation and divisions, thus undermining democracy. As is the case with digital literacy, fake news is not a new concept, and there are many examples of fake information being published deliberately to mislead the public throughout modern history, e.g., the Moon Hoax published by The Sun in 1835 in New York. After the 2016 and 2021 elections in the USA, Brexit and the COVID-19 pandemic, fake news entered common parlance (Pennycook/Rand 2021, p. 388). Fake news is defined as a deliberate attempt to deceive the public by presenting false information as news (Tandoc 2019, p. 2). Research shows that enabling factors for people to believe in fake news are a lack of "careful reasoning and relevant knowledge" as well as "familiarity and source." People are more likely to believe fake news if they have previously been exposed to it and if it comes from a source they know and trust (Pennycook/Rand 2021, pp. 392–393).

Another important aspect of the internet and social media is computer-mediated communication (CMC) or "netspeak," the term coined by Crystal in 2001 (2006). The main characteristics of CMC include: a) typography – the use of numbers, punctuation, and special symbols as well as nonstandard capitalisation, b) orthography – abbreviating words, special spelling to imitate pronunciation, etc., c) morphology – clipping words, blending or compounding them and using acronyms, d) syntax – brief, informal and, at times, sentences similar to spoken sentences, nonstandard use of prepositions followed by infinitive, etc. and e) use of emojis (Herring 2024, pp. 2–5). Although some see netspeak as a positive development, which adds to the linguistic wealth and exhibits users' creativity (Crystal 2006, pp. 274–275), there is evidence that the English language has become "significantly more informal," more negative, and emotional in the last two decades, moving out of the realm of CMC into the spoken language and having a negative effect on literacy among the youth (Herring 2024, pp. 5–6). Moreover, informal communication could erode language proficiency and professional communication in the workplace (Han 2024, pp. 216–217).

4.3 The challenges that online and social media bring

The hybridity of social media feeds, accompanied by the over-abundance of content, sources, platforms, and devices, makes it difficult for young people to become and remain news literate. A study has shown that young people choose to verify the news by informing themselves through multiple channels only if it seems suspicious. They take the messages of reputable brands or influencers with high numbers of followers for granted, rarely questioning their financial motives. Furthermore, they tend to mistrust certain social media (Facebook) because of the algorithms it uses but are less concerned about Instagram, although it belongs to the same company and uses similar mechanisms (Swart 2023, p. 506; p. 514).

Young adults come into contact with news as part of their daily social media habits (incidental news consumption). In this environment, flooded with other types of content, the news is neither taken seriously nor does the youth focus on it (Boczkowski/Mitchelstein/Matassi 2018). Furthermore, young people like googling for stories and using intermediaries such as Facebook or Google to get their news, but through this practice, they spend less time on the news and engage less with it than they would with traditional news (Antunovic/Parsons/Cooke 2018, p. 645). Since attention is dispersed on different online content, users tend to trust the people they know rather than journalists when choosing which stories to read (Boczkowsk/Mitchelstein/Matassi 2018).

Research has shown that online media have contributed to more active participation in political and civic life due to online petitions and other forms of political and civic engagement, which have translated into concrete forms of protest such as taking to the streets (Boulianne 2020, pp. 961–962). However, social media often affect the ability of young people to engage in online civic initiatives or discussions about controversial topics such as climate change or the migrant crisis because of privacy concerns and fear that their internet footprint might negatively affect their future, which is why they sometimes resort to pseudonyms and fake accounts (Swart 2023, pp. 516–517). Scholars have argued that social media could motivate young people to become more politically active because they could be used to express their opinions more easily, engage in debates, and connect with political actors. However, this does not seem to be the case as the entertainment content on social media may be numbing "the processing and salience of political considerations," which would, among other things, explain the low turnout among younger voters in elections in countries such as Germany, the US, Switzerland, etc. (Matthes 2022, p.7; p. 19).

Excessive use of social media has become an issue for public health. As reported in Poland (n – 330), 42 % of respondents (age 15–21) spend 3–4 hours on social media daily and 20 % more than 5 hours for communication with their friends and entertainment purposes, mostly on Facebook, YouTube and Instagram. This has brought about a lack of sleep (in 59 % of respondents), especially when using social media before going to bed, loss of focus when talking to another person (42 %), and not paying attention in school (43 %) (Wojdan et al. 2020, pp. 10–11).

Attentional overload – a situation in which one does not have enough cognitive resources to respond to the stimuli in the environment – is another serious problem caused by digital devices and social media. It leads to one's attention being divided on multiple tasks or stimuli at the same time which is also known as the "continuous partial attention." It leads to problems with deep concentration and to superficial understanding of information. One of the causes for this is the design of devices with all the notifications, personalised content, and alerts (Pennycook/Rand 2021), but also the mechanism of positive reinforcement when one finds something interesting online and reward in the forms of likes and comments (Albers 2017, p. 92; Newport 2019, pp. 18–20). Other problems linked with the excessive use of social media and digital devices include: digital dementia or overreliance on digital technology, changes in the areas of the brain and neurotransmitters responsible for decision-making and impulse control and reduced ability to regulate emotions (Chen/Dong/Li 2023, pp. 6–8; Shanmugasundaram/Tamilarasu 2023, pp. 3–4).

In summary, the effects of social media and digital technology are many and range from changes on how the information is served or changes in media consumption and information processing, over participation in political and civic life to attention disorder, to lack of sleep, emotion regulation and decision-making.

5. Do translators and interpreters need digital literacy?

According to the statistics from section 4.1, an average young person – perhaps a student starting their university programme or a young professional at the beginning of their career – spends a lot of time online, mostly on Instagram, TikTok, Snapchat, and YouTube, where they enjoy watching video content and engaging with others. This person likes listening to podcasts, does not watch linear TV, choosing streaming platforms and video-on-demand instead, is somewhat familiar with generative AI, but has negative attitudes toward it, does not read a lot, especially not the print media, and is not particularly interested in politics and current affairs.

Faculty staff, on the other hand, are by default older than the students and thus have entirely different media consumption habits and digital skills proficiency. Less than one-quarter of faculty staff aged 55–73 (baby boomers) have advanced digital skills as opposed to those aged 39–54 (generation X) where approximately one-quarter have advanced digital skills and those aged 23–38 (millennials) where one-half have advanced digital skills (Jorge-Vázquez et al. 2021, pp. 7–8).

One should be wary of generalisation but should also be realistic and not expect young translators or interpreters to be much different from the rest of their generation, even though the fact that they had decided to pursue this career presupposes solid general knowledge, an interest in international affairs and current issues. Concerns about how translation and interpreting students process information and the fact that there is room for improvement in their knowledge of history, current affairs and politics have been voiced as early as 2014 (Kalina 2014, pp. 19–20).

Although the following questions are yet to be empirically researched in translation and interpreting studies, it might be hypothesised that:

a) Prolonged exposure to shorter online forms (articles, videos, chats, etc.) negatively affects language skills, especially high-register language skills, which are important in translation and interpreting. Research shows this was the case with the general population (Herring 2024, pp. 5–6).
b) Lack of interest in the news and not reading enough because the focus lies on video and audio content might also negatively affect general knowledge and undermine familiarity with current issues.
c) Choosing online- and social media full of clickbait headlines, disinformation, fake news, and infotainment as the primary source of information might not only constitute a waste of time but negatively affect critical thinking and grasping of complex relations.
d) The dangers of information overload, superficial information processing, and attention disorders are not to be underestimated, especially in a profession that requires longer periods of intense concentration, e.g., during translation, simultaneous and consecutive interpreting.
e) In the era of constant photographing, recording, filming, sharing, posting and liking, there is a thin line between unprofessionalism and professionalism (netiquette), violation and respect of other people's privacy and intellectual property.
f) Finally, AI may offer many exciting opportunities but brings great risks: perpetuation of biases, hallucinations, and overreliance (Chan/Colloton 2024, pp. 57–61).

Research shows that interpreters have been somewhat slow to embrace new technologies (Corpas Pastor/Fern 2016, p. 36). Their approach to technology is still tempered with many willing to use the possibilities that technology has to offer, but emphasising the importance of the human factor. Many are aware of the ethical considerations regarding the use of AI tools and see AI as a "disruptive force" that might end up replacing them, which coincides with the attitudes on AI described in section 4.1 (Fan 2024, pp. 13–14; p. 17). Like many other professionals, translators and interpreters could benefit greatly from digital literacy.

It has been stated previously that translators and interpreters need information literacy, technology literacy, MT literacy, AI literacy and CAIL to be able to work in today's highly digital world. Being technology literate could help improve the uptake of new technologies (such as CAT and CAI tools, but also NMT and GenAI) and reduce the fear of translators and interpreters becoming redundant (see Djafri/Wahidati 2022; Drechsel 2019; Giustini/Dastyar 2024; Jin/Lee/Lee 2024; Krüger/Hackenbuchner 2022; Krüger 2023; 2024; O'Brien/Ehrensberger-Dow 2020). These literacies focus mostly on technical skills, which is not enough, given that translators and interpreters rely on the media in various aspects of their work and professional lives.

5.1 What can be done to strike the right balance?

The work of translators and interpreters should "always be based on verified and appropriate information" (Sales 2024, p. 745), therefore it is very important to be able to spot fake news, misinformation and disinformation.

Research shows that an important part of digital literacy – news literacy or media literacy – including the knowledge about how the news is produced makes a difference when deciding on the primary source of information. Those with more knowledge perceived social media as a supplementary source of information and pay attention to the source, media outlet, and the person sharing an article rather than the number of likes and comments (Schulz/Fletcher/Nielsen 2024).

Knowing what news is has proven important for combating fake news (Edgerly/Vraga 2020, p. 430), and being news literate would mean focusing more effort on "communicative and participatory practices" instead of "technological and critical thinking skills" (Swart 2023, p. 518). In this respect, the concept of social media information literacy (SMIL), which overlaps with digital literacy, can be helpful. Through its six areas – navigation, curation, appraisal, comprehension, creation, and interaction – it offers a model that could be helpful in combating information overload and, with that, news avoidance and conspiracy mentality (Heiss/Nanz/Matthes 2023).

A combination of digital literacy and algorithms deployed by the platforms to distinguish between formal and informal use of language could help prevent the erosion of language skills and communication (Han 2024, p. 217). With media literacy, fact-checking is the main weapon against fake news and disinformation (Larraz/Salaverría/Serrano-Puche 2024, p. 12; Vivona/Caranti 2020, pp. 25–26).

It is unrealistic to expect that the curricula of translation and interpreting studies will change overnight or fast enough to keep pace with the ever-changing media and digital environment we live in. It is, therefore, also up to the lecturers, the students and the professionals themselves to take steps to tackle the previously stated issues.

A simple way of doing this would be:

1) Resorting to massive online open courses (MOOCS) with a plethora of courses on critical thinking, digital literacy and AI. A simple class that is free of charge and four hours in duration might help realise how much is at stake (see Drechsel 2019, p. 260; Voudoukis/Pagiatakis 2022, p. 294).
2) Raising awareness of individual online- and social media consumption habits. This could be done with the help of a diary or by simply checking one's mobile phone settings or internet browser history, where a record of daily use is stored. Seeing how much time is spent mindlessly scrolling online over the course of a week could motivate many to change their habits (see the distraction tracker in Eyal Nir and Li 2019, pp. 62–63 and digital declutter Newport 2019, p. 64).
3) Emphasising and being aware of the need to diversify media sources. Instead of relying mostly on social media, online media outlets, and intermediaries, the goal is to have a balanced mix of legacy media, linear TV, radio, and online media (Swart 2023, p. 513).
4) Getting information on the new technologies and the many challenges they bring (such as privacy, trust, security and ethics), which could be done through interdisciplinary collaboration with research training groups and collaborative research centres from the field of IT, always in need of an audience for their seminars (see the call for a multidisciplinary approach to AI literacy in Giustini/Dastyar 2024, p. 206).
5) Putting more emphasis on learner autonomy, which could be beneficial at the university. For instance, allowing students to showcase in class how they use AI to help them with typical translation/interpretation issues might be helpful for students and teaching staff. Instead

of trying to test different possibilities of applying novel technology themselves, lecturers might get a better overview of the use of AI and could warn about the potential risks (see autonomy in Chan and Colloton 2024, p. 141).

6) Getting accustomed to using fact-checking tools, which could prove a powerful tool against fake news and disinformation (European Commission 2022, p. 29).

Finally, even a small step toward a better level of digital literacy counts and could help the entire community.

6. Conclusion

We live in a world dominated by all things digital: media, devices, AI. All of it is interconnected and all of it determines our everyday lives. An average individual spends hours online every day, most of it for entertainment purposes. These consumption patterns result in many problems: political polarisation, fake news, attention problems, and less engagement in democratic and civic activities. Moreover, these habits could numb the ability of people to analyse political issues. They could potentially make them disregard the most important concerns of today, such as the use of algorithms in the media and AI, violation of privacy, ownership structures of the social media platforms, and profitability issues as their main driver. This is why news literacy or media literacy including the knowledge about how the news is created and consumed as well as deciding on the primary source of information – is a valuable skill.

There are many different definitions and models of digital literacy in use. Many of them have been developed by organisations such as the OECD, UNESCO or the European Commission as a framework for the development of policies, achievement and measurement of goals such as the SDGs. Any of the models could be used to raise awareness and tackle the problems of the overuse of media and technology.

For translation and interpreting students and professionals alike, being digitally literate is important for their work on many levels: knowing what is going on in the world, improving language skills, getting the full picture on crucial issues, mastering digital tools and AI – all of this is vital for the success of the profession. Translators and interpreters need digital literacy, which, in addition to MT literacy and AI literacy emphasising the use of GenAI in translation and interpreting, comprises other literacies: information literacy, media literacy, balanced use of technology, safety, ethical concerns, creativity, etc. This is needed to keep up with the disruptions in the profession caused by new technologies and mitigate the negative consequences of media consumption habits.

Bibliography

Albers, Markus (2017): *Digitale Erschöpfung: Wie wir die Kontrolle über unser Leben* wiedergewinnen. München: Carl Hanser Verlag.

Antunovic, Dunja / Parsons, Patrick / Cooke, Tanner R. (2018): "'Checking' and googling: Stages of news consumption among young adults." *Journalism* 19(5), pp. 632–48. https://doi.org/10.1177/1464884916663625.

Baron, Robert J. (2019): "Digital literacy." In: Hobbs, Renee / Mihailidis, Paul (eds.): *The international encyclopedia of media literacy*. Hoboken: John Wiley & Sons. https://doi.org/10.1002/9781118978238.ieml0053.

Bawden, David (2008): "Origins and concepts of digital literacy." In: Lankshear, Colin / Knobel, Michele (eds.): *Digital literacies. Concepts, policies and practices.* New York: Peter Lang, pp. 17–32.

Beisch, Natalie / Koch, Wolfgang (2023): "ARD/ZDF-Onlinestudie: Weitergehende Normalisierung der Internetnutzung nach Wegfall aller Corona-Schutzmaßnahmen," retrieved on 27/10/2024 from https://www.ard-media.de/fileadmin/user_upload/media-perspektiven/pdf/2023/MP_23_2023_Onlinestudie_2023_Fortschreibung.pdf.

Belshaw, Douglas A. J. (2012): *What is 'digital literacy'? A pragmatic investigation.* Ph.D. thesis, Durham University, retrieved on 28/10/2024 from https://etheses.dur.ac.uk/3446/.

Boczkowski, Pablo J. / Mitchelstein, Eugenia / Matassi, Mora (2018): "'News comes across when I'm in a moment of leisure': Understanding the practices of incidental news consumption on social media." *New Media & Society* 20(10), pp. 3523–3539. https://doi.org/10.1177/1461444817750396.

Boulianne, Shelley (2020): "Twenty years of digital media effects on civic and political participation." *Communication Research* 47(7), pp. 947–966. https://doi.org/10.1177/0093650218808186.

Buckingham, David (2008): "Defining digital literacy." In: Lankshear, Colin / Knobel, Michele (eds.): *Digital literacies. Concepts, policies and practices*. New York: Peter Lang, pp. 73–89.

Buckingham, David (2010): "Defining digital literacy – what do young people need to know about digital media?" In: Bachmair, Ben (ed.): *Medienbildung in Neuen Kulturräumen*. Wiesbaden: VS Verlag für Sozialwissenschaften, pp. 59–71.

Chan, Cecilia Ka Yuk / Colloton, Tom (2024): "Strengths and weaknesses in embracing ChatGPT in curriculum design." In: Chan, Cecilia Ka Yuk / Colloton, Tom (eds.): *Generative AI in higher education*. London: Routledge, pp. 44–86. https://doi.org/10.4324/9781003459026-3.

Chen, Hao / Dong, Guijun / Li, Kefeng (2023): "Overview on brain function enhancement of internet addicts through exercise intervention: Based on reward-execution-decision cycle." *Frontiers in Psychiatry 14*. https://doi.org/10.3389/fpsyt.2023.1094583.

Chetty, Krish / Qigui, Liu / Gcora, Nozibele / Josie, Jaya / Wenwei, Li / Fang, Chen (2017): "Bridging the digital divide: Measuring digital literacy." *Economics Discussion Papers 69*. Kiel: Kiel Institute for the World Economy, retrieved on 27/10/2024 from https://hdl.handle.net/10419/169128.

Corpas Pastor, Gloria / Fern, Lily May (2016): "A survey of interpreters' needs and practices related to language technology," retrieved on 21/10/2024 from https://www.researchgate.net/publication/303685153_A_survey_of_interpreters%E2%80%99_needs_and_practices_related_to_language_technology.

Crystal, David (2006): *Language and the internet*. Cambridge: Cambridge University Press.

Degen, Matthias / Olgemöller, Max / Zabel, Christian (2024): "Quality journalism in social media – what we know and where we need to dig deeper." *Journalism Studies 25*(4), pp. 399–420. https://doi.org/10.1080/1461670X.2024.2314204.

Djafri, Fatmawati / Wahidati, Lufi (2022): "Examining digital technology literacy of professional Japanese language translator and interpreter." *Lingua Cultura 16*(1), pp. 89–96. https://doi.org/10.21512/lc.v16i1.7768.

"DQ (Digital intelligence)" (n.d.), retrieved on 27/02/2025 from https://live.dqinstitute.org/global-standards/#contentblock1.

"DQ Institute" (n.d.), retrieved on 20/10/2024) from https://live.dqinstitute.org/.

Drechsel, Alexander (2019): "Technology literacy for the interpreter." In: Sawyer, David B. / Austermühl, Frank / Enríquez Raído, Vanessa (eds.): *The evolving curriculum in interpreter and translator education*, pp. 259–268. https://doi.org/10.1075/ata.xix.12dre.

Edgerly, Stephanie / Vraga, Emily K. (2020): "Deciding what's news: News-ness as an audience concept for the hybrid media environment." *Journalism & Mass Communication Quarterly* 97(2), pp. 416–434. https://doi.org/10.1177/1077699020916808.

European Commission, Directorate-General for Education, Youth, Sport and Culture (2022): *Guidelines for teachers and educators on tackling disinformation and promoting digital literacy through education and training*. Luxembourg: Publications Office of the European Union. https://data.europa.eu/doi/10.2766/28248.

Eyal Nir / Li, Julie (2019): *Indistractable: How to control your attention and choose your life*. London et al.: Bloomsbury.

Fan, Damien Chiaming (2024): "Conference interpreters' technology readiness and perception of digital technologies." *Interpreting. International Journal of Research and Practice in Interpreting* 26(2), pp. 178–200. https://doi.org/10.1075/intp.00110.fan.

Gilster, Paul (1997): *Digital literacy.* New York: Wiley Computer Publishing.

Giustini, Deborah / Dastyar, Vorya (2024): "Critical AI literacy for interpreting in the age of AI." *Interpreting and Society* 4(2), pp. 196–213. https://doi.org/10.1177/27523810241247259.

Han, Yuxuan (2024): "The impact of digital media on language styles and communication methods based on text, image, and video forms." *Lecture Notes in Education Psychology and Public Media* 40(1), pp. 211–219. https://doi.org/10.54254/2753-7048/40/20240754.

Heiss, Raffael / Nanz, Andreas / Matthes, Jörg (2023): "Social media information literacy: Conceptualization and associations with information overload, news avoidance and conspiracy mentality." *Computers in Human Behavior* 148, 107908. https://doi.org/10.1016/j.chb.2023.107908.

Herring, Susan C. (2022): "Grammar and electronic communication." In: Chapelle, Carol A. (ed.): *The Encyclopedia of Applied Linguistics.*

Hoboken: Wiley-Blackwell, pp. 1–9. https://doi.org/10.1002/9781405198431.wbeal0466.pub2.

Hurcombe, Edward / Burgess, Jean / Harrington, Stephen (2021): "What's newsworthy about 'social news'? Characteristics and potential of an emerging genre." *Journalism* 22(2), pp. 378–394. https://doi.org/10.1177/1464884918793933.

"IEEE SA" (n.d.), retrieved on 20/10/2024 from https://standards.ieee.org/beyond-standards/new-standard-will-help-nations-accelerate-digital-literacy-and-digital-skills-building/.

International Panel on the Information Environment (2024): "Expert survey on the global information environment 2024," retrieved on 20/10/2024 from https://www.ipie.info/research/sfp2024-1.

Jin, Silhee / Lee, Junho / Lee, Juriae (2024): "What do interpreters expect of digital literacy training?" *FORUM. Revue Internationale d'interprétation et de Traduction / International Journal of Interpretation and Translation* 22(2), pp. 206–228. https://doi.org/10.1075/forum.23019.jin.

Jorge-Vázquez, Javier / Náñez Alonso, Sergio Luis / Fierro Saltos, Washington Raúl / Pacheco Mendoza, Silvia (2021): "Assessment of digital competencies of university faculty and their conditioning factors: Case study in a technological adoption context." *Education Sciences* 11(10), 637. https://doi.org/10.3390/educsci11100637.

Kalina, Sylvia (2014): "Interpreter training and interpreting studies – which is the chicken and which is the egg?" In: Andres, Dörte / Behr, Martina (eds.): *To know how to suggest: Approaches to teaching conference interpreting*. Berlin: Frank & Timme, pp. 29–33.

Krüger, Ralph (2023): "Artificial intelligence literacy for the language industry – with particular emphasis on recent large language models such as GPT-4." *Lebende Sprachen* 68(2), pp. 283–330. https://doi.org/10.1515/les-2023-0024.

Krüger, Ralph (2024): "Outline of an artificial intelligence literacy framework for translation, interpreting and specialised communication." *Lublin Studies in Modern Languages and Literature* 48(3), pp. 11–23. https://doi.org/10.17951/lsmll.2024.48.3.11-23.

Krüger, Ralph / Hackenbuchner, Janiça (2022): "Outline of a didactic framework for combined data literacy and machine translation literacy teaching." *Current Trends in Translation Teaching and Learning E.*, pp. 375–432. https://doi.org/10.51287/cttl202211.

Lankshear, Colin / Knobel, Michele (2007): *New literacies. Everyday practices and classroom learning.* New York: Open University Press.

Larraz, Irene / Salaverría, Ramón / Serrano-Puche, Javier (2024): "Combating repeated lies: The impact of fact-checking on persistent falsehoods by politicians." *Media and Communication* 12. https://doi.org/10.17645/mac.8642.

Law, Nancy / Woo, David / de la Torre, Jimmy / Wong, Gary (2018): "A global framework of reference on digital literacy skills for indicator 4.4.2." Montreal: UNESCO Institute for Statistics.

Long, Duri / Magerko, Brian (2020): "What is AI literacy? Competencies and design considerations." In: *Proceedings of the 2020 CHI Conference on Human Factors in Computing Systems*. New York: ACM, pp. 1–16. https://doi.org/10.1145/3313831.3376727.

Matthes, Jörg (2022): "Social media and the political engagement of young adults: Between mobilization and distraction." *Online Media and Global Communication* 1(1), pp. 6–22. https://doi.org/10.1515/omgc-2022-0006.

"Media & News Survey 2023 – November 2023 – Eurobarometer Survey" (n.d.), retrieved on 27/02/2025 from https://europa.eu/eurobarometer/surveys/detail/3153.

Newport, Cal (2019): *Digital minimalism: Choosing a focused life in a noisy world*. London: Penguin Random House.

Nichols, T. Philip / Stornaiuolo, Amy (2019): "Assembling 'digital literacies': Contingent pasts, possible futures." *Media and Communication* 7(2), pp. 14–24. https://doi.org/10.17645/mac.v7i2.1946.

O'Brien, Sharon / Ehrensberger-Dow, Maureen (2020): "MT literacy – a cognitive view." *Translation, Cognition & Behavior* 3(2), pp. 145–64. https://doi.org/10.1075/tcb.00038.obr.

Pennycook, Gordon / Rand, David G. (2021): "The psychology of fake news." *Trends in Cognitive Sciences* 25(5), pp. 388–402. https://doi.org/10.1016/j.tics.2021.02.007.

Rohleder, Bernhard (2023): "Wie die Deutschen Social Media nutzen," retrieved on 03/05/2025 from https://www.bitkom.org/sites/main/files/2023-02/BitkomChartsSocialMedia2023_0.pdf.

Ross Arguedas, Amy A. / Badrinathan, Sumitra / Mont'Alverne, Camila / Toff, Benjamin / Fletcher, Richard / Nielsen, Rasmus Kleis (2022): "'It's a battle you are never going to win': Perspectives from journalists in four countries on how digital media platforms undermine trust in news." *Journalism Studies* 23(14), pp. 1821–1840. https://doi.org/10.1080/1461670X.2022.2112908.

Salaverría, Ramón (2019): "Digital journalism: 25 years of research. Review article." *El Profesional de La Información* 28(1). https://doi.org/10.3145/epi.2019.ene.01.

Sales, Dora (2024): "Professional translators' and interpreters' views on information competence: An exploratory qualitative study from the Spanish context." *Journal of Librarianship and Information Science* 56(3), pp. 743–759. https://doi.org/10.1177/09610006231164147.

Schlude, Antonia / Schwind, Mara / Mendel, Ulrike / Stürz, Roland A. / Harles, Danilo / Fischer, Micha (2023): "Verbreitung und Akzeptanz generativer KI in Deutschland und an deutschen Arbeitsplätzen," retrieved on 03/05/2025 from https://www.bidt.digital/publikation/verbreitung-und-akzeptanz-generativer-ki-in-deutschland-und-an-deutschen-arbeitsplaetzen/.

Schulz, Anne / Fletcher, Richard / Nielsen, Rasmus Kleis (2024): "The role of news media knowledge for how people use social media for news in five countries." *New Media & Society* 26(7), pp. 4056–77. https://doi.org/10.1177/14614448221108957.

Setton, Robin / Dawrant, Andrew (2016): *Conference interpreting – a complete course*. Amsterdam: John Benjamins. https://doi.org/10.1075/btl.120.

Shanmugasundaram, Mathura / Tamilarasu, Arunkumar (2023): "The impact of digital technology, social media, and artificial intelligence on cognitive functions: A review." *Frontiers in Cognition* 2. https://doi.org/10.3389/fcogn.2023.1203077.

Spitzer, Manfred (2020): Digitales Unbehagen. München: mvg.

Stoll, Christoph (2009): *Jenseits simultanfähiger Terminologiesysteme: Methoden der Vorverlagerung und Fixierung von Kognition im Arbeitsablauf professioneller Konferenzdolmetscher*. Trier: WVT Wissenschaftlicher Verlag Trier.

Swart, Joëlle (2023): "Tactics of news literacy: How young people access, evaluate, and engage with news on social media." *New Media & Society* 25(3), pp. 505–21. https://doi.org/10.1177/14614448211011447.

Tandoc, Edson C. (2019): "The facts of fake news: A research review." *Sociology Compass* 13(9). https://doi.org/10.1111/soc4.12724.

Tinmaz, Hasan / Lee, Yoo-Taek / Fanea-Ivanovici, Mina / Baber, Hasnan (2022): "A systematic review on digital literacy." *Smart Learning Environments* 9(1), 21. https://doi.org/10.1186/s40561-022-00204-y.

UNESCO (n.d.): "SDG 4: Ensure inclusive and equitable quality education and promote lifelong learning opportunities for all," retrieved on 05/10/2024 from https://tcg.uis.unesco.org/wp-content/uploads/sites/4/2021/08/Metadata-4.4.2.pdf.

Vivona, Valentina / Caranti, Niccolo (2020): "The impact of digitalisation on media and journalism," retrieved on 28/10/2024 from https://dttools.eu/pdf/digit-al-io1-media-and-journalism.pdf.

Voudoukis, Nikolaos / Pagiatakis, Gerasimos (2022): "Massive open online courses (MOOCs): Practices, trends, and challenges for the higher education." *European Journal of Education and Pedagogy* 3(3), pp. 288–295. https://doi.org/10.24018/ejedu.2022.3.3.365.

Vuorikari, Rina / Kluzer, Stefano / Punie, Yves (2022): "DigComp 2.2 – the digital competence framework for citizens." Luxembourg: Publications Office of the European Union. https://doi.org/10.2760/115376.

Wojdan, Witold / Wdowiak, Krystian / Witas, Aleksandra / Drogoń, Justyna / Brakowiecki, Wojciech (2020): "The impact of social media on the lifestyle of young people." *Polish Journal of Public Health* 130(1), pp. 8–13. https://doi.org/10.2478/pjph-2020-0003.

An artificial intelligence literacy framework for translation, interpreting and specialised communication

Ralph Krüger
TH Köln – University of Applied Sciences

ABSTRACT
This chapter presents a domain-specific artificial intelligence (AI) literacy framework for translation, interpreting and specialised communication. Given that the degree of automation in the language industry can be increased considerably through recent general-purpose AI technologies, most notably multimodal large language models (MM-LLMs), translators, interpreters, technical writers and related actors require an extended set of AI-related competences if they want to participate successfully in AI-assisted language industry workflows. After sketching the potential LLM-fuelled automation in the language industry, the chapter goes on to discuss several predecessors of the proposed AI literacy framework and illustrates how they relate to and contribute to the proposed framework. Then, the individual dimensions of the framework will be discussed in detail. To conclude, the chapter discusses potential competence levels for the individual dimensions of the domain-specific AI literacy framework as well as plans for its didactic operationalisation.

Keywords: language industry, translation, interpreting, specialised communication, artificial intelligence, multimodal large language models, professional machine translation literacy, data literacy, artificial intelligence literacy

1. Introduction

The invention of the transformer architecture in 2017 (see Vaswani et al. 2017) represented a milestone in language-related artificial intelligence research. A specific neural network architecture specifically geared toward efficient natural language understanding and generation, the transformer, which had initially been conceived for neural machine translation (NMT), was quickly deployed as the base architecture of large language models such as OpenAI's GPT-4 and eventually shown to be capable of handling other modalities besides language. According to Stanford University's

Artificial Intelligence Index Report 2024, the transformer remains the leading base architecture of language-related and other AI technologies in 2024 (see Maslej et al. 2024, p. 63). The current state of the art are so-called *multimodal large language models* such as OpenAI's GPT-4o, which can integrate and process a range of different modalities (written language, images, audio and/or video)[1]. Due to their high versatility and wide scope of application, these models fall under the EU AI Act's definition of "general-purpose AI models," which "[display] significant generality and [are] capable of competently performing a wide range of tasks" (EU Artificial Intelligence Act 2024 Chapter I Article 3 Paragraph 63). Figure 1 provides an overview of the scope of application of general-purpose MM-LLMs in the language industry[2] and of the particular tasks in translation, interpreting and specialised communication that can potentially be (semi-)automated through these models:

---

1 In these multimodal LLMs, a unimodal LLM remains at the centre of the architecture (*LLM Backbone*). On the input side, this LLM is complemented by a *Modality Encoder*, which converts images, audio and/or video data into numerical vector representations (embeddings), and an *Input Projector*, which aligns these representations with the vector representations that the unimodal LLM has learned from textual data. On the output side, the LLM Backbone is complemented by an *Output Projector* and a *Modality Generator*, which are responsible for generating outputs in different modalities (see Zhang et al. 2024, pp. 2–4).

2 Angelone, Ehrensberger-Dow and Massey (2020, p. 1) define the language industry as comprising the GILT services (Globalisation, Internationalisation, Localization and Translation) as well as interpreting, consulting, project management and tool design. Major stakeholders are language service providers, vendors, translators, interpreters, revisers, terminologists, project managers, quality assurance specialists and consultants (ibid.). The current chapter also considers monolingual specialised communication (i.e., technical writing) as part of the language industry and hence technical writers (who often produce the source texts that feed into specialised translation) as further language industry stakeholders.

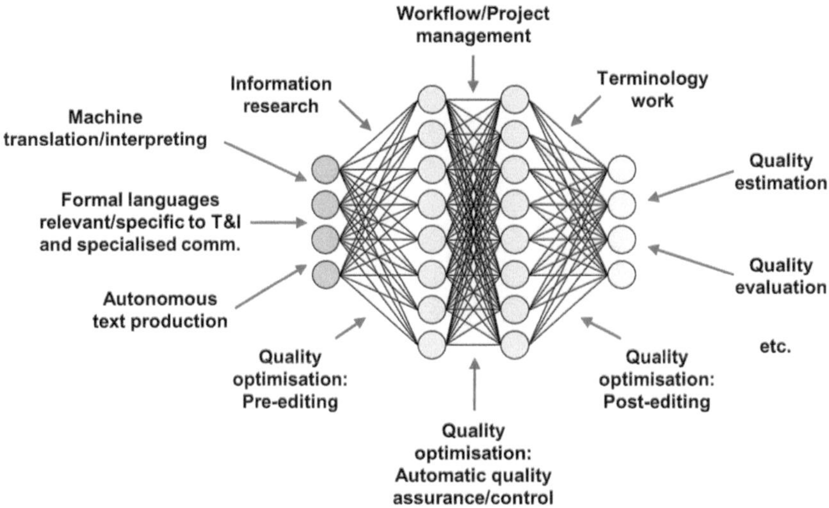

Figure 1: Potential scope of application of MM-LLMs in the language industry.

For example, in translation, multimodal LLMs can be employed both for "classic" machine translation (MT) and for other tasks such as quality evaluation or quality optimisation (pre-/post-editing for MT or automatic quality assurance/control of human translations). MM-LLMs which can process spoken language can potentially be used in machine interpreting and the ability of generative models to produce autonomous texts or to transform one monolingual text into another could also be harnessed in technical writing. In all three fields, these models can further be used for information research/terminology work or tasks related to project management (vendor communication, task planning, etc.). And since current LLMs are usually trained not only on natural language but also on formal languages (programming languages such as Python, markup languages such as XML or text patterns such as regular expressions), they can also assist in corresponding language industry workflows, e.g., when import filters for translation environment systems or search patterns for identifying and manipulating specific strings (such as e-mail addresses or URLs) have to be created. MM-LLMs capable of processing images and/or videos may also assist in multimodal text production/translation, e.g., by interpreting images (such as exploded drawings or flow-charts in technical writing/translation) or by producing such images.

Analysing this AI-fuelled automation of the language industry through a competence lens can broadly be approached in three ways. First, it could be asked which kind of translation, interpreting, and specialised communication competences will remain automation-resistant in light of current MM-LLMs and potential future AI technologies. This is the approach taken by Ayvazyan, Torres-Simón and Pym (2024), who query the US Department of Labor's Occupational Information Network (O*Net) database for the occupation *Interpreters and Translators* and extract data pertaining to the relative importance of *knowledges* (e.g., knowledge of the structure and content of source and target languages), linguistic, information processing and social communication skills and so-called "core" tasks (actually translating/interpreting texts, performing information research or terminology work, consulting reference materials, following ethical codes, etc.) (see ibid., pp. 126–131). The authors find that knowledges, linguistic skills and core tasks (with the exception of following ethical codes) can be largely automated by modern language-related AI technologies (with the possible level of quality achievable through such automation remaining unclear) but that information processing and social communication skills remain largely automation-resistant (see ibid.).

A second approach would be to focus on those human competences that – once they can be automated by a computer – are no longer required in humans and thus may get lost over time. This is what Sandrini (2022, p. 51) attempts to capture in his *translators' obsolescence cycle*, which models diminishing levels of competence brought about by increasing levels of automation. For example, the widespread introduction of terminology management systems in the 1980s made glossary creation largely redundant (see ibid.) while the introduction of NMT in the mid-2010s relieved translators of having to produce draft translations from scratch. Given the wide scope of application of general-purpose MM-LLMs as sketched above, the risk of technology-induced deskilling that Sandrini models with regard to translation will certainly become much broader as these and future AI technologies proliferate.

Such a deskilling perspective can be complemented by an upskilling perspective, which is the third broad approach to viewing AI-fuelled automation through a competence lens and the approach adopted in the present chapter. From this perspective, it can be argued that raising the degree of AI-fuelled automation in language industry workflows introduces new technological and process-related complexities and leads to a reconfiguration of the overall socio-technical systems in which these AI-assisted workflows are embedded. In order to master these complexities and to ensure that the full potential of general-purpose AI technologies can be harnessed in language industry workflows while taking into consideration the interests of all relevant stakeholders, revised, expanded or new competences on the part of relevant actors may be required. It is these competences which the domain-specific AI literacy framework discussed in section 3 aims to model.

2. Predecessors of the domain-specific AI literacy framework

This section provides a brief discussion of the conceptual predecessors of the AI literacy framework for translation, interpreting and specialised communication discussed in the next section. These are a professional MT literacy framework, an MT-specific data literacy framework and a generic AI literacy framework. The first two frameworks were developed as part of the DataLit^{MT} project (see Hackenbuchner/Krüger 2023), which created didactic resources for teaching data literacy in its translation-specific form of MT literacy to students of translation/specialised communication programmes at BA and MA levels. The third framework was developed by Long and Margerko (2020) independently of DataLit^{MT} and focuses on general AI literacy at societal level. The following discussion of the three frameworks will remain at a cursory level (they have been discussed extensively elsewhere and sources will be given in the corresponding sections) and mostly illustrate how these frameworks relate to and which elements they contribute to the domain-specific AI literacy framework proposed in this chapter.

2.1 Professional MT literacy framework

The term *professional MT literacy* is defined as "the full range of MT-related competences professional translators (and other language professionals) may require in order to participate successfully in the various phases of the MT-assisted professional translation process" (Krüger 2022a, p. 249). The framework depicted in Figure 2 operationalises this definition by distributing overall professional MT literacy over five dimensions:

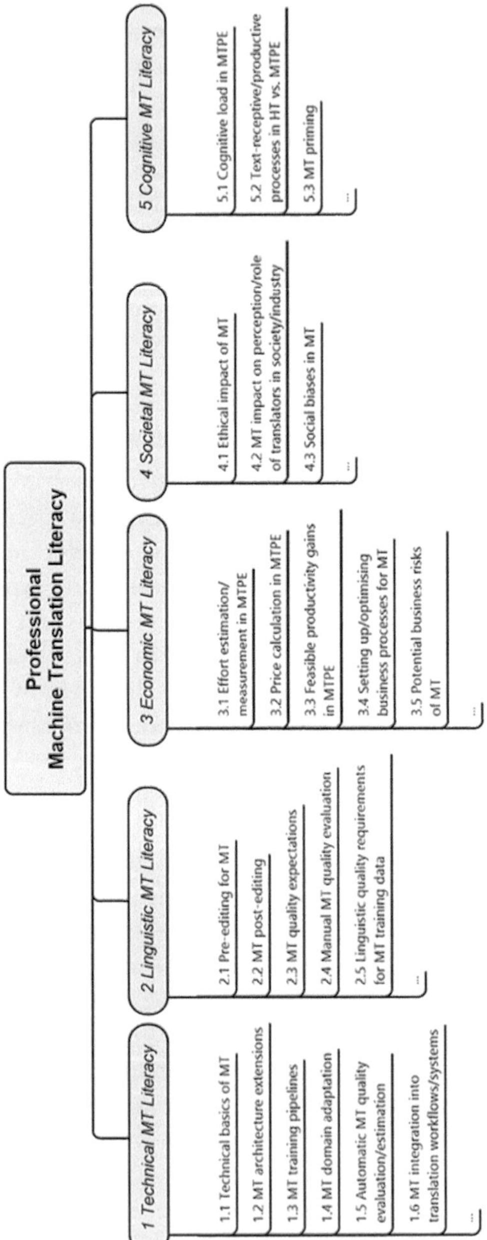

Figure 2: Professional MT literacy framework (Krüger 2022a, p. 250).

Technical MT literacy covers knowledge of the technical foundations of modern MT systems with a focus on NMT. *Linguistic MT literacy* mostly covers the "classic" MT-related competences translators were traditionally required to possess (pre-/post-editing, manual MT quality evaluation, etc.). Linguistic MT literacy illustrates quite well the technology-induced upskilling discussed in section 1, since linguistic competences geared toward MT now constitute only one of five dimensions of overall professional MT literacy. *Economic MT literacy* is concerned with implementing MT systems in language industry workflows and covers aspects such as effort measurement, price calculation and productivity gains in MT post-editing (MTPE) and potential business risks. *Societal MT literacy* is concerned with broader implications of MT use, particularly with its ethical dimension, shifts in professional/societal perceptions of the translation profession and social biases learned and reproduced by MT systems. *Cognitive MT literacy* is concerned with the cognitive impact of working with MT, such as cognitive load or potential priming effects exerted by an MT system[3].

Given that MM-LLMs – which are the currently dominant AI technology and hence also inform the domain-specific AI literacy framework to a certain extent (see section 3) – are derived from NMT and work in basically the same way (albeit having a much larger scope of application as discussed in section 1), there is a considerable overlap between professional MT literacy and AI literacy for translation, interpreting and specialised communication. Hence, the structure of the domain-specific AI literacy framework was heavily informed by the structure of the professional MT literacy framework. Specifically, the dimension *technical MT literacy* contributed to the dimension *technical foundations* (section 3.1), the dimension *economic MT literacy* inspired the dimension *implementation* (section 3.4) and the dimension *societal MT literacy* informed the dimension *ethical/societal aspects* (section 3.5) of the AI literacy framework. The dimensions *linguistic MT literacy* and *cognitive MT literacy* were mostly included in the dimension *interaction* (section 3.3) of the framework.

2.2 DataLit^MT framework

Data literacy is defined by Ridsdale et al. (2015, p. 11) as "the ability to collect, manage, evaluate, and apply data, in a critical manner." The DataLit^MT framework depicted in Figure 3 operationalises this definition with a focus on MT by distributing overall data literacy over five dimensions:

[3] An exhaustive discussion of the professional MT literacy framework is provided in Krüger (2022a, pp. 249–262).

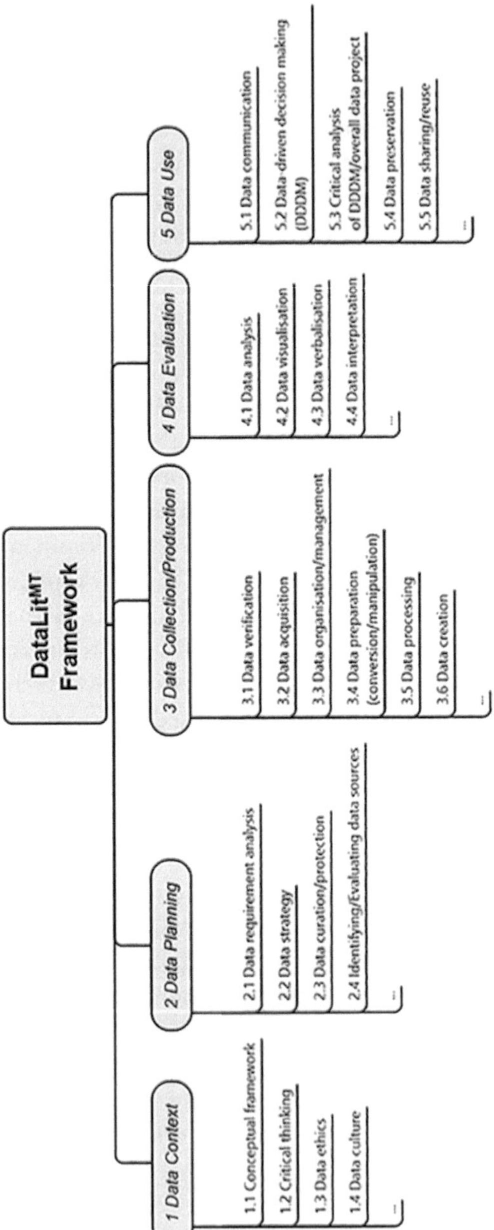

Figure 3: DataLit^{MT} framework (Krüger 2022a, p. 264).

The DataLit[MT] framework is an MT-specific data literacy framework, which depicts the typical lifecycle of data in an MT project/workflow. There is an immediate link between professional MT literacy and data literacy since modern MT systems such as NMT form part of the data-driven or corpus-based MT paradigm, which trains MT systems on large bi-/multilingual translation datasets or corpora (this interface provided the initial impetus for the DataLit[MT] project).

The *data context* provides an abstract, high-level framework for any data project, promoting a critical and ethical approach toward data and the need for establishing a data culture. *Data planning* involves identifying particular tasks or use cases that could be supported using data, establishing a data strategy to satisfy data needs, identifying/evaluating potential data sources, etc. *Data collection/production* in an MT context involves gathering and preparing data for training MT systems and producing new data (i.e., machine translations) using these systems. This new data feeds into the *data evaluation* stage (e.g., in MT quality evaluation), where it can be analysed, visualised/verbalised and interpreted. The results of the data evaluation stage then feed into the *data use* stage, where they may inform data-driven decision-making (e.g., deciding for or against implementing a certain MT system in production processes based on productivity and/or quality data).

In DataLit[MT], the individual (sub)dimensions of the DataLit[MT] framework (providing data competences to be taught) were mapped to corresponding (sub)dimensions of the professional MT literacy framework (providing application contexts in which to teach these competences); e.g., data evaluation was mapped to manual and automatic MT quality evaluation and to effort estimation/measurement and data use was mapped to price calculation in MTPE[4]. As such, the individual (sub)dimensions of the DataLit[MT] framework are mostly reflected in an indirect way in the domain-specific AI literacy framework (via their mapping to the professional MT literacy framework).

[4] The DataLit[MT] framework is discussed in detail in Krüger (2022a, pp. 262–269). The same paper provides an exhaustive discussion of the interface between the professional MT literacy framework and the DataLit[MT] framework (ibid., pp. 269–274).

A direct link between the DataLit^{MT} framework and the AI literacy framework is the subdimension *establishing a data culture*, which informs the subdimension *establishing an AI culture* as part of the *implementation* dimension of the AI literacy framework (section 3.4).

2.3 Generic AI literacy framework by Long and Magerko (2020)

The term *artificial intelligence literacy* is defined by Long and Magerko (2020, p. 1) as "a set of competencies that enables individuals to critically evaluate AI technologies; communicate and collaborate effectively with AI; and use AI as a tool online, at home, and in the workplace"[5]. Again, there are immediate links between this concept and both data and professional MT literacy. The link between AI and data literacy is provided by the machine learning (ML) paradigm, which is the currently dominant paradigm in overall AI research. In ML, AI systems are trained with large amounts of training data and learn representations and patterns from this data (e.g., corpus-based MT is a specific AI technology within the ML paradigm)[6]. The link between AI and professional MT literacy, on the other hand, is provided by LLMs, which, as discussed in sections 1 and 2.1, are derived from transformer NMT systems and share a similar operating principle with these systems.

Long and Magerko operationalise their definition of AI literacy by distributing it over five guiding questions, as depicted in Figure 4:

[5] The concept of AI literacy is also dedicated a separate article in the recent EU AI Act: "Providers and deployers of AI systems shall take measures to ensure, to their best extent, a sufficient level of AI literacy of their staff and other persons dealing with the operation and use of AI systems on their behalf, taking into account their technical knowledge, experience, education and training and the context the AI systems are to be used in, and considering the persons or groups of persons on whom the AI systems are to be used" (EU Artificial Intelligence Act 2024 Chapter I Article 4). This illustrates the urgency of developing and operationalising literacy frameworks such as those discussed in this chapter.

[6] On the close link between data and AI literacy see also Schüller et al. (2023, p. 426).

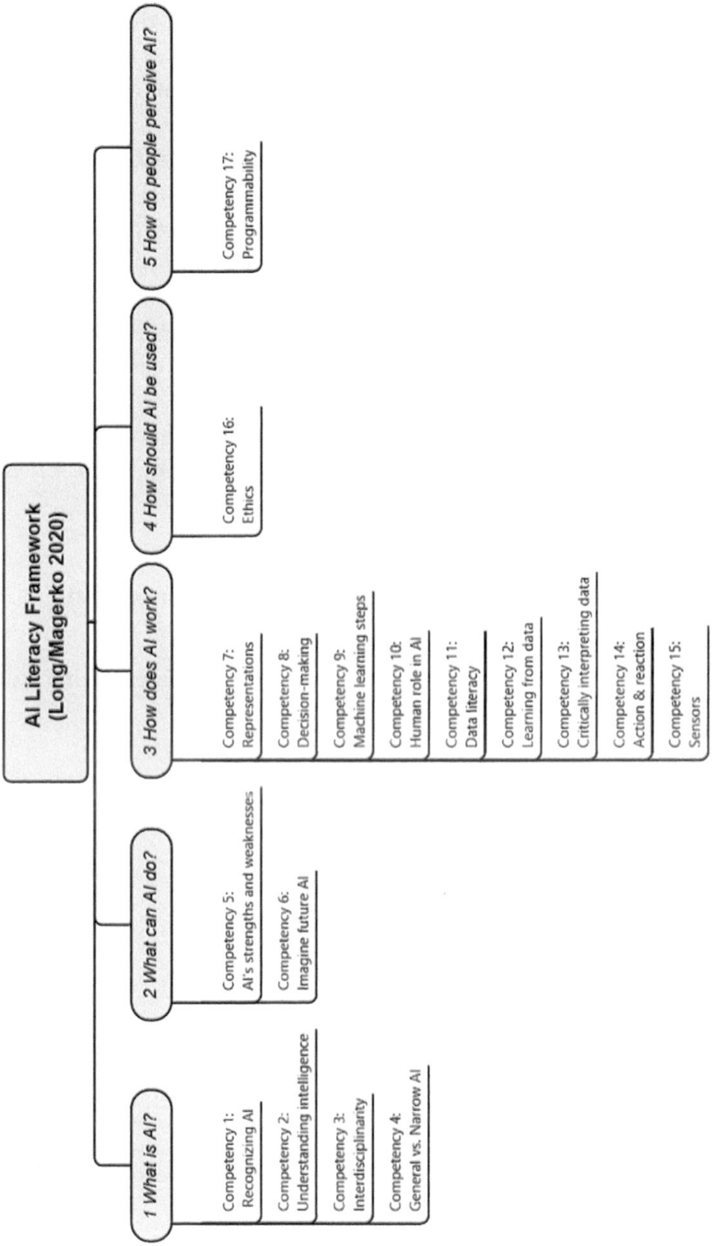

Figure 4: Generic AI literacy framework by Long and Magerko (2020, figure taken from Krüger 2023, p. 304).

Long and Magerko's AI literacy framework is generic in the sense that it is not tied to specific professional fields or domains, in contrast to the domain-specific AI literacy framework for translation, interpreting and specialised communication discussed in the following section. As such, the direct influence of this generic framework on the framework to be presented here is limited. The most direct link is provided by question 2 (*What can AI do?*), which informs the dimension *domain-specific performance* (section 3.2)[7]. The very important ethical question of *How should AI be used?* as well as the equally important aspect of human-AI interaction remain largely underdeveloped in Long and Magerko's generic framework. These two aspects are reflected to a much greater extent in the dimensions *interaction* (section 3.4) and *ethical/societal aspects* (section 3.5) of the domain-specific framework. Question 3 (*How does AI work?*) is covered mostly by the dimension *technical foundations* (section 3.1) of the framework.

3. AI literacy framework for translation, interpreting and specialised communication

The domain-specific AI literacy framework for translation, interpreting and specialised communication is depicted in Figure 5:

[7] This dimension was missing from the professional MT literacy framework, since the scope of application of expert systems such as MT is obvious. General-purpose AI technologies such as MM-LLMs, on the other hand, do not betray their affordances in any straightforward way. Since they can potentially be used for a vast array of tasks, determining their scope of application for particular professional fields is not a trivial undertaking (see also section 3.2).

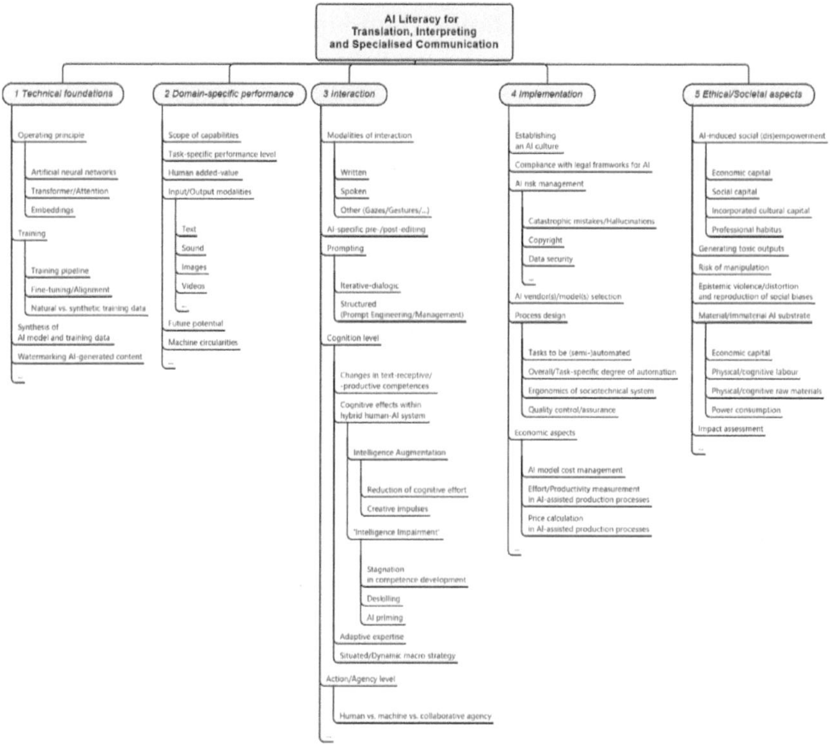

Figure 5: AI literacy framework for translation, interpreting and specialised communication.[8]

Although the framework is concerned with overall AI literacy for translation, interpreting and specialised communication and is therefore not tied to any specific AI technology, there is a certain focus on general-purpose MM-LLMs as the currently dominant AI technology (see section 2.1). The following discussion will also focus on these models. As AI research advances, the framework may have to be updated/revised accordingly.

8 A digital version of this framework is available under the following link: Retrieved on 26/07/2024 from th-koeln.de/itmk/ai-literacy.

3.1 Understanding the technical foundations of MM-LLMs

The first dimension of the framework is concerned with the technical foundations of multimodal LLMs. It can certainly be debated whether such technical knowledge is required by non-technical language industry actors such as translators, interpreters or technical writers, who are usually the end-users of these models[9]. However, if users perceive these technologies as a black box and do not understand their inner workings, this may curtail their agency when working with these models. This view is reinforced by Kenny (2019, p. 438), who claims, in the context of MT, that "[i]ncreased opacity [...] is a particular cause for concern for humans required to work with contemporary MT systems because it can limit their ability to intervene in translation workflows, thus undermining agendas of translator empowerment." Understanding the operating principle of MM-LLMs involves at least basic knowledge of neural networks, of transformers and attention mechanisms and of embeddings – not just word embeddings as used in unimodal LLMs but also image, audio and video embeddings as produced by the modality encoder of an MM-LLM (see section 1)[10]. Again, this dimension is a snapshot of the current AI landscape, which is still being dominated by the transformer architecture. However, other architectures are currently being researched and may compete with the transformer in the future, e.g., so-called *state space models*, which show promising performance in MT tasks (see Pitorro et al. 2024). Training LLMs is broadly comparable to training MT systems, with the exception that user-facing LLMs such as ChatGPT are usually fine-tuned for instruction following and aligned using techniques such as Reinforcement Learning from Human Feedback. When natural (i.e., human-generated) training data is not available in sufficient quantity and/or quality, synthetic (i.e., AI-generated) training data can be used. However, if such synthetic training data comes to dominate the overall training dataset at

---

[9] Potential competence levels for the framework will be discussed in more detail in section 4.

[10] DataLit^MT provides learning resources on word embeddings as used in NMT systems, retrieved on 26/07/2024 from (https://colab.research.google.com/drive/1BUCBwdD-nqyyFnJULtmLoxfqP8bZcBQMa?usp=sharing. These resources can be extended to cover embeddings of other modalities as processed by MM-LLMs.

the expense of natural data, model performance has been shown to degrade ("model collapse," see Shumailov et al. 2023)[11]. Awareness of this phenomenon may be important when the human-added value in light of high-performing AI technologies has to be articulated (see section 3.2). Finally, an awareness of the possibilities and limitations of watermarking AI content is important both in the context of current and future AI legislation (see section 3.4) and with regard to the risk of manipulation inherent in AI (see section 3.5).

3.2 Determining the domain-specific performance of MM-LLMs

As discussed briefly in section 2.3, determining the domain-specific performance of general-purpose MM-LLMs is not a trivial task, since they have a potentially very wide scope of application (see section 1), making their affordances somewhat opaque. Also, their task-specific performance level may depend on how well the models are prompted for a particular task (see section 3.3). Being able to identify the added value that humans continue to contribute to AI-assisted workflows is important for determining the optimum degree of automation of language industry workflows, for determining adequate prices in AI-assisted production processes and for establishing a proper AI risk management (see section 3.4). It is also important to counter potential AI-induced social disempowerment, which may manifest itself in reduced economic and social capital of professionals if their expert competences seem susceptible to being fully automated through AI (see section 3.5). In this context, Bubeck et al. (2023, p. 80) refer to Kahneman's (2011) distinction between *fast system 1 thinking* (which is instinctive, almost automatic and requires little to no cognitive effort) and *slow system 2 thinking* (which is rational, conscious, more effortful and involves complex decisions). According to this distinction, LLMs excel at system 1 "thinking" but lack the ability to switch to system 2 "thinking" while humans, although often being prone to system 1 thinking, can,

---

11 In this context, Thompson et al. (2024, p. 1) find that "[a] shocking amount of the web is machine translated" and raise "serious concerns about training models such as multilingual large language models on both monolingual and bilingual data scraped from the web" (ibid.).

if required, switch to system 2 thinking[12]. Determining domain-specific performance also requires knowledge of the input/output modalities a given model can handle, with the number of these modalities having increased recently with MM-LLMs. Given the high pace of AI research, it is also important to consider the future potential of AI and to be able to identify tasks which are still beyond current models such as GPT-4 but may well be within the scope of future models such as GPT-5 or GPT-6. Finally, the general-purpose character of MM-LLMs entails that complex process chains consisting of different sub-tasks (e.g., pre-editing, machine translating, and then post-editing a text) can, in principle, be supported or automated by one and the same model (see Figure 6), which may introduce unwanted machine circularities in language industry workflows. To avoid such circularities and achieve a proper risk diversification, the individual sub-tasks of such process chains should ideally be distributed over different technologies and/or human experts.

3.3 Interacting adequately with MM-LLMs

Interacting adequately with MM-LLMs first requires an awareness of the available modalities of interaction. Here, written (and perhaps spoken) interaction may dominate in the short to medium term, but at least in theory, MM-LLMs also allow for other means of interaction, such as gesture control. AI-specific pre-/post-editing is reminiscent of pre- and post-editing in the context of MT but can be wider in scope; e.g., in technical writing, notes taken by design engineers could be pre-edited and then passed to an LLM which transforms these notes into a draft operating manual (which would then be post-edited). At the moment of writing, prompting is the central method of human-LLM interaction, with the quality/informativeness of the prompt often correlating with the quality of the model output. Prompting can either be dialogical, meaning that users start with a naïve prompt and then

[12] See Bubeck et al. (2023, p. 80) in their performance analysis of an early version of GPT-4: "The model relies on a local and greedy process of generating the next word, without any global or deep understanding of the task or the output. Thus, the model is good at producing fluent and coherent texts, but has limitations with regards to solving complex or creative problems which cannot be approached in a sequential manner."

iteratively refine the model output through conversational interaction with the LLMs, or it can be structured, by adhering to best practices for prompting LLMs for a particular task (see e.g., the overview of best practice prompting LLMs for MT in Krüger 2023, pp. 311–317). Structured prompting (which may be followed by iterative refinement prompting) also includes methods such as Retrieval-Augmented Generation, where prompts are enriched with information from external knowledge sources. Cognition is also a very important dimension in human-LLM/AI interaction; e.g., translation process research has shown that translator-MT interaction can have both positive cognitive effects (such as a reduction in cognitive effort or creative impulses provided by the MT system) as well as negative cognitive effects (such as stagnation in competence development, deskilling or unwanted priming effects exerted by the MT system) (see the overview in Krüger 2022b, pp. 504–510). This requires a metacognitive awareness of these effects as well as the ability to articulate strategies to maximise positive and to minimise negative cognitive effects in human-LLM/AI interaction. Adaptive expertise "involves optimal performance in contexts where tasks are more ambiguous and when they call for novelty in problem solving" (Angelone 2022, p. 65). Adaptive expertise can be claimed to be an important competence in LLM-assisted language industry workflows since LLMs contribute to a phenomenon called *dejobbing*, meaning that these technologies make workflows more dynamic and "the responsibilities assigned to a given individual more challenging to recognise and define" (Herbert et al. 2023, p. 10). In other words, translators, interpreters and technical writers who want to participate successfully in dynamic LLM-assisted language industry workflows require adaptive expertise, which in turn requires an adequate domain-specific AI literacy. The aspect of developing a macro-strategy is informed by insights from translation process research, according to which expert performance is a form of strategic action where a macro-strategy guides micro-strategic decision-making. Sociocognitive translation studies also stresses the fact that such a macro-strategy is formed taking situational factors into consideration and that it may change dynamically over time (see Risku 2016, p. 59), which can be linked to the concepts of adaptive expertise and dejobbing discussed previously. Finally, another relevant aspect of human-LLM/AI interaction is that of human vs machine agency (again, see the MT-focused overview in Krüger 2022b, pp. 510–520), which is becoming more and more important as the autonomy of AI technologies increases[13]. An important competence in this regard is the ability to recognise when human intervention in LLM-assisted production processes is required and when LLMs can potentially complete certain tasks in an (almost) autonomous manner. Recently, there have been attempts at a joint conceptualisation of human and machine agency in human-LLM interaction under the term "collaborative agency" (see van Lier 2023, p. 80). In a collaborative agent system, the active human component supervises the non-autonomous/independent LLM component (see ibid.), which is compatible with human expert-in-the-loop approaches propagated for the language industry (see Slator 2022).

3.4 Implementing MM-LLMs in language industry workflows

The domain-specific (as opposed to generic) nature of the AI literacy framework discussed here is most obvious in the present dimension concerned with language industry workflow implementation. Setting up effective and efficient LLM/AI-assisted workflows presupposes an adequate AI culture in the organisation/company in which these workflows are to be implemented. This includes establishing guidelines for and providing training in the ethical and safe use of AI technologies. Compliance with legal AI frameworks and appropriate AI risk management have become pressing with the recent EU legislation on artificial intelligence. The EU AI Act, which constitutes the most significant legal framework on AI to date, defines four risk levels for AI systems: 1) minimal or no risk; 2) limited risk; 3) high risk; and 4) unacceptable risk (see EU Artificial Intelligence Act 2024 Compliance Checker). While systems posing unacceptable risks are prohibited, systems of the remaining risk levels have to satisfy certain requirements[14].

---

[13] Current LLM research is geared toward turning LLMs into autonomous agents which can be assigned complex process chains without the need for human supervision. E.g., Ng (2024) recently developed an agentic MT workflow where an LLM automatically performs the tasks of MT, quality evaluation and quality optimisation (however, see the remarks on machine circularities in section 3.2).

[14] Chatbot systems such as ChatGPT are considered as limited risk systems by the EU AI Act. These systems "must adhere to transparency obligations so users know they are not interacting with humans" (see EU Artificial Intelligence Act 2024 Compliance Checker). In the AI literacy framework, this is reflected in the subdimensions *Watermarking AI-generated content* (section 3.1) and *Risk of manipulation* (section 3.5).

Translation studies has already produced a considerable body of work on risk in the context of MT (e.g., Canfora/Ottmann 2020), which can inform LLM implementation in the language industry but potentially also in other industries. Choosing suitable AI vendors/models is informed by the subdimension identifying/evaluating data sources of the DataLitMT framework (see section 2.2). Process design depends, among other things, on the adequate identification of the necessary human-added value in order to find the optimal degree of automation of individual workflows (in this context, see also the discussion on machine circularities and LLM agents in sections 3.2 and 3.4). With regard to this added value of human experts-in-the-loop, ergonomic factors of process design, particularly at organisational and cognitive level also have to be taken into account (see the MT-oriented discussion in Krüger 2022b, pp. 493–496). Quality assurance/control and economic aspects are broadly comparable in MT- and LLM-assisted workflows, meaning that corresponding insights from MT research and translation studies (as reflected in the professional MT literacy framework) can again be incorporated here.

3.5 Considering ethical/societal aspects of MM-LLMs

The final dimension of the framework transcends its domain-specific character to a certain extent and incorporates wider ethical/societal aspects of current MM-LLMs and possible future AI technologies. Potential AI-induced social (dis)empowerment was already discussed briefly in the context of identifying human-added value in section 3.2. While translation and the language industry in general has been under high automation pressure and has had to counter corresponding discourses of marginalisation for quite some time, the general-purpose character and wide scope of application of MM-LLMs means that this automation pressure and the associated marginalisation tendencies now also spread to other professional fields, such as computer science or law (which may profit from corresponding insights gathered in translation studies). Having LLMs produce toxic outputs (discriminatory/hate speech, political misinformation, etc.) can be achieved via *Jailbreak Prompting* (see Yong/Menghini/Bach 2024), which circumvents the alignment of user-facing LLMs. In this context, awareness of jailbreak prompting strategies and potential countermeasures is important. The risk of manipulation via MM-LLMs is becoming more and more relevant the better these models are at imitating human texts, voices, faces etc., e.g., Jones and Bergen (2024) demonstrate that, in a Turing Test setting, people cannot confidently tell GPT-4 apart from a human interlocutor after having a 5-minute discussion with the model. This finding is exacerbated by research conducted by Salvi et al. (2024), which finds that LLMs can exhibit a high level of persuasiveness in conversations with humans, particularly when models are provided with personal information about their interlocutors. It is easy to conceive of possible misuse of these LLM capabilities, e.g., in translation project management, where LLMs could be used to manipulate translators into accepting unfavourable prices, deadlines or other job conditions. This requires an awareness of potential LLM-induced manipulation as well as strategies for watermarking AI-generated content (see section 3.1). Epistemic violence/distortion and reproduction of social biases refers to the risk that AI technologies may misrepresent reality, e.g., due to corresponding distortions in their training data (see e.g., Vanmassenhove 2024 on gender bias in MT and LLMs), which again requires an adequate awareness of this issue. Knowledge of the material and immaterial substrate of AI is particularly important in the context of environmental/climate protection, since training and deploying current AI technologies such as MM-LLMs requires high amounts of energy; e.g., Luccioni, Jernite and Strubell (2023, p. 1) compare the CO_2 emissions of MM-LLMs for different tasks and find that classification tasks (such as determining the sentiment expressed in a text) require less energy than generation tasks and that image generation is more energy-intensive than text generation. These aspects should also be considered when designing LLM-assisted language industry workflows. And finally, adequate AI literacy should also enable stakeholders to contribute to AI-focused impact assessments both at the level of individual professional fields and at overall societal level. Such an impact assessment "studies the effects of new technologies on the industry, the environment and society, evaluates such effects and develops instruments to steer technology development in more desired directions" (Brey 2012, p. 3). It could be argued that the field of translation studies may be an ideal contributor to a multifaceted AI impact assessment due to its extensive experience with analysing the manifold implications of MT-induced automation in the language industry.

4. Outlook: planned didactic operationalisation of the framework

The next steps toward operationalising the domain-specific AI literacy framework presented in the previous section include establishing competence levels and descriptors for the individual (sub)dimensions of the framework and combining these into a competence matrix, as was done in DataLit^{MT}:

DataLit^{MT} competence matrix: 3 Data collection/production		
	Basic level	***Advanced level***
3.1 Data verification	Can follow instructions to check MT training data quality for a given MT-assisted translation scenario in accordance with a range of pre-selected criteria.	Can critically evaluate MT training data quality for different MT-assisted translation scenarios, developing suitable assessment criteria and taking into account data-strategic considerations.
3.2 Data acquisition	Can follow instructions to collect MT training data for a given MT-assisted translation scenario.	Can identify and perform the steps required to collect MT training data for different MT-assisted translation scenarios, taking into account data-strategic considerations.

Figure 6: Excerpt from the DataLit^{MT} competence matrix (Krüger/Hackenbucher 2024, p. 261).

In the DataLit^{MT} matrix, the basic level competences correspond broadly to levels 1 to 3 of the European Qualifications Framework (EQF, see European Commission n. d.), ranging from "[b]asic skills required to carry out simple tasks" to various "cognitive and practical skills required to accomplish tasks and solve problems by selecting and applying basic methods, tools, materials and information" (ibid.). The advanced level competences correspond broadly to levels 4 to 6 of the EQF, ranging from various "cognitive and practical skills required to generate solutions to specific problems in a field of work or study" to "advanced skills, demonstrating mastery and innovation, required to solve complex and unpredictable problems in a specialised field of work or study" (ibid., levels 7 and 8 of the EQF were not covered by DataLit^{MT}). With regard to the domain-specific AI literacy framework, a finer-grained distinction of competence levels could be envisaged, in the spirit of the seven data and AI literacy levels proposed by Schüller et al. (2023, p. 429). Schüller et al. (ibid.) distinguish between the three roles 1) *informed prosumer*, 2) *skilled user* and 3) *expert creator and developer*. An informed prosumer is defined as "[a] person who produces and consumes data and AI in an informed way" (ibid.) and should master competence levels 1 (understand & recognise the overall relevance of AI and data), 2 (consume data and tools in a conscious way) and 3 (provide such data and tools in a conscious way). A skilled user is defined as "[a] person who uses data and AI in a skilled and responsible way, including application-relevant skills that go beyond consumption and sharing" (ibid.). In addition to competence levels 1 to 3, skilled users should master competence levels 4 (collect data), 5 (manage & provide data) and 6 (evaluate and analyse data). Finally, an expert creator is defined as "[a] person who creates insights, solutions, and tools with and based on data and AI." In addition to competence levels 1 to 6, expert creators should also master competence level 7 (create & develop). In a next step, the roles and competence levels proposed by Schüller et al. will be tailored to more specific language industry roles and competence levels, which will then be translated into individual competence descriptors that will allow for the didactic operationalisation of the framework, which again will be done in the spirit of DataLit^MT^.

A suitable vehicle for this operationalisation may be provided by the EU-funded Erasmus+ consortium *LT-LiDER: Language and Translation – Literacy in Digital Environments and Resources* coordinated by the Universitat Autònoma de Barcelona (see Sánchez Gijón et al. 2024). The LT-LiDER project, which runs from December 2023 until October 2026, aims, among other things, "to provide training materials to enhance digital and AI literacy skills among language and translation professionals and trainers" (ibid., p. 55)[15]. LT-LiDER and related initiatives can contribute to the development of AI-savvy professionals and citizens who are adequately equipped for an "AI-saturated world" (Markauskaite et al. 2022, p. 2), in which humans are working and living together with high-performing and ubiquitous AI technologies.

---

15 The LT-LiDER project website is available under the following link: Retrieved on 26/07/2024 from http://lt-lider.eu/. Project outcomes will be published on the website on an ongoing basis.

Bibliography

Angelone, Erik (2022): "Weaving adaptive expertise into translator training." In: Massey, Gary / Huertas-Barros, Elsa / Katan, David (eds.): *The human translator in the 2020s*. London: Routledge, pp. 60–73. https://doi.org/10.4324/9781003223344.

Angelone, Erik / Ehrensberger-Dow, Maureen / Massey, Gary (2020): "Introduction." In: Angelone, Erik / Ehrensberger-Dow, Maureen / Massey, Gary (eds.): *The Bloomsbury companion to language industry studies*. London: Bloomsbury Academic, pp. 1–14. https://doi.org/10.5040/9781350024960.0005.

Ayvazyan, Nune / Torres-Simón, Ester / Pym, Anthony (2024): "What kind of translation literacy will be automation-resistant?." In: Peng, Yuhong / Huang, Huihui / Li, Defeng (eds.): *New advances in translation technology. Applications and pedagogy*. Singapore: Springer, pp. 121–140. https://doi.org/10.1007/978-981-97-2958-6_7.

Brey, Philip A. E. (2012): "Anticipatory ethics for emerging technologies." *NanoEthics* 6, pp. 1–13. https://doi.org/10.1007/s11569-012-0141-7.

Bubeck, Sébastien / Chandrasekaran, Varun / Eldan, Ronen / Gehrke, Johannes / Horvitz, Eric / Kamar, Ece / Lee, Peter/ Tat Lee, Yin / Li, Yuanzhi / Lundberg, Scott / Nori, Harsha / Palangi, Hamid / Tulio Ribeiro, Marco / Zhang, Yi (2023): "Sparks of artificial general intelligence: early experiments with GPT-4." *arXiv*. https://doi.org/10.48550/arXiv.2303.12712.

Canfora, Carmen / Ottmann, Angelika (2020): "Risks in neural machine translation." *Translation Spaces* 9(1), pp. 58–77. https://doi.org/10.1075/ts.00021.can.

EU Artificial Intelligence Act (2024): *EU Artificial Intelligence Act Chapter I (General Provisions) Article 3 (Definitions) Paragraph 63*, retrieved on 16/07/2024 from https://artificialintelligenceact.eu/article/3/.

EU Artificial Intelligence Act (2024): *EU Artificial Intelligence Act Chapter I (General Provisions) Article 4 (AI literacy)*, retrieved on 22/07/2024 from https://artificialintelligenceact.eu/article/4/.

EU Artificial Intelligence Act (2024): *Compliance checker*, retrieved on 19/07/2024 from https://artificialintelligenceact.eu/assessment/eu-ai-act-compliance-checker/

European Commission (n. d.): *Description of the eight EQF levels*, retrieved on 25/07/2024 from https://europa.eu/europass/en/description-eight-eqf-levels.

Hackenbuchner, Janiça / Krüger, Ralph (2023): "DataLit^MT – Teaching data literacy in the context of machine translation literacy." In: Nurminen, Mary / Brenner, Judith / Koponen, Maarit / Latomaa, Sirkku / Mikhailov, Mikhail / Schierl, Frederike / Ranasinghe, Tharindu / Vanmassenhove, Eva / Alvarez Vidal, Sergi / Aranberri, Nora / Nunziatini, Mara / Parra Escartín, Carla / Forcada, Mikel / Popovic, Maja / Scarton, Carolina / Moniz, Helena (eds.): *Proceedings of the 24th annual conference of the European Association of Machine Translation* (EAMT 2023). European Association of Machine Translation, pp. 285–293, retrieved on 19/07/2024 from https://aclanthology.org/2023.eamt-1.28/.

Herbert, Sarah / do Carmo, Félix / Gough, Joanna / Carnegie-Brown, Anu (2023): "From responsibilities to responsibility: A study of the effects of translation workflow automation." *Journal of Specialised Translation* 40, pp. 9–35, retrieved on 29/07/2024 from https://www.jostrans.soap2.ch/issue40/art_herbert.pdf.

Jones, Cameron R. / Bergen, Benjamin K. (2024): "People cannot distinguish GPT-4 from a human in a Turing test." *arXiv*. https://doi.org/10.48550/arXiv.2405.08007.

Kahneman, Daniel (2011): *Thinking, fast and slow*. New York: Farrar, Straus and Giroux.

Kenny, Dorothy (2019): "Machine translation." In: Rawling, Piers / Wilson, Philip (eds.): *The Routledge handbook of translation and philosophy*. London/New York: Routledge, pp. 428–445.

Krüger, Ralph (2022a): "Integrating professional machine translation literacy and data literacy." *Lebende Sprachen* 67(2), pp. 247–282. https://doi.org/10.1515/les-2022-1022.

Krüger, Ralph (2022b): *Die neuronale maschinelle Übersetzung als Werkzeug fachübersetzerischen Handelns. Modellierung – 'Kompetenz'-/Performanzanalyse – didaktische Vermittlung*. Habilitation thesis, University of Mainz. https://doi.org/10.13140/RG.2.2.10106.91846.

Krüger, Ralph (2023): "Artificial intelligence literacy for the language industry – with particular emphasis on recent large language models such as GPT-4." *Lebende Sprachen* 68(2), pp. 283–330. https://doi.org/10.1515/les-2023-0024.

Krüger, Ralph / Hackenbucher Janiça (2024): "A competence matrix for machine translation-oriented data literacy teaching." *Target* 36(2), pp. 245–275. https://doi.org/10.1075/target.22127.kru.

Long, Duri / Magerko, Brian (2020): "What is AI literacy? Competencies and design considerations." In: Association for Computing Machinery: *CHI '20: Proceedings of the 2020 CHI conference on human factors in computing systems*. New York: Association for Computing Machinery, pp. 1–16. https://doi.org/10.1145/3313831.3376727.

Luccioni, Alexandra Sasha / Jernite, Yacine / Strubell, Emma (2023): "Power hungry processing: Watts driving the cost of AI deployment?." *arXiv*. https://doi.org/10.48550/arXiv.2311.16863.

Markauskaite, Lina / Marrone, Rebecca / Poquet, Oleksandra / Knight, Simon / Martinez-Maldonado, Roberto / Howard, Sarah / Tondeur, Jo / De Laat, Maarten / Buckingham Shum / Simon / Gašević, Dragan / Siemens, George (2022): "Rethinking the entwinement between artificial intelligence and human learning: What capabilities do learners need for a world with AI?." *Computers and Education: Artificial Intelligence* 3, pp. 1–16. https://doi.org/10.1016/j.caeai.2022.100056.

Maslej, Nestor / Fattorini, Loredana / Perrault, Raymond / Parli, Vanessa / Reuel, Anka / Brynjolfsson, Erik / Etchemendy, John / Ligett, Katrina / Lyons, Terah / Manyika, James / Niebles, Juan Carlos / Shoham, Yoav / Wald, Russell / Clark, Jack (2024): *The AI index 2024 annual report*. Stanford: Stanford University, retrieved on 26/07/2024 from https://aiindex.stanford.edu/report/

Ng, Andrew (2024): "Translation agent: Agentic translation using reflection workflow." *GitHub repository*, retrieved on 25/07/2024 from https://github.com/andrewyng/translation-agent

Pitorro, Hugo / Vasylenko, Pavlo / Treviso, Marcos / Martins, André F. T. (2024): "How effective are state space models for machine translation?." *arXiv*. https://doi.org/10.48550/arXiv.2407.05489.

Ridsdale, Chantel / Rothwell, James / Smit, Michael / Ali-Hassan, Hossam / Bliemel, Michael / Irvine, Dean / Kelley, Daniel / Matwin, Stan / Wuetherick, Bradley (2015): *Strategies and best practices for data literacy education. Knowledge synthesis report*. Dalhousie University, retrieved on 22/07/2024 from http://hdl.handle.net/10222/64578.

Risku, Hanna (2016): *Translationsmanagement. Interkulturelle Fachkommunikation im Informationszeitalter*. Tübingen: Narr Francke Attempto.

Salvi, Francesco / Horta Ribeiro, Manoel / Gallotti, Riccardo / West, Robert (2024): "On the conversational persuasiveness of large language models: A randomized controlled trial." *arXiv*. https://doi.org/10.48550/arXiv.2403.14380.

Sánchez Gijón, Pilar / Torres Simon, Esther / Vargas Urpí, Mireia / Aranberri, Nora / Ciobanu, Dragoş / Guerberof Arenas, Ana / Hackenbuchner, Janiça / Kenny, Dorothy / Krüger, Ralph / Moorkens, Joss / Rios Gaona, Miguel / Rivas Ginel, Isabel / Rossi, Caroline / Secară, Alina / Toral, Antonio (2024): "Literacy in digital environments and resources (LT-LiDER)." In: Song, Xingyi / Gow-Smith, Edward / Scarton, Carolina / Cabarrão, Vera / Chatzitheodorou, Konstantinos / Cadwell, Patrick / Lapshinova-Koltunski, Ekaterina / Bawden, Rachel / Sánchez-Cartagena, Víctor M./ Haddow, Barry / Kanojia, Diptesh / Nurminen, Mary / Moniz, Helena / Forcada, Mikel / Oakley, Chris (eds.): *Proceedings of the 25th annual conference of the European Association for Machine Translation (EAMT 2024)*. Sheffield: European Association for Machine Translation, pp. 55–56, retrieved on 26/07/2024 from https://eamt2024.github.io/proceedings/vol2.pdf.

Sandrini, Peter (2022): "'It's the economy, stupid'. Discussing the translator's business against the background of a changing techno-economic landscape." *Translation Matters* 4(2), pp. 49–62, retrieved on 26/07/2024 from https://ojs.letras.up.pt/index.php/tm/article/view/11620.

Schüller, Katharina / Ramplet, Florian / Henning, Koch / Schleiss, Johannes (2023): "Better ready than just aware: Data and AI Literacy as an enabler for informed decision making in the data age." In: Klein, Maike / Krupka, Daniel, Winter, Cornelia / Wohlgemuth, Volker (eds.): *INFORMATIK 2023, Lecture Notes in Informatics (LNI)*. Berlin: Gesellschaft für Informatik, pp. 425–430. https://doi.org/10.18420/inf2023_49.

Shumailov, Ilia / Shumaylov, Zakhar / Zhao, Yiren / Gal, Yarin / Papernot, Nicolas / Anderson, Ross (2023): "The curse of recursion: Training on generated data makes models forget." *arXiv*. https://doi.org/10.48550/arXiv.2305.17493.

Slator (2022): "Slator machine translation expert-in-the-loop report." *Slator*, retrieved on 30/07/2024 from https://slator.com/machine-translation-expert-in-the-loop-report/.

Thompson, Brian / Preet Dhaliwal, Mehak / Frisch, Peter / Domhan, Tobias / Federico, Marcello (2024): "A shocking amount of the web is machine translated: Insights from multi-way parallelism." *arXiv*. https://doi.org/10.48550/arXiv.2401.05749.

van Lier, Maud (2023): "Understanding large language models through the lens of artificial agency." In: Grahn, Håkan / Borg, Anton / Boldt, Martin (eds.): *35th annual workshop of the Swedish Artificial Intelligence Society (SAIS 2023)*, pp. 79–84. https://doi.org/10.3384/ecp199008.

Vanmassenhove, Eva (2024): "Gender bias in machine translation and the era of large language models." *arXiv*. https://doi.org/10.48550/arXiv.2401.10016.

Vaswani, Ashish / Shazeer, Noam / Parmar, Niki / Uszkoreit, Jakob / Jones, Llion / Gomez, Aidan N. / Kaiser, Łukasz / Polosukhin, Illia (2017): "Attention is all you need." In: Guyon, Isabelle / Luxburg, Ulrike / Bengio, Samy / Wallach, Hanna M. / Fergus, Rob / Vishwanathan, S. V. N. / Garnett, Roman (eds.): *Advances in neural information processing systems 30* (NIPS 2017), pp. 1–11, retrieved on 26/07/2024 from https://proceedings.neurips.cc/paper/2017/hash/3f5ee243547dee91fbd053c1c4a845aa-Abstract.html.

Yong, Zheng-Xin / Menghini, Christina / Bach, Stephen H. (2024): "Low-resource languages jailbreak GPT-4." *arXiv*. https://doi.org/10.48550/arXiv.2310.02446.

Zhang, Duzhen / Yu, Yahan / Dong, Jiahua / Li, Chenxing / Su, Dan / Chu, Chenhui / Yu, Dong (2024): "MM-LLMs: Recent advances in multimodal large language models." *arXiv*. https://doi.org/10.48550/arXiv.2401.13601.

Translation students' use of generative AI-driven tools for language learning and translation

Jim J. J. Ureel
University of Antwerp, Belgium

Enrique Cerezo Herrero
Universitat de València, Spain

Astrid Schmidhofer
University of Innsbruck, Austria

Melita Koletnik
University of Maribor, Slovenia
University of Vienna, Austria

ABSTRACT
Generative artificial intelligence (GenAI) is reshaping higher education (HE), offering new tools for teaching, learning and assessment (e.g., Fell Kurban/Şahin 2024, Kosslyn 2024, O'Dea/Ng 2025). Within translation and interpreting (TI) programmes, integrating GenAI tools raises significant questions about their role in developing language competence, translation competence and interpreting competence in students and preparing students for changing professional demands (Pym/Hao 2025). In our study, we examined students' self-reported use of GenAI tools and their perceptions of the value and impact of GenAI tools. We surveyed undergraduate and graduate students from four European countries – Austria, Belgium, Slovenia, Spain – to explore their familiarity with, attitudes towards and academic experiences with using GenAI tools. Our findings show that students use LLMs like ChatGPT mainly for language explanations, text editing and idea generation. However, although they perceive GenAI as a valuable resource for enhancing learning processes and future employability, they often lack formal training on ethical and effective GenAI use. We recommend further research to validate students' beliefs empirically and to explore TI trainer perspectives, since educators play a pivotal role in guiding responsible and effective use of GenAI tools. Furthermore, we emphasise the need for structured AI literacy teaching and assessment tailored to TI programmes, advocating for effective practices in AI literacy education to develop context-specific competences.

Keywords: generative artificial intelligence (GenAI), language teaching and learning, language competence, translation and interpreting programmes, foreign languages

1. Introduction

Generative artificial intelligence (GenAI)[1] has emerged as a transformative force across various domains, fundamentally altering the ways in which we live, work and learn, by, for example, personalising education, optimising workflows, improving accessibility and advancing creativity. The language industry, in particular, has been significantly impacted by its development, which has presented both ethical and practical challenges alongside valuable opportunities that demand careful consideration and risk mitigation. Given its profound impact on the industry, it is unsurprising that GenAI has also made significant inroads into higher education (HE) programmes focused on preparing future language professionals and enhancing their employability. Indeed, the Bologna Process underscores employability as a core objective of HE, aiming to equip students with the competences required to thrive in an ever-evolving job market. In this context, integrating GenAI into HE curricula, especially in language-related fields, directly addresses the demand for graduates who are not only proficient in their domain(s) and but also adept at navigating emerging technologies.

In HE, GenAI tools have gained considerable attention and are increasingly integrated into teaching, learning and assessment practices (e.g., Fell Kurban/Şahin 2024, Kosslyn 2024, Lin et al. 2024, O'Dea/Ng 2025, Plate et al. 2025, Pym/Hao 2025, Sidorkin 2024). The volume of academic and non-academic publications – both general and field-specific – exploring GenAI in HE is impressive and continues to grow. In this regard, AI literacy emerges as crucial, offering a comprehensive framework for evaluating and addressing the challenges and opportunities posed by GenAI, while aligning with the employability goals of the Bologna Process. By fostering AI literacy, HE institutions can ensure that students not only grasp the technological landscape but also develop the competences needed to leverage GenAI tools effectively, thereby enhancing their employability in an evolving labour

[1] We recognise the conceptual distinction between artificial intelligence (AI) and generative AI (GenAI), with GenAI referring to "a type of artificial intelligence that is able to generate new content using the provision by a user of inputs that could consist of text, pictures, audio or other data" (Shrier 2024, p. 32). While we focus on GenAI-driven tools for language learning and translation, we use the broader term *AI literacy* in our theoretical framework to align with standard terminology in the literature (see, for example, Long/Magerko 2020, Ng et al. 2021).

market. Understanding industry perspectives is crucial for developing AI literacy frameworks in HE, as these perspectives highlight the specific skills and competences that students must acquire to meet market demands.

To contribute further insight into this complex topic, in this chapter, we investigate the use of GenAI tools for language learning in the context of translation and interpreting (TI) university programmes[2]. We aim to explore the extent to which undergraduate and graduate TI students from four different European countries with different cultural backgrounds and educational traditions – Austria, Belgium, Slovenia, Spain – are accepting of and interact with GenAI tools in the contexts of language learning and translation training. For this purpose, we designed a survey, focusing on four key areas: (1) familiarity with GenAI tools, (2) academic experiences with the use of GenAI technologies, (3) attitudes towards GenAI technologies and (4) perspectives on GenAI tools as applied to learning. This study is part of a larger collaborative project conducted by researchers from four public universities from the countries mentioned above.

The background to our study is informed by industry perspectives, employability concerns and new learning outcomes related to GenAI, particularly the development of AI literacy. We outline our study's methodology, present our results and provide a discussion. We end our chapter with a conclusion drawn from the results and discussion.

2. Industry perspectives and employability

GenAI and the development of LLMs have significantly transformed the language industry. Serving a diverse range of clients, ranging from individuals to corporations and governments, the industry provides essential language services for content creators across various sectors. These services

[2] The term *translation and interpreting (TI) university programme* refers to both undergraduate and graduate programmes in translation and interpreting in HE. It includes country-specific programme titles, such as the *bachelor's programme of applied linguistics* in (Dutch-speaking) Belgium, where undergraduate TI education typically falls under applied linguistics programmes. In Slovenia, the term encompasses the *bachelor's programme in translation* and the *master's programme in translation studies*. In contrast, Austria and Spain offer discipline-specific bachelor's programmes in translation studies, along with master's programmes in translation and/or interpreting.

play a crucial role in overcoming linguistic and cultural barriers and facilitating internationalisation (Carr 2023). Krüger (2023) emphasises that the language industry has been at the forefront of AI-driven automation, especially with the advent of large language models (LLMs) like GPT-4. This has significantly redefined the required competences in the language industry, creating an urgent need for general and specialised AI literacy. The impact has been both positive and negative. On the negative side, authors frequently address ethical concerns such as bias, transparency, accountability and unintended societal consequences (Yi 2023), alongside practical challenges such as data privacy concern and the need for extensive computational resources (Paradkar 2024), all of which warrant careful consideration and risk mitigation. Conversely, GenAI and LLMs have created valuable opportunities, including cost reduction, increased efficiency and faster processing (Wolff 2024). To gain more nuanced insights into current trends, we examined the European Language Industry Survey (ELIS) for 2024 and the Nimdzi Language Technology Atlas/Radar.

ELIS is an annual initiative that has provided insights into trends, challenges and developments in the European language industry since 2013, when it was initiated by the European Union of Associations of Translation Companies. Currently, the survey is organised by various European language industry associations and networks, along with the European Commission's Language Industry Expert (LIND) group. ELIS engages a wide range of stakeholders, including language service companies, independent language professionals, translation and interpreting training institutes, language departments and others. The 2024 edition also focused on training and AI, introducing a dedicated survey for students in translation-related programmes.

The 2024 edition of ELIS did not explicitly address LLMS. Instead, they were included under the broader category of (generative) AI, under the theme "AI – The Elephant in the Room." According to the report, AI use was "still in its infancy" (ELIS Research 2024, p. 4) but rapidly increasing. AI overshadowed all other trends among language industry stakeholders and was viewed more positively by language service companies and (public service) language departments than by independent language professionals, university staff and students. AI also topped the ranking in first-time use and investment plans among independent professionals; 28 % used AI for the first time in 2023 and 21 % planned to invest in the technology in 2024. The report anticipated that by 2025, some form of machine translation or

AI would be used in more than 50 % of professional cases (ELIS Research 2024, ibid.).

Interestingly, GenAI was more prevalent in translation training programmes than in the language industry, with 63 % of participating students (352 students from 25 countries) confirming its inclusion in their studies. However, challenges persist, particularly in establishing clear guidelines for AI use, with only 43 % of university staff reporting such rules in place. Universities are also participating in AI-related initiatives through various European collaborative efforts (ELIS Research 2024, pp. 41–42).

The ELIS report also notes that stakeholders' reactions to AI resemble their responses to machine translation a few years ago. While some view AI as a tool to enhance efficiency and create new opportunities, the majority express concerns. Many independent language professionals, in particular, fear that improper use by untrained individuals could compromise quality. They also raise broader concerns that AI's acceptance may further devalue human translation work, potentially reducing appreciation and financial compensation (ELIS Research 2024, pp. 40–41). Nevertheless, some respondents remain hopeful, expecting that "the flaws in AI will re-ignite the appreciation for high quality human translation" (ELIS Research 2024, p. 4).

To meet the needs of the growing language industry, the language industry market research and consulting company Nimdzi has been publishing the freely accessible Language Technology Atlas on its website[3] since 2019. In 2024, the Atlas, which provided a snapshot of the language technology landscape at a given point in time, was replaced by the interactive and constantly updated Language Technology Radar. Both tools were created to enhance transparency in the language technology market and support technology providers, investors, linguists and language service buyers in their decision-making. Additionally, they serve as a valuable resource for language programme students, enabling them to explore various tools relevant to their future careers.

The 2023 Language Technology Atlas listed over 920 programmes and applications, with its creators surveying many more. They were classified into translation management systems, translation business management systems, interpreting systems, speech recognition solutions, audiovisual translation tools, machine translators, integrators, quality management, marketplaces and

---

[3] https://www.nimdzi.com/language-technology-atlas/

platforms, and multilingual content generators (MLCGs). With the advent of ChatGPT in November 2022 and the subsequent rise of LLMs, the MLCG category was added to the Atlas in 2023 (Akhulkova 2023), only to be split into two categories, namely multilingual creation tools and large language models (LLMs), in the 2024 Nimdzi Radar. As Ciesielski (2024, n. p.) aptly observed, "2024 might be the year of [their] real impact in language technology."

The new classification underscores, once again, the increasing importance of LLMs, which have, according to Akhulkova (2024), democratised language technologies with their versatility, accessibility and rapid proliferation, sparking widespread experimentation across the language industry. However, while offering immense potential, large-scale deployment of LLMs remains limited as organisations explore how to integrate them into workflows.

As GenAI continues to transform industries, including the language sector, HE must adapt to prepare students for these evolving professional landscapes. This transformation underscores the need to equip undergraduates and graduates with technological competences that align with market demands. Employability has always been a primary objective of the European Higher Education Area (EHEA), as outlined in the 1999 Bologna Declaration[4]. However, the challenges facing HE institutions in preparing graduates for the global workforce are now more pressing than ever. Technological competences are crucial for success in today's competitive world. As Do (2024) notes for translation programmes, there is a "(mis)match between university translation graduates' competences and market needs" (p. 224), particularly regarding technological skills. To address this mismatch, Pym and Hao (2025) recommend promoting AI literacy and teaching "translation technologies in *both* the additional-language class and the training of translators, in the hope of ensuring that literacy in translation technologies is as widespread as possible" (p. xix). However, how can we conceptualise AI literacy?

3. AI literacy

Defining constructs is essential in both theoretical and practical approaches, enabling practitioners and researchers to adopt perspectives – ranging from analytical to holistic – when addressing complex phenomena. This process

4 https://ehea.info/page-ministerial-conference-bologna-1999 (retrieved on 12/12/2024)

transforms abstract concepts into measurable and actionable frameworks, facilitating comprehensive investigation while focusing on relevant aspects of complex constructs (analytical investigation) and highlighting links between components for holistic investigation. Construct definition is crucial in assessment contexts, as it clarifies what we need to ask learners to demonstrate. In turn, this allows us to observe performance and draw conclusions about the extent to which learning outcomes are achieved.

Therefore, to investigate the operationalisation of AI literacy in translation and interpreting training, we first examine how models of communicative competence and translation competence have approached construct operationalisation. In second language acquisition (SLA), Canale and Swain's (1980) initial attempt at operationalising communicative competence laid the foundation for subsequent adaptations by themselves and other scholars (e.g., Bachman 1990). In the 1983 conceptualisation of communicative competence, Canale (1983) divided the construct into four components: (1) linguistic/grammatical competence, sociolinguistic competence, discourse competence and strategic competence (see also Kanwit and Solon 2023). Similarly, in translation studies (TS), the European Master's in Translation (EMT) model of translation competence effectively operationalises translation competence into a specific skill set, distinguishing five key areas in its 2022 version: (1) language and culture, (2) translation, (3) technology, (4) personal and interpersonal and (5) service provision (EMT 2022). Similarly, we use an existing model of AI literacy – Chan and Colloton's (2024) Dynamic AI Literacy Model for Specific Roles – in our study in the context of translation and interpreting (TI). This approach aims to contextualise and enhance training programmes by equipping professionals with the competences needed to navigate AI technologies effectively and responsibly.

Although AI literacy is a relatively new concept, several frameworks have already been established and explored to operationalise it (see, for example, Kandlhofer et al. 2016; Laupichler et al. 2022; Long/Magerko 2020; Ng et al. 2021). Collectively, they have contributed to the rapidly evolving discourse on AI literacy by emphasising aspects such as educational needs, workplace competences, ethical considerations and the integration of AI into everyday life. These frameworks highlight the complex and multidimensional nature of AI literacy, indicating that any universally accepted framework remains a work in progress due to the diverse needs and contexts in which

AI is developed, applied and studied. Krüger (2023) argues that AI literacy, particularly in the language industry, extends beyond general digital literacy, encompassing an understanding of the capabilities, limitations and ethical considerations of LLMs. This aligns with our study's focus on the importance of fostering AI literacy in translation and interpreting programmes. Building on these foundational models, we turn to the Dynamic AI Literacy Model (DAILM) as a context-specific framework designed to address the unique requirements of translation and interpreting professionals in the evolving AI landscape.

In this publication, we focus on a dynamic expansion of a Fundamental AI Literacy Framework following Chan and Colloton (2024). Their discussion of the Dynamic AI Literacy Model (DAILM) for Specific Roles builds upon the Fundamental AI Literacy Framework, which defines five essential components for understanding and responsibly interacting with AI technologies:

1. *Understanding AI concepts:* Understanding the basic principles of AI to facilitate informed decision-making and awareness of AI's capabilities and limitations.
2. *Awareness of AI applications:* Recognising AI's diverse applications in daily life and various domains, enabling individuals to use AI tools effectively and enhance their technological experiences.
3. *AI effectiveness for human emotions:* Understanding how AI interprets and responds to human emotions to foster empathetic and emotionally intelligent interactions with AI systems.
4. *AI safety and security:* Addressing potential risks, such as privacy breaches and algorithmic biases, to empower individuals to protect their data and make informed AI-related choices.
5. *Responsible AI use:* Encouraging ethical AI practices by recognising its limitations and biases to ensure fairness, transparency and accountability in AI systems.

Using Chan's Fundamental AI Literacy Framework (2024) as a foundation for developing learners' understanding of and engagement with AI technologies, Chan and Colloton (2024) propose a context-specific expansion called the Dynamic AI Literacy Model (DAILM) for Specific Roles (see Figure 1, with

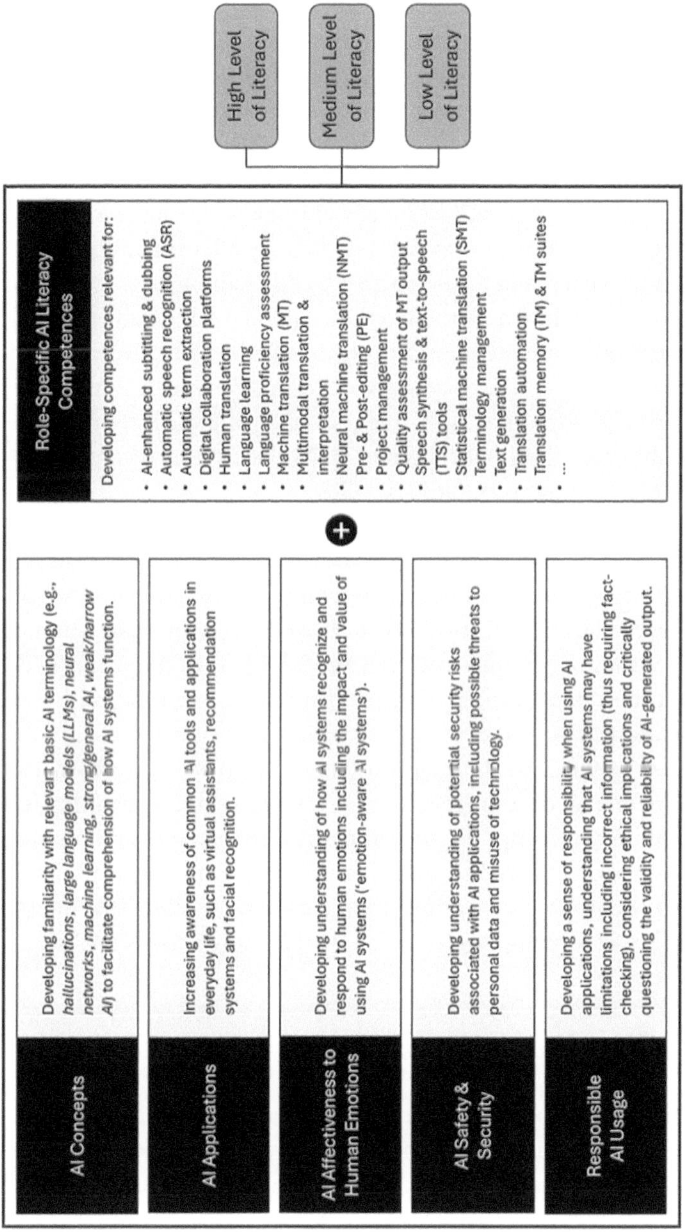

Figure 1: The Dynamic AI Literacy Model (DAILM) for Specific Roles: Translation & Interpreting (adapted from Chan/Colloton 2024).

role-specific AI literacy competences for translation and interpreting added by us). The DAILM applies the five foundational components above at varying levels of literacy (low, medium, high), based on professional needs. This tiered approach to AI literacy ensures that its development can be tailored to various professional contexts. The expanded DAILM model is flexible (i.e., dynamic), adapting to new roles as technology evolves. In essence, the DAILM adapts the Fundamental AI Literacy Framework to address the specific needs of various professions, making AI literacy relevant and practical for preparing individuals for a future shaped by AI technologies. Translator education is one such field where the DAILM's tailored approach is crucial, as it requires targeted competences to navigate AI tools effectively. In line with the DAILM's focus on developing specific competences, Pym (2023) identifies key principles for effectively integrating LLM tools into translator education, emphasising the importance of skills that are both transferable and adaptable to emerging technologies.

Although AI and LLMs significantly impact education across all fields, literature on their uses and risks in translator training remains relatively scarce. This gap underscores the value of applying the DAILM's context-specific approach in translator education, where Pym (2023) provides a practical example of how these principles can be implemented. In a seminal talk, Pym (2023) identifies two guiding principles for integrating LLM tools into translator education. The first principle involves training students to work with the technology and to understand its capabilities and limitations. The second principle focuses on developing interpersonal communication skills and expertise in prompt engineering, project management, as well as editing and revision tailored to specific end-users. Pym and Hao (2025, p. 45) highlight the importance of teaching transferable skills that enable students to access new technologies quickly and assess a tool's usefulness for specific tasks.

4. Our study

Building on the foundational exploration of AI literacy as a critical framework for navigating the complexities of using GenAI tools in HE, we investigated the use of GenAI tools for language learning in the specific context of TI programmes. In sections 1–3, we underscored the importance of AI literacy in addressing employability demands and equipping students with the competences to engage effectively and ethically with emerging GenAI technologies. Against this backdrop, we investigated how undergraduate and graduate TI students across diverse European educational contexts interact with and perceive GenAI-driven tools, providing empirical insights that align with and expand upon the theoretical considerations outlined above.

4.1 Methodology

As outlined in the introduction, the aim of this chapter is to analyse the extent to which AI-driven tools are used by students of TI for language learning. The primary focus of the survey was to investigate the use of LLM tools among students in TI programmes.

4.2 Sample

A total of 234 students participated in the study; all enrolled in either a bachelor's or master's programme in translation or interpreting. The average age of participants (n=197)[5] was 22 (SD = 4.0), ranging from 18 to 43 years at the time of completing the survey. Gender distribution (n=200) was as follows: female 80.0 %, male 17.0 % and other 3.0 %. Participants (n=199) were enrolled across four European countries: Austria (8.0 %), Belgium (30.2 %), Slovenia (14.6 %) and Spain (45.2 %)[6]. Regarding academic level (n=199), the majority (83.4 %) were undergraduate students, distributed as follows: first year (22.6 %), second year (19.1 %), third year (13.1 %) and fourth year (28.6 %)[7]. Graduate students comprised 16.6 % of the sample.

4.3 Instruments and procedures

This study employed a mixed-methods approach, collecting both quantitative and qualitative data. To achieve the study's objectives, an online *ad hoc* survey

5 The number of participants varies among individual questions as not all participants chose to answer all questions.

6 The remaining 2 % of participants were exchange students from France.

7 Fourth year applies only to Spain.

was designed to explore translation and interpreting students' experiences with and attitudes towards LLMs. Given the international scope of the study, the survey was administered in English.

The survey was created using the 1KA open-source application[8] and distributed to 575 people. Of these, 234 responses were fully or partially completed and subsequently analysed. The survey was relatively short, with an average completion time of 4 minutes and 33 seconds.

The survey included closed questions, such as yes/no, Likert-scale and multiple-choice formats, allowing respondents to select statements that best reflected their perspectives and use of AI tools. Additionally, the survey contained a few open-ended questions to allow students to elaborate on their responses to closed questions. The questionnaire was organised around the following key areas:

- Familiarity with AI tools
- Academic experiences with using AI tools
- Perspectives on AI tools as applied to learning
- Attitudes towards AI technologies

The questionnaire was initially reviewed by the four research team members, specialists in applied linguistics, translation and interpreting studies, who assessed its suitability and readability. Data collection occurred over a three-month period (May–July 2024). Participants were informed about the study's nature and assured that their data would remain anonymous and would be used solely for research purposes. They subsequently signed a consent form before completing the questionnaire.

4.4 Data analysis

All data were processed and analysed statistically using IBM SPSS Statistics 29. Due to space constraints, this chapter will present and discuss the overall results of the survey, focusing on the quantitative data only.

---

[8] https://1ka.arnes.si/

4.5 Results and discussion[9]

4.5.1 Familiarity with AI tools

Of the total number of students (n=234), the majority demonstrate a degree of familiarity with LLMs (see Figure 2). Specifically, 81.2 % (n=190) have used LLMs, while only 18.8 % (n=44) report having not used these tools. Consequently, for the remaining questions, only responses from students who answered affirmatively were considered, and those who answered negatively were excluded from the analysis.

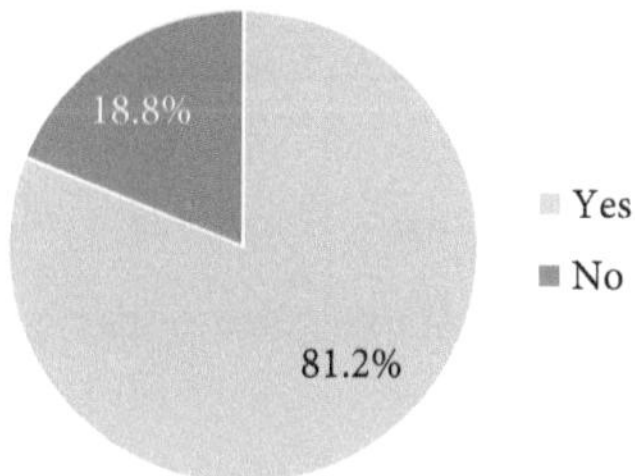

Figure 2: Prior use LLMs: "Have you used any large language models (LLMs) such as ChatGPT or Gemini?" (n=234).

Regarding which LLMs students have used and how frequently, ChatGPT emerges as the clear favourite among the majority of participants (Figure 3). Nearly the entire sample reports using ChatGPT for their academic tasks, with 70.2 % stating they use it at least monthly. Only 29.3 % indicate using it sporadically, and just one participant reported never having used the tool. Microsoft Copilot and Gemini follow in terms of preference, though with significantly lower usage rates and frequency. Lastly, only 14.5 % of participants report using other LLM tools.

In terms of how participants acquired the skills to use these tools, more participants reported learning through autonomous learning (28.0 %) than through formal training (18.7 %) (Figures 4 and 5). This could mean that students are not made aware of possible ethical issues, such as academic integrity and cognitive bias (UNESCO 2023). This suggests that there is still

9 Due to rounding, percentages may occasionally total slightly below 100 % (e.g., 99.9 %) or above 100 % (e.g., 100.1 %).

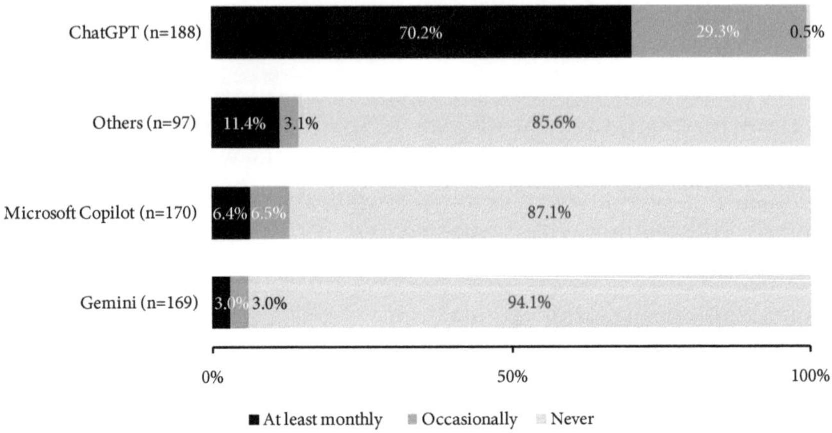

Figure 3: Type and frequency of LLM use: "Please specify which LLMs you have used and how frequently."

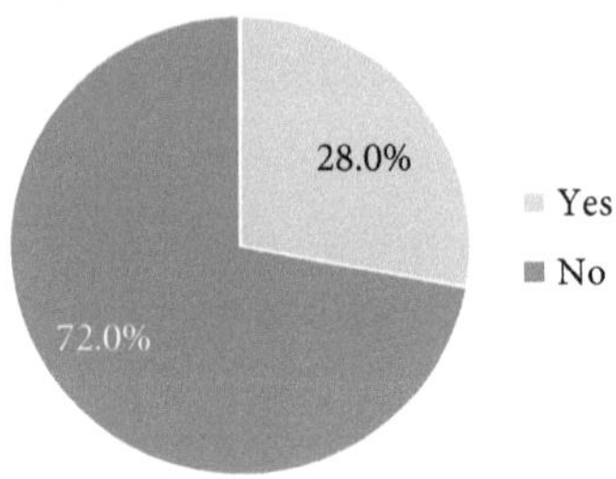

Figure 4: Autonomous learning: "Have you looked for information yourself on the use of LLMs (e.g., YouTube videos, online forums)?" (n=182).

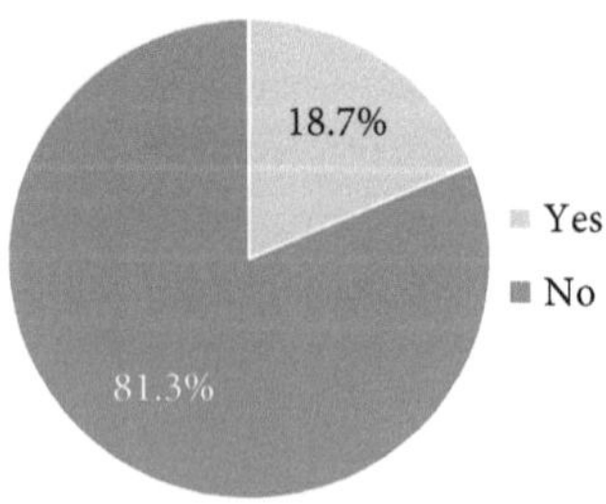

Figure 5: Formal learning: "Have you received any formal training on the use of LLMs (e.g., university courses, online courses)?" (n=182).

a sizeable gap in the provision of AI literacy among university students, which universities should seek to close. At least for our sample, this also does not confirm the findings of the 2024 ELIS report, in which 63 % of participating students reported that generative AI was already included in their training programmes.

4.5.2 Academic experiences with using AI tools

Within the academic environment, AI tools are regularly (i.e., daily, weekly, monthly) used primarily for language explanations (52.4 %), text reviewing and editing (48.8 %), generating ideas to assist with creative or academic writing tasks (41.5 %) and text production (41.0 %) (Figures 6 and 7). These tools are used to a lesser extent for translation (36.1 %) and research purposes, including searching for academic sources (35.1 %). The least frequent use is observed in generating practical exercises to consolidate acquired knowledge (22.2 %).

These findings underscore significant implications for education, particularly in HE. Firstly, LLMs have a clear and valuable application in foreign

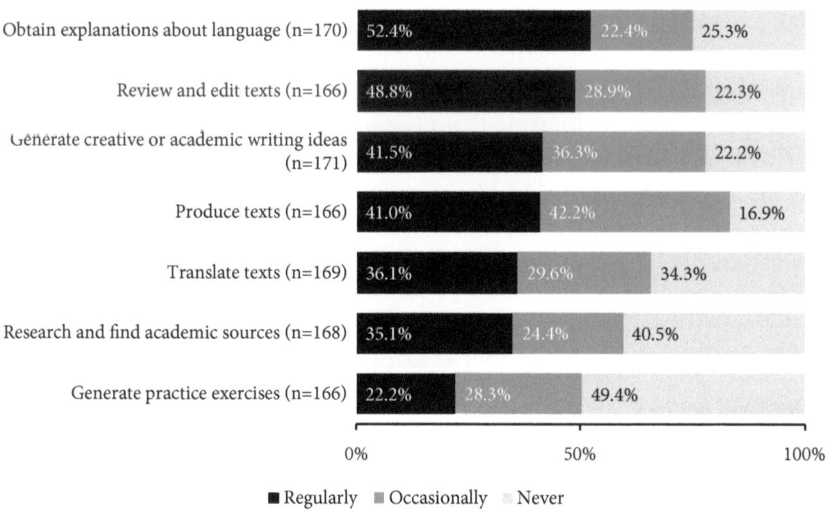

Figure 6: Academic experiences with AI tools (use and frequency): "Considering the LLM tool you use most often, what purposes do you primarily use it for?".

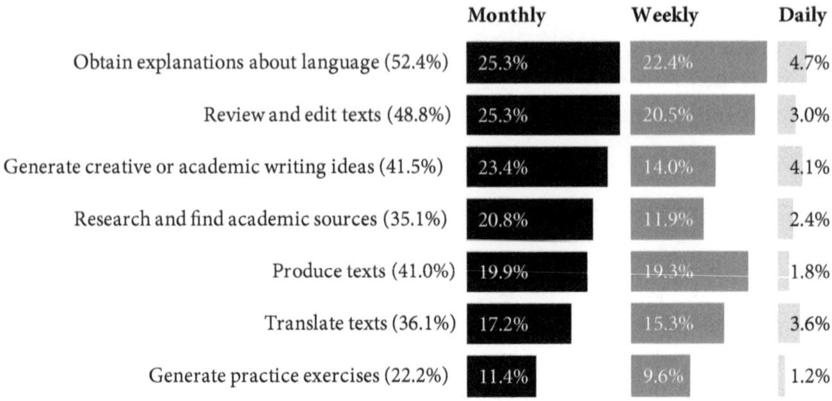

Figure 7: Academic experiences with AI tools (regular use: monthly, weekly, daily): "Considering the LLM tool you use most often, what purposes do you primarily use it for?"

language instruction and are extensively used by students, highlighting the need for their integration into curricula and teaching practices. Additionally, participants appear to recognise the importance of an active training process, using these technologies as complementary resources rather than relying on them passively. However, it is concerning that many students use these tools for language production, which could pose a risk to academic integrity. This emphasises the need to incorporate these tools into the classroom setting and to guide students in using them responsibly.

This widespread use may be attributed to the fact that most participants rate the linguistic output of LLMs as good to excellent (57.8 %), which encourages their use as a regular tool in academic tasks (Figure 8). Only 6.3 % of the participants believe that the quality of tool output fails to meet minimum academic standards.

4.5.3 Perspectives on AI tools as applied to learning

Following up on the previous question, students were asked to rate how helpful they consider these tools for the development of specific skills. Though critical evaluations prevail across all skills, there is an important difference between skills that involve written language use and those involving oral language use (Figure 9). In this vein, students rate LLM tools as significantly or moderately useful for improving writing (40.8 %), followed by translation

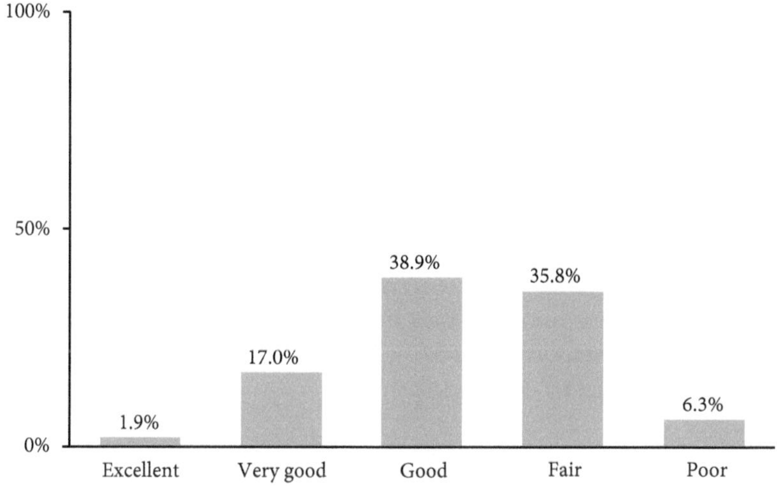

Figure 8: Student rating quality linguistic output LLM: "How would you rate the quality of the output produced by the LLM tool you use most frequently?" (n=159).

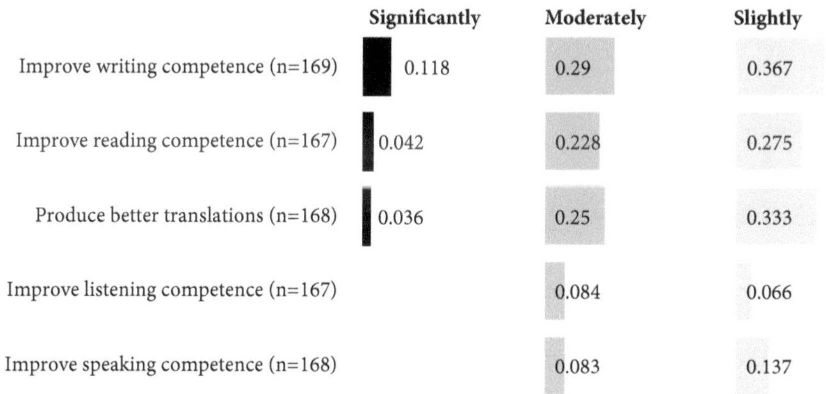

Figure 9: AI as applied to learning (degree of helpfulness): "Do you believe the LLM tool you use most frequently helps you ..."

(28.6 %) and reading (27.0 %). For listening and speaking, percentages are equally low (8.4 % and 8.3 %, respectively). These findings are further reinforced by the uncertainty expressed by approximately a quarter of the sample regarding the potential of LLMs to support the development of oral skills.

The following set of questions targeted the tools' usefulness at a broader level (Figure 10). In all instances, the significance of these tools across various fields of application is recognised. There seems to be ample awareness (considered *extremely* or *very* important) of the role of skilled prompt engineering (63.2 %) and high expectations regarding their relevance in a future career as a language professional (65.2 %), while their importance for academic performance is valued significantly lower (46.0 %). The usefulness attributed to these tools highlights the importance of mastering these technologies to prepare for a professional future increasingly shaped by them and to welcome them as pedagogical resources into the classroom. However, this need for training stands in stark contrast to the previously mentioned lack of formal instruction reported by the participants.

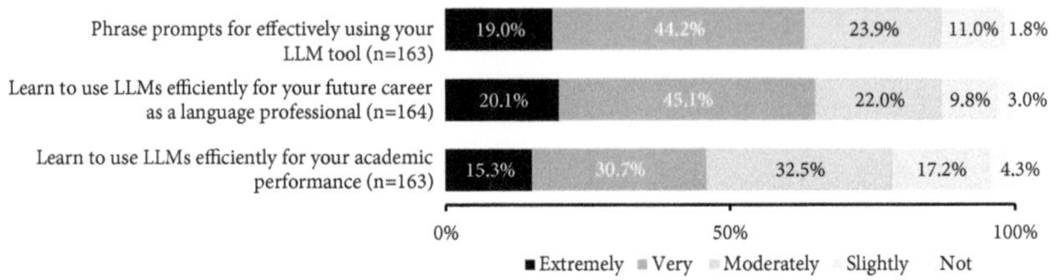

Figure 10: Tools' usefulness at a broader level: "To what extent do you agree with the following statements?"

4.5.4 Attitudes towards AI tools

The questions about attitudes offer a rather diverse range of answers (Figure 11). In general, students' attitudes are rather positive (represented in the answers *strongly agree* and *agree*), and a large ample majority considers LLMs to be useful tools for saving time (85.4 %), offering new ideas and perspectives (84.2 %), providing personalised immediate feedback (58.5 %) and answering questions they would not want to ask in class due to inhibition (55.4 %).

All of these data indirectly reflect the considerable level of trust placed in these technologies as academic support tools. On the downside, opinions differ significantly on whether LLMs can enhance future career prospects or facilitate networking. A considerable percentage (44.3 %) feel threatened in their professional development and think that LLMs can negatively impact their academic performance (56.4 %), which, to some extent, helps fuel the

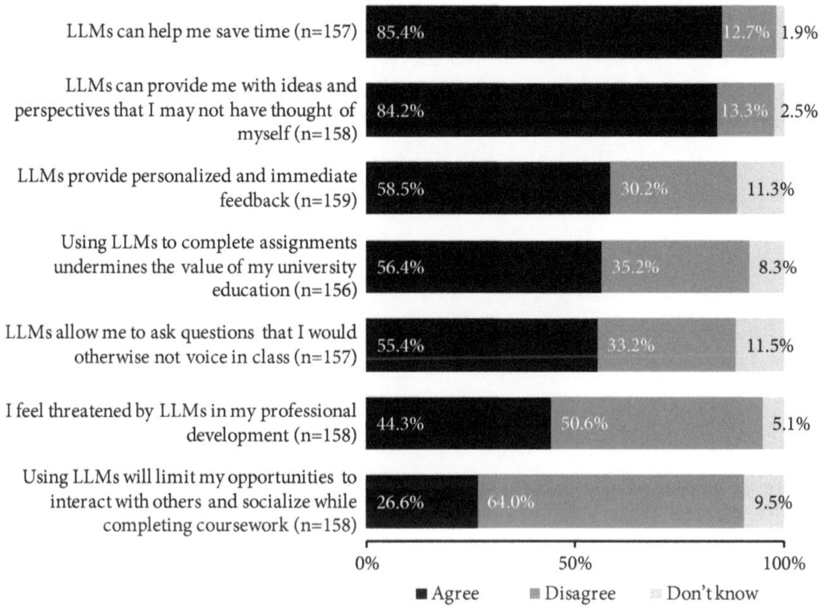

Figure 11: Attitudes towards AI tools: "To what extent do you agree with the following statements?"

heated debate about the role of these tools in academia. However, only a minority of students (26.6 %) believe that LLMs might have negative consequences for social interaction in the academic context.

The last question targeted ethical concerns related to the use of LLMs. As shown in Figure 12, around 58 % of the participants are aware of the ethical issues these technologies may pose in an academic setting. However, more than 40 % are unaware, indicating difficulty in discerning the boundaries between what is ethically acceptable and what is not when using these tools for academic purposes. This is particularly worrying in the light of the 2024 ELIS Report findings, where 57 % of university staff reported having no clear guidelines in place for AI use[10]. Nevertheless, these data are crucial, as

[10] Given the rapid changes in this domain, however, the situation might have changed already since data were published.

ethical considerations represent one of the most significant challenges these technologies bring to academia (see, for example, Li 2023). Once again, this lack of ethical awareness underscores the urgent need for training on the responsible use of LLMs for educational purposes, ensuring they never replace the active role students must play in their own learning process.

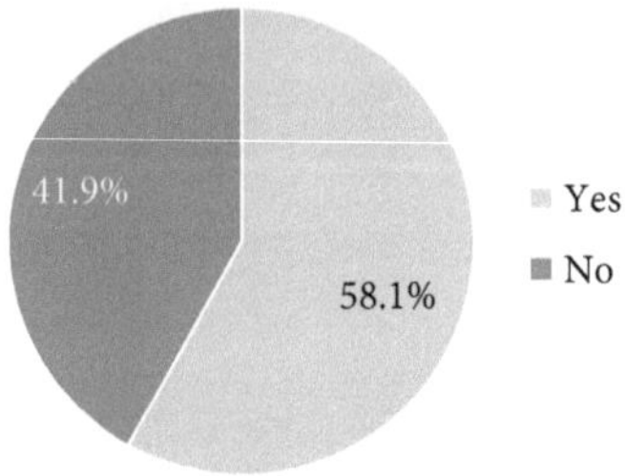

Figure 12: Ethical concerns: "Are you aware of any ethical concerns connected with the use of LLMs?" (n=160).

5. Conclusion

In this chapter, we investigated the use of GenAI tools for language learning in translation and interpreting (TI) programmes across four European countries (Austria, Belgium, Slovenia, Spain). Our primary aim was to explore graduate and undergraduate TI students' familiarity with use of and attitudes towards AI-driven technologies in their academic experiences. Our findings reveal a relatively high level of awareness and use of AI tools, particularly LLMs like ChatGPT, with most students actively using such tools for language explanations, text review, editing and generating ideas for academic writing. As data from the ELIS report show, GenAI seems to be widely addressed in training in some form. However, our findings indicate that the percentage of students who have attended formal training on AI literacy is considerably lower, with many students relying on self-learning to navigate these technologies.

Our study highlights the perceived positive impact of GenAI tools in supporting students' learning processes, as reported by participants. GenAI tools are viewed as enhancing academic performance and preparing students for future roles in the workplace. However, further research is needed to empirically assess the actual impact of GenAI use on these aspects. At the same time, our study raises concerns about ethical considerations, academic integrity and potential limitations in fostering essential skills like human interaction and communication.

One of the strengths of our study is its inclusion of students from diverse educational and cultural backgrounds, providing a broader perspective on the use of AI in translation and interpreting training. Additionally, our focus on multiple aspects of AI usage – ranging from academic experiences to attitudes – offers a comprehensive view that can inform curriculum development and pedagogical strategies. However, our study also has some limitations. First, our reliance on self-reported data introduces possible biases, since participants may overestimate or underestimate their familiarity with and use of AI tools. Second, while our study covers four European countries, our findings may not be fully generalisable to other regions with different educational systems or attitudes towards integrating, actively developing and/or assessing AI literacy in education. Future research could address these limitations by incorporating more objective measures of AI literacy and extending the study to include an even more diverse sample of students.

Overall, our study underscores the growing need for structured and strategic, needs-based AI literacy training in translation and interpreting programmes. It highlights the importance of integrating comprehensive and flexible AI literacy frameworks, such as the Dynamic AI Literacy Model (DAILM) for Specific Roles, into curriculum design. By focusing on context-specific and profession-focused learner needs, we can use and/or adapt frameworks to develop and assess the competences needed to navigate the evolving landscape of AI technologies. The DAILM framework, with its adaptable approach tailored to professional needs, provides a valuable model for fostering the competences necessary for effective and ethical engagement with AI in translation and interpreting training.

Bibliography

Akhulkova, Yulia (31/08/2023): The Nimdzi Language Technology Atlas. Nimdzi, retrieved on 20/08/2024 from https://www.nimdzi.com/language-technology-atlas/#about

Akhulkova, Yulia (01/09/2024): Nimdzi Language Technology Radar. Nimdzi, retrieved on 10/12/2024 from https://www.nimdzi.com/language-technology-tracker/#new-category-on-the-radar-llms

Bachman, Lyle F. (1990): *Fundamental considerations in language testing.* Oxford: University Press.

Canale, Michael (1983): "From communicative competence to communicative language pedagogy." In: Richards, Jack C. / Schmidt, Richard W. (eds.): *Language and communication*. London: Longman, pp. 2–27.

Canale, Michael / Swain, Merrill (1980): "Theoretical bases of communicative approaches to second language teaching and testing." *Applied Linguistics* 1(1), pp. 1–47. https://doi.org/10.1093/applin/I.1.1

Carr, Paul (14/08/2023): "Generative AI: Friend or foe for the translation industry?." Forbes, retrieved on 20/09/2024 from https://www.forbes.com/councils/forbestechcouncil/2023/08/11/generative-ai-friend-or-foe-for-the-translation-industry/

Chan, Cecilia Ka Yuk (2024): "AI literacy. AI in education", retrieved on 15/12/2024 from https://aied.talic.hku.hk/ai-literacy/

Chan, Cecilia Ka Yuk / Colloton, Tom (2024): *Generative AI in higher education: The ChatGPT effect*. London: Routledge. https://doi.org/10.4324/9781003459026

Ciesielski, Jourik (11/03/2024): LLM solutions and how to use them. Nimdzi. [Video], retrieved on 20/08/2024 from https://www.nimdzi.com/llm-solutions-and-how-to-use-them/

Do, Thu (2024): "Technological competence for graduate employability: Pedagogical and professional perspectives from cross-national translation working contexts." In: Le Ha, Phan / Bao, Dat / Windle, Joel (eds.): *Vietnamese language, education and change in and outside Vietnam*. Singapore, Springer, pp. 223–244. https://doi.org/10.1007/978-981-99-9093-1_11

ELIS Research (2024): *ELIS 2024 European Language Industry Survey*, retrieved on 20/08/2024 from https://elis-survey.org/

European Master's in Translation (EMT). (2022): Competence framework 2022, https://commission.europa.eu/system/files/2022-11/emt_competence_fwk_2022_en.pdf

Fell Kurban, Caroline / Şahin, Muhammed (2024): *The impact of ChatGPT on higher education: Exploring the AI revolution*. Leeds: Emerald. https://doi.org/10.1108/9781837976478

Kandlhofer, Martin / Steinbauer, Gerald / Hirschmugl-Gaisch, Sabine / Huber, Petra (2016): Artificial intelligence and computer science in education: From kindergarten to university. *IEEE Frontiers in Education Conference (FIE)*, pp. 1–9.

Kanwit, Matthew / Solon, Megan (eds.) (2023): *Communicative competence in a second language: Theory, method, and applications*. New York: Routledge. https://doi.org/10.4324/9781003160779

Kosslyn, Stephen M. (2024): *Active learning with AI: A practical guide*. Boston: Alinea Learning.

Krüger, Ralph (2023): "Artificial intelligence literacy for the language industry – with particular emphasis on recent large language models such as GPT-4." *Lebende Sprachen* 68(2), pp. 282–330. https://doi.org/10.1515/les-2023-0024

Laupichler, Matthias Carl / Aster, Alexandra / Schirch, Jana / Raupach, Tobias (2022): Artificial intelligence literacy in higher and adult education: A scoping literature review. *Computers and Education: Artificial Intelligence* 3, e100101. https://doi.org/10.1016/j.caeai.2022.100101

Li, Kang (2023): Determinants of college students' actual use of AI-based systems: An extension of the Technology Acceptance Model. *Sustainability*, 15(6), e5221. https://doi.org/10.3390/su15065221

Lin, Xi / Chan, Roy Y. / Sharma, Shyam / Bista, Krishna (eds.) (2024). *ChatGPT and global higher education: Using artificial intelligence in teaching and learning*. Baltimore: STAR Scholars Press. https://doi.org/10.32674/rh27qv16

Long, Duri / Magerko, Brian (2020): What is AI Literacy? Competencies and design considerations. In *Proceedings of the 2020 CHI Conference on Human Factors in Computing Systems*, New York: Association for Computing Machinery, pp. 1–16. https://doi.org/10.1145/3313831.3376727

Ng, Davy Tsz Kit / Leung, Jac Ka Lok / Chu, Samuel Kai Wah / Qiao, Maggie Shen (2021): Conceptualizing AI literacy: An exploratory review. *Computers and Education: Artificial Intelligence* 2, e100041. https://doi.org/10.1016/j.caeai.2021.100041

O'Dea, Xianghan / Ng, Davy Tsz Kit (2025): *Effective practices in AI literacy education: Case studies and reflections*. Leeds: Emerald. https://doi.org/10.1108/9781836088523

Paradkar, Sameer (2024): "Generative AI Applications – solutions, challenges and ethical considerations – Part 2." *Medium*, 23/1/2024 retrieved on 20/09/2024 from https://medium.com/oolooroo/generative-ai-applications-solutions-challenges-and-ethical-considerations-part-2-23f67c88b84c

Plate, Daniel / Melick, Elizabeth / Hutson, James / Edele, Susan (2025): *Generative AI in the English composition classroom: Practical and adaptable strategies*. New York: Routledge. https://doi.org/10.4324/9781003507949

Pym, Anthony (2023): "GPT in the training of translators." Presentation at the 60th anniversary of the Faculty of Translation and Interpretation at the Université de Mons, retrieved on 31/03/2024 from https://www.youtube.com/watch?v=b9U_FUaneso&t=45s

Pym, Anthony / Hao, Yu (2025): *How to augment language skills: Generative AI and machine translation in language learning and translator training*. London: Routledge. https://doi.org/10.4324/9781032648033

Shrier, David L. (2024): *Basic AI: A human guide to artificial intelligence*. London: Robinson.

Sidorkin, Alexander M. (2024): *Embracing chatbots in higher education: The use of artificial intelligence in teaching, administration, and scholarship*. New York: Routledge. https://doi.org/10.4324/9781032686028

UNESCO (2023): "ChatGPT and artificial intelligence in higher education: Quick start guide", retrieved on 09/10/2024 from https://unesdoc.unesco.org/ark:/48223/pf0000385146

Wolff, Rachel (2024): Machine translation (MT) vs generative AI for translation: Pros and cons. *Lokalise*, retrieved on 20/09/2024 from https://lokalise.com/blog/machine-translation-vs-ai-for-translation/

Yi, Michelle (2023): "The ethical challenges of generative AI applications." *Medium*, retrieved on 20/09/2024 from https://yulleyi.medium.com/the-ethical-challenges-of-generative-ai-applications-8478ecdfe2a4

Vorteile des Einsatzes von maschineller Übersetzung (MÜ) in den Anfangsphasen der Übersetzerausbildung: Mensch-Maschine-Interaktion in soziokonstruktivistischen Lehrveranstaltungen

Belén Lozano Sañudo
Universitat de València

ABSTRACT
In the age of artificial intelligence, translation students see their future work as that of mere "operators" (Rico Pérez 2017, p. 76), whose task is limited to the "validation" (Cid-Leal/Espín-García/Presas 2018, p. 190) of machine options devoid of communicative context. This view of their work as a purely mechanical activity, without emphasis on translator-relevant skills such as critical thinking and creativity, affects their self-esteem and is very demotivating. The widespread idea that MT shall lead in the near future to the obliteration of the translation profession relies on an overly simplistic view of human communication, which does not take into account that it is not based on a single semiotic system, verbal language, but that it rather involves other signs, sign systems and contextual elements that are essential for a correct interpretation of the message by the recipient. The didactic unit presented in this chapter aims at developing students' self-concept as future professionals who play a central role in all stages of the translation process and are responsible for the final product. By working on the most creative aspects of advertising texts, we aim at highlighting the significant benefits teacher-led experience with these systems offers for novice learners.

Keywords: Machine translation, translator training, self-concept, creativity, advertising translation

1. Einleitung

In den letzten Jahren haben wir einen schwindelerregenden Aufstieg der künstlichen Intelligenz (KI) erlebt, der durch das Zusammentreffen von drei Faktoren angetrieben wurde: der Verfügbarkeit riesiger Datenmengen (*big data*), dem Zugang zu großen, kostengünstigen Rechnerkapazitäten und der Entwicklung von Deep-Learning-Modellen auf der Grundlage neuronaler Netze. Während Gegner dieser Technologie befürchten, dass die Automatisierung vieler Aufgaben zum Verschwinden des Übersetzer- und Fremdsprachenlehrerberufs führt, argumentieren Befürworter, dass KI und insbesondere MÜ-Systeme erforderlich sind, um auf die aktuellen Bedürfnisse der mehrsprachigen Kommunikation zu reagieren. Im Informationszeitalter haben nämlich die Erfordernisse eines globalisierten Marktes in Verbindung mit der rasanten Entwicklung von Wissen und der Erstellung von Inhalten Institutionen, Agenturen und Sprachdienstleister gezwungen, maschinelle Übersetzung in ihre Arbeitsabläufe zu integrieren.

Diese umfassende Implementierung wurde auch durch das hohe Maß an Korrektheit und Flüssigkeit, das von neuronalen maschinellen Übersetzungssystemen erreicht wird, sowie durch die Flexibilisierung des Qualitätskonzepts, das in hohem Maße vom Zweck der Übersetzung abhängt, begünstigt. Dieser hohe Anwendungsgrad wird durch aktuelle Untersuchungen bestätigt, wie z. B. eine Studie über den Einsatz von MÜ im spanischen Sprachdienstleistungssektor. Sie ist Teil des Forschungsprojektes DITAPE (Docencia e Investigación en Traducción Automática y Postedición[1], González Pastor 2023). Laut der Studie bieten 66 % der Sprachdienstleister in Spanien Dienstleistungen im Bereich der MÜ an: 44,9 % maschinelle Übersetzung ohne Post-Editing, 63,3 % Post-Editing und 57,9 % Post-Editing-Revision. Interessant ist, dass 36,4 % der MÜ-Dienstleistungsanbieter eigene maschinelle Übersetzungssysteme verwenden. Bei den Freiberuflern beläuft sich der Prozentsatz, der Dienstleistungen im Bereich der MÜ anbietet, auf 51,5 %. Davon bieten 47,7 % Post-Editing und 41,5 % Post-Editing-Revision an, während der Anteil von denen, die MÜ ohne Post-Editing anbieten, mit 6,2 % eher gering ausfällt. Auf europäischer Ebene weist die Auswertung der Statistiken des ELIS-Berichts (European Language Industry Survey 2022, S. 25) ähnliche Ergebnisse auf. Daraus geht hervor, dass 58 % der Sprachdienstleister MÜ bereits in ihren Workflow integriert haben und 20 % eine solche Einführung in naher Zukunft planen. Bei den Sprachabteilungen internationaler öffentlicher Einrichtungen erreicht der Einsatz fast 90 %.

Vor diesem Hintergrund stimme ich der Schlussfolgerung von Melby und Hague (2019, S. 206) und Cid-Leal, Espín-García und Presas (2019, S. 191) zu, dass wir als Ausbildende im Fachgebiet des Übersetzens die Verantwortung

---

1 Lehre und Forschung in automatischer Übersetzung und Post-Editing (meine Übersetzung)

haben, unsere Studierenden auf einen Arbeitsmarkt vorzubereiten, in dem MÜ eine entscheidende Rolle spielt.

Wenn wir diese Verantwortung nicht zeitnah übernehmen, werden folgende zwei Hauptrisiken bestehen bleiben. Einerseits würde sich die Kluft zwischen den in der Ausbildung vermittelten technologiebezogenen Kompetenzen und den realen Marktanforderungen vergrößern (González Pastor/Rico 2021, S. 3), was sich wiederum auf die Beschäftigungsfähigkeit der Absolventen auswirken würde. Dies würde auch den aktuellen Trend verschärfen, den Übersetzerabschluss bei der Personalauswahl immer weniger als Mehrwert für am Übersetzungsprozess beteiligte Positionen zu betrachten (Krause 2017, S. 153). Laut DITAPE-Bericht halten Sprachdienstleister Vorkenntnisse in der MÜ und in der Post-Edition zwar noch nicht für unerlässlich, aber für wünschenswert. Arbeitgeber hingegen schätzen das Niveau der MÜ-Kenntnisse der Hochschulabsolventen als schlecht bzw. befriedigend ein (González Pastor 2023).

Andererseits vergleichen viele Übersetzer und Übersetzungsstudierende ihre Rolle im Übersetzungsprozess mit der eines bloßen „Operators“ (Rico Pérez 2017, S. 76), der sich infolge fehlender spezifischer MÜ-Technologieausbildung (Presas et al. 2016) darauf beschränkt, die von der Maschine angebotenen Optionen ohne kommunikativen Kontext zu „validieren“ (Cid-Leal/Espín-García/Presas 2019, S. 190). Diese Sichtweise ihrer Arbeit als rein mechanische Tätigkeit, bei der berufsrelevante Fähigkeiten wie kritisches Denken und Kreativität nicht im Vordergrund stehen, beeinträchtigt ihr Selbstwertgefühl und damit den sozioökonomischen Stand der Gruppe sowie die Zahl der Bewerber für den Studiengang Translationswissenschaft.

2. MÜ in der Übersetzerausbildung

Unter dem Druck einer Branche mit fest etablierten MÜ-Systemen diskutieren Translationswissenschaftler weltweit über den Stellenwert der MÜ in Übersetzerstudiengängen. Soll MÜ im Bachelor- oder Masterstudium, in einem bestimmten Fach oder fächerübergreifend in Übersetzungsfächern gelehrt werden? Welche Kompetenzen und Inhalte sollen in Verbindung mit MÜ vermittelt werden? Wie sollen Übersetzungsaktivitäten und Prüfungen ausgewählt und angeordnet werden, damit sie den neuen Anforderungen des Arbeitsmarktes entsprechen? Welche Rolle spielen

Übersetzungsschwierigkeiten und -probleme (Nord 2009, S. 233), die nicht von der Maschine gelöst werden und das Eingreifen der Studierenden mit ihrer Fähigkeit zum kritischen Denken erfordern? Das sind nur einige der diskutierten Fragen.

Derzeit laufen interessante Projekte, um diese Fragen zu beantworten, darunter eine Studie im Rahmen des Forschungsprojekts DITAPE. Sie wurde vom Instituto Interuniversitario de Lenguas Modernas y Aplicadas[2] (IULMA) und der CiTrans-Forschungsgruppe der Universität Valencia gefördert und von der Conselleria de Innovación, Universidades, Ciencia y Sociedad Digital der Generalitat Valenciana[3] finanziert. Die Studie besteht aus zwei Phasen: einer qualitativen ersten Phase und einer quantitativen zweiten Phase.

In der ersten Phase wurde mit Hilfe qualitativer Untersuchungstechniken der spontane Diskurs von Fachleuten in Unternehmen, unter Freiberuflern und Lehrern in der Branche aufgezeichnet. Er diente als Grundlage für den Entwurf eines Fragebogens, der in der zweiten, quantitativen Phase an die Befragten geschickt wurde. Umfragezeitraum war der 23. Mai bis 20. Juni 2022. Fast alle Lehrkräfte stimmten für eine Schulung der Studierenden in der Verwendung von arbeitsrelevanten Tools, so die Umfrageergebnisse (González Pastor 2023). Mehr als die Hälfte war der Meinung, Humanübersetzung solle weiterhin im Mittelpunkt der Ausbildung stehen im Gegensatz zu 26 %, denen zufolge die Humanübersetzung diese Hauptrolle verlieren sollte. Die restlichen 23,3 % sprachen sich weder dafür noch dagegen aus.

Diese Studie halte ich für besonders aussagekräftig, weil sie die Sichtweise der Lehrkräfte und die Art, wie sie diese Technologien vermitteln, berücksichtigt. Damit hebt sie sich von anderen Studien, die die gleiche Thematik behandeln, ab (z. B. Rico Pérez/García Aragón 2016 oder Presas et al. 2016). Dem DITAPE-Bericht zufolge unterrichtet fast ein Fünftel (19,2 %) der befragten Lehrkräfte das Fach Übersetzungstechnologien, in dem zu erwarten ist, dass zumindest die Entwicklung der MÜ mit den bisher existierenden Typen und ihren wichtigsten Merkmalen und Grenzen dargestellt wird. Laut dem

---

2 Interuniversitären Institut für moderne und angewandte Sprachen (meine Übersetzung)

3 Abteilung für Innovation, Universitäten, Wissenschaft und digitale Gesellschaft der Generalitat Valenciana (meine Übersetzung)

Bericht stimmen Übersetzungslehrer im Allgemeinen darin überein, dass die Verwendung von MÜ den Erwerb der Translationskompetenz einschränken könne. Aus diesem Grund betonen sie, dass die Anerkennung der Bedeutung der MÜ nicht vom Erkennen der Wichtigkeit der Humanübersetzung ablenken sollte. MÜ-Systeme und computergestützte Übersetzungssoftware werden von 50 % der Lehrkräfte im Unterricht genutzt, von denen wiederum die Hälfte grundsätzlich Post-Editing anwendet und Bewertung von maschinellen Übersetzungen vornimmt. Insgesamt ist diese Studie sehr hilfreich bei der Ermittlung der aktuellen Bedürfnisse und eine gute Grundlage für die Entwicklung von didaktischen Vorschlägen mit dem Ziel, die universitäre Übersetzerausbildung besser an die Realität der Arbeitswelt anzupassen. Es sind jedoch weitere Studien erforderlich, um die Ergebnisse zu konkretisieren.

Aus den Antworten geht jedoch nicht hervor, welche Art von MÜ-Aktivitäten im Unterricht durchgeführt werden und ob es sich um einmalige oder regelmäßige Kursaktivitäten handelt. So ist die Präsentation einer im Internet frei verfügbare MÜ-Maschine wie GoogleTranslate oder DeepL in einem Einführungskurs ins Übersetzen, bei der ihre Grenzen aufgezeigt werden, um von ihrer Verwendung abzuraten, nicht gleichbedeutend mit ihrer ständigen Verwendung in einem technischen Übersetzungskurs, in dem die Studierenden lernen, wie sie als Humanübersetzer in allen Phasen des Übersetzungsprozesses mit der Maschine interagieren können und sollen, um ihre Leistung als professionelle Übersetzer zu verbessern.

Betrachtet man die beiden Haupttätigkeiten der Lehrkräfte mit ihren Studierenden, Post-Editing und die Bewertung von Übersetzungen, so wird die MÜ als ein Produkt angesehen, das nach der Fertigstellung durch die Maschine von einem professionellen Humanübersetzer bewertet oder posteditiert wird. Diese Auffassung von MÜ als fertiges Produkt ist weitgehend für das Misstrauen der Akademiker gegenüber dieser Technologie verantwortlich.

3. MÜ als Prozess: neue Rollen und Kompetenzen des Humanübersetzers

Im Gegensatz dazu sieht Rico Pérez (2017, S. 77) die MÜ als zyklischen Prozess mit verschiedenen Phasen, in denen der Humanübersetzer und die Maschine interagieren müssen. Ihr Vorschlag verdeutlicht, dass die Rolle des Übersetzers viel breiter gefasst werden muss und die Einführung von MÜ-Systemen zur Entstehung neuer Berufsprofile jenseits des Post-Editors führen wird.

In ihrem Schema gibt es drei Arbeitszyklen, aus denen sich verschiedene Funktionen ableiten, die vom Humanübersetzer übernommen werden sollen. In der ersten Phase ist der Humanübersetzer für die Zusammenstellung von Korpora und Glossaren, die Bewertung ihrer Eignung und das Training von MÜ-Systemen zuständig. Im zweiten Schritt ist er für das Pre-Editing des Ausgangstextes verantwortlich, wenn er es zur Steigerung der Produktivität für sinnvoll erachtet. Der bewussten Entscheidung für oder gegen ein Pre-Editing sollte immer eine Abwägung des Kosten-Nutzen-Verhältnisses vorausgehen, d. h. der Zeitaufwand für das Pre-Editing ist gegen die Qualitätssteigerung des Zieltextes und die erwartete Zeitersparnis beim Post-Editing abzuwägen. In der zweiten Phase ist der Humanübersetzer auch für das Post-Editing der MÜ verantwortlich. Letztlich besteht in der dritten und letzten Phase die Aufgabe des Humanübersetzers darin, die Glossare zu aktualisieren und die Korpusdaten zu verbessern.

Aus diesen Funktionen ergeben sich neue Berufsprofile, unter ihnen der des Sprachberaters, ein Vorschlag von Melby und Hague (2019, S. 206). Zu seinen Hauptfunktionen gehört die Unterstützung der Kunden bei der Formulierung dessen, was die Autoren (ibid., S. 210) als strukturierte Übersetzungsspezifikationen bezeichnen, und zwar in einer Phase vor dem Eingang der Übersetzungsaufträge bei den Projektmanagern. Diese Spezifikationen basieren auf der internationalen Norm ASTM F2575-14 und werden verwendet, um die beste Lösung für jedes spezifische Projekt zu finden. Die Lösungen reichen von MÜ ohne menschliches Eingreifen über verschiedene Grade des Post-Editings, das unter anderem von der Funktion der Übersetzung und dem Risikoniveau potenzieller Übersetzungsfehler in der Übersetzung abhängt (Nitzke/Hansen-Schirra/Canfora 2019, S. 243), bis hin zu Humanübersetzung ohne MÜ-Systeme.

Nitzke, Hansen-Schirra und Canfora (ibid., S. 248), die MÜ als Prozess und nicht als Produkt betrachten, teilen diesen Ansatz mit Rico Pérez (2017) und schlagen ein Kompetenzmodell für Post-Editoren vor. Es umfasst vier Kernkompetenzen und acht Teilkompetenzen. Die Kernkompetenzen lassen sich in zwei zusammenfassen: Risikomanagementberatung und strategische Entscheidungsfindung sowie aktuelles und umfassendes Wissen über den

Übersetzungsmarkt und insbesondere über alle Aspekte im Zusammenhang mit MÜ und Post-Editing.

Von den acht Teilkompetenzen stimmen sechs mit denen eines Übersetzers überein: zweisprachige Kompetenz, außersprachliche Kompetenz (Weltwissen und Kenntnisse des Fachgebiets), instrumentelle Kompetenz (Verwendung von Textverarbeitungsprogrammen, Übersetzungsspeichern usw.), Dokumentationskompetenz, Revisionskompetenz und Übersetzungskompetenz. Daneben sollten zwei spezifische Kompetenzen für Post-Editoren in der Ausbildung erworben werden: MÜ-Kompetenz und Post-Editing-Kompetenz. Der Post-Editor muss über Kenntnisse der Funktionsweise verschiedener MÜ-Systeme verfügen, die es ihm ermöglichen, die typischen Fehler der einzelnen Systeme zu antizipieren, zu entscheiden, welches System für ein bestimmtes Projekt am besten geeignet ist, und MÜ-Systeme darüber hinaus zu trainieren. Laut Nitzke, Hansen-Schirra und Canfora „[...] knowing how MT is implemented helps to spot potential problems or difficulties. Ideally, in our view, a post-editor should be able to assess the quality of the MT training materials and even improve the training process if necessary" (2019, S. 250).

4. MÜ als Instrument in den Händen von Humanübersetzern

Im Ansatz des vorangegangenen Abschnitts, in dem MÜ als Prozess und nicht als Produkt dargestellt wird, steht der Humanübersetzer im Mittelpunkt und übernimmt die Verantwortung für jede Phase. MÜ wird als ein Werkzeug in den Händen des Übersetzers betrachtet, das es ihm ermöglicht, seine Produktivität erheblich zu steigern und die eher mechanischen Aspekte an die Maschine zu delegieren.

In der Wissenschaft herrscht aber auch Einigkeit darüber, dass die Übersetzung eine kreativere Seite hat, die die Arbeit von Humanübersetzern erfordert. Kay (1997, S. 3) schreibt:

> A computer is a device that can be used to magnify human productivity. Properly used, it does not dehumanize by imposing its own Orwellian stamp on the products of the human spirit and the dignity of human labor but, by taking over what is mechanical and routine and, if this were given over to a machine, the productivity of the translator would not only be magnified but his work would be more rewarding, more exciting, more human.

Nicht alle Textsorten eignen sich gleichermaßen gut für MÜ. Literarische oder Werbetexte erfordern in höherem Maße kulturelle Kenntnisse, Sensibilität und Kreativität, als es die MÜ leisten kann. Es geht also nicht darum, dass Maschinen den Menschen ersetzen, sondern um eine Aufgabenteilung, um der wachsenden Nachfrage nach Übersetzungsdienstleistungen gerecht zu werden.

In Übereinstimmung mit obigem Zitat von Kay argumentiert Foti (2021, S. 13) folgendermaßen:

> La traducción es difícil. Todos lo sabemos. Y la transcreación y la localización lo son aún más. Los conocimientos culturales y la sensibilidad que un traductor aporta a un texto son un acto de creación. Ahora bien, a menudo hay poco tiempo, y no todos los textos necesitan tratamiento completo. Aquí es donde la traducción automática encuentra su nicho[4].

5. MÜ im Rahmen des soziokonstruktivistischen Ansatzes

Die objektivistische Erkenntnistheorie beschränkt den Lehr- und Lernprozess auf die bloße Weitergabe von Wissen durch den Lehrer, der im Besitz der statischen und objektiven absoluten Wahrheit ist, an die Lernenden, die eine begrenzte Anzahl von Fähigkeiten und Daten passiv absorbieren. Sie wird dem Ausbildungsprofil von Fachleuten in unserer sich ständig weiterentwickelnden Gesellschaft nicht gerecht.

Der soziokonstruktivistische Ansatz von Kiraly (2000), bei dem Lernende Wissen durch Interaktion und Teilnahme an kooperativen, zwischenmenschlichen und erfahrungsbasierten Aktivitäten aufbauen, die in realen oder simulierten beruflichen Kontexten stattfinden, wird als geeignetste Methodik zur Bewältigung der aktuellen Ausbildungsherausforderungen postuliert.

Die von mir vorgestellte didaktische Einheit basiert auf Kiralys Konzepten des *empowerments* und des *translator's self-concept* sowie auf seiner

---

4 „Übersetzen ist schwierig. Das wissen wir alle. Und Transkreation und Lokalisierung sind sogar noch schwieriger. Das kulturelle Wissen und die Sensibilität, die ein Übersetzer in einen Text einbringt, sind ein Schöpfungsakt. Doch oft ist die Zeit knapp, und nicht alle Texte müssen vollständig bearbeitet werden. Hier findet die maschinelle Übersetzung ihre Nische". (meine Übersetzung)

Unterscheidung zwischen Übersetzungskompetenz und Kompetenz des Übersetzers (ibid., S. 13). Das Konzept des *empowerment* wird definiert als „[…] acquiring the expertise and thus the authority to make professional decisions; assuming responsibility for one's actions; and achieving autonomy to follow the path of lifelong learning" (ibid., S. 1). Das *translator's self-concept* bezieht sich auf das Bild, das die Studierenden von sich selbst als zukünftige Fachleute und vom Beruf haben. Übersetzungskompetenz definiert Kiraly (ibid., S. 13) als Gesamtheit der Fähigkeiten, die eine Person in die Lage versetzen, einen akzeptablen Zieltext in einer Sprache auf der Grundlage eines in einer anderen Sprache verfassten Textes zu erstellen. Die Kompetenz des Übersetzers hingegen umfasst nicht nur die oben genannten Fähigkeiten, sondern setzt auch voraus, dass der Übersetzer in der Lage ist, Mitglied von Fachgemeinschaften zu werden, wie etwa jene für die seine übersetzten Texte bestimmt sind, oder von Gruppen professioneller Übersetzer, und dass er sich in diesen Gemeinschaften mit der erforderlichen Gewandtheit bewegen kann. Um beruflich erfolgreich zu sein, muss ein Übersetzer nach seiner Ausbildung über beide Kompetenzen verfügen. Kiraly schreibt:

> It is clear that today, high levels of translation competence, foreign language competence and native tongue competence are in themselves insufficient, albeit essential, features of the translator's overall professional profile. But the translator's marketability also depends on his or her ability to use modern tools of the trade in a professional manner, to research new topics quickly and efficiently, to justify one's work when necessary, to negotiate and collaborate with other translators and subject matter experts to accomplish tasks at hand. What is essential for graduates is that they be competent enough to tackle a wide variety of assignments and that they be confident to undertake new language-related tasks that may not have even existed when they were studying. (ibid., S. 13)

6. Didaktische Einheit zur Entwicklung des beruflichen *self-concept*

Ein Schlüsselbegriff in der Pädagogik ist die Motivation. Ohne Motivation fällt Lernen schwer. Wie also motivieren wir Lernende, deren Beruf von den Medien und der Gesellschaft immer wieder als mechanische Tätigkeit dargestellt wird, die in naher Zukunft von Maschinen übernommen wird? Aus diesem Grund habe ich es mir zum Ziel gesetzt, meinen Studierenden in allen Lehrveranstaltungen die zentrale Rolle bewusst zu machen, die sie als Humanübersetzer im Übersetzungsprozess spielen.

Ich unterrichte Allgemeines Übersetzen 1 Deutsch-Spanisch/Valencianisch im ersten Semester des zweiten Studienjahres im Studiengang Übersetzen und Sprachmittlung an der Universität Valencia. Die Studierenden werden in diesem Kurs zum ersten Mal im Studium mit praktischen Übersetzungsübungen konfrontiert.

Die Teilnehmenden arbeiten mit Werbetexten, die normalerweise in allgemeinen Übersetzungskursen verwendet werden, weil für sie keine Kenntnisse in einem bestimmten Fachgebiet vorausgesetzt werden muss. Ziel der Aktivität ist es, den Studierenden an aktuellen realen Textbeispielen bewusst zu machen, wie komplex die Transkreation in der Werbung ist und welch hohes Maß an sprachlichem Feingefühl und Kreativität der Humanübersetzer benötigt, um diese Aufgaben erfolgreich zu bewältigen, ganz im Sinne des obigen Zitats von Foti. Sie soll auch zum Nachdenken über die Grenzen der MÜ anregen. Das soll sich positiv auf das berufliche Selbstverständnis (translator's self-concept) der Studierenden auswirken und ihnen die nötige Motivation geben, ihre Übersetzungskompetenz weiter auszubauen.

Ich stütze mich dabei auf folgende theoretische Grundlagen:

a) den funktionalistischen Übersetzungsansatz von Nord (2009). Wir konzentrieren uns auf die in Werbetexten wichtigste Funktion, nämlich die appellative. Diese Funktion stellt die Perspektive des Empfängers in den Mittelpunkt und ist aus Sicht der Übersetzung am interessantesten, da sich die Ausgangslage des Empfängers bei jeder Interaktion mit unterschiedlichem Übersetzungsmaterial anders ist. Selbst wenn das Zielpublikum der Übersetzung und das ursprüngliche Publikum der gleichen Altersgruppe angehören, einen ähnlichen sozialen Status genießen, das gleiche Bildungsniveau haben und sogar den gleichen Beruf ausüben, kann aufgrund der Tatsache, dass sie aus unterschiedlichen Gesellschaften kommen, nicht davon ausgegangen werden, dass sie einen gemeinsamen kulturellen Hintergrund, gemeinsame Überzeugungen, Empfindungen, Erfahrungen und Werteskalen, d. h. Weltanschauungen haben (Nord 2010, S. 246);
b) Nords Konzept der nicht-sequenziellen vertikalen Übersetzungseinheit, die aus über den gesamten Text verteilten funktionalen Markern besteht (Nord 1998. S. 69);

c) Cesteros (2006, S. 57) sehr weit gefasste Definition der nonverbalen Kommunikation als „todos los signos y sistemas de signos no lingüísticos que comunican o se utilizan para comunicar“[5], wobei die Autorin kulturelle Gewohnheiten und Bräuche einschließt;
d) die Konzepte der semantischen oder kontextuellen Deautomatisierung und der kreativen strukturellen Modifikation phraseologischer Einheiten von Sánchez-López (2018); und
e) die Grenzen der neuronalen maschinellen Übersetzung (Lozano Sañudo 2023, S. 178–182).

An der Lehrveranstaltung *Allgemeines Übersetzen 1* nahmen ca. 20 Studierende teil; ein Viertel von ihnen waren Erasmus-Studenten aus Österreich oder Deutschland. Ich teilte sie in Vierer-Gruppen ein, wobei jede Gruppe eine Person mit Deutsch als Muttersprache umfasste. Jede Gruppe übersetzte ein Werbeplakat der deutschen Schokoladenmarke *Ritter Sport* und hatte die folgenden vier Teilaufgaben zu lösen:

1. Identifizieren der appellativen Marker des Originals.
2. Übersetzen des Textes durch DeepL.
3. Analysieren, ob die appellative Wirkung beibehalten wurde. Wenn nicht, reflektieren und diskutieren: warum nicht? Wenn ja: wie?
4. Vorschlagen einer alternativen Übersetzung, wenn das System keine funktionierende Option anbieten konnte.

Gruppe 1 sollte in der ersten Teilaufgabe die phraseologische Einheit „jemand kommt zum Zug“ identifizieren (Abbildung 1). Nachdem wir im Unterricht das Kapitel von Sánchez López (2018) gelesen und kommentiert hatten, sollte die Gruppe erkennen, dass die appellative Ressource in diesem Beispiel auf dem Spiel mit Polysemie (phraseologische oder globale Bedeutung und kompositorische Bedeutung) beruhte. Hier handelt es sich um semantische oder kontextuelle Deautomatisierung. Wenn wir mit einer phraseologischen Einheit konfrontiert werden, interpretieren wir sie normalerweise gemäß ihrer globalen Bedeutung. In diesem Fall jedoch deautomatisieren

[5] „alle nicht-sprachlichen Zeichen und Zeichensysteme, die kommunizieren oder zur Kommunikation verwendet werden“. (meine Übersetzung)

Abbildung 1: Ritter-Sport-Plakat im Bahnhof. Bei uns kommen alle zum Zug.

die deiktischen lokalen Koordinaten mit dem Bahnhof als Ort des kommunikativen Akts die Interpretation mit der globalen Bedeutung und aktivieren die Bedeutung der Elemente, in diesem Fall „Zug". Der Ausdruck „jemand kommt zum Zug" bedeutet, jemand ist an der Reihe; jemand wird als nächster bedient; jemand erhält die Möglichkeit, sich aktiv an etwas zu beteiligen und davon zu profitieren. Im Kontext heißt es weiter: „Wir setzen auf langfristige Partnerschaften im Kakaoanbau". Die Gesamtbedeutung der phraseologischen Einheit bezieht sich auf den fairen Handel, nämlich darauf, dass Kakaoproduzenten in vielen Ländern, darunter Ghana und die Elfenbeinküste, die oft nicht an der internationalen Wirtschaft teilhaben dürfen, die Möglichkeit erhalten, Teil der Produktionskette zu sein und davon zu profitieren. Ritter Sport setzt auf transparente Lieferketten, um mit seinem Kakaoangebot positiven Einfluss auf die sozialen, ökonomischen und ökologischen Bedingungen des Kakaoanbaus in Entwicklungsländern zu nehmen. Einerseits ist die globale Bedeutung des Ausdrucks „bei uns gewinnt jeder, jeder hat eine Chance"; andererseits heißt die wörtliche, kompositorische oder summative Bedeutung der Teile, dass alle zum Zug kommen, was mit dem lokalen Kontext *Bahnhof* spielt.

DeepL schlug für „Bei uns kommen alle zum Zug" „*Con nosotros todos tienen una oportunidad*" vor. Diese Übersetzung ist verständlich und erfasst die Idee, die vermittelt werden soll.

In der dritten Teilaufgabe stellten die Studierenden fest, dass der durch die kontextuelle Deautomatisierung der phraseologischen Einheit ausgelöste Appelleffekt des Wortspiels in der Übersetzung verschwunden war. An diesem Punkt wurde eine Debatte über die Grenzen der MÜ eröffnet. Die MÜ übersetzt segmentweise ohne Informationen über den räumlich-zeitlichen Kontext, in dem der kommunikative Akt stattfindet, und ist daher nicht in der Lage, das Spiel mit der Polysemie und das semantische Feld der Züge zu erkennen. Bei Eingabe des gesamten Textes lautete die von von DeepL vorgeschlagene Übersetzung: „*Todo el mundo tiene una oportunidad con nosotros. Apostamos por asociaciones a largo plazo en el cultivo de cacao*". Die Bedeutung ist richtig erfasst, allerdings fehlt die appellative Wirkung.

In der vierten Teilaufgabe schlugen die Studierenden Optionen vor wie zum Beispiel: „*Con nosotros todo el mundo tiene la oportunidad de subirse al tren. Apostamos por proveedores de cacao a largo plazo*".

Gruppe 2 bekam ein Poster zugewiesen, dessen Slogan *Fahr doch mal die vegane Schiene* lautete[6]. Im Text der Gruppe 2 spielte der lokale pragmatische Parameter ebenfalls eine wichtige Rolle, denn auch hier finden wir die Werbung in Form eines Plakats im Bahnhofsgebäude. Bei der textuellen Äquivalenz spielen die deiktischen Koordinaten des Kontexts eine grundlegende Rolle (Mellado Blanco 2015, S. 154). „Fahr doch mal die vegane Schiene" basiert auf der phraseologischen Einheit „eine bestimmte Schiene fahren" und bedeutet, etwas auf eine bestimmte Art und Weise tun; sich auf etwas spezialisieren; eine Neigung für etwas haben. Wenn wir uns jedoch die Bestandteile ansehen, finden wir das Substantiv „Schiene". „Schiene" spielt mit dem semantischen Feld der Züge, ebenso wie „fahr". Das Erkennen des Zusammenspiels zwischen der Gesamtbedeutung der Einheit und der Bedeutung ihrer Bestandteile bringt Sender und Empfänger einander näher, da letzterer sich der gleichen sprachlich-kulturellen Gemeinschaft zugehörig fühlt wie ersterer.

Für „Fahr doch mal die vegane Schiene" schlägt DeepL „*¿Por qué no te haces vegano?*" vor und greift damit die phraseologische Bedeutung sehr gut auf. Das Spiel mit der kompositorischen Bedeutung, die durch den lokalen Kontext aktiviert wird, ginge aber verloren, was zu einem erheblichen Verlust der appellativen Wirkung führen würde. Interessant ist, dass, wenn wir die gesamte Anzeige in DeepL eingeben, d. h. „Fahr doch mal die vegane Schiene. Lecker, vegan und mit Kakao aus 100 % zertifiziert und nachhaltigem

[6] Es war uns leider nicht möglich, dieses Poster in der erforderlichen Auflösung zu erhalten.

Bezug", sich der Vorschlag der Maschine ändert: „*¿Por qué no optar por la vía vegana? Deliciosos, veganos y con cacao procedente de fuentes 100 % certificadas y sostenibles*". In dieser zweiten Option haben wir das Wort „vía", sodass, obwohl wir nur eine Komponente haben, die die Bedeutung mit den lokalen deiktischen Koordinaten aktiviert, nämlich „vía", und nicht zwei wie im deutschen Ausgangstext, nämlich „fahr" und „Schiene", ein gewisses Maß an appellativer Wirkung erhalten bleibt.

In der Werbung spielen jedoch Konnotationen eine entscheidende Rolle, und wenn man spanische Muttersprachler bittet, den Ausdruck „optar por la vía" zu vervollständigen, wird eine große Mehrheit höchstwahrscheinlich das Adjektiv „fácil" hinzufügen. Dieser Ausdruck hat im Spanischen die pejorative Bedeutung „aufgeben".

Um das Spiel mit der Polysemie aufrechtzuerhalten, könnten die Studierenden Übersetzungen vorschlagen wie „*Súbete al tren vegano*", die auch bedeuten würde, dass es sich um einen aktuellen Trend handelt und somit die positive Konnotation hätte, trendy zu sein.

Abbildung 2: Ritter-Sport-Slogan Bahnbrechend lecker.

Im dritten Beispiel (Abbildung 2) „Bahnbrechend lecker" haben wir ein lexikalisiertes Adjektiv, bestehend aus „Bahn" + „brechen" + Suffix „d" zur Bildung des zusammengesetzten Präsenspartizips. Das etymologische Wörterbuch von Kluge (2011) erklärt, dass es von der Kollokation „eine Bahn brechen" abgeleitet ist, von der wiederum die phraseologische Einheit „sich Bahn brechen“ mit der Bedeutung „sich durchsetzen“ oder „sich etablieren“ abgeleitet ist. Der Ausdruck bedeutet also, sich durch seinen unübertroffenen Geschmack gegenüber der Konkurrenz durchzusetzen. Auch hier finden wir das Substantiv „Bahn“, das mit dem räumlichen Kontext spielt. DeepL schlägt „*Innovadoramente delicioso*“ vor, unabhängig davon, ob wir nur den Slogan „Bahnbrechend lecker“ oder den gesamten Text eingeben. Diese Übersetzung spielt nicht mit der Polysemie und kompensiert sie auch nicht durch andere Wortspiele. Im Unterricht sollten die Studierenden die appellativen Ressourcen des Spanischen nutzen und nach Lösungen suchen, um den Verlust der appellativen Wirkung zu kompensieren wie z. B. die lexikalische Kreation „*un sabor que marca trendencia*“.

Abbildung 3: Kreative strukturelle Modifikation. Ritter Sport-Slogan Erdnuss gut, alles gut.

Im vierten Werbetext (Abbildung 3) wird wie in den Beispielen 1-3mit der globalen Bedeutung und den Teilbedeutungen gespielt. Diesmal ist es keine semantische oder kontextuelle Deautomatisierung, sondern eine kreative Modifikation. „Erdnuss gut, alles gut“ ist eine Abwandlung des deutschen Idioms „Ende gut, alles gut“. Das erste Wort „Ende“ wurde durch „Erdnuss“ ersetzt, was mit dem Kontext übereinstimmt, da auf der Verpackung zwei Stück mit Erdnüssen gefüllte Schokolade abgebildet sind. Die Aufnahme dieses Wortes deautomatisiert die Gesamtinterpretation und macht Platz für eine wörtlichere „Wenn die Erdnuss gut ist, ist alles gut“. Die zugrundeliegende Botschaft ist, dass Ritter

Sport-Schokoladen gut sind, weil die Zutaten von hoher Qualität sind. Darüber hinaus ist das Wort „gut" im Sinne von gut schmeckend und „gut" im Sinne von „nicht schädlich für Tiere und Pflanzen" zu verstehen.

Unabhängig davon, ob nur der Slogan, „Erdnuss gut, alles gut" oder die gesamte Anzeige in DeepL eingegeben wird, lautet die vorgeschlagene Übersetzung: „*Maní bueno, todo bien. También bueno: la mitad de nuestra finca de cacao permanece intacta para animales y plantas*". Abgesehen von den Problemen, die mit der spanischen Variante zusammenhängen, erfüllt diese Option nicht die appellative Funktion. Zum einen, weil die Polysemie mit der phraseologischen Bedeutung verloren geht. Zum anderen, weil die Wiederholung von „gut" verschwindet. Der Humanübersetzer kann versuchen, kreativere Ideen zu entwickeln, was ein hohes Maß an Einfallsreichtum erfordert.

In vielen Fällen stellten die Lernenden fest, dass es nicht möglich war, eine phraseologische Einheit zu finden, um ein paralleles Wortspiel im Spanischen vorzuschlagen. Sie sahen sich gezwungen, in Übereinstimmung mit der von Nord (2010, S. 254) geäußerten Idee auf andere diskursive Strategien zurückzugreifen. In diesem Beispiel entschieden sie sich für einen Klangeffekt wie Reime, der in Slogans sehr häufig verwendet wird, weil er länger im Gedächtnis des Empfängers hängen bleibt: „*Calidad suprema y respeto al ecosistema: ese es nuestro lema*".

Abbildung 4: Kreative strukturelle Modifikation. Ritter Sport-Slogan Schmeckt auch Mutter Erdnuss.

Im letzten Beispiel (Abbildung 4) wird der Ausdruck „Mutter Erde“ verwendet. Auf Spanisch würde er wörtlich „*Madre Tierra*“ heißen, aber häufiger findet man „*Madre Naturaleza*“. Dieses Äquivalent basiert auf der griechisch-römischen Personifizierung der Natur. Im Slogan wurde die zweite Komponente *Erde* verändert und durch *Erdnuss* ersetzt. Die Erdnuss erscheint auch visuell auf dem Bild, damit ihre Bedeutung aktiviert wird. Die Gesamtbedeutung „Es gefällt der Natur“ gewinnt an Gewicht, wenn wir den Rest des Texts lesen: „Die Hälfte unserer Kakaofarm bleibt unberührt für Tiere und Pflanzen“. Damit wird zum Ausdruck gebracht, dass Ritter Sport umweltfreundlich ist. Unter den möglichen Synonymen für das Verb „mögen“ wird hier „schmecken“ verwendet. Es ist etwas, das man über die Geschmacksknospen wahrnimmt und als angenehm empfindet. Man mag den Geschmack von etwas, weshalb es hier idealerweise mit (Tafeln) Schokolade assoziiert wird. Auch für diesen Slogan gibt es nicht nur eine Übersetzungslösung. Ein möglicher Vorschlag, der auch mit Reimen spielt, wäre: „*Un sabor que lo peta y respeta el planeta: esa es nuestra meta*“.

7. Fazit

MÜ ist eine effektive Möglichkeit, die Arbeit der Übersetzer zu beschleunigen und zu erleichtern. MÜ ist inzwischen unverzichtbar, stellt meiner Ansicht nach aber keine Gefahr für den Übersetzerberuf dar. Sie sollte bereits in der Anfangsphase der Übersetzerausbildung gezielt vermittelt werden. Anhand realer Textbeispiele aus meinen Lehrveranstaltungen habe ich aufgezeigt, welche Vorteile entsprechende Übersetzungsaufgaben in den Anfängerkursen bieten. Dazu gehören:

1. Sensibilisierung der Studierenden dafür, dass MÜ ihren festen Platz in der Praxis erobert hat, der Übersetzer aber die Schlüsselfigur im Übersetzungsprozess bleibt. Daraus resultiert höhere Motivation zum Lernen und zur ständigen Verbesserung der Übersetzungsfertigkeiten.
2. Bewusstmachung der Komplexität der Übersetzertätigkeit, wodurch die Studierenden lernen, ihr berufsbezogenes *self-concept* zu präzisieren. Das wirkt sich positiv auf den sozioökonomischen Status des Berufszweiges aus.
3. Kenenlernen der Vielfalt der Übersetzertätigkeit, die zum einen aus Routinearbeiten besteht, die an Maschinen delegiert werden können,

und zum anderen aus Teilen, die eine Humanübersetzung erfordern. MÜ sollte frühzeitig in die Übersetzerausbildung integriert und überlegt eingesetzt werden, sodass ihre Grenzen und die Notwendigkeit der menschlichen Komponente deutlich werden. Die gewählten Werbetexte verdeutlichen die Rolle der menschlichen Komponente mit intellektuellen Fähigkeiten wie logisches Denken, interkulturelle Kompetenz und Kreativität.

Meine Lehrerfahrung hat gezeigt, dass der Einsatz von MÜ in der Anfangsphase der Ausbildung die Entwicklung von Übersetzungskompetenz in keiner Weise behindert, sondern fördert.

Die maschinelle Übersetzung ist auf dem Vormarsch, und wir als Lehrkräfte sehen uns dadurch einer großen Herausforderung gegenüber. Wir müssen unsere Studierenden darauf vorbereiten, in allen Phasen des Übersetzungsprozesses mit der Maschine zu interagieren, damit sie ihr Potenzial voll ausschöpfen und sich auf die kreativsten Aspekte konzentrieren können. Es bedarf eines fruchtbaren Austauschs zwischen Forscher, Dozenten und Institutionen, um unausweichliche Fragen zu beantworten, bspw. wann der beste Zeitpunkt in der Ausbildung ist, um die Arbeit mit MÜ einzuführen und wie wir die Arbeit mit MÜ integrieren können, ohne die Entwicklung der Übersetzungskompetenz zu beeinträchtigen.

Quellenverzeichnis

Cestero Mancera, Ana M. (2006): „La comunicación ni verbal y el estudio de su incidencia en fenómenos discursivos como la ironía". *ELUA. Estudios de Lingüística* 20, S. 57–77.

Cid-Leal, Pilar / Espín-García, Maria Carmen / Presas, Marisa (2019): „Traducción automática y posedición: Perfiles y competencias en los programas de formación de traductores". In: Tolosa Igualada, Miguel / Echeverri, Álvaro (Hrsg.): *Porque algo tiene que cambiar. La formación de traductores e intérpretes: Presente & futuro / Because something should change: Present & Future Training of Translators and Interpreters. MonTI* 11, S. 187–214. https://doi.org/10.6035/MonTI.2019.11.7.

ELIS European Language Industry Survey (2022): *Trends, expectations and concerns of the European language industry*, abgerufen am 30.09.2024 auf https://elis-survey.org/wp-content/uploads/2022/03/ELIS-2022-report.pdf?utm_source=elis-repository&utm_medium=website&utm_campaign=elis-report22&utm_id=elis-report-22.

Foti, Markus (2021): „La traducción y la máquina“. *Puntoycoma. Boletín de los traductores españoles en las instituciones de la Unión Europea* 170, S. 13–15.

González Pastor, Diana (Hrsg.) (2023): *El impacto de la traducción automática en la traducción profesional en España: tendencias, retos y aspectos socioprofesionales. El proyecto DITAPE.* Berlin et al.: Peter Lang.

González Pastor, Diana / Rico, Celia (2021): „POSEDITrad: la traducción automática y la posedición para la formación de traductores e intérpretes“. *RIDU Revista Digital en Docencia Universitaria,* 15(1), S. 1–13, https://doi.org/10.19083/ridu.2021.1213.

Kay, Martin (1997): „The proper place of men and machines in language translation“. *Machine Translation*, 12(1/2), S. 3–23.

Kiraly, Donald (2000): *A social constructivist approach to translator education. Empowerment from theory to practice.* Manchester (UK) / Northampton (MA): St. Jerome Publishing.

Kluge, Friedrich (2011): *Etymologisches Wörterbuch der deutschen Sprache.* Berlin et al.: De Gruyter.

Krause, Alexandra (2017): „Program designing in translation and interpreting and employability of future degree holders“. In: Valero Garcés, Carmen / Pena Díaz, Carmen (Hrsg.): *AIETI 8: Superando límites en traducción e interpretación = Além dos limites em traduçao e interpretaçao = Beyond limits in Translation and Interpreting.* Genf: Tradulex, S. 147–158, abgerufen am 24.04.2025 auf http://www.tradulex.com/varia/AIETI8.pdf.

Lozano Sañudo, Belén (2023): „Retos y futuro de la traducción automática“. In: González Pastor, Diana (Hrsg.): *El impacto de la traducción automática en la traducción profesional en España: tendencias, retos y aspectos socioprofesionales. El proyecto DITAPE.* Lausanne et at.: Peter Lang, S. 169–190.

Melby, Alan K. / Hague, Daryl R. (2019): „A singularity preoccupation. Helping translation students become language-services advisors in the age of machine translation“. In: Sawyer, David B. / Austermühl, Frank / Enríquez Raído, Vanessa (Hrsg.): *The evolving curriculum in the interpreter and translator education*. Amsterdam: John Benjamins, S. 205–229.

Mellado Blanco, Carmen (2015): „Parámetros específicos de equivalencia en las unidades fraseológicas (con ejemplos del español y el alemán)“. *Revista de filología* 33, S. 153–174.

Nitzke, Jean / Hansen-Schirra, Silvia / Canfora, Carmen (2019): „Risk management and post-editing competence“. *The Journal of Specialised Translation*, 31, S. 239–259.

Nord, Christiane (1998): „La unidad de traducción en el enfoque funcionalista“. *Quaderns. Revista de traducció* 1, S. 65–77.

Nord, Christiane (2009): „El funcionalismo en la enseñanza de traducción“. *Mutatis Mutandis* 2(2), S. 209–243. https://doi.org/10.17533/udea.mut.2397.

Nord, Christiane (2010): „Las funciones comunicativas en el proceso de traducción: un modelo cuatrifuncional“. *Núcleo* 27, S. 239–255.

Presas, Marisa / Torres-Hostench, Olga / Cid-Leal, Pilar (2016): “Las empresas de servicios lingüísticos ante la traducción automática. Retos y obstáculos para su implantación”, Präsentation, Congreso Internacional de Traducción e Interpretación, CITI7, abgerufen am 08.07.2024 auf https://www.researchgate.net/publication/301699036.

Rico Pérez, Celia (2017): „La formación de traductores en traducción automática“. *Revista tradumàtica Tecnologies de la traducció* 15, S. 75–96. https://doi.org/10.5565/rev/tradumatica.200.

Rico Pérez, Celia / García Aragón, Álvaro (2016): *Análisis del sector de la traducción en España (2014–2015).* Universidad Europea: Madrid, abgerufen am 24.04.2025 auf http://hdl.handle.net/11268/5057.

Sánchez López, Elena (2018): „Claves para entender el fenómeno de la variación en fraseología“. In: Mogorrón Huertas, Pedro / Albaladejo Martínez, J. Antonio (Hrsg.): *Fraseología, Diatopía y Traducción / Phraseology, Diatopic Variation and Translation.* Amsterdam / Philadelphia: John Benjamins, S. 243–262.

NMT and AI in undergraduate translation courses (English/Serbian)

Borislava Eraković
University of Novi Sad

ABSTRACT
The growing use of artificial intelligence (AI) and neural machine translation (NMT) in the language industry – and students' easy access to such tools – underscores the importance of integrating them early in translator training. This chapter reports on action research involving 67 students enrolled in News Translation and Specialised Translation courses at the University of Novi Sad during the 2023/2024 academic year. The courses followed a collaborative, social constructivist framework, incorporating AI and NMT into varied assignments. The research focuses on two key competences: information mining (IM) and post-editing (PE). The qualitative analysis of IM competence explores students' ability to recognise translation problems, evaluate online sources, and choose appropriate solutions. For PE, the study looks at the types of binary errors students identify in NMT (Google Translate) and AI (ChatGPT) outputs, and how they evaluate their translation performance with and without these tools. The results suggest that students need guidance in both areas. While students recognise the benefits of NMT and AI in improving translation quality, they also note that these tools can limit their creativity and self-reliance. Finally, the chapter proposes assignment types that incorporate NMT and AI to help students develop their IM and PE competencies.

Keywords: translator training, Google Translate, ChatGPT, information mining competence, post-editing competence

1. Introduction

Since the release of the first AI-based chatbot in November 2023, claims about AI's potential to replace human translators have generated significant hype. Initially, this sparked concerns among translation professionals (ELIS Survey Partners 2024), but recent studies (see Ehrensberger-Dow/Delorme Benites/Lehr 2023) and discussions at the 2024 Translating Europe Forum suggest these fears have subsided. The prevailing view at the Forum was that while AI's role is growing, human translators remain in the loop and hopefully "in the cockpit" (Pantcheva 2024). Despite advances in adaptive NMT, AI and CAT (computer-aided translation) tools, which have transformed translation workflows and reduced translators' autonomy (see Omazić/Pavlović 2022, pp. 18–20), human expertise is still necessary to assess NMT quality and determine required revisions. As future pre- and post-editors of NMT, students need to be equipped to anticipate and identify NMT errors and recognise critical elements in the source text that require closer examination.

AI in translation workflows is typically seen as a way of "augmenting" human capabilities. However, O'Brien (2023, p.13) notes that in the language industry, "augmented translation" primarily refers to improving efficiency for market-driven purposes rather than enhancing human cognitive abilities. This underscores the importance of translator training, which can provide students with the opportunity to explore whether and how AI tools can support their cognitive abilities and when to verify AI-generated information through other resources. Although students are often seen as digital natives, they may lack key research skills to perform this task (see Eraković/Radić Bojanić 2023) and require targeted support.

This paper examines the areas where the second- and third-year students in the *News Translation* (T2) and *Translation of Specialized Texts* (T3) courses at the University of Novi Sad, Serbia, required guidance and practice in information mining (IM) and recognising binary errors in post-editing (PE) of NMT. The findings highlight students' blind spots in verifying AI-generated solutions and identifying NMT errors, while also offering an example of how such tools can be introduced early in translator training.

Following a brief introduction to IM and PE competence, the next sections provide an overview of the educational context, an analysis of students' decision-making in IM, the types of NMT errors identified, and how they assess the impact of the tools they used on their decisions.

1.1 Information mining competence

In the latest edition of the EMT Competence Framework (EMT Board 2022), translation competence encompasses strategic, methodological and thematic competences. The methodological part, which was previously listed as the "ability to interact with MT" (EMT 2017, p. 7), has been updated to "MT literacy and awareness of MT's possibilities and limitations" (EMT Board 2022, p. 7). This competence is elaborated in the third learning outcome, which highlights the importance of evaluating the relevance and reliability of information sources (ibid., p. 8). Technology competence, which includes proficiency in using search engines and corpus-based tools, was first introduced in the 2009 EMT Framework (EMT Expert Group 2009) as "information mining competence." In the 2017 and 2022 editions, this was integrated into the methodological dimension of translation competence. For the purposes of this study, the 2009 definition remains the most relevant, as it outlines a concrete set of skills tested in this study: 1) identifying information and documentation needs, 2) developing strategies for documentary and terminological research, 3) evaluating the reliability of documentary sources, and 4) effectively using tools and search engines (e.g., terminology software, electronic corpora, electronic dictionaries) (EMT Expert Group 2009, p. 6).

Based on these skills, the guiding research questions concerning the students in T2 and T3 were: 1) What types of translation problems do students identify as searchable online? 2) Which search strategies and actions do they employ? 3) How relevant are the sources they find?

1.2 Post-editing of NMT: binary errors

Literature on teaching PE skills suggests these should be introduced at later stages of translator training (FIT 2022, p. 3; Guerberof-Arenas/Moorkens 2019, p. 232). Yamada (2019, p. 87) found that student competence in PE NMT matches human translation competence – in other words, to post-edit NMT effectively, students should first be highly competent translators. However, Mossop (2020, p. xxvi), advises that PE practice texts should be tailored to students' translation and PE competence levels. Furthermore, in everyday classroom experience, NMT has become an unavoidable tool in all translation classes, regardless of level, as students regularly resort to it.

In the current four-year BA English Language and Literature programme, the T2 and T3 courses are among the first translation courses students take. They therefore focus on raising awareness of factors influencing translation expectations across fields (literary, specialised, news, legal). At this stage, students are learning translation techniques and when to apply them, and their approach to translation errors is still elementary. As a result, PE tasks focus on binary errors (Pym 1992) – segments that are clearly and unambiguously wrong. In the context of this study, binarism is linked to what students were taught to regard as non-negotiable. For example, in the T2 course, students were introduced to the main stylistic features of hard news and were required to apply them in their translation and PE assignments. These features included keeping paragraphs to two or three sentences, limiting sentence length to 30 words, and avoiding colloquial expressions, scientific terms or anglicisms when a standard Serbian equivalent was available. Additionally, foreign names had to be transcribed into Serbian according to the guidelines in the *Orthography of the Serbian Language*. These instructions were regularly checked in class, and any deviations were corrected. Failure to follow them was, therefore, considered a binary error (i.e., an objectively incorrect choice).

The English-to-Serbian NMT output for hard news typically contained the types of errors that students had practised avoiding throughout the course. Thus, in addition to practising PE, identifying binary errors in such texts helped raise awareness of NMT's limitations, and trained students to focus on key aspects when reviewing their own translations.

2. Educational context

In the BA English Language and Literature programme students take two mandatory translation courses in the second year (Translation of Fiction and News Translation) and can choose additional translation courses in the third and fourth year, which focus on specialised texts, official documents, EU law and consecutive interpreting. All courses are introductory, designed to raise awareness of how text genre and function shape translators' decisions.

The pedagogical approach aligns with social constructivist epistemology (Kiraly 2000) and discovery learning, which emphasise students' autonomous learning through collaborative work on identifying translation problems, mining information from various sources, and translation in small teams. The teacher's primary role is to facilitate this process by setting the scene, monitoring each team's progress, and intervening when necessary.

Courses are delivered face-to-face but are supported by an online Moodle platform where students can access materials and Google Docs links. These platforms enable collaboration within teams, sharing final versions for class discussions, reviewing other teams' work, and seeking the teacher's guidance during or between sessions.

The action-research project described here was conducted with 23 students enrolled in the T3 course in the fall of 2023 and 44 students enrolled in the T2 course in the spring of 2024. The research was motivated by two key observations: first, students often struggled to identify which segments of the source text required further investigation, where to search for relevant information, and how to evaluate it; second, their home assignments reflected uncritical reliance on Google Translate, as if they feared to introduce corrections into translations that appeared fluent.

In the introductory phase, students were familiarised with to essential strategies for information mining on the internet through discussions and reading assignments. Topics included Google search operators, formulating effective queries, identifying authoritative terminology sources, and assessing the relevance of parallel texts.

2.1 Classroom scenarios and content

2.1.1 News translation (T2)

The course began with an analysis of AI tools (ChatGPT[1] and Gemini[2]) for summarising longer news stories and translating them from English into Serbian. Since news translation requires ordering information based on its relevance to the target audience, AI-generated summaries often fell short. They tended to preserve the source text's order of information, keep the irrelevant details, and omit crucial ones. Additionally, AI translations contained errors in register, sentence and paragraph length, name and title transcriptions, verbal aspect and other areas. Initial exercises showed that while students could identify most of these errors in both the summaries and translations, this did not always imply they could correct them.

After the introductory phase, the course focused on news stories selected by students. At the start of each session, students spent a few minutes searching for the latest news stories that interested them. The first three suggestions were then put to a vote, and the chosen text became the translation assignment for the class. Students first worked on their individual translations and then collaborated with other team members to compose their team's final version. This version was expected to resemble a typical hard news story: up to 200 words in length, with a title, a lead summarising the main points, and the inverted pyramid structure for the ordering of information, moving from general to specific. Paragraphs were to contain no more than two sentences, each concise (no longer than 30 words), with factual content, and avoiding anglicisms, colloquialisms, and overly technical terminology.

---

1 https://chatgpt.com/ (retrieved on 06/05/2025)
2 https://gemini.google.com/app (retrieved on 06/05/2025)

Upon completion, teams submitted their anonymous final versions to a shared Google Doc for class-wide analysis and discussion. During the class discussion, all team translations, including the Google-translated version, were analysed, highlighting successful solutions and potential errors. The class then collectively discussed the strengths and challenges of each translation.

2.1.2 Translation of specialised texts (T3)

The T3 course was structured around the translation of a longer text (604 words) that included terminology from media studies and socio-political discourse regarding the spread of conspiracy theories online (Tuters 2020). The version provided to students was edited to exclude references to conspiracy theories related to Donald Trump's first presidential election campaign. The text was assessed at the C2 CEFR level for readability using the free readability analyser Lumos Write Metrics[3]. The text was divided into eight sections, each containing one paragraph paired with a Google-translated version alongside another paragraph that the students were required to translate from scratch.

In preparation for the translation task, teams were assigned to find Serbian equivalents for all specialised terms in the text. During this phase, students tested ChatGPT as a terminology extraction tool, conducted Google searches, and consulted Serbian lexicographical resources, such as corpora and language guidebooks. They compiled the terminology and corresponding source links to a shared Google Doc, which served as the preliminary terminology resource and remained open for revision throughout the course.

Students worked individually on translations during class. Following this, the teacher provided feedback in the form of questions and prompts, encouraging students to reconsider and discuss inadequate solutions, which were marked but not explicitly corrected. Group discussions were held in class and students revised their translations based on these discussions before moving on to the next section of the text.

---

3 Lumos Write Metrics: Free readability checker online, retrieved on 20/12/2024 from https://www.lumoslearning.com/llwp/free-readability-checker-online.html.

2.1.3 Final tests

The expected learning outcomes for these courses were to increase students' awareness of the fallibility of NMT and AI translation through the development of PE and IM skills. Two tests were designed to assess these outcomes.

Information mining test. Students in T2 and T3 were given an English text containing at least five translation problems that required online research. Nord (2005, p. 167) defines translation problems as objective tasks that have to be solved by any translator, regardless of their level of competence, and categorises them as pragmatic, convention-related, linguistic, and text-specific. For this test, the instructions were simplified: students were asked to identify problems that could not be solved with a general bilingual dictionary but required research in other online sources. Students had 90 minutes to complete the test in a computer classroom. They were required to list the concepts they searched for, provide the exact phrasing of their search queries, list the sources that contained the translation equivalents or relevant information, and explain their reasoning when multiple solutions were possible.

Recognition of binary errors. The tasks for recognising binary errors in NMT varied between T2 and T3 students. T2 students were asked to identify and correct errors in a Google-translated news story. Their performance is presented as percentages, reflecting their success in identifying and correcting the errors.

T3 students participated in an awareness-raising exercise. After completing the translation of the text they had worked on throughout the semester, students reflected on how NMT influenced their translations, based on feedback from the teacher and class discussions. They answered the following questions in writing:

1) What types of errors did you make when NMT was provided versus when it was not?
2) When did you make more errors in meaning?
3) When did you make more orthographic errors?
4) When did you make more idiomatic errors?
5) Looking at your translations, when did you find it easier to find solutions for segments that could not be translated literally – when NMT was provided or when it was not?

Their responses are summarised and contrasted with the teacher's analysis of the type of errors students made with and without NMT.

3. Results and discussion

3.1 Information mining test

3.1.1 What types of translation problems do students identify as searchable online?

The results of the students' internet search tests are presented as percentages to illustrate the prevalence of certain types of their responses. These findings are specific to the groups in this study and are not intended to be generalisable. Rather, they should be viewed as examples of the challenges students may encounter, which should be examined with each new cohort to determine whether similar or different issues arise.

In the texts provided, students identified several categories of translation problems that could be researched online. These included:

- translation norms, particularly the transcription of personal names into the Cyrillic alphabet and finding Serbian equivalents for toponyms or institutional names;
- textual equivalents, involving terms and phrases with equivalent meanings in the same type of text, typically specialised terms;
- natural phrasing, concerning expressions and collocations that would sound unidiomatic if translated literally into Serbian;
- culture-specific realities, such as identifying cultural reference and determining if there is a standardised Serbian translation.

Table 1 presents the percentages of students who identified the specified number of searchable items in the text, found relevant sources for their translations and successfully solved them:

Table 1: Information mining: problems and solutions

	T3	T2	T3	T2
	Problems identified		Sources relevant	
4 & 5	45 %	56 %	22 %	32 %
2 & 3	34 %	39 %	65 %	50 %
0 & 1	17 %	2 %	17 %	15 %

The results are clustered into three groups: 4/5, 2/3 and 0/1. A single mistake may be accidental, while two or three suggest students had difficulty in identifying certain problems but were successful with others. Four or five unidentified searchable issues suggest that students in general had problems with identifying what to search for. The percentages indicate that searching for information on the internet and finding a solution was a challenging task for a significant number of students. Approximately half of the students in both T2 and T3 were able to identify the required number of searchable problems (4 or 5: T2 – 56 %, T3 – 45 %), but only about half of those were able to find a successful solution in the sources (T2 – 32 %, T3 – 22 %).

Several recurring issues were observed, with the most common ones outlined below. A key difficulty appears to be determining what makes an expression search-worthy. Specifically, students struggled with questions such as:

- Does extratextual information about an item influence the choice of translation technique? For example, in the case of the document titled *World Heritage Tentative List*, the word *tentative* should be researched in relevant sources and applied appropriately, rather than translated directly.
- Is a word or expression a concept/specialised term or a general language expression? For instance, *a cultural dope* is a sociological concept that needs to be researched in parallel texts rather than translated freely.
- Is an expression a fixed phrase, or does it require creative paraphrasing since literal translation would be unidiomatic? For example, a literal translation of *rabbit hole* into Serbian would not convey its meaning as "world where rules do not apply."

A related issue was determining what should be discovered about an expression. For instance, when dealing with the name of an institution such as the International Organization for Migration, students easily found it in the English and Serbian Wikipedia (*Međunarodna organizacija za migracije*), but they did not investigate further to check whether alternative translations were more commonly used in authoritative documents. They did not explore whether *internacionalna* or *međunarodna* was preferred, or which abbreviation (the English IOM or the translated MOM) was standard. This problem, along with an overreliance on bilingual dictionaries, reflects a view of translation as primarily a linguistic task rather than a cultural one, aligning with similar findings in the literature on students' search strategies (see Zanettin 2002, p. 3, 7).

3.1.2 Which search strategies and actions do they employ?

Students had difficulty deciding what type of search to conduct and the sequence of steps to follow. A typical example involves translating the religious title of a church dignitary, such as "dean." While its primary meaning in English refers to the education sector (*dekan* in Serbian), there is also a second, religious meaning that students need to recognise. To solve this problem, students would need to:

- identify the meaning of the title in English;
- search for texts in Serbian that reference this religious function (e.g., *Dean of Westminster*);
- if multiple translation variants exist (e.g., *đakon, dekan, upravitelj*), perform a frequency check to determine the most commonly used translation in relevant texts.

However, few students conducted a series of different types of searches for a single expression.

Students also checked how frequently a term or an expression appeared in online sources. A common issue with these frequency checks was that they were often incomplete: once one solution was confirmed to be in use, no further checks for alternative solutions were conducted. For example, when dealing with a borrowing, students might check if *emotikon* was used for *emoji*, but fail to explore other possible translations. Similarly, when examining the standard Serbian title for the *National Geographic* journal, they might confirm *Nacionalna geografija*, but not consider the transcribed version. Additionally, when identifying one collocate in a collocation, students often did not explore whether other collocates might also be appropriate.

Such examples suggest that students lack clear criteria for determining when they have sufficiently explored options and can stop searching. The issue may not be technical, but rather theoretical – more specifically, understanding the types of questions translators need to ask beyond simply determining the meaning of an unknown word or expression. As Guerberof-Arenas, Valdez and Dorst (2024, p. 88) note, some students' explanations suggest that they are not using resources to support their decision, but rather relying on their own proficiency and intuition.

To address this, students need to be repeatedly provided with examples of the different types of questions translators should ask when working on a text, along with sample "conversations" the teacher has had with ChatGPT. Research on professional translators' workflows (see Gough 2016, p. 243) shows that translators typically spend about a third, and sometimes even half, of their time on research. Highlighting this can help students gain perspective on how much time they might devote to researching or even just formulating questions.

3.1.3 How relevant are the sources they find?

In terms of the types of sources students utilised, the most frequently consulted were authoritative parallel texts in Serbian, followed by specialised dictionaries for terminological issues and the Serbian orthography manual for the transcription of proper names. Table 2 presents the percentages of the types of sources used by students:

Table 2: Information mining: types of sources

Types of sources	T3	T2
Specialised dictionary or Serbian orthography manual	43 %	50 %
Corpora (concordances)	0 %	6,5 %
Authoritative parallel texts	86 %	73 %
Frequency on Google: 1 expression	60 %	47 %
Frequency on Google: 2 expressions	43 %	47 %
Defined region in frequency search	0 %	17 %

Regarding the authority and reliability of the sources, students often did not consider whether the page they found was an automatically generated translation or an authentic parallel text. Automatically generated translations have become common on the internet and they display easily recognisable features. This emphasises the need to practice traditional text analysis, including examining cohesive devices, adherence to standardised orthography, and other indicators of a coherent text.

The least frequently consulted source was the electronic corpus of Serbian, mainly due to its limited availability. Only one web-based corpus exists, and it offers no significant advantages over a standard Google search.

Approximately half of the students used Google to verify the frequency of words or expressions in Serbian. However, despite introductory presentations, some technical search-related issues persisted in these searches until the end of the course. Specifically, students were unfamiliar with how search operators (such as "" and *) function. For instance, many did not realise that searching for "sanitarni radnik" with and without quotes yielded different results or that the asterisk (*) could help identify more frequent collocates. Their limited experience with Google searches was also evident in difficulties recognising when to add keywords to narrow results and how to select appropriate ones. Additionally, only a small number utilised Google's advanced settings to limit searches to the Serbian region. This was a surprising finding, revealing the limits of students' internet literacy and highlighting the need for a sustained focus on the technical aspects of online searches. It also underscores the importance of continuous reminders that searches should aim to capture cultural differences (hence the relevance of delimiting the region), not just linguistic equivalents.

3.2 Post-editing binary errors in NMT

Regarding the ability to identify and edit binary errors in NMT and AI translations, we present the percentages reflecting the T2 group's success in identifying and correcting binary errors in NMT, and a summary of the T3 group's self-assessment on how NMT and AI impacted the occurrence of errors in their translations.

3.2.1 Identification and correction of binary errors in a Google-translated text (T2)

In the raw Google-translated (NMT) news story, 44 T2 students were tasked with identifying and correcting binary errors. As a group, the students identified the following types of errors:

- stylistic: Issues with sentence and paragraph length as well as register (including the presence of anglicisms, colloquialisms and specialised terminology);
- grammatical: errors stemming from differences in verb transitivity between English and Serbian;

- idiomatic: unidiomatic collocations resulting from the literal translation of fixed phrases and idioms;
- translation norms: improper transcription of personal names from English and other languages, as well as journal titles.

Table 3 shows the percentages of students who identified and successfully corrected these errors:

Table 3: PE – identification and correction of binary errors

T2 (44 students)	% of students who identified the error	% of students who corrected the error
idiomatic I: idiom	80	55
idiomatic II: collocation	68	43
norm: transcription	60	20
style: sentence length	48	48
style: register	18	9
grammar: verb form	38	32

The results indicate that while a considerable number of students were able to identify unnatural phrasing (80 % for idioms, 68 % for collocations), producing accurate corrections proved more challenging (55 % for idioms, 43 % for collocations). Grammatical errors related to verb transitivity were identified and corrected to a moderate degree, while inappropriate levels of formality and colloquial expressions also posed difficulty. All these errors affect the stylistic features of a text, an area where AI tools could be highly useful and regularly tested in class.

For transcription errors, 60 % of students identified them, but only 20 % successfully corrected them, suggesting insufficient use of resources such as transcription dictionaries and Serbian orthographic manuals.

Students were more successful with sentence length issues, likely because they recalled this as a required textual feature that is easy to spot in a short text and address effectively, as indicated by equal success rates in identification and correction. The ability to identify such errors is particularly important in contexts where AI is used, as AI chatbots offer little assistance if the translator is unaware of the required features of the target text.

3.2.2 Self-assessment of the influence of NMT on errors

Students in T3 were asked to reflect on the feedback received from the teacher and during class discussions and write their conclusions on how NMT influenced the types of errors they made during translation (semantic, orthographic, grammatical, and idiomatic). They also considered how these tools affected their creativity when literal translation was not possible. Thirteen students submitted responses, summarised in Table 4 alongside the teacher's analysis of errors identified in 20 completed translations.

Table 4: The impact of NMT on students' translations – students' and teachers' perspectives

	Students (13)		Teacher (evaluation of 20 translations)			
What type of errors are more common?	**+NMT**	**−NMT**	**+NMT**	**−NMT**	**No difference**	**No errors**
Semantic	8	4	10	5	5	–
Idiomatic	12	2	5	2	12	2
Orthographic	–	4	–	1	8	11
Word order	2	–	2	1	15	2
Omission	–	1	2	6	12	2
(−)Consideration of extratextual context			10	4	5	1
(−)Missing or inadequate textual connector			–	4	6	10

Labels:
+/−NMT: students did (+) or did not (−) use NMT.
No difference: the teacher did not find that the use of NMT coincided with a greater or smaller number of errors.
No errors: the teacher did not find errors of the specified type.

Both student responses and teacher evaluations align in noting that more semantic errors occurred when NMT was provided. However, while students believed NMT had a negative influence on idiomatic accuracy, the teacher's analysis did not confirm this (Label: No difference). The teacher also observed that students paid less attention to context when translating paragraphs with NMT and struggled with the logical organisation of the text, particularly the use of textual connectors, regardless of whether NMT was used.

On the positive side, students highlighted several benefits of using Google Translate: the tool provided initial ideas for further research on Google or ChatGPT, sped up the search process, and helped them identify unidiomatic or nonsensical translations into Serbian. In class discussions, students explained this effect with a psychological rationale – unnatural expressions were easier to spot in someone else's translation, which they could evaluate with fresh eyes, compared to their own work.

Among the drawbacks of NMT use, students reported the following challenges: It was harder to think of alternative translations when one was already suggested, focusing on context became more difficult, they conducted less research, their translations tended to be more literal, they more easily accepted unidiomatic expressions as plausible, and they overlooked semantic errors more often. Interestingly, in a similar recent study, Zhang (2023) found that undergraduate translation students expressed concerns about MT negatively affecting their independent and critical thinking but did not report adverse effects on their language skills or translation competence.

4. Conclusions

Recognising students' propensity to use AI and NMT tools as a given, this chapter advocates for their early integration into translator training rather than postponing their use until advanced levels. These tools could be introduced systematically across relevant tasks to ensure meaningful engagement. AI chatbots can aid information mining by assisting in term extraction, providing definitions, suggesting key terms for further research and offering initial links. However, these tools often need to be paired with proficient internet browsing to ensure effectiveness. It is important to guide students how to recognise automatically machine-translated pages and differentiate them from authentic parallel texts. This study also highlights the importance of continuously addressing search syntax, source types, their characteristics and reliability.

Formative and summative assessments of information mining competence can reveal that, despite being digitally savvy, students may lack proficiency in internet research for translation purposes. Difficulties arise not only with *how* to search (e.g., selecting strategies, performing frequency checks, or crafting queries) and *where* to search (e.g., choosing appropriate regions, domains, parallel texts, or online lexicographical resources), but also in *what* to search (e.g., identifying translation problems) and *why* (e.g., understanding how search results inform translation decisions). The *what* and *why* are directly tied to the ability to identify and assess translation problems, and determine their relevance for translation strategies, making these skills essential in every translation assignment rather than being confined to separate courses.

As AI and NMT technologies continue evolving, translators need to critically assess their relevance and impact on professional practices (EMT 2022, Technology competence points 15, 16, 18). One way to foster this critical awareness is by incorporating NMT post-editing tasks alongside translation from scratch. Focusing on clearly defined types of binary errors in introductory courses, students practise MT PE, which helps them recognise the limitations of NMT and AI tools from early on.

Since PE competence is closely linked to translation competence – and neither is fully developed at the undergraduate level – it is reasonable to prioritise core types of binary errors typical of specific text genres. The study results indicate that students need training not only in identifying errors but also in correcting them, which often involves improving their use of resources.

This action research also found that students identified errors in NMT-generated texts more easily than in their own translations. This suggests that incorporating NMT and AI tools into class assignments, using the same text students have previously translated from scratch, could be valuable. Comparing these versions can raise awareness of both NMT's limitations and the importance of creativity in translation.

Since 2023, AI and NMT cannot be sidestepped in current workflows or in translator training. If students are to "build their self-concept as human translators in the age of MT" (Öner Bulut/Alimen 2023, p. 379), they need to understand these tools' limitations and advantages from early on as well as the enduring necessity of human expertise.

Bibliography

ELIS Survey Partners (2024): *European language industry survey 2024: Trends, expectations and concerns of the European language industry*, retrieved on 20/12/2024 from tinyurl.com/5796y8ke.

Ehrensberger-Dow, Maureen / Delorme Benites, Alice / Lehr, Caroline (2023): "A new role for translators and trainers: MT literacy consultants."

The Interpreter and Translator Trainer 17(3), pp. 393–411. https://doi.org/10.1080/1750399X.2023.2237328.

EMT Expert Group (2009): *Competence for professional translators, experts in multilingual and multimedia communication*. Brussels: European Commission.

EMT Board (2017): *European Master's in Translation competence framework 2017*. Brussels: European Commission, retrieved on 20/12/2024 from tinyurl.com/38tzjc79.

EMT Board (2022): *European Master's in Translation competence framework 2022*. Brussels: European Commission, retrieved on 20/12/2024 from tinyurl.com/2umek6vh.

Eraković, Borislava / Radić Bojanić, Biljana (2023): "The intersection of digital and translation competence in students of translation." *Ars & Humanitas* 17(1). https://doi.org/10.4312/ars.17.1.125-138.

FIT (2022): *FIT position paper on educating the next generation of translators*, retrieved on 20/12/2024 from https://library.fit-ift.org/public/Publications/positionpapers/PDP_202204_Educating_Next_Generation_Translators_ENFR.pdf.

Guerberof-Arenas, Ana / Moorkens, Joss (2019): "Machine translation and post-editing training as part of a master's programme." *The Journal of Specialised Translation* 31, pp. 217–238. https://doi.org/10.26034/cm.jostrans.2024.4712.

Guerberof-Arenas, Ana / Valdez, Susana / Dorst, Aletta G. (2024): "Does training in post-editing affect creativity?." *The Journal of Specialized Translation* 41, pp. 74–97. https://doi.org/10.26034/cm.jostrans.2024.4712.

Gough, Joanna (2016): *The patterns of interaction between professional translators and online resources*. Ph.D. thesis, University of Surrey, retrieved on 20/12/2024 from http://epubs.surrey.ac.uk/813254/.

Kiraly, Donald (2000): *A social constructivist approach to translator education: Empowerment from theory to practice*. Manchester: St. Jerome Publishing.

Mossop, Brian (2020): *Revising and editing for translators*. London / New York: Routledge.

Nord, Christiane (2005): *Text analysis in translation*. Amsterdam: Rodopi.

O'Brien, Sharon (2023): "Human-centered augmented translation: Against antagonistic dualisms." *Perspectives* 32(3), pp. 391–406. https://doi.org/10.1080/0907676X.2023.2247423.

Omazić, Marija / Pavlović, Nataša (2022): "Prevođenje u digitalnom okruženju: utjecaj prijevodnih tehnologija na praksu i teoriju prevođenja." In: Glušac, Maja / Mikić Čolić, Ana (Eds.): *Jezik u digitalnom okruženju.* Zagreb: Hrvatsko društvo za primijenjenu lingvistiku. pp. 11–26.

Öner Bulut, Senem / Alimen, Nilüfer (2023): "Translator education as a collaborative quest for insights into the re-positioning of the human translator (educator) in the age of machine translation: The results of a learning experiment." *The Interpreter and Translator Trainer* 17(3), pp. 375–392. https://doi.org/10.1080/1750399X.2023.2237837.

Pantcheva, Marina (2024): *Compete, collaborate, or take control: The role of linguists in an AI future.* Keynote presentation at the Translating Europe Forum 2024, retrieved on 20/12/2024 from tinyurl.com/3nsd7rkt.

Pym, Anthony (1992): "Translation error analysis and the interface with language teaching." In: Dollerup, Cay / Loddegaard, Anne (Eds.): *The teaching of translation*. Amsterdam: John Benjamins, pp. 279–288.

Tuters, Marc (2020): "How conspiracy theories spread online – it's not just down to algorithms." *The Conversation*, retrieved on 20/12/2024 from https://theconversation.com/how-conspiracy-theories-spread-online-its-not-just-down-to-algorithms-133891.

Yamada, Masaru (2019): "The impact of Google neural machine translation on post-editing by student translators." *The Journal of Specialised Translation* 31, pp. 87–106.

Zhang, Jia (2023): "Exploring undergraduate translation students' perceptions towards machine translation: A qualitative questionnaire survey." In: Yamada, Masaru / Do Carmo, Felix (Eds.) *Proceedings of Machine Translation Summit XIX, Vol. 2: Users Track.* Macau SAR, China: Asia-Pacific Association for Machine Translation, pp. 1–10, retrieved on 20/12/2024 from https://aclanthology.org/2023.mtsummit-users.1.pdf.

Zanettin, Federico (2002): "DIY corpora: the WWW and the translator." In: Maia, Belinda / Haller, Johann / Ulrych, Margherita (Eds.) *Training the language services. Provider for the new millennium.* Porto: Universidade do Porto, pp. 239–248.

“I feel somewhat constrained by the raw output…”: a case study on teaching post-editing in translator training

Maria Elisa Fina
Ca’ Foscari University of Venice

ABSTRACT
The widespread adoption of neural machine translation (NMT) and large language models (LLMs) has intensified the need to include post-editing (PE) training in translation curricula. Despite the availability of guidelines and skill sets for PE in the existing literature, the teaching of PE presents numerous challenges, particularly for translation students encountering PE for the first time.

This paper describes a PE course offered at Ca’ Foscari University of Venice in the 2023–2024 academic year for master’s students of translation. Particular attention is given to the approach developed to address students’ initial resistance to PE and the issue of subjectivity in the PE process.

Following an overview of the existing literature on PE training, the course objectives and contents are outlined, and the practical tasks proposed to the students are described in detail. These tasks are discussed with reference to the PE-related skills and competences available in the literature, as well as to the challenges encountered by the students. The discussion then focuses on the results of a task-based survey that was carried out to explore students’ acquired attitudes toward PE and its relationship with translation. Finally, the concluding section discusses key considerations for future training.

Keywords: post-editing, machine translation, training in PE, translator training, post-editing competences

1. Introduction

More than 20 years have passed since O’Brien’s paper (2002) on teaching post-editing (hereafter “PE”), in which she argues the need for specific training in PE to meet the growing demand for translation services, and 10 years have passed since Gaspari, Almaghout and Doherty’s paper (2015), in which they highlight the impact of familiarity with translation technology on the employability of future translators. According to do Carmo and Moorkens (2021, p. 39), PE has been incorporated in many translation programmes’ curricula since at least 2009 and is listed as part of the translation competences in the European Master’s in Translation Competence Framework

(EMT Board and Competence Task-Force 2022)[1]. The transition from statistical machine translation (hereafter "SMT") to neural machine translation[2] (hereafter "NMT"), which produces better-quality outputs, and the increasing presence of both MT and PE in the translation industry (Ginovart Cid/Colominas 2020, p. 283) has made the need for training in PE even more crucial. Cid-Leal, Espín-García and Presas (2019, p. 100) speak in terms of "a shift from computer-assisted human translation to human-assisted machine translation," which poses new challenges to translator training programmes. This challenge is also due to the lack of agreement in the ISO 18587 (2017)[3] on PE-related skills, as the five topics that should be covered in the training – advanced use of translation memory and MT, advanced terminology work, advanced text-processing skills, practice in both light and full PE, and use of Quality Assessment tools – are only briefly described in an Annex (Ginovart Cid/Colominas 2021, p. 227). The inclusion of training in PE in translation programmes has posed the crucial issues of defining sets of skills and competences that post-editors should acquire or integrate and designing course contents accordingly.

But designing the training involves a further issue: resistance to PE. According to O'Brien (2002, p. 100), translators who are not skilled in PE tend to develop hostility to MT technology. Narratives of resistance to PE can be found in Allen (2003) and Austermühl (2013), mainly in reference to the identity crises that translators may face because of industry pressures; the causes of translators' resistance to PE have been studied as well (Cadwell/O'Brien/Teixeira 2018; Moorkens/Way 2016). A different, new view of PE is provided by do Carmo and Moorkens (2021, p. 39), who claim that "PE needs to be studied in more detail, beyond the acceptance/resistance divide" to shed light on the actual impact of technological advances on the translator's work and on the type of professionals the language industry is actually seeking.

In the light of these preliminary observations, the following question can be raised: in line with the current best practices and skill sets, what contents should be designed and proposed to students for them to perceive

---

1 Retrieved on 10/04/2022 from https://commission.europa.eu/system/files/2022-11/emt_competence_fwk_2022_en.pdf.

2 For an overview, see Kenny (2018).

3 This Standard is currently under revision.

and approach PE as an *enriched evolution* of the translator profession rather than a practice that is disruptive to the translation profession?

Starting from this issue, the aim of this paper is to share experiences from a PE course arranged at Ca' Foscari University of Venice in the 2023–2024 academic year as part of the training offered in the Translation and Interpretation master's degree programme. In the following sections, the course contents proposed to the students will be presented, ranging from theoretical knowledge to practical tasks aimed at raising awareness and building competence. These contents will be discussed in reference to the PE-related skills and competences available in the existing literature, as well as to the students' perceptions of PE and the challenges they encountered.

2. Literature review

2.1 PE skills and competences

Ginovart Cid and Colominas (2021, p. 227) classify the skill sets available in the literature "into two different types depending on the function attributed to the post-editor." While some skill sets seem to attribute "limited or reductive roles" (Kenny/Doherty 2014, p. 290) to the post-editor, others suggest "a more extensive job profile" (Ginovart Cid/Colominas 2021, p. 227).

In her proposed outline for a course module in PE, O'Brien (2002) lists as necessary skills knowledge of MT, terminology management skills, pre-editing/controlled language skills, programming skills, and text linguistic skills. She also stresses the importance of a positive attitude toward MT (ibid., p. 102).

Another interesting skill set is provided by Rico and Torrejón (2012), who divide the necessary PE skills into three groups:

- core competences: "attitudinal or psycho-physiological competences" which relate to dealing with subjectivity in PE specifications, client expectations and uncertainty, and the "strategic competence" necessary to "arrive at *informed decisions* when choosing among different PE alternatives (Rico/Torrejón 2012, p. 170, emphasis in the original);
- linguistic skills: the linguistic, communicative and textual skills required of a translator (ibid.);
- instrumental competence: understanding MT technologies, terminology management, corpora, controlled language and basic programming skills (ibid.).

An important contribution also comes from Pym (2013), who emphasises skills relating to quickly acquiring mastery of new software and tools as well as the ability to evaluate tools and MT suggestions. He also includes revision skills aimed at correcting punctuation and improving cohesion and style, as well as working as a part of a review team and carrying out revision according to specified quality levels. In other publications, the proposed skill sets include the ability to balance PE speed and invested effort with respect to required quality (Doherty/Gaspari 2013) and the ability to minimise the technical (keyboarding) effort (Krings 2001) and measure effort and quality to determine fair prices (Guerberof Arenas/Depraetere/O'Brien 2012).

More recent contributions are those by Nitzke, Hansen-Schirra and Canfora (2019) and Ginovart Cid and Oliver (2020). Nitzke, Hansen-Schirra and Canfora (2019) outline a PE competence model by adapting PACTE's (2003) translation competence model and Robert, Remael and Ureel's (2017) revision competence model. The authors propose a set of four core competences (risk assessment competence; strategic competence; consulting competence; service competence) and a set of eight subsidiary sub-competences: bilingual competence; extralinguistic competence; instrumental competence; research competence; revision competence; translation competence; MT competence; post-editing competence (for a full account, see Nitzke/Hansen-Schirra/Canfora 2019, pp. 248–250). Regarding the post-editing competence, the authors stress the fact that, since the NMT output is more fluent and contains fewer mistakes, the post-editor needs to be trained in "spotting exactly [...] more fine-grained problems" (ibid.).

Ginovart Cid and Oliver (2020), instead, provide a survey-based list of PE skills considered to be the most important for a professional post-editor. These include the ability to carry out both light and full PE, adhere to guidelines, decide when to work on a segment or discard it, identify MT output errors, and apply the right correction strategy.

Although the proposed professional skills are useful for course content design, the author of this paper agrees with Ginovart Cid and Colominas (2021, p. 227) on the fact that "neither the industry nor the research community seem to have reached consensus on their specific definition or delimitation." However, the proposed skill sets mentioned above can be condensed into a unified set, where the "core competences" can be summarised as follows: translation competence, risk assessment competence, critical knowledge of MT systems, the ability to adhere to client-provided guidelines, technology competence (the ability to quickly acquire mastery of and evaluate software and tools), the ability to balance PE speed and effort in relation to the required quality.

2.2 Course contents in PE training

The existing literature also includes a few publications focused on PE-related course contents and tasks to be offered in PE training. In this regard, O'Brien's paper (2002) can be considered seminal as, along with the set of competences described in section 2.1, she also provides a list of course contents, both theoretical and practical, that match her proposed set of skills reported in sub-section 2.1 (for a full account, see O'Brien 2002, pp. 104–105). Absolon (2018) proposes a training plan featuring a series of exercises aimed at developing the three groups of skills in his model (linguistic, technical, and decision-making); Koponen (2015) shares her experience in building a PE course module in Finland, from course objectives and topics to course assignments to evaluation of the practical organisation of the course as well as of learning outcomes; Doherty and Kenny (2014) outline a syllabus covering also topics such as ethics, payment and collaboration; Flanagan and Christensen (2014) describe a MT and PE course module with assignments involving PE according to the PE guidelines provided by TAUS (Massardo et al. 2016); Rossi (2017) describes a course on SMT and PE.

More recently, survey based research has provided interesting results. Ginovart Cid, Colominas and Oliver (2020, p. 299) report that the elements recurring in training courses at the time of their research are PE levels (light and full PE), PE guidelines, PE attitude, PE risks, PE techniques, practical PE exercises. In their survey-based, mixed-method study on MTPE skills, course descriptions and educators' thoughts, Ginovart Cid and Colominas (2021) observe very interesting trends regarding PE training elements, skills and tasks. These are only a few: the task-based – rather than project-based – course tends to be preferred by a significant number of educators; almost half of the respondents do not have a structured exercise for error categorisation of the MT output (ibid.); assignments or activities on pre-editing tend not to be included; the post-edited texts tend not to be evaluated; only in a few cases MTPE is included in "regular" or "traditional" translation courses (for a full account, see pp. 240–244). If we now relate the results of these survey-based studies to the proposed course contents mentioned in the previous paragraph, the offered PE training appears to emphasise different levels of intervention on the MT output (light vs full PE), adherence to provided guidelines, and prioritising the PE process over the assessment of the final product. Overall, not all the suggested skills and competences seem to be (fully) covered in PE courses. This is not surprising, given the inherent challenges in implementing a holistic pedagogical approach (Ginovart Cid/Colominas 2021, p. 145), likely due to time constraints, the varying objectives of degree programmes, the educators' own competences, and related issues.

2.3 Other relevant literature

As far as methods and processes of PE are concerned, a few contributions have focused on PE time for measuring PE effort (Krings 2001; Specia 2011; Tatsumi/Roturier 2010, among others), while others on the steps involved in the PE process (e.g., Rico/Díez Orzas 2013). In Popović et al. (2014), the technical effort is represented by five types of edit operations: correcting word form, correcting word order, adding omission, deleting addition, correcting lexical choice. do Carmo and Moorkens (2021, p. 44) describe four types of editing actions – or "edits" – and classify them as primary and secondary: "deletion" and "insertion" are primary editing actions, while "replacement" and "movement" are secondary editing actions. However, they acknowledge that this is "a simplification of a complex process" (p. 45), as "when editing [...] translators manipulate segmentation" (ibid.)

Regarding PE operations, particularly interesting is Nitzke and Gros' (2021) study on preferential changes in revision and post-editing, which they call "over-editing." An interesting result found by the authors comparing light PE and full PE is that more syntactic and grammatical flaws were corrected in the light PE task, although they were not supposed to be corrected in light PE (p. 31). As far as the product of PE is concerned, a few studies have analysed the presence of "post-editese" – i.e., "the existence of features of post-edited machine translation output (MTPE) that distinguish it from human translated text (HT)" (Farrell 2023, p. 52) – in post-edited texts (Castilho/Resende 2022; Volkart/Bouillon 2022).

Finally, a few publications have also investigated the state of the art of training courses in PE offered by training centres and universities. MTPE at university seems to be offered mainly at master's level (Plaza-Lara 2019); from a practical perspective, Ginovart Cid, Colominas and Oliver (2020, p. 286) mention the MTPE courses (also online) implemented by Trados (n.d.)[4] and TAUS (Massardo et al. 2016).

3. MT and PE teaching in Italian universities

A brief overview of the teaching of MT and PE in Italian master's degree programmes will now be provided. As expected, all degree programmes in translation offer a course on translation technologies. Among these, all the programmes that are part of the EMT Network (2024–2029) cover MT and PE (in addition to CAT tools and other technology-related topics). In three cases the word "post-editing" appears in the course name, and in almost all the courses PE is explicitly mentioned as part of the course contents. In the very few instances in which PE is not explicitly mentioned, the inclusion of artificial intelligence (hereafter AI) and MT suggests that PE is covered as well. Other recurring topics listed in the course contents include CAT tools, programming languages, corpora, and tools for terminology management.

4. Course description

The course "Translation technologies and post-editing" is offered as a core training[5] to the second-year students of the MA course in Translation and Interpretation at Ca' Foscari University of Venice. It was officially introduced in the academic year 2023–2024 after a major reorganisation of the study plan aimed at complying with the competence framework of the EMT network[6]. It is divided into two modules of 30 hours and six credits each: module 1 was taught in the first semester (September to December 2023) by an adjunct lecturer; module 2 was taught in the second semester (February to May 2024) by the author of this paper. The two lecturers had previously agreed on distributing contents as follows: module 1 would focus on CAT

4 Formerly SDL. See https://www.trados.com/training/post-editing-machine-translation/ (retrieved on 10/12/2024).

5 The official classification in Italian is "*caratterizzante*."

6 The curricula Italian/English/Spanish and Italian/English/Italian Sign Language have obtained the EMT status for 2024–2029.

tools (specifically Trados), while module 2 would focus mainly on MT and PE. However, the author decided to include in module 2 also a corpus-driven translation task from Italian into English[7]. The Moodle platform was used for distributing materials and collecting assignments.

4.1 Students

The course was compulsory[8] for the students of the two curricula characterising the MA programme: the English/Spanish/Italian Sign Language curriculum[9] and the Chinese/English/Italian curriculum. The students' background knowledge is supposed to be averagely the same as far as courses focused on translation are concerned. In all three curricula core translation courses – in their respective language pairs – are offered in the fields of tourism and cultural heritage, politics and economics, and translation for the publishing industry. The expression "translation technologies" appears only in the course name discussed in this paper; however, NMT systems as well as generative AI are introduced and marginally covered in the "traditional" translation courses. The extent to which the students were previously exposed to MT and PE cannot be precisely determined, which led the author to start from scratch in teaching PE to the students.

Most of the students were native speakers of Italian, six students were native speakers of Chinese and one student was a native speaker of Russian. In line with the students' preferences – including the international students' – the course was held in Italian, although the relevant terminology was provided in English.

Enrolment to the MA programme is limited to a fixed number of students; furthermore, candidates for the English/Spanish curriculum are required to have at least C1 level proficiency in English, while those applying for the Chinese/English/Italian curriculum are required to have at least B2 level proficiency in English. The actual level of proficiency in English was difficult

---

7 This part will not be treated in this paper due to space constraints and little actual relevance to the part relating to MT and PE.

8 Attendance is not compulsory, albeit strongly recommended. However, the course-related final exam is compulsory.

9 In turn, this is subdivided into English/Spanish, English/Italian Sign Language and Spanish/Italian Sign Language.

to detect, as the students came from different background in terms of BA studies and had varying levels of exposure to the English language.

4.2 Course objectives and topics

The course aimed to introduce the students to the use of MT and PE in the translation industry. The MT- and PE-related objectives stated in the course syllabus can be synthesised as follows[10]:

- Acquiring knowledge of the key ISO 18587 guidelines for PE
- Acquiring knowledge of different MT tools
- Being able to carry out MTPE at varying levels of intervention
- Being able to evaluate whether the MT output is appropriate/correct and or requires human translator intervention
- Being able to evaluate pros and cons of MT systems
- Being able to efficiently and effectively work in a team.

To acquire these skills, the course combined theoretical background and practical tasks.

The theory was kept to the minimum, not because it was not valued as a core content as much as the practical component, but merely due to time constraints as well as the students' need to practise as much as possible. Furthermore, thanks to events and seminars organised throughout the academic year, students had the opportunity to acquire some essential background on the history of MT. Thus, at the beginning of the course the students were requested to acquire the background knowledge on their own and were provided with recommended readings on the history of MT, on the different types of MT systems (rule-based vs statistical vs neural), and on generative AI. Then, the students were introduced to the key concepts and terminology regarding MT and PE. In the second and third lessons, the following contents were delivered: all the definitions regarding MT and the related acronyms, the definition of PE, the types of PE (light vs full), the differences between PE, translation, review, revision and proofreading, based on the ISO 18587 (2017) and the ISO 17100 (2015). The differences

[10] In the syllabus, the learning outcomes are stated according to Dublin Descriptors.

between light PE and full PE developed by Massardo et al. (2016) and the competences of the post-editor were also covered. Along with, and as part of, the required competences listed in the ISO 18587[11], important skills such as attention to detail, critical thinking, time management, and communication skills were also brought to the students' attention. Far from being presented as abstract concepts, these were illustrated in a way that is pragmatic (i.e., explaining what they mean in practice), provoking (i.e., pushing the students to reflect on their actual level of competence and possible weaknesses), and operational (i.e., encouraging "reparatory" actions for possible weaknesses). For example, the students were shown punctuation mistakes made by other students in translation assignments and were hence invited to self-assess their *actual* mastery of their own mother tongue at all linguistic levels[12]; they were given practical examples of non-effective time management in PE tasks (e.g., spending excessive time on a low-priced PE job in the field of expertise); they were presented with more educational uses of social media – as opposed to the common trends of showing-off or sharing private aspects of life – to learn about new trends in the language industry, follow professional accounts, and/or networking with other professionals for sharing best practices.

As far as the practical component is concerned, the very first tasks were aimed at detecting genuine attitudes toward MT and PE (these are analysed in sub-section 4.3). To this purpose, *before* providing the above-mentioned background, very short texts in English on general interest topics (e.g., misuse of antibiotics or descriptions of tourist destinations) were machine translated into Italian using both NMT systems (DeepL) and generative AI (Gemini and ChatGPT). The PE task was followed by a discussion of the (perceived) quality of MT outputs and of the PE-related process enacted by the students. After the PE guidelines were provided, the students were given very short texts (e.g., instructions for re-setting a password or information regarding admission to a museum) on which they were asked to perform both light PE and full PE, so that they could get acquainted with the two processes involved. During this first part of the course, the students shared various doubts (see sub-section 4.3), which were all annotated and used for subsequent task design. After this

11 Translation competence; linguistic and textual competence; competence in research; information acquisition and processing; cultural competence; technical competence; domain competence.

12 Misuse of the Italian language very often occurs also in professional contexts.

preliminary phase, the students were required to self-select into groups of four or five students and were regularly assigned tasks on full PE to be carried out in a collaborative manner. The students were encouraged to work individually at first and then to share their work to produce a collectively agreed version of MTPE. There were four major PE tasks, each involving a 350-word text on the following topics: 1) London streets markets; 2) Covid-19 translation challenges; 3) public transport in Venice; 4) digital media addiction. The assignments were completed as homework and subsequently discussed in the classroom.

Due to time constraints, several topics listed in the existing literature as part of course content were either not covered or only briefly addressed. These topics include pre-editing, PE effort, terminology management, and programming. Terminology management had already been addressed by a colleague in a course titled "Research Methodologies and Documentation for Translation"; as a result, students were encouraged to apply the knowledge and skills acquired in that course to the practice of PE. Programming fell outside the lecturer's expertise, and there was insufficient time to bridge this gap. PE effort was informally addressed during classroom discussions, where some students expressed concerns about the "optimal" execution time compared to the actual time they had spent on tasks. Pre-editing was not covered for two primary reasons: first, NMT and translation produced by generative AI do not appear to be affected by typos or major grammatical errors; second, Koponen, in her teaching experience in Finland, noted that students "did not consider pre-editing particularly beneficial" (2015, p. 8). However, students were advised to always review the source text (ST) for errors or inaccuracies.

4.3 Students' response to MT and PE[13]

Most of the students had a pre-formed general understanding of potential benefits as well as the "problems of hallucinations and bias" (Moorkens/Guerberof Arenas 2024, p. 78) associated with NMT and generative AI. During the first lesson, when asked about their use of MT and AI and their general attitudes, most students appeared uncertain or reluctant to disclose their "relationship" with these tools[14]. The general impression that emerged was a need to gain a deeper understanding of MT's practical contribution

[13] The lessons were recorded as additional material for weak categories of students. The students' statements, observations, and doubts were retrieved from the recordings.

[14] An anonymous survey would have been useful and will be adopted in next academic year.

to a translator's work, coupled with a strong interest in hands-on practice to address uncertainty and make informed decisions.

As a result of the discussions held with the students throughout the course, three main issues could be identified. The first one is "resistance" to PE (see section 1). During the first PE tasks carried out before providing the theoretical background, the students *verbally* expressed their "unease" in their new role of post-editors. They reported feeling uncomfortable doing PE, as it seemed to conflict with their long-developed translation skills. Additionally, they perceived their role as translators to be diminished (see Doherty/Kenny 2014). Later in the course, they also reported the urge to intervene unnecessarily on the raw MT output. They also said they were unable to understand the boundaries between translator's intervention and post-editor's intervention and, regarding TAUS guidelines, they found it difficult to ignore grammatical and syntactical errors in light PE. According to Nitzke and Gros (2021, p. 31) this behaviour could be due to the fact that "it is odd for translators to keep syntactically and grammatically unusual or even incorrect units in the final text, even if the content is still conveyed." The students' difficulty also seems to confirm that "in actual practice, the distinction between these levels [light vs full PE] is not straightforward, and the use of light post-editing in particular appears to be somewhat unclear" (do Carmo/Koponen 2024, p. 206).

Another issue that was observed in the early phase of the course is subjectivity. When questioned about unnecessary interventions on the raw MT output, the students brought explanations based on personal preferences – especially lexical and stylistic ones. For example, ChatGPT literally translated the ST segment "drugs used to treat infections" as "*farmaci utilizzati per trattare le infezioni*." A few students suggested editing the verb *trattare* ("to treat") into the verb *curare* ("to cure") as they deemed it more "appropriate" for the context, thus disregarding the slight difference in nuance between *trattare* and *curare*. In line with Nitzke and Gros' view that "one focus of training in revision and post-editing should be on suppressing personal preferences […], especially regarding lexical choices and style" (2021, p. 32), this was deemed a major issue to be dealt with during the course and to be considered when designing PE tasks.

The last major issue is related to communication skills. After PE assignment 2, most students reported difficulties with style-related issues, such as applying italics or punctuation marks where they would normally be used (e.g., italics for foreign words) and admitted that they intentionally refrained from emailing the lecturer for clarifications. This aspect also stimulated reflection, not only on the reasons why students chose not to contact the lecturer, but also on how to train the students to confidently share their doubts with a client in a real job context and to convey authority and competence in their communications.

In the light of these major issues, the PE assignments were developed according to a specific structure that required the students to proceed step by step and were supplemented with additional sub-tasks.

4.4 Structure of the PE assignments

Before delving into the structure of the major PE assignments, the sub-tasks they contained and how these relate to PE competences and the issues reported in section 4.3, a few aspects need to be clarified:

- for each ST, the source of the excerpt and the place of publication of the post-edited version were indicated in order to simulate a real assignment and allow the students to define the type of receivers of the final text;
- all the STs were in English, and their raw MT outputs in Italian were provided with the assignments[15];
- the texts were characterised mainly by common language, but also featured a few potentially problematic segments (geographical names, in one case wordplay, and few occurrences of domain-specific jargon or specialised vocabulary);
- before carrying out the assignment, the students were strongly recommended to read about the topic of the text in both Italian and English to acquire sufficient knowledge and relevant vocabulary in the two languages, read the "Instructions" file and stick to the order in which the sub-tasks were presented in the assignment file;
- no CAT tools with integrated MT were used for performing MTPE. This gap was due to technical issues the lecturer encountered with the CAT

15 MT may produce slightly different raw outputs of the same text. For this reason, rather than having the ST submitted in the MT system by each student, the raw output was provided by the lecturer.

software available at university, which were resolved only when the course was nearing its conclusion.

The method adopted for training students is "split training" (Absolon 2019, in Ginovart Cid/Colominas 2021, p. 244), which involves "dividing skills into subskills to a more or less granular level and [...] attributing a tailored practical exercise to each subskill" (ibid.). Four sub-tasks were designed and included in the PE assignments. Each will be described in the following sub-sections.

4.4.1 Sub-task 1: MT output analysis

The first sub-task involved comparing the ST and the raw MT output. More specifically, the students were required to use different colours as follows: red for mistakes or inaccuracies to be corrected; yellow for segments about which they were uncertain and to be checked; cyan for segments that they accepted and retained in the PE, but that they would have translated differently if the original task had involved *translating the ST from scratch* rather than post-editing its MT. The main aim of this first sub-task is to favour familiarisation with MT, which relates to the instrumental competence (Rico/Torrejón 2012). Detecting mistakes was expected to enhance the students' ability to identify the main weaknesses of different MT systems, although they soon realised that generalisation is not possible due to the many aspects that come into play (e.g., domain, degree of technicality). Mistakes were easily identified by most of the students. One example is provided in Table 1:

Table 1: Example of MT mistake detection (PE assignment 2)

ST	Raw MT output (DeepL)	Error
[...] from handwashing posters to social distancing tape [...]	[...] dai manifesti per il lavaggio delle mani ai nastri per prendere le distanze dai social [...]	nastri per prendere le distanze dai social [back trans.: ribbons to distance oneself from social media]

This is an excerpt from PE assignment 2 on Covid-19 translation challenges. The meaning of the ST segment "social distancing tape" was completely distorted in the raw MT output and hence marked in red by the students. Other mistakes usually detected involved punctuation marks (for example *em* and *en* dashes, which are almost never used in Italian). This first sub-task is also relevant to the attitudinal/psychological competence (Rico/Torrejón 2012): in order to prevent the students from producing versions that are "inspired by the MT" (Koponen 2015, p. 11)[16] rather than post-edited, they had to use their research skills to filter subjectivity out of the PE process. In this way, they would make informed decisions based on *objective evidence* (research competence) rather than personal preferences. No limitations were imposed regarding the type of tools allowed for linguistic evidence: online dictionaries, terminology databases, web-based research in general. Interaction with AI was also allowed, but with the strong advice to use it as a starting point for further research rather than the only source or the ending point. An example of edit justified with web-based evidence is shown in Table 2:

Table 2: Example of edit (PE assignment 4)

ST	Raw MT output (DeepL)	Full PE
[…] (which proves people will get anything *inked* on their biceps).	[…] (a riprova del fatto che la gente si fa *incidere* qualsiasi cosa sul bicipite).	[…] (a riprova del fatto che la gente si fa *tatuare* qualsiasi cosa sul bicipite.

This is an excerpt from PE assignment 4 on digital media addiction. In this full PE the edit involves a replacement (do Carmo/Moorkens 2021), with the verb "*tatuare*" replacing the verb "*incidere*" provided by the raw MT. The edit was justified by the students in a footnote comment, followed by the sources that they searched for linguistic evidence. The comment reads as follows[17]:

> The English expression "to get something inked" literally means "to get something tattooed." The Italian verb "*incidere*" does not necessarily carry this meaning, and it could even sound overly strong: although a tattoo is as permanent as an incision, "incision" on the arm carries a negative connotation and could allude to the idea of a wound or a surgical operation.

---

16 This expression was used by one of the students who took part in Koponen's PE course.

17 Translated from the original comment in Italian.
https://www.treccani.it/vocabolario/incidere2_(Sinonimi-e-Contrari)/ (retrieved on 10/04/2025).
https://www.treccani.it/enciclopedia/incisione/ (retrieved on 10/04/2025).

https://www.treccani.it/vocabolario/incidere2_(Sinonimi-e-Contrari)/
https://www.treccani.it/enciclopedia/incisione/

Drawing on their sensitivity as translators, the students felt that the MT segment required correction. Consequently, they consulted authoritative online dictionaries to verify the meaning of the verb "*incidere*" and the related noun "*incisione*." However, they did not investigate the usage of "*incidere*" in web-based texts related to tattoos.

4.4.2 Sub-task 2: light vs full PE[18]

The second sub-task involved carrying out both light PE and full PE following TAUS guidelines. The ST and its MT were provided in a table – respectively in column 1 and column 2 – and the light and full PE were to be inserted respectively in column 3 and column 4. This task relates to core competences (Rico/Torrejón 2012), as applying both light and full PE "forces" the students to strictly follow the guidelines and hence to evaluate, case by case, when one PE alternative would be more suitable than the other. The table format was chosen purposely, in order for students to better observe the differences between the two PE alternatives as well as to always keep an eye on the ST. As mentioned in section 4.3, there was a general tendency to over-edit in light PE, as exemplified in Table 3:

Table 3: Example of light vs full PE (PE assignment 2)

ST	Raw MT output (DeepL)	Light PE	Full PE
Services like Google Translate support only 100 languages, give or take. What about the thousands of other languages – spoken by people just as vulnerable to this crisis?	Servizi come Google Translate supportano solo 100 lingue, più o meno. Che dire delle migliaia di altre lingue parlate da persone altrettanto vulnerabili a questa crisi?	Servizi come Google Translate, supportano più o meno 100 lingue. E le migliaia di altre lingue parlate da persone altrettanto esposte a questa crisi?	Servizi come Google Translate, includono circa 100 lingue. E le altre migliaia parlate nel mondo ed altrettanto esposte alla crisi?

18 In PE assignments 2, 3, and 4, due to time constraints, only full PE was required. However, the students were encouraged to perform light PE on their own and discuss any doubts with the lecturer.

In this excerpt from PE assignment 2 on Covid-19 translation challenges, instances of over-editing in the light PE are the elimination of the *em* dash (—), the elimination of "*più o meno*" ("give or take") and of "*Che dire delle*" ("What about the"), which has been condensed into the conjunction "E"[19]. The segment has been further rephrased from "*le migliaia di altre lingue*" ("the thousands of other languages") in the light PE to "*le altre migliaia*" ("the other thousands") in the full PE, in which the repetition of the word "*lingue*" from the previous sentence has been avoided. In general, the lecturer placed great emphasis on the importance of providing linguistic evidence for edits in the full PE, especially when operating replacement at the lexical level. Indeed, this activity was deemed useful not only for building PE competence, but also for favouring the shift in the students' mindset from resistance to PE to a view of the post-editor as a professional who has acquired further skills that may contribute to increasing productivity and being more attractive to the language industry.

Half-way through the course, when several students raised issues about how to make decisions in the absence of specific instructions, a more detailed "Instructions" file was provided, which included a list of terms not to be translated as well as instructions on formatting and style (e.g., spacing, where to use italics, organisation into paragraphs, etc). To avoid confusion, the formatted version was to be reproduced on a new page, outside the table. This aspect was introduced as part of the core competences to help the students deal with subjectivity (psycho attitudinal competence) and strictly follow instructions (strategic competence). In particular, the do-not-translate-terms list was considered useful to simulate a real PE task and to increase students' attention to detail.

4.4.3 Sub-task 3: PE vs translation

This sub-task builds on the first one (ST vs MT comparison) and specifically concerns the MT segments that the students highlighted in cyan. These segments were accepted by the students in the full PE, but they would have translated them differently if the task had involved translating from scratch. In this third sub-task, the students were required to compile all the cyan-highlighted

[19] In this context the conjunction "E" has a strong disjunctive connotation, with the implicit meaning being "*Ma*" ("But").

segments into a pre-designed table and provide their own translations along with evidence-based justification. This task was developed in response to the students' initial resistance to PE and their struggle with their "inner translator." Focused on the attitudinal competence (Rico/Torrejón 2012, p. 170), this sub-task aims to shift the students' mindset regarding PE and translation. The underlying belief is that, by allowing them to experience first-hand how their choices – especially when it comes to lexical or stylistic issues – are often influenced by subjectivity, they are more likely to perceive PE as an evolution of the translator's work rather than as a disruptive shift toward a diminished role of the translator. Providing justification was the most challenging aspect for the students. In many cases, they were unable to provide proper web-based evidence, and during classroom-based discussion most admitted that their suggested translations arose naturally from their intuition as native speakers of Italian. When provided, evidence comes mostly from authoritative dictionaries or encyclopaedia, Google frequences, and/or context-based research. An example of proposed translation is shown in Table 4:

Table 4: Example of sub-task three (PE assignment 4)

ST segment	MT segment accepted in the full PE	Suggested translation
[...] we can find *those, and much more besides*, with the click of an app.	[...] noi possiamo trovare *queste e molte altre cose* con un semplice clic su un'applicazione.	[...] possiamo trovare *tutto questo e molto altro* con un semplice click su un'app.

This is an excerpt from PE assignment 4 on digital media addiction. The students motivated their proposed translation in the third column as follows[20]:

> "Tutto questo e molto altro": a common expression in Italian, it flows more naturally than the literal translation proposed by the raw output. Below is the frequency:
>
> "tutto questo e molto altro" site:it = about 1,240,000 results
> "queste e molte altre cose" site:it = about 31,000 results.
>
> The numerical frequency is not significant, but the translator's linguistic sensitivity prevails.

[20] Translated from the original comment in Italian.

As can be seen, the Google-based research seems to confirm the appropriateness of their suggested translation. However, the students made a point of specifying that what prevailed was their "linguistic sensitivity," i.e., their intuitive judgement as translators.

4.4.4 Sub-task 4: accompanying e-mail

The students were required to write an accompanying e-mail for a hypothetical client. In such an e-mail, they would make inquiries about issues where the instructions were not clear or might not be appropriate, and/or briefly illustrate how they had proceeded. In general, the students were taught to always ensure, for the future, that they and their clients "speak the same language" in any revision or PE task and, if necessary, to explain the differences between the various revision alternatives. Here is an example of accompanying e-mail[21] produced by one of the groups:

> Dear …,
> Please find attached the file containing the full PE of the text you commissioned. We would also like to take this opportunity to raise a few questions that arose during the work:
>
> 1. Regarding the title of Anna Lembke's book *Dopamine Nation*, do you prefer that we use the official Italian translation or the English title?
> 2. Should English borrowings (*smartphone*, *partner*, *online*, and *scrolling*) not included in the *do not translate* list be formatted in italics?
>
> We look forward to your kind reply and thank you in advance.
>
> Best regards
> [names of the students]

As for question 1, the official Italian translation of the book was not mentioned at all in the instructions. This means that the students carried out some research about the book. As for question 2, formatting instructions were provided for several digital media-related terms (e.g., *binge watch*, *like*, *e-commerce*) to be italicised in the full PE. However, no instructions were given regarding the English borrowings in Italian mentioned in the e-mail.

---

[21] Translated from the original e-mail in Italian.

The omissions in the instructions were intentional, designed to train attention to detail and encourage students to identify the gap and seek clarification. In general, the students were trained to communicate in a clear, polite and concise manner, and to justify their personal initiatives – if any – with objectivity.

4.5 Other aspects of the course

A few considerations are necessary regarding the following aspects: evaluation of PE and time management. The evaluation of the post-edited texts submitted by the students was focused on two main criteria: MT error detection and the quality of evidence supplied. The ability to immediately identify the errors made by the MT system was emphasised as *essential*, with failure to detect errors in the exam resulting in exam failure. This approach was adopted to discourage "lazier" students from over-relying on MT, although this scenario was unlikely given the general resistance to PE. The students were basically trained according to the following principle, developed by the lecturer herself: "often doubt, always check, never neglect." Emphasis was also placed on the quality of the evidence provided by the students to justify their edits, in order to encourage them to filter subjectivity and personal taste out of the PE process. To this end, PE tasks submitted by different groups were compared and discussed (see Ginovart Cid/Colominas 2021, p. 244). During these discussions, students frequently asked for feedback on the evidence they had provided. For this reason, the comparison involved not only the ST vs MT vs PE, but also the evidence submitted by different groups for the same edit.

Another important aspect was time management. The students were given an ideal timeframe for completing the PE task, but many admitted they were unable to finish within the suggested timeframe due to the research required to provide linguistic evidence. While effective time management is crucial in real professional settings, in the specific context of introducing translation students to PE the quality of the process and the development of students' awareness were prioritised over strict adherence to time constraints.

5. PE vs translation: survey

Unlike Koponen (2015), who used reflective essays to collect students' responses to the course, an informal anonymous survey was used in this course. The survey was administered toward the end of the course as the final step of an assignment that involved both translation and PE. Each group of students was split into two sub-groups and assigned the same text on transport in Venice (PE assignment 3). One sub-group post-edited the MT output of the text following sub-tasks 1, 2, and 3 (described earlier), while the other translated the text from scratch without access to the raw MT output. The two sub-groups then exchanged and analysed their work before completing a survey tailored to their specific tasks.

Two separate surveys were administered: one for the students who post-edited the text and another for those who translated it from scratch. The surveys had a similar structure, consisting of a series of statements to be rated on a Likert scale (1 = strongly disagree to 5 = strongly agree). Each survey included two statements comparing translation and PE, two addressing the effort involved in translation versus PE, and two focusing on the time required for each task. Additionally, the survey for post-editors included two statements about the constraints posed by PE, while the survey for translators featured two statements regarding the quality of the raw MT output.

The surveys were administered *not* with the aim to provide statistics, but to track the students' attitudes toward PE and its relationship with translation. In the survey for the post-editors, most students reported feeling tempted to intervene on the raw MT output to improve its quality, despite its overall good quality. Additionally, the majority indicated that a well-executed full PE is sufficient to produce a TT comparable to one produced by a human translator. Opinions regarding effort and time are divided: most students disagree that translating that text from scratch would have required less effort and time, yet these responses are not reflected in the opposite statements, where the students' answers are evenly distributed across the 1 to 5 scale.

Regarding the survey for the translators, most students agree that their translations are of better quality than the full PE carried out by the post-editors. They also feel that the PE of the MT output is *not* sufficient to produce a translation comparable to one created by human translation. In terms of effort, most students agree that MTPE of that text would have required more effort.

Finally, the comment box provided for each question revealed a few interesting points raised by the students. These include the importance of the post-editor's domain expertise (see Faes/Massey 2024, p. 31) and its impact on effort, as well as the observation that a lack of practice in PE makes the task more time-consuming compared to translating from scratch.

6. Future improvements and concluding remarks

The course described in this paper represents the author's first experience teaching PE. Thus, the students' responses and reflections are crucial for making improvements in future teaching. During the discussion held in the final lessons, most students stated that they had gained a clearer understanding of the PE process and of the skills required of a post-editor. However, they admitted that they still found it challenging to adhere to the light PE guidelines and were often tempted to perform more creative forms of PE, inspired by the MT output rather than strictly based on it. They also mentioned having developed a better understanding of MT limitations (for example, noticing that MT tends to replicate the syntactical structure of the ST) as well as its potential benefits in terms of productivity. Additionally, the students expressed appreciation for the activities that required adherence to specific instructions and the inclusion of the do-not-translate-terms list. They found simulating communication with a client particularly useful, as it helped them identify weaknesses in their communication skills. Surprisingly, they did not raise concerns regarding the absence of CAT tools with integrated MT, probably because they recognised the importance of developing a clear understanding of MT and PE before incorporating the technology itself. Regarding subjectivity in PE, the students noted that searching for evidence to justify their edits and suggested translations (sub-task 3) helped them filter out subjectivity. However, they often found it challenging to provide evidence for syntactical reformulations or stylistic issues.

In section 1, the following question was raised: "In line with the current best practices and skill sets, what contents should be designed and proposed to students for them to perceive and approach PE as an *enriched evolution* of the translator profession rather than a practice that is disruptive to the translation profession?" The experience shared in this paper suggests that including translation-related processes like sub-task 3 in the practical component could be effective in fostering a neutral, if not positive, attitude toward MT and PE. Possible improvements to this PE course could include the following: introducing the concept of "risk" (Nietzke/Hansen-Schirra/

Canfora 2019) and explaining its relevance to informed decision-making regarding whether to translate or post-edit as well as selecting appropriate PE alternatives; incorporating technology featuring integrated MT for MTPE workflows; teaching the types of edit usually involved in PE; practising PE at a wider range of intervention levels than the standard light vs full PE guidelines; emphasising the need to filter subjectivity out of PE processes, for instance, by showing examples of over-editing by previous students. It would also be interesting to analyse students' behaviours and responses to a broader, more complex project involving both translation and PE. In such a project, they would be required to decide which documents to post-edit (and which type of PE to perform) and which to translate, while adhering to specific formatting instructions and do-not-translate-terms lists. Last, but not least, students should be made aware of the importance of having "a razor-sharp focus on keeping the language correct" (Faes/Massey 2024, p. 31) as well as of developing domain expertise, as the combination of linguistic and domain knowledge is key to employability (ibid.).

Based on this experience, the issue seems to extend well beyond the mere definition of skill sets and course contents. For future post-editors to perceive themselves "not only as mere proof-readers of machine output, but as competent language consultants and experts in creating PE processes" (Nietzke/Hansen-Schirra/Canfora 2019, p. 251), two key factors should be taken into consideration: *when* to introduce MT and PE (see O'Brien 2002) in translator training, and *who* should train translation students in these areas. The hypothesis proposed here is that students are less likely to develop resistance to PE if training in MT and PE is integrated alongside their translation studies. Therefore, BA translation students should be introduced to the fundamentals of MT and PE during their third year. This could include short tasks that involve analysing raw MT output, identifying MT errors, and discussing the advantages and limitations of MT, along with basic PE exercises. At the MA level, it is crucial for lecturers teaching "traditional" translation and those teaching translation technologies to collaborate so as to ensure that students do not learn about MT and PE solely within the technology course. Ideally, students should incorporate MT into their translation courses as well, experimenting with MT systems across various subject domains and critically evaluating the output. Furthermore, it is essential to expose students to the latest trends in the language industry while encouraging them to stay informed independently, for example, by using social media to stay updated. With regard to who is best qualified to train translation students in MT and PE, it is the author's strong belief that, when the course is taught by academics, it is essential to involve professionals from the language industry. These professionals could contribute by conducting practical seminars or workshops, providing students with the opportunity to address real-world challenges such as time management, PE effort, pricing and integrating technologies.

In conclusion, the author of this paper endorses Ginovart Cid, Colominas and Oliver's (2020, p. 300) assertion that it is vital to "keep updating our views, resources and methods in the best way possible." Additionally, the author aligns with do Carmo and Koponen's (2024, p. 206) perspective that, rather than rigidly distinguishing between light and full PE, "a corresponding 'PE continuum' may also be defined." Such a PE continuum would enable students to engage with varying degrees of PE intervention, ranging from a simple "sanity check" (ibid.) to "more creative editing processes in which machine translation only provides a starting point" (ibid.).

Bibliography

Absolon, Jakub (2018): *The need for competency-based selection and training of post-editors*. Nitra: ASAP-translation.com, ISBN: 978-80-89970-00-1.

Absolon, Jakub (2019): *Human translator 4.0. Manual of effective use of machine translation for a modern translator.* Online: ASAP-translation.com.

Allen, Jeffrey (2003): "Post-editing." In: Somers, Harold (Ed.): *Computers and translation: A translators guide.* Amsterdam: John Benjamins, pp. 297–317. https://doi.org/10.1075/btl.35.19all.

Austermühl, Frank (2013: "Future (and not-so-future) trends in the teaching of translation technology." *Tradumàtica: tecnologies de la traducció* 11, pp. 326–337, retrieved on 10/12/2024 from https://revistes.uab.cat/tradumatica/article/view/n11-austermuehl/pdf.

Cadwell, Patrick / O'Brien, Sharon / Teixeira, Carlos (2018): "Resistance and accommodation: Factors for the (non-) adoption of machine translation among professional translators." *Perspectives* 26(3), pp. 301–321. https://doi.org/10.1080/0907676x.2017.1337210.

Castilho, Sheila / Resende, Natália (2022): "Post-editese in literary translations," *Information* 13(2), 66, pp. 1–22. https://doi.org/10.3390/info13020066.

Cid-Leal, Pilar / Espín-García, María-Carmen / Presas, Marisa (2019): "Traducción automática y posedición: perfiles y competencias en los programas de formación de traductores" [Machine translation and post-editing: Profiles and competencies in translator training programmes]. *MonTI* 11, pp. 187–214.

do Carmo, Felix / Koponen, Maarit (2024): "Revisers and post-editors: The guardians of quality." In: Massey, Gary / Ehrensberger-Dow, Maureen / Angelone, Erik (Eds.): *Handbook of the language industry: Contexts, resources and profiles*. Berlin et al.: De Gruyter Mouton, pp. 203–224.

do Carmo, Félix / Moorkens, Joss (2021): "Differentiating editing, post-editing and revision." In: Koponen, Maarit / Mossop, Brian / Robert, Isabelle S. / Scocchera, Giovanna (Eds.): *Translation revision and post-editing. Industry practices and cognitive processes*. London: Routledge, pp 35–49. https://doi.org/10.1515/9783110716047-010.

Doherty, Stephen / Gaspari, Federico (2013): "Effective post-editing in human & machine translation workflows: Critical knowledge & techniques," retrieved on 10/04/2024 from https://www.readkong.com/page/effective-post-editing-in-human-machine-translation-9550669.

Doherty, Stephen / Kenny, Dorothy (2014): "The design and evaluation of a statistical machine translation syllabus for translation students." *The Interpreter and Translator Trainer* 8(2), pp. 295–315. https://doi.org/10.1080/1750399X.2014.937571.

EMT Board and Competence Task-Force (2022): *European Master's in Translation Competence Framework 2022*, retrieved on 13/12/2024 from https://commission.europa.eu/system/files/2022-11/emt_competence_fwk_2022_en.pdf.

Faes, Florian / Massey, Gary (2024): "Charting the language industry: Interview with an industry observer." In: Massey, Gary / Ehrensberger-Dow, Maureen / Angelone, Erik (Eds.): *Handbook of the Language Industry: Contexts, Resources and Profiles*. Berlin, Boston: De Gruyter Mouton, pp. 17–31. https://doi.org/10.1515/9783110716047-002.

Farrell, Michael (2023): "Current evidence of post-editese: Differences between post-edited neural machine translation output and human translation revealed through human evaluation." In: Orăsan, Constantin / Mitkov, Ruslan / Corpas Pastor, Gloria / Monti, Johanna (Eds.): *The international conference on Human-informed translation and interpreting technology (Hit-IT 2023), Proceedings*. Shoumen: INCOMA Ltd., pp. 52–63, retrieved on 10/04/2025 from https://hit-it-conference.org/wp-content/uploads/2023/07/HiT-IT-2023-proceedings.pdf.

Flanagan, Marian / Christensen, Tina Paulsen (2014): "Testing post-editing guidelines: How translation trainees interpret them and how to tailor them for translator training purposes'." *The Interpreter and Translator Trainer* 8(2), pp. 257–275.

Gaspari, Federico / Almaghout, Hala / Doherty, Stephen (2015): "A survey of machine translation competences: Insights for translation technology educators and practitioners." *Perspectives* 23(3), pp. 333–358. https://doi.org/10.1080/0907676X.2014.979842.

Ginovart Cid, Clara / Colominas, Carme (2021): "The MT post-editing skill set. Course description and educators' thoughts." In: Koponen, Maarit / Mossop, Brian / Robert, Isabelle S. / Scocchera, Giovanna (Eds.): *Translation revision and post-editing. Industry practices and cognitive processes*. London: Routledge, pp. 226–246.

Ginovart Cid, Clara / Colominas, Carme / Oliver, Antoni (2020): "Language industry views on the profile of the post-editor." *Translation Spaces* 9(2), pp. 283–313. https://doi.org/10.1075/ts.19010.cid.

Ginovart Cid, Clara / Oliver, Antoni (2020): "The post-editor's skill set according to industry, trainers and linguists." In: Portsiel, Jörg (Ed.): *Maschinelle Übersetzung für Übersetzungsprofis*. Berlin: BDÜ Weiterbildungs- und Fachverlagsgesellschaft mbh, pp. 305–322, retrieved on 10/04/2025 from https://repositori-api.upf.edu/api/core/bitstreams/16e833bb-41fd-4099-b4c6-e5d5233ffc49/content.

Guerberof Arenas, Ana / Depraetere, Heidi / O'Brien, Sharon (2012): "What we know and what we would like to know about post-editing." *Tradumàtica: tecnologies de la traducció* 10, pp. 211–218, retrieved on 10/04/2025 from https://revistes.uab.cat/tradumatica/article/view/n10-guerberof-depraetere/pdf.

ISO 17100 (2015): *Requirements for translations services*. Geneva: International Organization for Standardization.

ISO 18587 (2017): *Translation services – Post-editing of machine translation output – Requirements*. Geneva: International Organization for Standardization.

Kenny, Dorothy (2018): "Sustaining disruption? The transition from statistical to neural machine translation." *Tradumàtica: tecnologies de la traducció* 16, pp. 59–70. https://doi.org/10.5565/rev/tradumatica.221.

Kenny, Dorothy / Doherty, Stephen (2014): "Statistical machine translation in the translation curriculum: Overcoming obstacles and empowering translators." *The Interpreter and Translator Trainer* 8(2), pp. 276–294. https://doi.org/10.1080/1750399X.2014.936112.

Koponen, Maarit (2015): "How to teach machine translation post-editing? Experiences from a post-editing course." In: O'Brien, Sharon / Simard, Michel (Eds.): *Fourth workshop on post-editing technology and practice, Proceedings*. Miami: Association for Machine Translation in the Americas, pp. 2–15, retrieved on 10/04/2025 from https://aclanthology.org/2015.mtsummit-wptp.1.pdf.

Krings, Hans P. (2001): *Repairing texts: Empirical investigations of machine translation post-editing processes*. Koby, Geoffrey S. (Ed.). Kent, Ohio et al.: Kent State University Press.

Massardo, Isabella / van der Meer, Jaap / O'Brien, Sharon / Hollowood, Fred / Aranberri, Nora / Drescher, Katrin (2016): "TAUS MT post-editing guidelines", retrieved on 10/12/2024 from https://www.taus.net/resources/reports/mt-post-editing-guidelines.

Moorkens, Joss / Guerberof Arenas, Ana (2024): "Artificial intelligence, automation and the language industry." In: Massey, Gary / Ehrensberger-Dow, Maureen / Angelone, Erik (Eds.): *Handbook of the language industry: Contexts, resources and profiles*. Berlin et al.: De Gruyter Mouton, pp. 71–98. https://doi.org/10.1515/9783110716047-005.

Moorkens, Joss / Way, Andy (2016): "Comparing translator acceptability of TM and SMT outputs." *Baltic Journal of Modern Computing* 4(2), pp. 141–151, retrieved on 10/04/2025 from https://aclanthology.org/W16-3404.pdf.

Nitzke, Jean / Gros, Anne-Kathrin (2021): "Preferential changes in revision and post-editing." In: Koponen, Maarit / Mossop, Brian / Robert, Isabelle S. (Eds.): *Translation revision and post-editing. Industry practices and cognitive processes*. London: Routledge, pp. 21–34.

Nitzke, Jean / Hansen-Schirra, Silvia / Canfora, Carmen (2019): "Risk management and post-editing competence." *The Journal of Specialised Translation* 31, pp. 239–259, retrieved on 10/04/2025 from https://jostrans.soap2.ch/issue31/art_nitzke.php.

O'Brien, Sharon (2002): "Teaching post-editing: A proposal for course content." In *Proceedings of the 6th European Association for Machine Translation (EAMT) Workshop: Teaching machine translation*. Manchester: EAMT, pp. 99–106, retrieved on 10/04/2025 from https://aclanthology.org/2002.eamt-1.11.pdf.

Plaza-Lara, Cristina (2019): "Análisis DAFO sobre la inclusión de la traducción automática y la posedición en los másteres de la red EMT" [SWOT analysis of the inclusion of machine translation and post-editing in the Master's degrees offered in the EMT network]. *The Journal of Specialised Translation* 31, pp. 260–280, retrieved on 10/04/2025 from https://jostrans.soap2.ch/issue31/art_plaza.php.

Popović, Maja / Lommel, Arle / Burchardt, Aljoscha / Avramidis, Eleftherios / Uszkoreit, Hans (2014): "Relations between different types of post-editing operations, cognitive effort and temporal effort." In: Cettolo, Mauro / Federico, Marcello / Specia, Lucia / Way, Andy (Eds.): *Proceedings of the 17th conference of the European Association for Machine Translation*. Dubrovnik: European Association for Machine Translation, pp. 191–198, retrieved on 20/12/2024 from https://aclanthology.org/2014.eamt-1.41.pdf.

Pym, Anthony (2013): "Translation skill-sets in a machine-translation age." *Meta* 58(3), pp. 487–503, retrieved on 20/12/2024 from https://www.erudit.org/en/journals/meta/2013-v58-n3-meta01406/1025047ar.pdf.

Rico, Celia / Díez Orzas, Pedro Luis (2013): *D4.1.4. Annex I. EDI-TA: Post-editing methodology for machine translation*. MultilingualWeb-LT (LT-Web), retrieved on 10/04/2025 from https://www.w3.org/International/multilingualweb/lt/wiki/images/1/1f/D4.1.4.Annex_I_EDI-TA_Methology.pdf.

Rico, Celia / Torrejón, Enrique (2012): "Skills and profile of the new role of the translator as MT post-editor." *Revista Tradumática* 10, pp. 166–178, retrieved on 10/12/2024 from https://abacus.universidadeuropea.com/bitstream/handle/11268/657/CR2012.pdf?sequence=1&isAllowed=y.

Robert, Isabelle S. / Remael, Aline / Ureel, Jim J. J. (2017): "Towards a model of translation revision competence." *The Interpreter and Translator Trainer* 11(1), pp. 1–19. https://doi.org/10.1080/1750399x.2016.1198183.

Rossi, Caroline (2017): "Introducing statistical machine translation in translator training: From uses and perceptions to course design, and back again," *Revista Tradumàtica* 15, pp. 48–62.

Specia, Lucia (2011): "Exploiting objective annotations for minimising translation post-editing effort." In: Forcada, Mikel L. / Depraetere, Heidi / Vandeghinste, Vincent (Eds.): *Proceedings of the 15th conference of the European Association for Machine Translation*. Leuven: European Association for Machine Translation, pp. 73–80, retrieved on 10/04/2025 from https://aclanthology.org/2011.eamt-1.12.pdf.

Tatsumi, Midori / Roturier, Johann (2010): "Source text characteristics and technical and temporal post-editing effort: What is their telationship?." In: Zhechev, Ventsislav (Ed.): *Proceedings of the second joint EM+/ CNGL workshop "Bringing MT to the user: Research on integrating MT in the translation industry" (JEC ' 10)*. Denver: Association for Machine Translation in the Americas, pp. 43–51, retrieved on 10/04/2025 from https://aclanthology.org/2010.jec-1.6.pdf.

Volkart, Lise / Bouillon, Pierrette (2022): "Studying post-editese in a professional context: A pilot study." In: Moniz, Helena / Macken, Lieve / Rufener, Andrew / Barrault, Loïc / Costa-jussà, Marta R. / Declercq, Christophe / Koponen, Maarit / Kemp, Ellie / Pilos, Spyridon / Forcada, Mikel L. / Scarton, Carolina / Van den Bogaert, Joachim / Daems, Joke / Tezcan, Arda / Vanroy, Bram / Fonteyne, Margot (Eds.): *Proceedings of the 23rd annual conference of the European Association for Machine Translation*. Ghent: European Association for Machine Translation, pp. 71–79, retrieved on 10/12/2024 from https://aclanthology.org/2022.eamt-1.10.pdf.

Target text didacticisation for learning and teaching translation concepts: comparative analysis of human vs machine translations for the assessment of asymmetrical text interpretations

Juan Antonio Albaladejo Martínez
University of Alicante

ABSTRACT
Placed within Applied Translation Studies (TS), this paper explores the concept of "interpretative anisomorphism" (IA) through the design of a didactic unit (DU) with a task-based approach (TBA) destined for the bachelor's course *Translation Theory and History*. Students shall learn key concepts in TS by merging theoretical and historical elements. This is achieved through the didacticisation of professional target texts (TTs). Given the ever-increasing competitiveness of machine translation (MT) and the recent irruption of artificial intelligence (AI), this DU combines human translations (HTs) with MT/AI-generated TTs for a comparative analysis. Methodologically, we resort to a case study to analyse a series of translation problems (TPs) and the solutions offered in the TTs. A paratext from *Peter Schlemihls wundersame Geschichte* (2013) was chosen as ST, because it lends itself well for the didactic design given its self-containment and high proportion of TPs. By contrasting the interpretations of the TPs, students are encouraged to determine the existence of the IA and the shareability of MT/AI-generated interpretations compared with human ones. The result of the analysis shows a similar percentage of sharable interpretations in MT/AI-generated TTs and in HTs. The joint didacticisation of HTs and MT/AI-generated TTs provides some innovative findings in the field of didactics.

Keywords: interpretative anisomorphism, target text didacticisation, human translation, machine translation, didactic unit

1. Introduction

This paper presents the design for a DU in the field of TS based on the didacticisation of TTs generated by human and machine translators. The motivation for this proposal arose during a recent period of teaching performed in June 2024 in the framework of the Erasmus+ Programme at Higher Education Institutions and is destined to become a DU for the bachelor's course *Theory and History of Translation* at the University of Alicante, specifically for the German section.

The course aims at introducing students to key theories and concepts of TS by blending theoretical and historical aspects. The DU that is the subject of this paper centres on the concept of *anisomorphism* (asymmetry), especially the IA[1].

One of the basic requirements for proving the existence of the IA through a comparative analysis is the selection of an appropriate ST. Our main criteria are the existence of various TTs produced by different (human) translators and their easy accessibility and usability in the classroom. This is the main reason for choosing classic literary texts. Another argument is the higher density of TPs in literature because there language is used in a way that favours multiple meanings. Words and expressions characterised by polisignation (Abrams/Harpham 2013, p. 14) pose an important challenge in the hermeneutic process.

This DU resorts to a fragment of the German novella *Peter Schlemihls wundersame Geschichte* (2013 [*The wonderful history of Peter Schlemihl*]), originally published in 1814 and written by Adelbert von Chamisso (1781–1838), given its large number of Spanish retranslations (north of 20), and more specifically to a letter which accompanies the main text and is part of a paratextual complex which is also present in most of the Spanish versions. Genette (1997) defines paratext as "a heterogeneous group of practices and discourses" (p. 2) which "is fundamentally heteronomous, auxiliary, and dedicated to the service of something other than itself that constitutes its raison d'être. This something is the text" (p. 12). The genre "letter" lends itself particularly well as a unit of analysis in this didactic proposal given its brevity and self-containment. There were other reasons that motivated the choice of this particular novella: on the one hand, the presence of numerous TPs, many of which arise from instances of indeterminacy (Iser 1978, p. 24) that tend to induce differing solutions; on the other hand, the intention of bridging the gap between professional translation and translation teaching; and finally, the fact that the novella has been translated by the teacher (the book is currently in press). Being conscious of the difficulty to comply with Kiraly's (2000, p. 43) maximalist approach of offering students authentic translation briefs in the classroom setting for didactic purposes, we align ourselves with Vienne's (1994) more

[1] Hermeneutic anisomorphism is a synonym.

feasible proposal of designing learning and teaching (L&T) activities that recreate (professional) tasks previously carried out by the teacher, or with "simulated real life situations" consisting of "tasks that replicate professional requirements" (Inoue/Candlin 2017, p. 58).

This DU replaces the traditional teacher-centred teaching perspective with a student-centred semi-autonomous learning model. It involves the transition from the conventional transmissionist approach to blended models that strive to combine transactional and transformational approaches, based on cooperative and collaborative learning (González Davies 2004, p. 14), in line with Kiraly's (2000) and Kelly's (2005) social constructivism. The resulting L&T model of our DU applies a TBA. The idea is to connect students with real products of the outside world of translation and to generate learning projects that are meaningful and relevant for them, since that is the basis for effective learning (Caine/Caine 1994, p. 90).

In this respect, it seems more and more obvious that the sweeping changes MT is causing nowadays in the professional (and didactic) translation landscape require a matching respond in the realm of translator training programmes. This is the reason why we include TTs generated by MT in this DU that focuses on a comparative text analysis.

Though the usefulness of MT in literary translation has traditionally been questioned and still is by some experts (Koehn 2020, p. 21), others are highlighting its benefits in translation productivity (Toral/Wieling/Way 2018, p. 10), especially since the introduction of neural MT. The recent emergence of AI and its derived potential use as a translation tool through chatbots like ChatGPT offers an interesting new alternative to traditional MT services like Google Translate or DeepL (to name just two popular programmes many students rely on). In light of the rapid adoption of all kinds of AI applications, and having verified, through several personal tests, the potential usefulness of GPT translations, we decided to include the TT generated by this tool in the comparative analysis of the DU.

2. Concept of anisomorphism

This Greek term is made up by the negative prefix "a-," followed by a linking "n" and the main word "isomorphism", which is being negated. "Isomorphism" literally means "equal form" (Gregory 1987, p. 395), thus "anisomorphism" can be equated to "not equal form." Dictionaries tend to offer, if at all, a definition of "isomorphism". Crystal (2008, pp. 256–257) defines it as "a property of two or more structures whose constituent parts are in a one-to-one correspondence with each other, at a given level of abstraction." According to Alcaraz Varó and Martínez Linares (1997, p. 308), it refers to the symmetry or parallelism that can be established between two systems.

Beginning with Delabastita (1993, p. 17), the term "anisomorphism" is being used in TS to refer to the causes for the lack of identity (or total symmetry) between ST and TT. While Delabastita (1993) made reference to two types of anisomorphism (linguistic and cultural), which cause TPs, Franco Aixelá (1996) added two new types (pragmatic, interpretative). These four asymmetries are responsible for the ever-present differences between ST and TT (Alcaraz Varó/Martínez Linares 1997, p. 54).

The asymmetric nature of languages results from the fact that they are not objective reflections of reality, but rather taxonomies. Von Humboldt (2009, pp. 101–102) and Ortega y Gasset (1983, p. 436) already established the linguistic anisomorphism in all its significance for the translation process.

Newmark (1988, p. 94), for his part, points to the cultural anisomorphism when he divides language into three different categories: "universal", "cultural" and "personal." Cultural language tends to pose TPs given its idiosyncratic nature, which reveals itself mainly through culture-bound terms.

Pragmatic anisomorphism makes reference to rhetoric text conventions which tend to differ from one language to another (Franco Aixelá 1996).

Finally, the IA results from the fact that "perception and comprehension are not qualities inherent in the objects themselves" (Iser 1978, p. 64) and that "the relative indeterminacy of a text allows a spectrum of actualizations" (ibid., p. 24). Meanings are not fixed magnitudes inscribed in a text, they are rather the result of the interaction between text and reader in the reading process (Iser 1975, p. 229). This is why Reiß and Vermeer (2014, p. 68) defined texts as "offer of information." Due to its relative openness, "any receiver (among them, the translator) chooses the items they regard as interesting, useful or adequate to the desired purposes" (Nord 1997, pp. 25–26). While the ST is an offer of information in the source language and culture, the TT becomes a new offer of information in the target language and culture based on the initial offer of the ST (Reiß/Vermeer 2014, p. 69).

3. L&T method

Before getting into the topic of the specific L&T method, it seems necessary to explain the rationale of the didacticisation of real TTs in the classroom. The advantages of using real products of historic translation processes are manifold. If we agree with Toury's idea that "[w]hat trainees really need is an opportunity to abstract *their own guiding principles and routines* from actual instances of behaviour, with the help of responses to their performance" (2012, p. 291), e.g., through feedback by teachers, it seems equally advantageous that they get to compare these acquired conceptions with those embodied in the solutions of professional translators. Thus, in the case of the IA, they can test their skills of text interpretation against the backdrop of the ones that reveal themselves throughout the history of translation. After all, "interpretation takes place within historical situations" (Iser 2000, p. 6), which means that the results of our current hermeneutic process tend to contrast with the ones obtained by translators in different moments of history.

As far as methodology is concerned, we preferably use two L&T models that have gained traction in the translation classroom in recent years: (1) TBA; (2) project-based approach (PBA). We share the believe that these models should not be seen as antagonistic but complementary (Kelly 2005; Marco 2004) and that the difference between them is "simply a question of level / stage of training, that is of sequencing" (Kelly 2005, p. 116).

Therefore, we reserve the PBA for a research project on a topic of translation theory or history which is carried out by students in small working groups (aided by the teacher). It represents their first ever term paper which requires students to abide by strict academic criteria and is located at a later stage in the course schedule as it requires a greater degree of autonomy and responsibility on the part of the learners.

The DU presented in this paper resorts to a method which we call "task-based learning and teaching approach," in analogy to Ellis' (2003) "task-based language learning and teaching" term. This terminology is more representative since it includes both dimensions of the pedagogical process (L&T).

3.1 Course design

The course shows a hierarchical structure since "toda programación general de un curso suele compartimentar sus contenidos en una serie de unidades didácticas"[2] (Pastor Cesteros 2004, p. 273), which in turn are structured into tasks. Each DU "debe determinar sus propios objetivos, tener una estructura pedagógica e incluir una evaluación"[3] (ibid., p. 274) and it represents "un conjunto de tareas encaminadas a la consecución de los objetivos elegidos"[4] (Hurtado 1999, p. 50). Applying a sequence of tasks helps to "organize a body of knowledge into manageable components, thus making a challenging activity one which is eminently more achievable" (D'Andrea 2003, p. 30).

The course *Theory and History of Translation* at the University of Alicante was originally designed using the "intellectual approach" (ibid., p. 29), which focuses on disciplinary content, and since its inception in 2011 has been taught according to this rationale. Having come to the conclusion that the transmissionist, teacher-centred and lecture-based model does neither satisfy the current teachers' nor the students' expectations, in 2023 we decided to implement a progressive design change by adopting the systematic approach. According to D'Andrea (ibid., p. 29), it "proceeds from identifiable needs to predictable outcomes. It follows a planning sequence with a feedback loop for changing and improving the design each time the course is taught." Initially, two DUs were adapted to conform to the new paradigm. The ultimate goal is the phased replacement of all teaching units in a few years' time.

3.2 TBA in translation

Coming from second language teaching (see Estaire/Zanon 1994; Nunan 1989; Willis 1996), at the turn of the Millenium translation scholars (González Davies 2003a, 2004; Hurtado 1999; Kelly 2005) started to apply the TBA to translation teaching. In this realm, the method consists of "pautar tareas en el aula de traducción que condujeran, por etapas y de manera progresiva, a la consecución del objetivo específico propuesto"[5] (Marco 2004, p. 82). The task

---

[2] "any general course programme tends to compartmentalize its contents into a series of didactic units" (our translation).

[3] "must determine its own objectives, have a pedagogical structure and include an assessment" (our translation).

[4] "a set of tasks aimed at achieving the chosen objectives" (our translation).

[5] "setting tasks in the translation classroom that achieve, in stages and in a progressive manner, the outlined specific goal" (our translation).

is articulated through "una cadena de actividades relacionadas entre sí que, una vez acabadas, permiten que el alumno haya ampliado su conocimiento"[6] (González Davies 2003b, p. 13).

Talking about their structure, González Davies (2004) defines a task as "a chain of activities with the same global aim and a final product" (ibid., p. 23). When she indicates that "the full completion of a task usually takes up several sessions" and that "on the way, both procedural (know how) and declarative (know what) knowledge are practised and explored" (ibid.), she is referring to the didactic process. Breen (1989) already distinguished between "task-as-workplan" (i.e., structure and design) and "task-as-process." The first includes 1) learning content, and 2) instructions. The second stands for the activity students carry out when they perform the task (Ellis 2018, p. 23). The actual process may or may not unfold as initially planned in the workplan. The resulting feedback helps to readjust, if necessary, the design of the DU.

The TBA constitutes both a methodological and a curricular design framework that makes it possible to interweave the different elements that make up the L&T process: objectives, content, materials, sequencing and development of the work, and assessment. Another essential didactic principle is to place learners at the centre of the process and help them play a greater role by offering "a collaborative learning environment in which tasks are pedagogically sequenced to scaffold acquisition" (Inoue/ Candlin 2017, p. 58).

There are different types of tasks: Nunan (1989) distinguishes pedagogic from real-world tasks. The first is aimed at "stimulating internal processes of acquisition," the second "require[s] learners to approximate, in class, the sorts of behaviours required of them in the real world beyond the classroom" (p. 40). Hurtado (2019) applies the terms "enabling" and "preparatory" tasks for Nunan's pedagogic type and "final" task for his real-world task. The first type serves as preparation for the second one; the final task consists, e.g., in translating a certain text genre (ibid., pp. 59–60). As far as the type of activities translation tasks may include, Hurtado mentions: analysis, comparison, revision / correction applied to texts in the source and target language, as

6 "a chain of interrelated activities, which, once completed, allow the learner to have broadened his or her knowledge" (our translation).

well as to STs and TTs; questionnaires; documentation; contrastive exercises; fact sheets for conceptual issues; etc. (ibid., p. 60). In our DU, we will refer to the first type as "propaedeutic" and to the second type as "performance" task (this one in accordance with the terminology by McTighe and Wiggins 1999, pp. 139–140).

As far as the learning process of our students is concerned, our approach seeks to improve their translation competence in all its five sub-components plus the psychophysiological component (see PACTE 2011, pp. 318–319).

3.3 DU design

Based on Anthony's (1963, pp. 63–67) proposal, Richards and Rodgers (2014 [1986]) established three concepts for the description and definition of the different levels of conceptualisation and organisation of a teaching method: (1) approach, (2) design, and (3) procedure. The nature of their relationship would be as follows: "a method is theoretically related to an approach, is organizationally determined by a design, and is practically realized in procedure" (ibid., p. 22).

The approach refers to the theories concerning the nature of the discipline and the "philosophy" of the L&T model with its specific practices and principles (ibid.). The design represents the level of implementation of the theoretical principles and is therefore the link between the approach and the pedagogical procedures. It defines the objectives, contents, L&T tasks and activities, the roles of teachers and learners and the L&T materials (ibid., p. 29). Finally, the procedure describes the materialisation in the classroom of the approach and design of the method, i.e., how tasks and activities are integrated into DUs (ibid., p. 35). Table 1 shows the central aspects of the DU:

Table 1: Schedule and methodological aspects of the DU

L&T mode	L&T method	Course schedule
Participatory lecture + cooperative learning	Task-based approach: Learner-centred setting based on short lectures, followed by practical hands-on sessions (students work in peer groups guided by the teacher)	15 week course DU No. 7: "IA" 3 hrs classwork 4,5 hrs homework

3.4 Tasks and activities

What follows (tables 2 to 5) is a breakdown of the workplan of the four tasks with their respective activities that make up the DU:

Table 2: Propaedeutic task "The IA concept"

Task 1: propaedeutic: "Determine the 'IA' concept"	
Activity 1.1.	Brainstorming exercise: What is "IA"?
Objectives	Determining the student's state of knowledge
Content	IA
Material	Blackboard & notebook
Setting	Classroom: plenary session
Teacher's / Learner's role	Organiser & facilitator / Active participant
Time	20 minutes
Activity 1.2.	Reading and comprehension exercise: How to explain the "IA"?
Objectives	Understanding the nature of the "IA" Strengthen skills in text analysis
Content	IA
Material	(1) Franco Aixelá (1996, pp. 50–63) (2) Reiß/Vermeer (2014, pp. 18–19) (3) Iser (1975, pp. 228–231)
Setting	Classroom: groupwork
Teacher's / Learner's role	Facilitator & guide / autonomous learner
Time	70 minutes

Table 3: Performance task "Spotting, analysing and solving TPs"

Task 2 (performance): Find, analyse and solve TPs present in the ST.	
Activity 2.1.	Reading comprehension and text analysis
Objectives	Determining student's skills in finding, analysing and solving TPs
Content	ST comprehension and analysis
Material	ST: "An Julius Eduard Hitzig von Adelbert von Chamisso"
Setting	Classroom + homework (groupwork)
Teacher's / Learner's role	Facilitator and guide / autonomous learner
Time	30 min. (classroom) + 60 min. (homework)

(Continued)

Table 3: (*Continued*)

Activity 2.2.	Personal text interpretation and translation of the ST
Objectives	Developing students' interpretative skills Developing student's transfer skills
Content	Text interpretation and interlinguistic translation
Material	ST: "An Julius Eduard Hitzig von Adelbert von Chamisso"
Setting	Homework (groupwork)
Teacher's / Learner's role	Facilitator and guide / autonomous learner
Time	75 minutes
Assessment	What?: ST comprehension, spot TPs, shareable interpretation, transfer skills How (Who)?: Observation and analysis of students' work and participation (teacher) + self- and peer-assessment (students)

Table 4: Performance task "Creating a TT corpus"

Task 3 (performance): Set up a TT corpus for the qualitative comparative text analysis.	
Activity 3.1.	Producing TTs generated by MT & AI tools
Objectives	Developing students' instrumental skills
Content	Use of IT tools
Material	ST: "An Julius Eduard Hitzig von Adelbert von Chamisso"
Setting	Homework (groupwork)
Teacher's / Learner's role	Facilitator and guide / autonomous learner
Time	15 minutes
Activity 3.2.	Generating a table for the qualitative comparative text analysis
Objectives	Developing students' instrumental skills
Content	Use of IT tools
Material	ST: "An Julius Eduard Hitzig von Adelbert von Chamisso" TTs: didactic, human and machine translation(s)
Setting	Homework (groupwork)
Teacher's / Learner's role	Facilitator and guide / autonomous learner
Time	45 minutes
Assessment	What?: Instrumental skills, documentation skills How (Who)?: Analysis of students' work (teacher) + self- and peer-assessment (students)

Table 5: Performance task "Comparative analysis of TTs"

Task 4 (performance): Analyse: compare human (didactic & professional) vs MT/AI TTs.	
Activity 4.1.	Determine the existence and scope of the IA
Objectives	Developing students' analytical skills
Content	TT analysis
Material	ST + TTs + Documentation
Setting	Homework (groupwork)
Teacher's / Learner's role	Facilitator and guide / autonomous learner
Time	45 minutes
Activity 4.2.	Shareability of MT/AI-interpretations vs human ones
Objectives	Developing students' analytical skills
Content	TT analysis
Material	ST + TTs + Documentation
Setting	Homework (groupwork)
Teacher's / Learner's role	Facilitator and guide / autonomous learner
Time	30 minutes
Assessment	What?: Analytical skills. How (Who)?: Analysis of students' work (teacher) + self- and peer-assessment (students)

The closing activity of the DU consists of a 60 min. final plenary debate and assessment session in the classroom. In total, the DU comprises 180 minutes of classroom and 270 minutes of homework L&T. In accordance with the social constructivist approach, assessment becomes a collaborative task in which students participate. For the teacher's assessment of the work done by the students, each work group hands in the results of the tasks together with a short report on the completion of the activity and their self- and peer-assessment.

4. Procedure: partial exemplification of task 4

In order to understand the rationale behind task 4 (the most decisive one for the issue at hand), in this section we analyse the differing interpretations concerning the most salient TPs contained in the ST by contrasting solutions provided by HTs[7] and MT/AI. The analysis seeks to demonstrate the existence

[7] Since this paper presents only the design of the DU, it does not include didactic TTs as part of the HTs. As a result, this exemplified analysis compares only professional translations with TTs generated by MT/AI tools.

of the IA and provide answers on the potential usefulness of MT/AI-generated interpretations in the realm of literary translation.

4.1 ST

In this first sub-section we present the ST (Table 6). We have numbered and highlighted in bold the analysed TPs in order to make it easier for the reader to follow the explanations.

Table 6: Source text: An Julius Eduard Hitzig von Adelbert von Chamisso

An Julius Eduard Hitzig von Adelbert von Chamisso
Du vergissest niemanden, Du wirst Dich noch eines gewissen Peter Schlemihls erinnern, den Du in früheren Jahren ein paar Mal bei mir gesehen hast, ein langbeiniger Bursch, den man ungeschickt glaubte, weil er linkisch war, und der wegen seiner Trägheit für faul galt. Ich hatte ihn lieb, - Du kannst nicht vergessen haben, Eduard, **wie er uns** (TP2a) einmal **in unserer grünen Zeit** (TP1) **durch die Sonette lief** (TP2b), ich brachte ihn mit auf einen der **poetischen Tees** (TP3), wo er mir noch während des Schreibens einschlief, ohne das Lesen abzuwarten. Nun erinnere ich mich auch eines Witzes, den Du auf ihn machtest. Du hattest ihn nämlich schon, Gott weiß wo und wie, in einer alten schwarzen Kurtka gesehen, die er damals freilich immer noch trug, und sagtest: „der ganze Kerl wäre glücklich zu schätzen, wenn seine Seele nur halb so unsterblich wäre, als seine Kurtka." So wenig galt er bei euch. – Ich hatte ihn lieb. – Von diesem Schlemihl nun, den ich seit langen Jahren aus dem Gesicht verloren hatte, rührt das Heft her, das ich Dir mitteilen will. – Dir nur, Eduard, meinem nächsten, innigsten Freunde, meinem beßren Ich, vor dem ich kein Geheimnis verwahren kann, teil ich es mit, nur Dir und, es versteht sich von selbst, unserm Fouqué, gleich Dir in meiner Seele eingewurzelt – aber in ihm teil ich es bloß dem Freunde mit, nicht dem Dichter. – Ihr werdet einsehen, wie unangenehm es mir sein würde, wenn etwa **die Beichte** (TP4a), die ein ehrlicher Mann im Vertrauen auf meine Freundschaft und Redlichkeit **an meiner Brust abgelegt** (TP4b), in einem **Dichterwerke** (TP5) an den Pranger geheftet würde, oder nur wenn überhaupt unheilig verfahren würde, wie mit dem Erzeugnis schlechten Witzes, mit einer Sache, die das nicht ist und sein darf. Freilich muß ich selbst gestehen, daß es um die Geschichte Schad ist, die unter des guten Mannes Feder nur albern geworden, daß sie nicht von einer geschickteren fremden Hand in ihrer ganzen komischen Kraft dargestellt werden kann. – Was würde nicht Jean Paul daraus gemacht haben! – Übrigens, lieber Freund, mögen hier manche genannt sein, die noch leben; auch das will beachtet sein. –
Noch ein Wort über die Art, wie diese Blätter an mich gelangt sind. Gestern früh bei meinem Erwachen gab man sie mir ab, - ein wunderlicher Mann, der einen langen grauen Bart trug, eine ganz abgenützte schwarze **Kurtka** (TP6) anhatte, eine botanische

Kapsel darüber umgehangen, und **bei dem feuchten, regnichten Wetter** (TP7) **Pantoffeln** (TP8) über seine Stiefel, hatte sich nach mir erkundigt und dieses für mich hinterlassen; er hatte, aus Berlin zu kommen, vorgegeben.

Kunersdorf, den 27. September 1813

Adelbert von Chamisso

P.S. Ich lege Dir eine Zeichnung bei, die der kunstreiche Leopold, der eben an seinem Fenster stand, von der auffallenden Erscheinung entworfen hat. Als er den Wert, den ich auf diese Skizze legte, gesehen hat, hat er sie mir gerne geschenkt.

4.2 TTs and their selection

Given the spatial limitations of this paper, we cannot reproduce the TTs in their entirety, which is why in Table 7 we only include those sentences where TPs are present. As far as the TT selection is concerned, we have prioritised recent versions (von Chamisso/Xandru 2019, HT2 and von Chamisso/Barja/Lanceros 2020, HT3) and one with a high level of circulation (von Chamisso/Michael/Valdés 1994, HT1). In the first case, one can expect translators to have checked prior versions when encountering interpretation problems. In the second case, it is reasonable to assume that a widespread circulation fosters specific lines of interpretation.

4.3 TT analysis

What follows is a brief analysis of eight TPs that reveal the existence of the IA and help to assess the viability of MT/AI-generated interpretations as potential enhancers of HT productivity.

TP1 is solved in two different ways: all HTs interpret *in unserer grünen Zeit* ("in our green time[s]") as a synonym for "youth" by association with the colour (HT2 is less specific with its "in the good old days," but it seems reasonable to assume it refers to that time of life). And although neural MT has diminished the traditional tendency toward verbatim solutions, both MT/AI-generated versions are literal renderings. Both solutions are shareable, the first being compatible with the communicative, the second with the philological translation method (Hurtado 2001; Nord 1997). The communicative approach produces the loss of the biographical implicit ("green time[s]" refers to the period in which von Chamisso and his friends published their first poems in a literary almanac with a green cover).

Table 7: HTs vs MT/AI TTs

HT1 (1994)	HT2 (2019)	HT3 (2020)	MT (DeepL, 2024)	AI (GPT3.5, 2024)
[…] Yo le quería (TP1), y tú, Eduard, no puedes haber olvidado que **en los tempranos días de nuestra juventud** (TP1) una vez **fue objeto de nuestros sonetos** (TP2). En una ocasión le llevé a una de nuestras **tertulias poéticas** (TP3) y se quedó dormido mientras escribíamos, sin esperar a la lectura. […] Ambos comprenderéis cuan desagradable sería para mí que la confesión [Ø] (TP4) hecha por este hombre sincero, confiando en mi amistad y honradez, una vez vertida a la **poesía** (TP5) fuera expuesta a la picota de la crítica; o bien fuera tomada despiadadamente, como producto	[…] Yo le tenía cariño. No puedes haber olvidado, Eduard, cómo una vez, **en los buenos tiempos** (TP1), **se zafó de nuestros sonetos** (TP2): yo lo había traído a uno de nuestros **tés poéticos** (TP3) y se me quedó dormido mientras escribíamos, sin esperar a la lectura. […] Comprenderéis la repulsión que me produciría que la confesión, por llamarla así, que un hombre honorable depositó **en mí** (TP4), confiando en mi amistad y en mi rectitud, fuese puesta en la picota en su condición de **obra literaria** (TP5), o simplemente si sucediera alguna desgracia como consecuencia de un mal chiste	[…] Yo le tenía aprecio, e imagino que no habrás olvidado cómo, **en los años de nuestra juventud** (TP1), cuando **tanto él como nosotros corríamos detrás de los sonetos** (TP2), me lo llevé conmigo a una ***soirée* de aficionados a la poesía** (TP3); y él se durmió mientras escribíamos sin esperar siquiera a la lectura… […] ambos tendréis que comprender lo improcedente que sería que la confesión que un hombre honesto ha vertido **en mi pecho** (TP4) confiando en mi franqueza y amistad se viniera a poner en la picota, una vez editada, encuadernada como **un mero**	[…] Le tenía cariño. No puedes haber olvidado, Eduard, cómo una vez **recorrió nuestros sonetos** (TP2) **en nuestros días verdes** (TP1); lo llevé a uno de los **tés poéticos** (TP3), donde se quedó dormido mientras yo seguía escribiendo, sin esperar a leer. […] Te darás cuenta de lo desagradable que sería para mí que la confesión que un hombre honrado, confiado en mi amistad y en mi honradez, hizo **a mi pecho** (TP4), fuera puesta en la picota en una **obra de poesía** (TP5), o sólo si fuera tratada impúdicamente en absoluto, como con el producto de un mal ingenio, con una	[…] Yo lo quería. No puedes haber olvidado, Eduard, cómo una vez **en nuestros años verdes** (TP1) **nos deleitó con los sonetos** (TP2), lo llevé a una de las **tertulias poéticas** (TP3), donde se quedó dormido mientras escribía, sin esperar a que leyéramos. […] Comprenderás lo desagradable que sería para mí si la confesión que un hombre honesto depositó **en mi pecho** (TP4) confiando en mi amistad y honestidad, fuera ridiculizada en una **obra poética** (TP5), o si se tratara de manera profana, como con una broma de mal gusto, con algo que no es y no debe ser así. […]

HT1 (1994)	HT2 (2019)	HT3 (2020)	MT (DeepL, 2024)	AI (GPT3.5, 2024)
de un chiste malo, cosa que ni es ni debe ser. […] Un extraño personaje de largas barbas grises, vistiendo una ***kurtka*** (TP6) negra raída por el uso, llevando una caja de herborizar colgada en bandolera y quien, **a pesar del** (TP7) tiempo húmedo y lluvioso, calzaba unas **pantuflas** (TP8) por encima de sus botas, había preguntado por mí […].	acerca de algo que ni es ni puede ser motivo de burla. […] un hombre extravagante, que llevaba una larga barba gris y vestía una **chaqueta** (TP6) negra totalmente desgastada, sobre la que llevaba en bandolera una cesta de botánico, y con unos **chanclos** (TP8) sujetos a las botas, **a causa del** (TP7) tiempo húmedo y lluvioso, había preguntado por mí […].	**invento de escritor** (TP5), o malévolamente se entendiese como fruto de una broma de mal gusto, cosa que ni es ni puede ser. […] un tipo raro que lucía una larga barba gris, llevando un **kurtka** (TP6) negro y muy gastado, con un estuche de los de herborizar que traía colgado por encima y **pantuflas** (TP8) sobrepuestas a las botas – **por el tiempo** (TP7), húmedo y lluvioso […].	cosa que no es ni debe ser tal. […] un extraño hombre de larga barba gris, vestido con una **kurtka** (TP6) negra muy gastada, una cápsula botánica encima y **zapatillas** (TP8) sobre las botas **en un** (TP7) clima húmedo y lluvioso, había preguntado por mí […].	un hombre extraño, con una larga barba gris, llevaba una **chaqueta** (TP6) negra completamente desgastada, una cápsula botánica colgada sobre ella, y **en el clima húmedo y lluvioso** (TP7), **zapatillas** (TP8) sobre sus botas, se había informado por mí […].

Wie er uns durch die Sonette lief ("how he ran through our sonnets") is probably the most difficult TP in this text. Our own interpretation would be that he [Schlemihl] was literarily processed in the sonnets. HT1 attributes a figurative meaning ("he was the subject of our sonnets") and MT a literal version ("he ran through our sonnets"), both being shareable (to some extent, the latter lacks comprehensibility), while none of the other three TTs offers an interpretation that fits the meaning and syntax in the ST.

The expression *literarischer Tee* (TP3) refers to the concept "literary salon." All TTs offer a shareable interpretation: "poetic gathering" (HT1, AI) and "soirée of poetry lovers" (HT3) are typical communicative translation techniques (explicitation and description); the second type of solution is the verbatim translation: "poetic tea" (HT2, MT).

As to TP4, *die Beichte an meiner Brust ablegen* ("make a confession at/on/ to my breast"), the major challenge is how to express the final part. HT1 and HT2 choose to avoid the problem by omitting the expression either completely or partially (a questionable procedure in literary translation). The other three TTs offer literal translations with varying degrees of naturalness.

In *Dichterwerk* (TP5), only HT2 renders the more general meaning "literary work" instead of the more limited "poetic work." Given the specific reference to the story of Peter Schlemihl, it is quite clear that von Chamisso is not talking about a work of poetry, which is why, except HT2, all other TTs have failed to interpret the text in the right way.

For the culture-specific item *kurtka* (TP6) the TTs present two types of solution, both being shareable: either the borrowing (TH1, TH3, MT) or the generalisation "jacket" (TH2, AI). The first adheres to an exoticising approach (philological method), the second to a domesticating one (communicative method).

At first glance, *bei dem feuchten, regnichten Wetter* ("given that damp, rainy weather"), does not seem to qualify as TP. The TTs, however, present contradictory solutions that seem to point to the existence of a TP. The explanation lies within the context of the story: Schlemihl wears slippers over his seven-league boots in order to be able to make small steps (the slippers are a tool for limiting the boots' movements). When von Chamisso sees the strange figure wearing slippers over his boots, he seems surprised given that the weather is damp and rainy. In this context, we consider only HT1 a correct interpretation ("despite the wet and rainy weather"), while HT2 and HT3 produce a contradiction in terms ("because of the wet and rainy weather"). MT and AI err both when selecting the preposition ("in") and the term "climate" (instead of "weather").

Finally, TP8 becomes a problem when translators try to make sense of wearing slippers over the boots. This leads HT2 to render "clogs" for *Pantoffeln* instead of slippers. As in the case of TP7, TP8 would not be considered a TP in a nonfictional context.

5. Results and final remarks

The primary aim of this paper was to outline a didactic proposal capable of introducing students to the concept of IA, not just in a theoretical way but through a hands-on practical exercise that applies a TBA. The joint didacticisation of professional, didactic and MT/AI-generated TTs was another cornerstone of the DU destined to provide realism and answers to the usability of non-human interpretations concerning TPs, specifically in the realm of literature (presumably the least suitable type of texts for MT). By exemplifying the central task, we have tried to illustrate how the didactic design can be applied in the classroom.

The TT analysis shows to a certain extent predictable outcomes. On the one hand, it provides sufficient evidence to postulate the existence of the IA; on the other hand, it confirms the increased quality of machine-driven interpretations. If we establish the shareability of the interpretation of TPs as the defining criterion for the assessment of the usability of MT/AI-generated TTs as auxiliary tools in HT, we come to the conclusion that the results of the analysis seem to back up the idea of their usefulness. Judging by the shareability index (the proportion of feasible vs unfeasible interpretations), the specific case reveals no substantial difference between HT- and MT/AI-generated interpretations: HT1 (6/2), HT2 (4/4), HT3 (5/3), MT (6/2), AI (5/3).

Of course, we have to bear in mind that this sample is rather small. And since the DU is based on a case study, the results concerning the usability of MT/AI-generated interpretations cannot be extrapolated to all types of literature, not even to the field of prose texts as a whole. It provides, however, some insight into the changing patterns of machine-driven text interpretation and its potential use as enhancer of HT productivity. Finally, the comparison between the translation techniques applied by MT vs AI seems to suggest a heavier reliance on verbatim renderings by the first, while the second shows more balanced results that combine to a larger extent literal and descriptive translations.

Bibliography

Abrams, Meyer / Harpham, Geoffrey (2013): *A glossary of literary terms*. Stamford: Cengage Learning.

Alcaraz Varó, Enrique / Martínez Linares, María Antonia (1997): *Diccionario de lingüística moderna*. Barcelona: Ariel.

Anthony, Edward M. (1963): "Approach, method and technique." *ELT Journal* 17(2), pp. 63–67.

Breen, Michael (1989): "The evaluation cycle for language learning tasks." In: Johnson, Robert Keith (Ed.): *The Second Language Curriculum*. Cambridge: Cambridge University Press, pp. 187–206.

Caine, Renate N. / Caine, Geoffrey (1994): *Making connections: Teaching and the human brain*. Menlo Park: Addison-Wesley.

Crystal, David (2008): *A dictionary of linguistics and phonetics*. Oxford: Blackwell.

D'Andrea, Vaneeta-Marie (2003): "Organizing teaching and learning: Outcomes-based planning." In: Fry, Heather / Ketteridge, Steve / Marshall, Stephanie (Eds.): *A Handbook for Teaching & Learning in Higher Education*. London: Kogan Page, pp. 26–41.

Delabastita, Dirk (1993): *There's a double tongue: An investigation into the translation of Shakespeare's wordplay, with special reference to Hamlet*. Amsterdam: Rodopi.

Ellis, Rod (2003): *Task-based language learning and teaching*. Oxford: Oxford University Press.

Ellis, Rod (2018): *Reflections on task-based language teaching*. Bristol: Multilingual Matters.

Estaire, Sheila / Zanon, Javier (1994): *Planning classwork: A task based approach*. Oxford: Macmilan Publishers.

Franco Aixelá, Javier (1996): *Condicionantes de traducción y su aplicación a los nombres propios (inglés-español)*. Alicante: Universidad de Alicante.

Genette, Gerard (1997): *Paratexts: Thresholds of interpretation*. Cambridge: Cambridge University Press.

González Davies, María (2003a): "Introducción: principios pedagógicos." In: González Davies, María (Ed.): *Secuencias: Tareas para el aprendizaje interactivo de la traducción especializada*. Barcelona: Octaedro, pp. 11–18.

González Davies, María (2003b) (Ed.): *Secuencias: Tareas para el aprendizaje interactivo de la traducción especializada*. Barcelona: Octaedro.

González Davies, María (2004): *Multiple voices in the translation classroom: Activities, tasks and projects*. Amsterdam / Philadelphia: John Benjamins.

Gregory, Richard L. (1987) (Ed.): *The Oxford companion to the mind*. New York: Oxford University Press.

Hurtado Albir, Amparo (Ed.) (1999): *Enseñar a traducir: metodología en la formación de traductores e intérpretes*. Madrid: Edelsa.

Hurtado Albir, Amparo (2001): *Traducción y traductología: introducción a la traductología.* Madrid: Cátedra.

Hurtado Albir, Amparo (2019): "La investigación en didáctica de la traducción. Evolución, enfoques y perspectivas." *MonTI* 11, pp. 47–76.

Inoue, Izumi / Candlin, Christopher N. (2017): "Applying task-based learning to translator education: Assisting the development of novice translators' problem-solving expertise." In: Colina, Sonia / Angelelli, Claudia V. (Eds.): *Translation and interpreting pedagogy in dialogue with other disciplines*. Amsterdam / Philadelphia: John Benjamins, pp. 55–82.

Iser, Wolfgang (1975): "Die Apellstruktur der Texte: Unbestimmtheit als Wirkungsbedingung literarischer Prosa." In: Warning, Rainer (Ed.): *Rezeptionsästhetik*. München: Wilhelm Fink Verlag, pp. 228–252.

Iser, Wolfgang (1978): *The act of reading: A theory of aesthetic response*. Baltimore et al.: Johns Hopkins University Press.

Iser, Wolfgang (2000): *The range of interpretation*. New York: Columbia University Press.

Kelly, Dorothy (2005): *A handbook for translator trainers*. London et al.: Routledge.

Kiraly, Donald (2000): *A social constructivist approach to translator education; empowering the translator*. Manchester (UK) / Northampton (MA): St. Jerome.

Koehn, Philippe (2020): *Neural machine translation*. New York: Cambridge University Press.

Marco, Josep (2004): "¿Tareas o proyectos? ¿Senderos que se bifurcan en el desarrollo de la competencia traductora?." *TRANS* 8, pp. 75–88.

McTighe, Jay / Wiggins, Grant (1999): *The understanding by design handbook*. Alexandria: ASCD.

Newmark, Peter (1988): *A textbook of translation*. New York: Prentice Hall.

Nord, Christiane (1997): *Translating as a purposeful activity: Functionalist approaches explained*. Manchester (UK) / Northampton (MA): St. Jerome.

Nunan, David (1989): *Designing tasks for the communicative classroom*. Cambridge: Cambridge University Press.

Ortega y Gasset, José (1983): "Miseria y esplendor de la traducción." In: Ortega y Gasset: *Obras completas*. Vol. V. Madrid: Alianza, pp. 431–452.

PACTE (2011): "Results of the validation of the PACTE translation competence model: Translation problems and translation competence." In: Alvstad, Cecilia / Hild, Adelina / Tiselius, Elisabet (Eds.): *Methods and strategies of process research*. Amsterdam / Philadelphia: John Benjamins, pp. 317–343.

Pastor Cesteros, Susana (2004): *Aprendizaje de segundas lenguas: lingüística aplicada a la enseñanza de idiomas*. Alicante: Servicio de Publicaciones Universidad de Alicante.

Reiß, Katharina / Vermeer, Hans (2014): *Towards a general theory of translational action*. London et al.: Routledge.

Richards, Jack C. / Rodgers, Theodore S. (2014): *Approaches and methods in language teaching. A description and analysis*. Cambridge: Cambridge University Press.

Toral, Antonio / Wieling, Martijn / Way, Andy (2018): "Post-editing effort of a novel with statistical and neural machine translation." *Frontiers in Digital Humanities* 5(9), pp. 1–11.

Toury, Gideon (2012): *Descriptive translation studies and beyond*. Amsterdam / Philadelphia: John Benjamins.

Vienne, Jean (1994): "Pour une pédagogie de la traduction en situation." In: Snell-Hornby, Mary / Pöchhacker, Franz / Kaindl, Klaus (Eds.): *Translation studies: An interdiscipline*. Amsterdam / Philadelphia: John Benjamins, pp. 421–429.

von Chamisso, Adelbert / Michael, Ulrike (trans.) / Valdés, Hernán (trans.) (1994): *La maravillosa historia de Peter Schlemihl*. Madrid: Siruela.

von Chamisso, Adelbert (2013): *Peter Schlemihls wundersame Geschichte*. Frankfurt a. M.: Suhrkamp.

von Chamisso, Adelbert / Fernández, Xandru (trans.) (2019): *La maravillosa historia de Peter Schlemihl*. Barcelona: Navona.

von Chamisso, Adelbert / Barja, Juan (trans.) / Lanceros, Patxi (trans.) (2020): *La extraordinaria historia de Peter Schlemihl*. Madrid: Abada.

von Humboldt, Wilhelm (2009): "Vorrede zur Agamemnon-Übersetzung." In: Kitzbichler, Josefine / Lubitz, Katja / Mindt, Nina (Eds.): *Dokumente zur Theorie der Übersetzung antiker Literatur in Deutschland seit 1800*. Berlin et al.: Walter de Gruyter, pp. 95–113.

Willis, Jane (1996): *A framework for task-based learning*. Harlow: Longman.

The educational value of post-editing automated poetry translations in early stage translator training

Katharina Walter
Universität Innsbruck

ABSTRACT
Post-edited literary translations are on the rise, although literature was long regarded as a stronghold of the human voice, even when other translatorial domains had already become heavily technologised. Focusing on a classroom experiment from 2023, this contribution examines the value of AI tools such as DeepL and ChatGPT for translating poetry. Both applications are oblivious to poetic form in a source text and cannot thus reliably recreate it in a target text. ChatGPT, however, can be prompted to partially reconstruct poetic form in a separate step after translation. The experiment analysed in this chapter echoes previous research about the limiting effect that automated translation of full poems and other literary texts tends to have on human translators' creativity. Nevertheless, the use of AI tools for inspiration has also been shown to facilitate the translation of particularly challenging terms or passages in such texts. It is now widely accepted that aspiring translators need to learn about the possibilities and limitations of automated translation as part of their education. This contribution aligns with this perspective in showing that, in our AI-saturated age, experimenting with automated poetry translation and subsequent post-editing has educational value, even at an early stage of translator training.

Keywords: AI and data literacy, automated translation, creativity, translator training, poetry translation

1. Introduction

Drawing on PETRA-E's framework of reference for the education and training of literary translators, this contribution examines to which extent translation tools based on artificial intelligence (AI) can assist prospective language professionals in developing their skillset. At the core of the analysis is an experiment on poetry translation with and without DeepL that was carried out in the translator training classroom in 2023, but the performance of neural machine translation (NMT) tools such as DeepL in poetry translation will also be compared to that of large language models (LLMs) such as ChatGPT.

As far as the quality of automated poetry translation is concerned, this contribution mainly examines whether automated translation output hinders creativity by leading to more homogeneous translations than humans would produce without machine assistance or, on the contrary, fosters creativity by allowing humans to focus on particularly challenging sections in a text and even encouraging them to use more literal translations of unconventional expressions than humans normally produce. This phenomenon was observed by Kolb, Dressler and Mattiello (2023) in their study of human- and machine-translated English-language versions of Nestroy's play *The Talisman*. It was found that NMT systems such as DeepL and Google Translate sometimes offer literal and thus novel target-language equivalents for occasionalisms, neologisms Nestroy often only used on a one-off basis, for which human translators mostly chose naturalising equivalents. However, other studies on literary prose (Guerberof-Arenas/Toral 2022, p. 207; Guerberof-Arenas/Toral 2024, p. 240; Kolb 2023, p. 65) established that post-edited texts tend to manifest less creativity overall and engage their readers less than human translations.

In this contribution, translatorial creativity is defined with Bayer-Hohenwarter as a manifestation of "creative shifts," which occur when translators abandon the linguistic structures found in source texts to be translated (2011, p. 669). In addition, this contribution also takes into account the interplay between the separate dimensions of the acceptability or purposefulness, flexibility or inclination toward creative shifts, novelty or uniqueness and fluency or inclination toward reproductive strategies in a translation discussed by Guerberof-Arenas and Toral (2022, p. 186). The implications of Kolb, Dressler and Mattiello's (2023) and Guerberof-Arenas and Toral's (2022) studies will be analysed with a view toward the translation of poetry, a literary genre that is often regarded as particularly challenging to translate, mainly due to the complex interplay between content and form that can be difficult to recreate in a language other than the original one. From the point of view of automated translation, this difficulty is enhanced by the fact that tools such as DeepL and ChatGPT, while continually improving as translation aids at the levels of expression, grammar and syntax, are still unable to reliably recognise poetic form in a source text and transfer it into a target-language version. While, for now, DeepL and other NMT systems offer no possibility whatsoever to translate poetic form, task-specific prompting in ChatGPT and other LLMs allows for some adjustment of poetic form in a translation.

The obliviousness of AI-based translation tools to poetic form is probably the main reason why comparatively little research has been published to date about automated or technology-enhanced poetry translation. Examining the perceived usefulness of technology from the viewpoint of Dutch literary translators, for instance, Daems highlights that text segmentation at sentence level is a key issue that hinders translators of poetry from using CAT tools (2022, p. 59), a limitation that also applies to most current NMT systems. Nevertheless, in a study on poetry translation between Croatian and German, Seljan, Dunđer and Pavlikovski conclude that rough translations prepared with NMT systems are somewhat useful (2020, p. 1044). The experiment analysed here echoes this finding, especially as the main goal was not to increase productivity or improve translation quality but to facilitate prospective translators in developing the skills required to critically assess the potentials and limitations of translation technology.

Apart from the circumstances under which automated translation can potentially enhance or impair creativity, another important question addressed in this contribution is at which stage in training it is appropriate to add AI-based translation tools to prospective translators' toolkits, especially in the context of literary translation. In integrity with Nitzke, Hansen-Schirra and Canfora's (2019) and Hackenbuchner and Krüger's (2023) emphasis on the importance for language professionals to develop a comprehensive understanding of automated translation, this contribution argues that translators in training should be confronted with AI technologies from the start of their education and in a large variety of contexts, including unconventional ones, such as poetry translation. Arguing that both lay people and language professionals require a solid amount of AI and data literacy, Hackenbuchner and Krüger propose that for a professional use of automated translation a differentiated understanding of the available technology is required that entails technical, linguistic, economic, social and cognitive skills, as well as data literacy (2023, pp. 285–292). Hands-on experience and critical discussion of translation technology in a translator training environment are essential aspects of this educational process.

While it is beyond question that AI and data literacy should be a key aspect of specialised translator training at all levels, literary translation continues to be less technologised than other domains. Nevertheless, PETRA-E's framework of reference for the education and training of literary translators establishes the need for language professionals working in this field to familiarise themselves with language technology. The framework outlines eight competences: 1. Transfer competence, 2. Language competence, 3. Textual competence, 4. Heuristic competence, 5. Literary-cultural competence, 6. Professional competence, 7. Evaluative competence and 8. Research competence. For each of these competences, translators can identify their level of proficiency based on the respective descriptors on a scale from L1 (Beginner) to L5 (Expert). Currently, the framework highlights technological skills for the following categories:

3. Textual competence: From L2 level (Advanced Learner) onwards, familiarity with automatisation processes in the field of literary translation is required as part of textual competence, which “consists of the knowledge of literary genres and styles and the ability to apply this knowledge in the analysis of source texts and the production of target texts.” L3 level users (Early Career Professionals) also have to be able to proficiently evaluate automatically translated output. (PETRA-E)
4. Heuristic competence: In the general description of this competence, it is stated that literary translation must entail “the ability to develop strategies for an efficient use of (digital) information sources.” Consequently, familiarity with CAT tools is required as of L2 level. (PETRA-E)

According to the descriptors used by PETRA-E, the very heterogeneous group of undergraduate students that participated in the translation experiment outlined in the next section were mostly at beginners’ level. In integrity with PETRA-E’s framework, this implies that automated translation should only feature occasionally in the training of future translators of literary and other texts, and mainly with a view toward facilitating their awareness of the potentials and limitations of automated translation.

2. Classroom experiment on poetry translation with(out) DeepL

2.1 Experiment design

On June 23, 2023, twelve undergraduate students of diverse linguistic backgrounds and at different levels of their studies who, with one exception, were enrolled in a translation studies degree course at the University of

Innsbruck or elsewhere, rendered a short poem from German into English in an experiment that was conducted on a creative writing course for future language professionals. Some experiment participants were not allowed to use NMT, while others had to. After translating the poem, the students also answered questions about their translation process. Originally, translation was not supposed to feature on this creative writing course, except for two sessions on interlingual creative transfers often referred to as transcreation. However, when an international competition for poetry translation was mentioned in class, some students explicitly asked for poetry translation to be covered. Therefore, the experiment was planned to reconcile the students' interest with the need for future language professionals to reflect on the implications of AI-based translation tools for creative processes. At the core of the experiment and analysis lay the following key questions:

(1) Is machine output an obstacle to creativity because it leads to more homogeneous translations than humans would produce without machine support?
(2) Or, on the contrary, does automated translation enhance creativity by allowing humans to create target texts at greater speed, some of which may contain novel suggestions that humans might not otherwise consider?
(3) To what extent and in which contexts are automated translation tools valuable aids for poetry translation at undergraduate level?

In the translation experiment analysed in this contribution, participants rendered "(Thema)," a poem by the contemporary German author Durs Grünbein that is not available online in English translation, from German into English during a 90-minute course session. The original poem is available online on a platform called Lyrikline, which "aims to enhance the dissemination, degree of popularity and reception potential of contemporary poetry throughout the world and to foster an international exchange of poets, poems and translations" ("The Lyrikline Network"). "(Thema)," which had originally been published by Suhrkamp in 1999 as part of a collection entitled *Nach den Satiren*, was interesting for this experiment for various reasons. The poem is relatively short and accessible, even though Grünbein uses some unusual language with novel metaphors. In addition, the poem also contains some elements of traditional poetic form, such as rhyme. For the students' translation experience, these factors meant that the given task was achievable, so long as it was clear to them that the main focus was going to be on the process and not on the result, as most students would have needed substantially more time to create a polished version of the assignment. At the same time, due to some unusual stylistic features in the original text and the implications of poetic form, translation with DeepL was always only going to be of limited use at best, so that one key message for the students involved was not to over-rely on technology.

The experiment participants were randomly divided into two groups. Group A (human translators or HT) translated the poem without the help of DeepL, while Group B (post-editors or PE) had to work with DeepL in a first step. In integrity with the key aims of the experiment outlined above, students were ensured that the purpose of the exercise was not to assess performance, but to get an insight into poetry translation and to look at different translation processes and results when including or excluding machine assistance. Participants did not submit their translations anonymously, but their work has been anonymised for this contribution.

The resources students were allowed to use to complete their translations were limited for better comparability of the results. The HT group was allowed to use the following monolingual and multilingual dictionaries as needed: *Duden*[1], *Macmillan*[2], *Cambridge* GE-EN/EN-GE[3], and *Rhyming Dictionary*[4]. The PE group was told to use the same resources as the HT group and additionally translate the poem with DeepL in a first step.

2.2 Analysis

While the HT group produced more varied and personalised translations overall, the PE group also changed the machine output significantly. In integrity with Kolb's observations on literary translators being "primed"

---

1 https://www.duden.de/woerterbuch (retrieved on 07/05/2025)

2 https://www.macmillandictionary.com/ (The website of the electronic dictionary and the blog were closed on June 30, 2023.)

3 https://dictionary.cambridge.org/de/worterbuch/deutsch-englisch/ (retrieved on 07/05/2025)

4 https://www.rhymezone.com/ (retrieved on 07/05/2025)

by automated translation output, meaning that it they may struggle to emancipate themselves from a proposed translation once they have seen it (2023, p. 61), the poems translated without machine assistance were more diverse than the PE versions at the level of expression. At the same time, the HT versions tended to preserve obvious features of poetic form such as rhyme to a greater extent. This is probably because those rhymes are not retained in the unmodified DeepL version, as the included sample DeepL translation from June 23, 2023, the day of the experiment, shows. Overall, the experiment participants' translations indicate that it was more difficult to insert rhymes in the PE versions retroactively than to consider features of poetic form from the beginning of the translation process, as the HT group seemingly did. Even though the translation task for the experiment was unspecific in that respect, the translation drafts indicate that all participants were aware of poetic form when translating. While some students were at early stages of their degree course and most of them had little general background in literary studies or literary genres, poetic form had been previously discussed on the creative writing course the poetry translation experiment formed part of, with an emphasis on the sonnet and ballad forms. Thus, all experiment participants knew that the meaning in a poem was informed by a particularly strong interplay between content and formal features.

In order to illustrate the different tendencies that distinguished the PE versions from the HT versions, the six opening lines from both groups are shown in Table 1[5]. The PE group tended not to dissociate themselves very much from lexical choices pre-empted by DeepL. This is shown by the italicised passages in Table 1, which contain the rhymes in the original poem and the equivalent passages in translation, as well as one particular expression and its English translations.

5 In order to facilitate comparison of these versions, their formatting was partly homogenised (using the same font and font size but not, for instance, ignoring students' individual formatting choices with regard to indentations and line breaks).

Table 1: Opening lines of poem: HT versions

Grünbein	Und dann kommt der heitere Teil vom Sterben. *Versöhnt* Mit dem Tag der Geschäfte verspricht und Verträge *bricht*, Drehst du dich früh aus dem Spiegel. Dein gebrauchtes *Gesicht*, Scharf rasiert, das dem *Quengeln* von innen *höhnt*, Gehört dem Empfangschef, der die Verhandlungen führt.
DeepL (June 23, 2023)	And then comes the cheerful part of dying. Reconciled With the day that promises business and breaks contracts, You turn early from the mirror. Your used face, Shaved sharp, that scoffs at the *querulous* from within, Belongs to the receptionist who negotiates.
HT a	And then you have the peaceful side of dying. Reconciliate With the day that promises success and breaks pacts of *grace* You turn to the mirrow (sic). See your tired *face*, Sharply shaved, depiction of your *sad faith* It belongs to the boss, him who decides what will be us.
HT b	And then comes the light part of dying. Already made up with the day planting seeds and forgetting *about*, Quite early, you move out the *mirror.* Your face *worn-out*, tightly shaved, jeering all that inner *whining*, and owned by the chief bouncer, negotiating with *valour.*
HT c	And then comes the joyful part of death. Reconciliation With a day that promises business and breaks contracts, You turn away from the mirror early. Your spent face, sharply shaven, which from within taunts *questioners*, Belongs to the administrator who negotiates.
HT d	And then comes the best part of dying. *Reconciled* With the day that promises profit and contracts *erase* You turn out of the mirror Your used *face* Sharp shaved, that mock you from inside the *whined* Owned by the receptionist, who the negotiations guided.

HT e	And then came the cheerful part of dying. *Reconciled* On the day of promised business and endless *breaches* You roll out of bed early. Your tired worn-out *features* Clean shaven, mocking inside which *wailed*, belongs to the receptionist, who leads negotiations.
HT f	And then comes the pleasant part of dying. *Reconcile* With the day that promises deals and breaks *agreements*, You turn away from the mirror early. Your used *appearance*, sharply shaved, to mock the internal *whine*, belongs to the receptionist who runs the negotiation.

Choices such as "breaks pacts of grace" and "forgetting about" as equivalents for "Verträge bricht" show that the HT group tended to focus on the overall meaning of the poem, rather than on individual words or expressions. In integrity with Guerberof-Arenas and Toral's observations, the HT group used reproductive translation strategies less often than the PE group, thus producing more creative translations overall (see 2022, p. 186). In addition, the HT group also showed greater awareness of poetic form as part of the overall message and effect of the text than the PE group. Only one participant did not use rhyme, while four preserved all rhymes from the original excerpt. In general, the HT versions show greater diversity at the lexical level, as a comparison of the translations for the word "Quengeln" highlights: "sad," "whining," "questioners," "whined," "wailed" and "whine" include three different word categories. Although different forms of "whine," a translation for the verb "quengeln" suggested prominently in bilingual dictionaries, are used in three out of six translated versions, none of the translations are identical to each other.

In comparison to the versions that were created without machine assistance, the translations offered by the experiment participants who used DeepL in a first step were more homogenous regarding expression but less form-conscious[6] (Table 2):

6 Again, in order to facilitate comparison of these versions, the formatting was partly homogenised. For more detailed information, see previous footnote.

Table 2: Opening lines of poem: PE versions

Grünbein	Und dann kommt der heitere Teil vom Sterben. *Versöhnt* Mit dem Tag der Geschäfte verspricht und Verträge *bricht*, Drehst du dich früh aus dem Spiegel. Dein gebrauchtes *Gesicht*, Scharf rasiert, das dem *Quengeln* von innen *höhnt*, Gehört dem Empfangschef, der die Verhandlungen führt.
DeepL (June 23, 2023)	And then comes the cheerful part of dying. Reconciled With the day that promises business and breaks contracts, You turn early from the mirror. Your used face, Shaved sharp, that scoffs at the *querulous* from within, Belongs to the receptionist who negotiates.
PE a	And then comes the cheerful part of dying. Reconciled With the day that *makes* and *breaks* promises and, You turn away early from the mirror. Your used face, Sharply shaved, that scoffs at the *querulous* from within, Belongs to the chief receptionist who leads the negotiation.
PE b	And then comes the cheerful part of dying. Reconciled with the day that offers *trade* and breaks contracts *unpaid*. You turn from the mirror. Your worn off face, sharply shaved, which *wines* (sic) from within, belongs to the solicitor who negotiates.
PE c	And then comes the cheerful part of dying. *Reconciled* With promised wealth and broken contracts in just one *touch*, You quickly turn away from the mirror, early. Your face has seen too *much*, Shaved too sharp, the *tears* that inside you are *piled*, To the receptionist who does the negotiating it belongs.
PE d	And then comes the cheerful part of dying. *Reconciled* With the day that promises *business* and broken contracts in a *briefcase*, You turn early from the mirror. Your used face, Sharp-shaven, that scoffs at the *querulous* from within, Belongs to the receptionist who *filed*.
PE e	And then comes the cheerful part of dying. Reconciled with the day when business may be *made* and contracts *fade*, You turn early from the mirror. Your used face, Shaved sharp, scoffing at the *querulous* from the inside, Belongs to the receptionist who negotiates.

PE f	And now follows the fun part of dying. Reconciled With the day that promises *deals* and breaks former *seals*, You turn away from the mirror. Your hollowed face, Shaved to a sharp edge, mocking the *whining* emerging from within, Belongs to the receptionist who leads negotiations.

Only one PE version contains four end rhymes like the original German version, and even though all translations include at least some internal rhymes, as the bold passages show, the students in this group generally placed less emphasis on poetic form than the participants working without machine assistance. Both the translated poems and the students' comments that will subsequently be discussed in more detail indicate that the main reason for this obliviousness toward poetic form was the fact that the original DeepL output was unrhymed. As is manifest in the choices of terms used to replace the German "Quengeln," for which *Cambridge Dictionary* suggests "whimper" and "whine" as translations, participants had difficulties dissociating themselves from the DeepL output. Three out of six PE versions still contain "the querulous," the nominalised form of this adjective from the NMT output, which is highly unusual and was probably generated by DeepL as a grammatical equivalent for the nominalised form of the German verb "quengeln" that features in the original poem.

Even though the limiting effect of machine output on creativity is notable in the PE versions, sometimes a reproductive rendering of phrases from a source text encouraged by machine output may also enhance creativity, as the example of "scharf rasiert" shows. In German, this is an infrequent but established expression indicating that someone is "clean-shaven," a naturalising English-language equivalent that features in HT e, for instance. The DeepL output included a reproductive translation for this German phrase that does not quite work, "[s]haved sharp." However, in version PE e the original machine output was rendered into something similar that has potential in the given context: "[s]haved to a sharp edge." Even though this phrase is not normally used to refer to a beard, except if it is shaved to a straight line, the expression is familiar from contexts referring to tools or sharp weapons, such as the "wooden horse," a historical torture device[7]. Depending on how one interprets Grünbein's poem, the raw image suggested by the phrase "shaved to a sharp edge" could thus be a valid equivalent. This finding dovetails with Kolb, Dressler and Mattiello's argument that reproductivity in automated translation can potentially encourage creativity (2023, p. 543), which will be discussed in more detail in a subsequent section.

After translating the poem, the experiment participants also answered questions about their translation process, which are given in Table 3. An English translation is included alongside the original German versions of these questions.

Table 3: Follow-up questions to the poem translation

German	English
Zum Übersetzungsprozess: Wie haben Sie den Text übersetzt? Bitte unterstreichen Sie die zutreffende Option. Ohne maschinelle Unterstützung Mit maschineller Unterstützung (DeepL, https://www.deepl.com/de/translator) Wie lange haben Sie für die Übersetzung gebraucht? Beschreiben Sie in groben Zügen den Prozess, der Sie zur endgültigen Version Ihrer Übersetzung geführt hat. Welche Schwierigkeiten sind im Zuge der Übersetzung aufgetreten und wie haben Sie diese bewältigt? Welche zusätzlichen Hilfsmittel haben Sie benutzt, um den Text ins Englische zu übertragen? Ergänzen Sie die zutreffenden Optionen.	About the translation process: How did you translate the text? Please underline the appropriate option. Without machine support With machine support (DeepL, https://www.deepl.com/de/translator) How long did the translation take you? Describe in broad terms the process that led you to the final version of your translation. Which difficulties arose during the translation process and how did you overcome them? Which additional tools did you use to translate the text into English? List the ones you used here.

[7] See https://www.parallelparliament.co.uk/lord/lord-thomas-of-gresford2/dept-debates/scotland-office?page=4 (retrieved on 07/05/2025)

German	English
Zur Person:	About the person:
Absolvieren Sie derzeit ein Bachelorstudium am INTRAWI[8]? Unterstreichen bzw. ergänzen Sie die zutreffenden Optionen.	Are you currently completing a bachelor's degree at INTRAWI? Underline or add the appropriate options.
Ja	Yes
Nein	No
Wenn ja, mit welchen Sprachen?	If yes, with which languages?
Wenn nein, was ist Ihre Studienrichtung?	If no, what is your field of study?
Im wievielten Semester sind Sie?	How many semesters have you been studying for your degree?

The answers to these questions highlight the diversity of the experiment participants' profiles. Except for one contributor, who was enrolled at another faculty but had selected our creative writing course as an elective module, all participants were pursuing a degree in translation studies either at the University of Innsbruck or elsewhere. They included students whose first language was German and who had selected English as one of their working languages alongside both regular and exchange students who were translating between two foreign languages. One student explicitly stated that they had transferred the poem from German to English via their mother tongue, Russian. Some experiment participants were only in their second semester, while others were at the final stages of their undergraduate degree. One participant also had a disability that required working at a slower pace. The diversity of this group could be seen as a limitation of the experiment, but as focus was not on analysing the experiment participants' performance, their diverse profiles can also be regarded as an asset, as in its heterogeneity the group is certainly representative of the cohort of students pursuing an undergraduate degree in translation studies. Nevertheless, the translation results have to be evaluated in light of the circumstances, which included varied prerequisites and levels of motivation for completing the task within the allocated time.

[8] Acronym stands for: Institut für Translationswissenschaft, University of Innsbruck, Austria

The time students stated to have invested in translating the poem or post-editing the automated translation ranged from approximately 30 minutes to 74 minutes. One participant from the PE group remarked that they did not even have remotely enough time to finish the task. As one of the main reasons mentioned for using NMT and other translation technologies even in literary translation, which was long regarded as one of the last resorts for HT, it is worth mentioning that the participants from the PE group complained as much about time constraints as the HT group. One member from the PE group explicitly stated that it was difficult to create a form-conscious version from the DeepL output, as it limited their choices, which can be regarded as echoing research about "priming effects" (see Kolb 2023, p. 55).

3. Theoretical foundation: a brief excursion to poetry translation with LLMs

While neither NMT systems nor LLMs can reliably recognise formal features in a source text and replicate them in translation, task-specific prompting allows users to introduce some formal elements in translation with LLMs. However, the output quality strongly depends on the quality of the prompts used. On October 30, 2024, the Grünbein poem that formed part of the classroom experiment outlined above was translated into English with ChatGPT 4o using two different prompts. To show the variability in performance, the same lines from the poem that were analysed previously will be displayed in Table 4 as they featured in the original poem, the unmodified DeepL version from June 23, 2023, and in two different LLM translations from October 30, 2024. The two LLM translations will also be accompanied by the associated prompts.

Table 4: DeepL vs ChatGPT results for the translation of Durs Grünbein's poem

Grünbein	Und dann kommt der heitere Teil vom Sterben. *Versöhnt* Mit dem Tag der Geschäfte verspricht und Verträge *bricht*, Drehst du dich früh aus dem Spiegel. Dein gebrauchtes *Gesicht*, Scharf rasiert, das dem *Quengeln* von innen *höhnt*, Gehört dem Empfangschef, der die Verhandlungen führt.

DeepL (June 23, 2023)	And then comes the cheerful part of dying. Reconciled With the day that promises business and breaks contracts, You turn early from the mirror. Your used face, Shaved sharp, that scoffs at the *querulous* from within, Belongs to the receptionist who negotiates.
ChatGPT 4o, version 1 (October 30, 2024)	*Prompt, Oct. 30, 2024, version ChatGPT 4o: "Please translate the following poem by Durs Grünbein into English:"* And then comes the cheerful part of dying. Reconciled With the day that promises deals and breaks contracts, You turn early away from the mirror. Your worn face, Clean-shaven, that sneers at the *whining* from within, Belongs to the receptionist who conducts the negotiations.
ChatGPT 4o, version 2 (October 30, 2024)	*Prompt, Oct. 30, 2024, version ChatGPT 4o: "You are an author and translator of poetry. Contemporary German poetry is your special area of interest. Please translate the following poem by Durs Grünbein into English, and try to find an equivalent for the poetic form used in the source text. In particular, try to recreate the occasional rhymes from the source text in your English translation. Take your time:"* And then comes the lighthearted side of dying, *resigned* To the day that makes deals and leaves contracts *behind*, You step out of the mirror. Your worn-out *face*, Smoothly shaved, mocks the inner *disgrace*, Belongs to the clerk who mediates talks.

While the limited space available in this contribution does not allow for a detailed discussion of the two LLM translations, some notable details will be highlighted. To begin with, version 1 created with ChatGPT 4o is very similar to the DeepL translation from 2023. This demonstrates that automated translation continues to homogenise translation output (see Daems 2022; Farrell 2018; Kolb 2023; Taivalkoski-Shilov 2019), which in the case of literary texts, unlike other domains, can substantially decrease the value of a translation. Furthermore, version 1 created with ChatGPT 4o does not contain any elements of poetic form, even though the prompt explicitly stated that the text to be translated was a poem. A more task-specific prompt like the one used to generate version 2, which gives the model an expert role and instructs it to generate a rhymed target text, allows users to create a translation which, like the original text, contains some end rhymes. However, as the end rhymes in the translation are not in the places that rhyme in the original poem, it can safely be assumed that ChatGPT 4o still lacks the analytical capacity to determine the form of a poem.

4. Recent research on Johann Nestroy's *Der Talisman* for an alternative outlook on literary translation with machine assistance

While in the classroom experiment presented in this contribution, the poem translations prepared without DeepL contained more creative shifts and adhered more closely to the poetic form used in the original poem, it should not be assumed that machine output is generally counterproductive in literary translation. Kolb, Dressler and Mattiello highlight the potentials of machine assistance in their research on English-language versions of Johann Nestroy's 1840 play *Der Talisman*, which several translators rendered into English, and of which a significant part is not written in standard German. Focusing on occasionalisms or neologisms of "temporary function" (2023, p. 543) that frequently occur in Nestroy's play, Kolb, Dressler and Mattiello found that automated translation occasionally offered literal and therefore novel target-language equivalents that human translators tended to avoid in favour of normalising translations.

Kolb, Dressler and Mattiello show that many of Nestroy's occasionalisms are compounds, meaning that the playwright often used a comparatively widespread word formation strategy in German that tends to be used with less liberty in English. Where such occasionalisms occurred, the target-language versions produced by DeepL and Google Translate fell into four different categories:

1. occasionalistic or literal translation (e.g., analogous compound in the target language, such as "hair powder soul," which was the DeepL output for "Haarpuderseele")
2. non-occasionalistic translation (e.g., syntactic phrase or other normalising strategy; one example is Google Translate's "hairdressing equipment" for "Friseurkastln")

3. omission (partial or full; for instance, DeepL suggested "ordinary soul" for "Ordinariseelerl," omitting the diminutive suffix in the second part of the compound)
4. errors (no examples included) (Kolb/Dressler/Mattiello 2023, p. 11).

Even though the examples mentioned here do not suggest that the machine output can be used unmodified by human translators where these occasionalisms are concerned, they indicate that these translations can sometimes serve as a source of inspiration. Kolb, Dressler and Mattiello conclude that "some literally translated occasionalistic MT compounds can indeed convey more of the humor, satire, and linguistic and philosophical wit contained in the original than normalising target solutions" (ibid., p. 25). In light of Kolb, Dressler and Mattiello's findings, the evidence gathered from the poetry translation experiment analysed in this contribution suggests that the value of automated translation for literary texts depends on the literary genre, the degree of originality of the source text and on the linguistic area of focus in question.

5. Conclusion

The analysis presented in this contribution allows the following preliminary conclusions to be drawn: Although automated translation may generally speed up translation processes, the amount of time saved strongly depends on the source text. Translation can probably be best accelerated for prose texts with few unconventional features, whereas the increase of translation speed is negligible when form-conscious texts are translated, especially if their degree of stylistic novelty is above average, as is the case with Grünbein's poem. The limitations an AI-assisted transfer imposes on literary translators for these text types mainly stems from the fact that automated translation tools are oblivious to formal stylistic devices, such as rhyme or metre, which are frequently used in poetry.

At a more general level, machine output can also be problematic because it pre-empts lexical and syntactic choices for which human translators might otherwise consider multiple varieties. Not only does this make it more difficult for translators to find their own literary voice, but it also obliterates the original authors' stylistic preferences. As far as a translator's creativity is concerned, the use of automated translation often has a homogenising and thus limiting effect. Despite the inevitable "priming" associated with post-editing literary translations (Kolb 2023, p. 55), when used purposefully, automated translation can also foster creativity in translation, even of poetry. As has been shown, this is especially the case at the level of expression. The observations gathered in this contribution indicate that the maximum benefits can be incurred from automated translation when, rather than transferring entire texts or passages, translators use automated translation for short passages or specific phrases from a text. In order to be able to make informed choices about when and where to use AI-based translation tools, however, prospective translators require hands-on, practical experience and critical reflection as an integral part of their training.

PETRA-E's framework of reference for the education and training of literary translators suggests that even at an early training stage (L2 level) literary translators should be familiar with CAT tools and be aware of the advancing automatisation of literary translation (PETRA-E). Thus, translator training should facilitate the skilful use of and critical reflection on automated translation tools for a variety of text types and at all stages of training. While both NMT systems and LLMs are currently oblivious to poetic form, which they cannot reliably analyse and replicate in translation, specific prompts allow users to create form-conscious target-language versions of the underlying source texts. This shows that it is vital for future language professionals to train efficient prompting as a skill. In conclusion, it can be established that in our increasingly AI-saturated world future translators must experiment with AI-based translation tools, even and especially when working on text types that highlight the limitations of these tools and the importance of well-informed human input.

Bibliography

Bayer-Hohenwarter, Gerrit (2011): "'Creative shifts' as a means of measuring and promoting translational creativity." *Meta* 56(3): pp. 663–92. https://doi.org/10.7202/1008339ar.

Daems, Joke (2022): "Dutch literary translators' use and perceived usefulness of technology." In: Hadley, James Luke / Taivalkoski-Shilov, Kristiina / Teixeira, Carlos S. C. / Toral, Antonio (Eds.): *Using technologies for creative-text translation*. New York / London: Routledge, pp. 40–65. https://doi.org/10.4324/9781003094159-3.

Farrell, Michael (2018). "Machine translation markers in post-edited machine translation output." In: Chambers, David / Drugan, Joanna / Esteves-Ferreira, João / Macan, Juliet M. / Mitkov, Ruslan / Stefanov, Olaf-Michael (Eds.): *Proceedings of the 40th Conference Translating and the Computer*, pp. 50–59, retrieved on 07/04/2025 from https://www.asling.org/tc40/wp-content/uploads/TC40-Proceedings.pdf.

Grünbein, Durs "(Thema)." *Lyrikline*, retrieved on 26/09/2023 from https://www.lyrikline.org/de/gedichte/thema-77.

Guerberof-Arenas, Ana / Toral, Antonio (2022): "Creativity in translation: Machine translation as a constraint for literary texts." *Translation Spaces* 11(2), pp. 184–212. https://doi.org/10.1075/ts.21025.gue.

Guerberof-Arenas, Ana / Toral, Antonio (2024): "To be or not to be: A translation reception study of a literary text translated into Dutch and Catalan using machine translation." *Target International Journal of Translation Studies* 36(2), pp. 215–244. https://doi.org/10.1075/target.22134.gue.

Hackenbuchner, Janiça / Krüger, Ralph (2023): "DataLitMT – Teaching data literacy in the context of machine translation literacy." In: Nurminen, Mary / Brenner, Judith / Koponen, Maarit / Latomaa, Sirkku / Mikhailov, Mikhail / Schierl, Frederike / Ranasinghe, Tharindu / Vanmassenhove, Eva / Vidal, Sergi Alvarez / Aranberri, Nora / Nunziatini, Mara / Escartín, Carla Parra / Forcada, Mikel / Popovic, Maja / Scarton, Carolina / Moniz, Helena (Eds.): Proceedings of the 24th annual conference of the European Association for Machine Translation, pp. 285–93, retrieved on 07/04/2025 from https://aclanthology.org/2023.eamt-1.28.

Kolb, Waltraud (2023): "'I am a bit surprised'." In: Rothwell, Andrew / Way, Andy / Youdale, Roy (Eds.): *Computer-assisted literary translation: The state of the art*. New York / London: Routledge, pp. 53–68. https://doi.org/10.4324/9781003357391-4.

Kolb, Waltraud / Dressler, Wolfgang U. / Mattiello, Elisa (2023): "Human and machine translation of occasionalisms in literary texts." *Target International Journal of Translation Studies* 35(4), pp. 540–572. https://doi.org/10.1075/target.21147.kol.

Krüger, Ralph (2023): "Artificial intelligence literacy for the language industry – with particular emphasis on recent large language models such as GPT-4." *Lebende Sprachen* 68(2), pp. 283–330. https://doi.org/10.1515/les-2023-0024.

Nitzke, Jean / Hansen-Schirra, Silvia / Canfora, Carmen (2019): "Risk management and post-editing competence." *The Journal of Specialised Translation* 31, pp. 239–259. https://www.jostrans.org/issue31/art_nitzke.pdf.

PETRA-E. "Framework of reference for the education and training of literary translators," retrieved on 26/10/2024 from https://petra-educationframework.eu/.

Seljan, Sanja / Dunđer, Ivan / Pavlovski, Marko (2020): "Human quality evaluation of machine-translated poetry." *IEEE Conference Publication / IEEE Xplore*, pp. 1040–1045. https://ieeexplore.ieee.org/document/9245436.

Taivalkoski-Shilov, Kristiina (2018): "Ethical issues regarding machine(-assisted) translation of literary texts." *Perspectives* 27(5), pp. 689–703. https://doi.org/10.1080/0907676x.2018.1520907.

"The Lyrikline Network," retrieved on 27/10/2024 from https://www.lyrikline.org/en/about/.

"quengeln." *Cambridge Dictionary*, Cambridge UP, retrieved on 03/10/2023 from https://dictionary.cambridge.org/de/worterbuch/deutsch-englisch/quengeln.

Zwischen „Horror“ und „Achterbahn der Gefühle“. Zur Einstellung von Studenten gegenüber dem Einsatz von KI-Lösungen im interlingualen Untertitelungsprozess

Marco Agnetta
Universität Innsbruck

ABSTRACT
This chapter presents a study on the attitudes of audiovisual translation students toward the use of AI within the interlingual subtitling process. It presents an experiment conducted in subtitling courses in four language pairs. The students' experience with AI solutions was reconstructed on the basis of notes and semi-structured focus group discussions and compared with data from screen recordings. The results of this first experiment with young prospective subtitlers show a rather negative attitude toward the use of AI in subtitling. Most participants prefer to do their own subtitling from scratch with little or no use of automated solutions. The reason for this lies in the multi-step nature of the machine process and its increased susceptibility to cascade errors, which stands in the way of a holistic human work process. The (multiple) pre- and post-editing of machine output, here referred to as "inter-editing," appears to be more time-consuming and cognitively demanding than a fully human translation. The participants also feel restricted in their choice of translation solutions.

Keywords: subtitling, AI, effort, inter-editing, user experience, AVT didactics

1. Zur Einführung

Die Modi der audiovisuellen Übersetzung (AVT), allen voran die Synchronisation und die Untertitelung, richten sich seit jeher nach den zeitgenössischen und sich stetig weiterentwickelnden technischen Möglichkeiten[1]. Doch es ist der Einsatz von KI-Lösungen – eine der neuesten Errungenschaften der Technik auf dem Gebiet der Texterstellung und des Kommunikationsdesigns im Allgemeinen –, der gegenwärtig in Begriff ist, das gesamte Ökosystem der transnationalen Film-, Fernsehen- und Webkultur zu verändern. Und das ist nicht nur die Folge der erheblichen Verbesserungen des maschinellen

[1] Bei den vorliegenden Ausführungen handelt es sich um eine erweiterte und ins Deutsche übersetzte Version von Agnetta (2025 i. Dr.).

Outputs, sondern auch der nennenswerten Entwicklungen auf dem Feld der intermodalen Transfers[2]: Automatic Speech Recognition (ASR), Speech-to-Text (STT), Text-to-Speech (TTS) usw.

Von der Erstellung bis zur Ausstrahlung audiovisueller Produkte werden etliche Prozesse zunehmend automatisiert. Gerade der Einsatz maschineller Übersetzungssysteme könnte dabei helfen, der mittlerweile sehr großen Nachfrage nach lokalisiertem audiovisuellem Material (vgl. Nikolic/Bywood 2021, S. 51) zu begegnen. Jedoch herrschen in einer Zeit, in der durch Menschen und vollautomatisch untertitelte Videos gleichzeitig existieren, ganz unterschiedliche Qualitätsstandards. Wie die mittlerweile flächendeckende automatische Untertitelung im Laienbereich, genauer auf den sozialen Plattformen, zeigt, stehen Fehlerfreiheit und Idiomatizität hinter einer ungefähren Verstehbarkeit häufig zurück. Auch fehlerhafte automatische (intralinguale) Untertitelungen werden als nützliches Zusatzangebot erachtet. Hier wird in der Regel kein Aufwand einer Überarbeitung des automatisch generierten Outputs betrieben. Untertitel für die Film-, Fernseh- und Festivalindustrie müssen hingegen nicht zuletzt als bezahlte Dienstleistung höheren Qualitätsansprüchen genügen.

Obwohl die Qualität des maschinengenerierten Outputs nicht einwandfrei ist, ist bei Kunden und in ‚der Öffentlichkeit' häufig die Rede davon, ein Post-Editing (PE) (seltener ein Pre-Editing) würde den Übersetzungsaufwand minimieren und damit zeitliche und finanzielle Ressourcen schonen. Abschnitt 2 der vorliegenden Untersuchung gibt Hinweise darauf, inwiefern wissenschaftliche Studien diese Ansicht stützen. Die Erfahrungen der professionellen Untertitler selbst, die in den Berufsverbänden eine Stimme finden, scheinen die Hypothese einer Effizienzsteigerung durch (teil-)automatisches Übersetzen jedenfalls nicht zu bestätigen, zumal Post-Editing-Aufträge in der Regel (viel) schlechter remuneriert werden als Übersetzungs- bzw. Untertitelungsprojekte (vgl. AVTE-MT 2021, S. 10). Schließlich fiele der Aufwand, der beim Untertiteln mittels KI eingespart würde, spätestes

2 Ausführungen Rokebys (o. J.) folgend, werden mit dem Begriff der „intermodalen" Übersetzung jene Transfers bezeichnet, die auf eine Änderung des Rezeptionsmodus (auditiv→visuell, visuell→taktil usw.) abzielen. Diese zur Reduktion kommunikativer Barrieren eingesetzten Verfahren sind zwar eng mit dem „intersemiotischen" Übersetzen (Jakobson 1959/1974: 155) verwandt, aber nicht deckungsgleich.

bei der Qualitätskontrolle durch den Redakteur wieder ins Gewicht (vgl. ibid., S. 7). Was für Produzenten scheinbar eine logistische und finanzielle Erleichterung darstellt, ist somit für die gesamte Menge an angestellten und selbständigen Dienstleistern sowie letztlich auch für den anspruchsvollen Rezipienten allerdings kaum hinnehmbar. Im Laienbereich hingegen, das heißt in audiovisuellen Produktionen von und/oder für Laien, die nicht den auf dem Filmmarkt gültigen Qualitätsmaximen entsprechen, scheint die vollständige Automatisierung der Untertitelung gegenwärtig ihren Siegeszug zu feiern. Während vorher die Produzenten solchen Materials offene Untertitel selbst erstellen mussten, bieten neuerdings immer mehr Plattformen (bspw. *Instagram*, *TikTok*) den *Creators* und neuerdings auch ganze Betriebssysteme (bspw. *Android*) allen Endnutzern eine automatische Untertitelung jeglicher Sprachausgabe an. Diese Funktion kann meistens nach Belieben hinzu- oder abgeschaltet werden. Die Auswirkungen dieser neuen Technologien auf den Arbeitsmarkt sind gewaltig, wie nicht zuletzt die alarmierenden Meldungen von den Arbeitnehmerverbänden zeigen (vgl. Agnetta 2025a). Für den Aufbau und Erhalt eines nachhaltigen, die Interessen aller Beteiligten im Auge behaltenden AVT-Marktes ist die Erforschung von Einstellungen gegenüber KI-Anwendungen in den Arbeitsläufen entsprechend tätiger Übersetzer essentiell.

Die folgenden Ausführungen limitieren sich auf die Darstellung der Einstellungen angehender Untertitler zum Einsatz von KI-Systemen bei der interlingualen Untertitelung. Sie ergänzen, wie der Stand der Forschung zeigt (Abschnitt 2), bereits existierende Untersuchungen zur Nutzererfahrung professioneller Untertitler. Dieser Fokus ergibt sich aus der häufig geäußerten Beobachtung, jüngere Untertitlergenerationen seien technikaffiner und tendierten im Untertitelungsprozesses damit auch zur selbstverständlichen Verwendung von KI-Tools (vgl. Jaki/Bolz/Röther 2024, 330). Er folgt zudem aus der Notwendigkeit, die Didaktik in diesem Bereich nach den Bedürfnissen dieser neuen Untertitler-Community auszurichten. Zunächst werden in Abschnitt 3 einige Unterschiede zwischen den durch Menschenhand und der maschinell erstellten Untertitel vorgestellt. Darauf aufbauend wird ein im Sommersemester 2024 an der Universität Innsbruck durchgeführtes Experiment vorgestellt, in dem beide Vorgehensweisen durch Studenten auf den Prüfstand gestellt wurden (s. Abschnitt 4). Insbesondere wurden studentische Erfahrungen mit dem Einsatz (semi-)automatischer Werkzeuge im Untertitelungsprozess gesammelt und dokumentiert. Im Vordergrund steht die Frage, ob eine Automatisierung einiger Schritte der interlingualen Untertitelung den Übersetzern die Arbeit erleichtert und ökonomischer gestaltet oder ob selbige dadurch eher aufwändiger wird (s. Abschnitt 5). Die Studie wird durch ein Fazit abgerundet, das auch einer AVT- und genauer einer Untertitelungsdidaktik, Anknüpfungspunkte liefert, um Studenten in diesem Feld zu den gegenwärtigen Potenzialen und Herausforderungen im Umgang mit KI-Systemen zu sensibilisieren.

2. Zum Stand der Forschung

Ganz oder teilweise maschinell erzeugte und gegebenenfalls durch einen humanen Akteur post-editierte Untertitel sind ein spannender Forschungsbereich, der sich methodologisch an der Schnittstelle zwischen produkt-, prozess- und akteursorientierten Ansätzen befindet. Produktorientiert ist die Beschreibung der Merkmale des maschinellen Outputs sowie die Rekonstruktion und Überprüfung der Faktoren, die dieses beeinflussen. Prozessorientiert ist bspw. der Nachvollzug des Ablaufs des Post-Editions-Prozesses, d. h. der humanen Interventionen, um maschinelles Output publikationsreif zu gestalten. Akteursorientiert ist der Ansatz, wenn er die Bedürfnisse, Einstellungen und das Verhalten der involvierten Parteien in den Vordergrund rückt.

Schon seit den 2000er Jahren wird zur Integration von MT in Untertitelungsabläufen geforscht (vgl. Bywood/Etchegoyhen/Georgakopoulou 2017; Melero/Oliver/Badia. 2006; Volk et al. 2010). Bei der Bewertung der Potenziale und Grenzen, die KI-Systeme für die AVT und insbesondere für die Untertitelung bieten, stellt sich nicht nur die Frage nach einer Produktivitätssteigerung. Im Sinne einer nachhaltigen, d. h. die Anliegen und Ängste aller involvierten Akteure berücksichtigenden, Lösung müssen auch die Erfahrungen von Humanübersetzern mit diesen Werkzeugen in den Fokus rücken. Die Produktivität von KI-Lösungen hängt nämlich nicht zuletzt auch davon ab, ob und wie sie sich in der Praxis bewähren, und das bedeutet unter anderem, ob Untertitler in ihrer Anwendung einen gesteigerten Wert sehen und KI-Lösungen daher freiwillig in ihren Arbeitsabläufen integrieren.

Eine erste Untersuchung zur Einstellung von Untertitlern zur MT ist im Rahmen des EU-geförderten SUMAT-Projekts entstanden (vgl. Etchegoyhen et al. 2014). Analysiert wurde hier die (statistische) maschinelle Untertitelung in 7 Sprachenpaaren und 11 Übersetzungsrichtungen (en→nl, en↔fr, en↔de, en→po, en↔es, en→sv; sr↔sl), die dann von professionellen Untertitlern evaluiert wurden. Die Übersetzung der von einem Menschen erstellten intralingualen Untertitel wurde durch ein satzbasiertes statistisches maschinelles Übersetzungsverfahren erstellt; die dafür benötigten Korpora wurden für das Projekt eigens zugeschnitten[3]. Die Datenerhebung erfolgte mittels Fragebögen. Eines der bemerkenswerten Ergebnisse dieser Studie ist, dass die Arbeit mit der maschinell erzeugten Übersetzung (mit 2.37 von 5 Punkten) sowie deren Qualität (mit 2.18 von 5 Punkten) tendenziell negativ bewertet wurde, obwohl es durchschnittlich zu einer nicht unerheblichen Produktivitätssteigerung (ca. 40 % mehr Untertitel in der gleichen Zeit) kam (vgl. Etchegoyhen et al. 2014, S. 50 und 52–53).

Matusov, Wilken und Georgakopoulou (2019) gehen prinzipiell davon aus, dass nur „customized systems“, d. h. individuell zugeschnittene Übersetzungssysteme, zu einer erhöhten Bereitschaft bei Untertitlern führen, KI-Lösungen in ihren Arbeitsabläufen zu integrieren. Dementsprechend dient die Nutzerbefragung (zwei professionelle Untertitler, ein Sprachenpaar und eine Übersetzungsrichtung: en→le) am Ende ihrer Studie hauptsächlich dazu, ein individualisiertes neuronales System hinsichtlich der allgemeinen Qualität sowie der vorgeschlagenen Lösung zur Segmentierung von Untertiteln zu evaluieren. Bei den beiden Studienteilnehmern ließ sich eine geringfügige Effizienzsteigerung und Zeitersparnis vor allem bei der Verwendung solcher personalisierter Systeme beobachten. Auch hier waren von einem Menschen erstellte ausgangssprachliche Untertitel die Basis für die maschinelle Übersetzung in die Zielsprache.

Eine weitere Studie zur Nutzererfahrung von zwölf professionellen Untertitlern in zwei Sprachenpaaren und vier Übersetzungsrichtungen (fi↔en, fi↔sv) präsentieren Koponen et al. (2020). Die Teilnehmer mussten

---

[3] Zur individuellen Anpassung statistischer maschineller Übersetzungssysteme und deren Nutzen für den Untertitelungsprozess vgl. Müller/Volk (2013) und de Sousa/Aziz/Specia (2011, S. 98).

maschinell übersetzte Untertitel post-editieren und ihre Erfahrungen dokumentieren. Auch hier basierten die maschinell erzeugten zielsprachlichen Untertitel auf ausgangssprachlichen Untertiteln, die von einem Menschen erstellt wurden. Ihre Daten erhoben die Autoren mittels Keylogging sowie Fragebögen und Interviews. Die benutzten Untertitelungsprogramme waren Wincaps Q4 oder Spot.

Ähnlich ist auch der Ansatz von Karakanta et al. (2022). Diese führten eine Befragung von 22 professionellen Untertitlern durch, die in sieben Sprachenpaaren und 8 Übersetzungsrichtungen (es↔en, es→it, es→de, it→fr, en→fr, en→pl, en→nl) tätig sind[4]. Die Datenerhebung erfolgte über Fragebögen, die nach der Durchführung eines Übersetzungsauftrags mit Hilfe des Untertitelungs-Tools *Matesub* zu beantworten waren. Während die bisher vorgestellten Untersuchungen auf das Post-Editing von maschinell übersetzten Untertiteln, die allerdings auf von einem Menschen erstellten intralingualen Untertiteln basieren, präsentieren Karakanta et al. die Einstellungen der Versuchsteilnehmer hinsichtlich gänzlich maschinell erzeugter, das bedeutet auch automatisch transkribierter, gespotteter und segmentierter, Untertitel. In ihrem Versuchsaufbau bewerten die Übersetzer die automatischen Untertitel eher neutral bis positiv und damit als annehmbaren Ausgangspunkt für den eigenen Untertitelungsprozess.

Zuletzt ist die Studie von Orel Kos (2024) zu erwähnen. Sie vergleicht den Translationsprozess (hier insbesondere die Entscheidungsfindung) und die Merkmale des Translationsprodukts von 10 Übersetzungsstudenten im ersten Masterjahr, die Untertitel mithilfe des maschinellen Übersetzungstools DeepL erstellen sollten (Experiment von 2022/23), mit dem von 15 Studenten, die diese ohne den Rekurs auf neuronale MÜ verfassten (Experiment von 2021). Die verwendete Untertitelungssoftware war *Subtitle Edit*; jedoch sollten die Versuchsteilnehmer im Experiment von 2023 nicht die integrierten Transkriptions- und Übersetzungsfunktionen verwenden, sondern bei der Übersetzung der gelieferten zeitkodierten englischen Untertitel auf das neuronale Online-Übersetzungstool DeepL zurückgreifen, das Output post-editieren und gemäß den üblichen formalen Vorgaben dem Master-Template

4 Fragebogen und Auswertung finden sich auf folgender Seite: <https://github.com/fatalinha/subtitlers-have-a-say> (26.07.2024).

anpassen. Als zu untertitelndes Material dienten in beiden Experimenten Szenen aus der Liebeskomödie *And So It Goes* (2014). An dieser kleinen Population ließen sich bereits einige interessante, aber noch zu verifizierende Beobachtungen anstellen: Bei den Studenten, die mit der Post-Edition beauftragt wurden, ließen sich klare Priming-Effekte erkennen (Orel Kos 2024, S. 192–193), die sich auf ein Übervertrauen (*overreliance*)[5] auf die maschinell erzeugte Ausgabe zurückführen lassen (ibid., S. 198) und die sich in einer auffälligen, häufig unidiomatisch zu nennenden Nähe zum Ausgangstext manifestieren. Währenddessen gelangten die von Null auf selbst übersetzenden Studenten auf der Basis der eigenen Erfahrung[6] zu idiomatischeren und zugleich kreativeren Lösungen. Überdies wurden Merkmale der Filmdialoge ausfindig gemacht, bei denen die neuronale MÜ an ihre Grenzen stößt und die für Humanübersetzer mit einer gewissen Kontextsensibilität nicht oder nur selten ein Problem darstellen, nämlich im Bereich von Geschlechterzuweisungen, Numerus (ibid., S. 195), Förmlichkeitsmarker und Anredeformen, Modalverben, Polysemie, bildliche Sprache sowie Schimpf- und Tabuwörter (ibid., S. 194–200).

Die vorliegende Untersuchung möchte in mehrfacher Hinsicht die beschriebenen Ansätze ergänzen, und zwar sowohl hinsichtlich der Zielsetzung, der erforschten Gruppe, des eingesetzten Programms zur automatischen Untertitelung als auch der Datenerhebungsmethode. Mit den erhobenen Daten sollen im vorliegenden Artikel die Einstellungen von Untertitelungsstudenten gegenüber dem Post-Editing automatisch erstellter Untertitel gesammelt und in ihren Tendenzen beschrieben werden (s. Abschnitt 5.1). Um nicht allein subjektive Einschätzungen zu beschreiben, wird in einem weiteren Schritt exemplarisch untersucht, inwieweit diese Einschätzungen mit real messbaren Größen in Verbindung stehen – in diesem Fall wurden perzipierter und realer zeitlicher Aufwand zueinander in Beziehung gesetzt (s. Abschnitt 5.2).

---

5 Dieses Übervertrauen ist nicht nur im Übersetzungsbereich, sondern auch bei maschinengestützten Dolmetschen zu beobachten (vgl. Defrancq/Fantinuoli, 2021, S. 92–93, 98–99; Prandi 2015, S. 53–54; Prandi 2023, S. 242).

6 Auf die Wichtigkeit des Erfahrungsschatzes eines Übersetzers, dessen Fehlen sich bei der KI-gestützten oder generierten Übersetzung fatal auswirkt, weist Mjölsnes (2022, S. 23–26) hin.

Viele der bisherigen Arbeiten rücken mit den professionellen Untertitlern zu Recht die Berufsgruppe in den Fokus, die wohl primär von den gegenwärtigen technischen Neuerungen bei der Untertitelung betroffen ist. In der vorliegenden Studie stehen hingegen wie bei Orel Kos (2024) angehende Untertitler im Mittelpunkt. Diese werden jetzt schon, spätestens aber in ihrem Arbeitsalltag sicherlich mit den rasanten Entwicklungen im Bereich der Untertitelung mittels KI in Berührung kommen. Die Einstellung gegenüber den sich abzeichnenden Tendenzen beeinflusst u. a. den Studienabschluss und die anschließende Berufswahl. Davon ausgehend, dass Studenten mit der Zeit und insbesondere seit der Pandemie ohnehin maschinelle Übersetzungssysteme verwenden, ist eine Thematisierung und eine konstruktive Arbeit mit dieser Technologie im Untertitelungsunterricht in hohem Maße gewinnbringend (Orel Kos 2024, S. 189) – und zwar nicht nur für die Studenten selbst, sondern auch für die sich in diesem Bereich verortende AVT-Didaktik und die entsprechende Forschung.

Es sei explizit erwähnt, dass es hier vordergründig um die Einstellungen angehender Humanübersetzer gegenüber KI-generierter Untertitel geht. Eine allgemeine Evaluation jeder Form von digitaler Arbeitsumgebung, die für die meisten Untertitler wohl jetzt schon die Realität darstellt, steht hier nicht zur Debatte. Die Anwendung von (lokalen oder cloud-basierten) CAT-Tools und Translationsmanagement-Systemen ist in der AVT nun schon längere Zeit gang und gäbe. Deren Nutzen – gemessen an Produktivitäts- und Effizienzsteigerung – für den Untertitler ist bekannt (vgl. Georgakopoulou 2019, S. 519; Granell/Chaume 2023, S. 21). Wie die Statements der AVT-Verbände zeigen, bezieht sich die Kritik der Arbeitnehmer an maschinellen Übersetzungssystemen (die u. a. auf generative KI zurückgreifen) ohnehin nicht so sehr auf die Tools und deren Weiterentwicklung selbst, sondern darauf, dass diese Entwicklungen von bestimmten Akteuren (Kunden, Entwicklern und sogar der Öffentlichkeit) auf mehreren Ebenen dazu genutzt werden, die Bezahlung der und die Wertschätzung gegenüber den in der Branche Tätigen herabzusetzen (vgl. Agnetta 2025a: 20).

Auch die Zielsetzung der folgenden Ausführungen ist im Vergleich zu den oben angeführten Studien eine andere: Sie münden nicht in konkreten Vorschlägen zur Verbesserung von untertitelungsspezifischen KI-Lösungen, sondern sie wollen rein deskriptiv vorgehen und lediglich punktuell einige Ausgangspunkte für den Umgang der AVT-Didaktik mit diesem Thema erwähnen.

3. Zur automatischen Untertitelung

Die interlinguale Untertitelung ist eine komplexe Operation, die vom Untertitler gleich mehrere Rücksichtnahmen einfordert (vgl. exemplarisch Díaz-Cintas/Remael 2021, S. 91–144). Ihre Automatisierung macht eine Umstrukturierung des Untertitelungsprozesses erforderlich, die im Wesentlichen in einer strikten Aufteilung dieser Aufgabe in separate und aufeinander aufbauende Arbeitspakete besteht.

Ein mit untertitelungsspezifischen CAT-Tools ausgestatteter Humanübersetzer ist zumeist nicht auf die durchgehende und kleinschrittige Aufteilung seiner Arbeit angewiesen. Zwar sind das Hörverstehen, die eventuelle Transkription des Originaldialogs, die Übersetzung, das Spotting (d. h. die Synchronisierung des Titels mit dem Bildmaterial) und Splitting (d. h. die Aufteilung der Untertitel in semantisch zusammengehörende Segmente) sowie die Kürzung Phasen, die im wissenschaftlichen Diskurs und im untertitelungsdidaktischen Kontext als getrennte Aufgaben konzeptualisiert und zunächst auch separat voneinander eingeübt werden können. Jedoch ist die Arbeitsweise (erfahrener) Untertitler in der Regel eine ganzheitliche: All die oben genannten Operationen werden nahezu simultan für jeden einzelnen Untertitel durchgeführt. Wenn dem Untertitler nicht bereits eine in Form eines Master-Templates vorgespottete Filmdatei vorliegt, ist das Spotting dank Wave-Darstellung des Audio-File trotzdem vergleichsweise einfach zu bewerkstelligen. Hierbei kann der Humanübersetzer leicht zwischen Dialogen, Musik und anderen Geräuschen unterscheiden, sodass ein fehlerhaftes Spotting die Ausnahme ist. Eine Rückbindung an das polysemiotische bzw. multimodale Ganze ist hier jederzeit gegeben. Auf eine Transkription des Originaldialogs wird, zumal wenn ein Dialogbuch oder ein Skript vorliegt, in der Regel gänzlich verzichtet. Die Originalaussage wird intuitiv (d. h. ganzheitlich) erfasst und durch eine zielsprachliche Formulierung wiedergegeben, die dem Register des Originals Rechnung trägt. Der Einsatz von Termdatenbanken, Translation-Memory-Systemen, Wörterbüchern und anderen Recherchewerkzeugen läuft nebenbei und kommt – je nach Filmgenre – mehr oder weniger punktuell zum Tragen. Eine erste zielsprachliche Lösung, die nicht den spatio-temporalen Erfordernissen der Untertitelung entspricht (Anzahl der Zeichen und Zeilen, CPS – *characters per second*, Standzeiten etc.), kann gerade in einer computergestützten Arbeitsumgebung sukzessive angepasst werden.

Die Qualitätssicherung erfolgt in der Regel durch einen Untertitlerkollegen oder Redakteur.

Eine automatisierte Untertitelung muss demgegenüber kleinschrittiger vorgehen. Und in dieser Mehrschrittigkeit liegt u. a. auch die Fehleranfälligkeit der maschinellen Untertitelung begründet. Es entsteht ein Kaskadenmodell wie das folgende: Zunächst muss der gesamte (eingespeiste) Originaldialog über eine automatische Spracherkennung (ASR) verarbeitet werden. Dabei werden den gesprochenen akustischen Signalen Zeitstempel (*time stamps*) zugewiesen (ähnlich dem Timecode, mit dem in nahezu allen Modi der AVT gearbeitet wird). Der erkannte Dialog wird in eine Textdatei umgewandelt (STT). Diese Textfassung fungiert als intralingualer Untertitelungstext, der in einem weiteren Schritt zwar in eine andere Sprache übersetzt, jedoch nicht mehr zeitlich angepasst wird. Ein falsches Spotting, das sich u. a. in *false negatives* (das Fehlen von Untertiteln, wenn gesprochen wird) oder *false positives* (das Vorliegen von Untertiteln, wenn nicht gesprochen wird) (vgl. Karakanta et al. 2022, S. 266) manifestiert, ist daher in der zielsprachlich untertitelten Version nicht unüblich. Die Übersetzung läuft als separater Schritt maschinell ab. Heutzutage scheint die neuronale MT die (satz- oder text-basierte) statistische MT, die hier längere Zeit maßgebend war, weitgehend abgelöst zu haben[7]. Was bei der Spracherkennung als erstem Schritt schon nicht richtig erkannt wurde, kann auch nicht richtig übersetzt werden. Auch kann es trotz richtiger ASR zu falschen Übersetzungen kommen, etwa wenn das Übersetzungsprogramm eine Übersetzungslösung vorschlägt, die nicht kontextsensibel ist und/oder nicht den sonstigen visuellen und akustischen Komponenten des zu untertitelnden Materials passt. Insgesamt scheinen Übersetzungen eher wörtlich angelegt zu sein. In der Regel passen die in der Praxis genutzten Programme die Untertitel nur sehr bedingt an die Richtlinien und Gegebenheiten des audiovisuellen Materials an. Die in jedem Untertitelungsauftrag an einigen Stellen unausweichlichen Kürzungen oder Umformatierungen und individuelle Positionierungen von Untertiteln müssen daher weiterhin von menschlichen Akteuren vorgenommen werden. Letzteres würde eine automatische Bilderkennung voraussetzen und damit

[7] Zu den unterschiedlichen Formen der MT im Bereich der Untertitelung vgl. Karakanta (2022, S. 92–93).

potenziell eine weitere Variable in den Workflow integrieren, die sowohl zur Verbesserung des Outputs führen als auch eine neue Fehlerquelle hinzufügen kann.

Die Maschine benötigt also all diese Zwischenstationen, weil die Ausgabe eines Verfahrens den Input für das nächste darstellt. Ein Merkmal solcher maschineller Kaskadenprozesse ist dabei, dass jede einzelne der oben genannten Operationen von der Maschine für den ganzen Text durchgeführt wird, bevor die nächste begonnen wird. Und bei jedem Schritt wird mit dem Output weitergearbeitet, der im vorausgegangenen Schritt ausgegeben wurde – unabhängig von dessen Qualität. Auf diese Weise kommt es häufig zu Kaskadenfehlern, also Fehlern, die auf einen vorausgegangenen Arbeitsschritt zurückzuführen sind. Das maschinell erzeugte Endprodukt ist umso besser, je besser das Ergebnis der einzelnen Teilschritte ist. Derart plakativ konstatiert scheint dies eine Binsenwahrheit zu sein. Bei solch mehrschrittigen Verfahren wie der eben beschriebenen automatischen Untertitelung hat eine solche Beobachtung allerdings weitreichende Konsequenzen. Zwar bedeutet das, dass man durch geeignete Maßnahmen bei der Vorbereitung des Inputs und der Nachbereitung des Outputs das Ergebnis eines jeden Teilschrittes steuern kann, etwa durch die Anpassung der für das Training neuronaler Netzwerke notwendigen annotierten Korpora, durch die Benutzung von Aufnahmen in Studioqualität ohne Störgeräusche, die Vereinfachung des Ausgangstextes usw. Doch dies bedeutet auch, dass ein zufriedenstellendes Ergebnis gegenwärtig nur durch die ressourcenintensive Hintereinanderschaltung mehrerer Pre- und Post-Editing-Schleifen erreicht werden kann, die bis dato der Aufmerksamkeit (mindestens) eines menschlichen (Untertitelungs-)Experten bedürfen. Das Post-Editing des ASR-Outputs ist zugleich ein Pre-Editing des zu übersetzenden Textes. Wir sprechen daher im Weiteren in Bezug auf diese zwischengeschalteten qualitätssichernden Maßnahmen von einem Zwischen- oder Inter-Editing.

Auch wenn die Maschine die Zwischenschritte innerhalb von Sekunden durchführt, stellt sich bei alledem doch die Frage, ob ein (menschliches) Zwischen-Editing von Teilergebnissen, wie etwa einer Speech-to-Text-Transkription, den Aufwand rechtfertigt, den es verursacht. Eine kleinschrittige Arbeit erscheint den im Kontext dieser Studie befragten Untertitlern meistens eher kontraproduktiv. Eine (zumindest perzipierte) Effizienzminderung ist denn auch der von den Versuchsteilnehmern am häufigsten genannte

Grund dafür, dass sie von maschinellen Untertitelungslösungen bisher nicht überzeugt sind. Dies schlägt sich in einer eher negativen Grundeinstellung der Übersetzer gegenüber den in der Untertitelungssoftware eingebetteten KI-Lösungen nieder. Der punktuelle Einsatz externer KI-Lösungen (etwa das Youtube-Transkript oder DeepL-Übersetzungen[8]) gilt hingegen als weniger problematisch – wahrscheinlich weil er nur auf bestimmte Passagen limitiert ist und daher auch kognitiv weniger Ressourcen bindet.

Daraus ergibt sich folgende Beobachtung: KI-Systeme werden dort konsultiert, wo das Output vielversprechend erscheint. Eine mögliche Lösung für die Schonung zeitlicher und kognitiver Ressourcen beim Zwischen-Editing, die sicher weiterzuverfolgen ist, ist daher die des „Filtering", die man bei Etchegoyhen et al. (2014, S. 49–50, 52) beschrieben findet: Dort ließ sich eine Produktivitätssteigerung bei der semiautomatischen Untertitelung dadurch erzielen, dass dem Untertitler nur jene maschinell übersetzten Textelemente vorgesetzt wurden, die nach einer automatisch durchgeführten Qualitätseinschätzung einen gewissen Wert nicht unterschritten. Es werden also nur diejenigen Ergebnisse weitergetragen, die eine gewisse Qualität und damit eine erhöhte Chance auf Beibehaltung haben. An dem Grad der Beibehaltung bzw. an der Notwendigkeit anzubringender Veränderungen wird ja für gewöhnlich ein verminderter Aufwand und damit eine gute Qualität des maschinellen Outputs gemessen. Dieses Filtering könnte bezüglich jedes automatischen Zwischenschritts, also nicht nur bei der Übersetzung, vorgenommen werden, etwa bei der Bewertung der automatischen Spracherkennung und des automatischen Spotting bzw. Splitting.

Beim Vergleich menschlicher und automatischer Übersetzungsprozesse ist man manchmal dazu verleitet, die Mängel im maschinellen Output auf die Schwierigkeit des Übersetzungsmodus zurückzuführen. Es ist zwar wahr, dass Textverständnis, Spotting und Splitting auch für den selbständig untertitelnden Humanübersetzer herausfordernd sind, wie eine Versuchsperson bestätigt (ES-DE_A_01: „Der […] Redner hat sehr schnell und ohne Pausen geredet, es war schwer, alles unterzubekommen und richtig zu spotten"). Allerdings besteht ja gerade die hermeneutische Aufgabe und das Ethos des

---

[8] In unserem Korpus waren dies ES-DE_A_01 (DeepL), DE-FR_A_01 (Youtube).

Untertitlers darin, angesichts der Herausforderungen des Materials, funktionierende (Kompromiss-)Lösungen zu finden. Dem Übersetzer die Mittel an die Hand zu geben, um entsprechende Entscheidungen zu treffen und so zur Mündigkeit zu verhelfen, ist ja gerade der höhere Zweck der (universitären) Translatorenausbildung. Die Maschine ist nicht dahingehend konzipiert, auf der Grundlage statistischer Wahrscheinlichkeiten ausgewählte Übersetzungslösungen zu hinterfragen. Wenn nicht ein humaner Akteur eingreift, arbeitet sie auch mit fehlerhaften Ergebnissen weiter.

4. Zum Experiment

Das nachfolgend beschriebene Untertitelungsexperiment wurde im Sommersemester 2024, genauer in den Monaten Mai und Juni, am Institut für Translationswissenschaft der Universität Innsbruck durchgeführt. Es fand in zwei aufeinanderfolgenden Sitzungen (30 + 90 Minuten) im Rahmen von regulären, d. h. über das ganze Semester laufenden Untertitelungskursen statt. Diese werden in Innsbruck sprachenpaarspezifisch angeboten und sind unmittelbar praktisch angelegt. Studenten des Masterstudiengangs *Translationswissenschaft* lernen in diesem Kurs die spezifischen Herausforderungen des Untertitelns sowie den Umgang mit Untertitelungssoftwares. Viele von ihnen sind in der Spezialisierung *Literarisches und Audiovisuelles Übersetzen* eingeschrieben und können potenziell als angehende Untertitler betrachtet werden. Sie sind geradezu prädestiniert für eine Befragung hinsichtlich der aktuellen technischen Möglichkeiten auf dem Gebiet der interlingualen Untertitelung – u. a. weil gerade jüngere Translatorengenerationen Berührungen mit KI-gestützten Anwendungen nicht scheuen (vgl. Karakanta et al. 2022, S. 268; Orel Kos 2024, S. 199). Je nach Studienkombination können im Studiengang *Translationswissenschaft* einer bis vier Untertitelungskurse (je zwei in den zwei Arbeitssprachen) belegt werden. Insgesamt haben 24 Studenten aus fünf Kursen am Experiment teilgenommen. Zwei Datensätze waren aufgrund fehlerhafter Bildschirmaufzeichnung nicht auswertbar. Wir arbeiten im Folgenden daher mit 22 Datensätzen.

In der ersten der beiden für dieses Experiment veranschlagten Unterrichtsstunden (ca. 30 Min.) hat der Autor dieser Studie die Untertitelungssoftware und die darin enthaltenen Funktionen zur automatischen Texterkennung und Übersetzung vorgestellt. Für das Experiment wurde das Desktop-Programm *Subtitle Edit* verwendet, das als Open-Source-Lösung bereits seit längerem Bestandteil der Untertitelungskurse in Innsbruck ist und – anders als die ebenfalls benutzte, offen zugängliche Software *Aegisub* – seit der 3.6.5-Version (März 2022) auch die automatisierte Erstellung von Speech-to-Text-Transkriptionen sowie die neuronale maschinelle Übersetzung von und in die hier analysierten Sprachen (EN, DE, IT, ES, FR) integriert. In dieser Unterrichtsstunde hatten die Teilnehmer genügend Zeit, sich mit dem Tool auseinanderzusetzen und Rückfragen zu stellen, damit jeder für den eigentlichen Untertitelungsauftrag gerüstet war, der als Heimarbeit zu bearbeiten war. Die Spracherkennung erfolgte über die Audio-to-text-library und das Toolkit Vosk/Kaldi, die Übersetzung über das integrierte lizenzfreie MT-System Google Translate (V1 API). Damit ist eine Softwarelösung favorisiert worden, in der die Daten, mit denen die Maschine trainiert wird, nicht individuell auf die Untertitelungsaufgabe zugeschnitten worden sind. Zwar ist es wahr, dass sowohl bei ASR als auch bei MT die Qualität des maschinellen Outputs von der Quantität und Qualität des Materials abhängt, mit dem man das System trainiert hat, und dass die Güte der vom Programm generierten Untertitel ebenso unmittelbar davon abhängt. Wir verlassen uns hier aber bewusst auf die Lösungen einer handelsüblichen und in der Übersetzerzunft verbreiteten Software, die sowohl ein automatisches intralinguales Transkript der Videodatei als auch eine automatische Übersetzung in die gewünschte Zielsprache verspricht.

Der Auftrag bestand darin, eine hochwertige, genaue und idiomatische interlinguale Untertitelung eines ca. 1,5-minütigen Ausschnitts von Youtube-Videos zu erstellen und sich dabei mit einem Screen-Recorder aufzunehmen (hier wurde die Software *oCam* vorgeschlagen). Zweck dabei war, den gesamten Untertitelungsprozess nachvollziehen zu können und zu bestimmen, welche Tools im Verlaufe der Untertitelung von den Studenten genutzt werden.

Die zu untertitelnden Videos wurden über Link verschickt und mussten von den Teilnehmern heruntergeladen werden. Im Hinblick auf Thema und Genre der Videos wurde auf Einheitlichkeit gesetzt: In ihnen kommen informierte Laien oder Experten im dokumentarischen Stil zu den Auswirkungen des KI-Einsatzes für kreative Berufszweige zu Wort. Durch die Wahl vergleichbarer Videos wurde nicht nur der Aktualitätsbezug, sondern auch eine gewisse Neuartigkeit der verwendeten Terminologie garantiert. Insgesamt wurde bei der Auswahl der Videoausschnitte darauf geachtet, dass sie bestimmte Herausforderungen bereithalten, etwa eine hohe Informationsdichte und Schnelligkeit des Gesprochenen, Fachsprachlichkeit, Verwendung von Eigennamen etc., um evaluieren zu können, wie Mensch und Maschine mit diesen umgehen. Es wurden allerdings nur in Studioqualität aufgenommene Videos ausgewählt, in denen sich der Sprecher klar und akzentlos in der jeweiligen Standardvarietät zum Thema äußert. Damit wurde von Vornherein ein fehlerreduziertes Ergebnis bei der automatischen Spracherkennung angestrebt. In der Gruppendiskussion (s. u.) wurde jedoch explizit darauf hingewiesen, dass bei anderen Medien Rauschen, Hintergrundgeräusche, Akzente, Stimmverzerrung, Gesang etc. die Spracherkennung womöglich trüben können.

Um die sprachenübergreifende Vergleichbarkeit der Untertitelungen zu gewährleisten, wurden auch die Einstellungen im Programm einheitlich gehalten. Diese mussten vor dem Untertitelungsauftrag auf folgende Werte gesetzt werden: Die Untertitel durften maximal zweizeilig sein; die Einzelzeile durfte eine Länge von 40 Zeichen (inklusive Leerzeichen) nicht überschreiten. Optimalerweise musste mit 15 CPS, maximal aber mit 17 CPS gearbeitet werden. Die Untertitel mussten mindestens eine Sekunde und durften höchsten 6 Sekunden eingeblendet sein. Der Abstand zwischen zwei Untertiteln sollte mindestens 15 Millisekunden betragen. Für die Bearbeitung des Untertitelungsauftrags wurden kein Zeitlimit gesetzt: Jeder Untertitler durfte daheim in seinem eigenen Tempo arbeiten und auch Pausen machen. Einzige Bedingung war, dass die Bildschirmaufnahme immer dann mitlief, wenn an der Untertitelung gearbeitet wurde.

Die Teilnehmer durften sich selbständig in zwei etwa gleich große Gruppen aufteilen: Gruppe A (n_A=9) sollte ohne die Zuhilfenahme automatischer Untertitelungs-Tools arbeiten und von Grund auf selbständig spotten und übersetzen. Online-Wörterbücher und andere Recherchewerkzeuge waren erlaubt. Gruppe A diente in diesem Versuchsaufbau als Kontrollgruppe[9]. Gruppe B (n_B=13) sollte hingegen mit den automatischen Untertitelungs-Tools von *Subtitle Edit* arbeiten, d. h. die Studenten sollten die im Programm

---

9 Zwei der neun Studenten der Gruppe A entschieden sich beim Untertiteln von der Pike auf für die Arbeit mit der ihnen bekannteren Software *Aegisub*, was angesichts der Ähnlichkeit zu *Subtitle Edit* in dieser Gruppe nicht ins Gewicht fiel.

eingebettete automatische Texterkennung (Vosk/Kaldi) und automatische Übersetzung (Google Translate V1 API) durchführen. Die Aufgabe war in dieser Gruppe also weniger eine reine Übersetzungs- als eine Post-Editing-Aufgabe. Da das Ergebnis in beiden Gruppen eine genaue und idiomatische Untertitelung darstellen sollte, musste es sich in Gruppe B um ein *full post-editing* handeln[10]. Auch hier war die Benutzung von Online-Wörterbüchern und anderen Recherchewerkzeugen zusätzlich erlaubt.

Unter Berücksichtigung der Sprachenpaare – untertitelt wird in der Regel in die Muttersprache, und die Kurse wurden nicht nur von deutschen Muttersprachlern belegt – sowie der Aufteilung auf die Gruppen A und B ergibt sich folgende Verteilung der Versuchsteilnehmer (Tabelle 1):

Tabelle 1: Teilnahmen am Experiment nach Sprachenpaar, Übersetzungsrichtung und Aufteilung in Gruppe A (ohne KI) und Gruppe B (mit KI)

Sprachenpaar	Übersetzungs richtung	Gruppe A	Gruppe B	Total
en↔de	en→de	3	5	**8**
	de→en	1	1	**2**
es↔de	es→de	1	3	**4**
	de→es	–	1	**1**
fr↔de	fr→de	1	1	**2**
	de→fr	1	1	**2**
it↔de	it→de	1	1	**2**
	de→it	1	–	**1**
		9	**13**	**22**

Jedem Teilnehmer wurde nach folgendem Muster ein Kürzel zugewiesen, bspw. „EN-DE_B_05", was so viel bedeutet wie: Übersetzungsrichtung Englisch→Deutsch, Gruppe B, Teilnehmer 5. Zwei Studenten haben zweimal am Experiment teilgenommen, und zwar in unterschiedlichen Sprachenpaaren und unterschiedlichen Gruppen (EN-DE_A_02 = ES-DE_B_02; EN-DE_B_03 = FR-DE_A_01).

[10] Zu den verschiedenen Arten des Post-Editings vgl. Nitzke/Hansen-Schirra (2021, S. 29–33).

Während des Untertitelungsprozesses (oder unmittelbar danach) sollten die Versuchsteilnehmer Selbstreports[11] zu den gemachten Erfahrungen abfassen, die einer späteren Gruppendiskussion dienen konnten. Diese fand in der Stunde nach der Heimarbeit statt (90 Min.). In dieser Gruppendiskussion wurden die Ergebnisse der praktischen Arbeit mit dem Untertitelungstool gesammelt und zur Diskussion gestellt. Dieses Gruppengespräch wurde vom Versuchsleiter und Autor des vorliegenden Artikels aufgenommen. Die Teilnehmer wurden über Sinn und Zweck des Experiments aufgeklärt. Sowohl die Teilnahme an der Gruppendiskussion als auch die Abgabe der Bildschirmaufzeichnungen, der Untertiteldateien und der Notizen zu den eigenen Erfahrungen waren stets freiwillig. Die thematische Auswertung der Gruppendiskussion erfolgte nach der Transkription in anonymisierter Form. Von allen Teilnehmern liegen Einverständniserklärungen zur Nachnutzung der erhobenen Daten vor.

Die im Kontext des beschriebenen Experiments erhobenen Forschungsdaten umfassen also die Untertitelungsdateien und die Bildschirmaufzeichnungen aller Teilnehmer, in Gruppe B darüber hinaus auch die vom Programm erzeugte STT-Datei sowie die von acht Teilnehmern zur Verfügung gestellten Selbstreports[12]. Die Bildschirmaufnahmen ermöglichen eine detaillierte Erforschung des Untertitelungsprozesses, während die Reports und die Diskussion eher Aussagen über die Einstellungen zum automatischen Untertiteln zulassen. Die erhobenen Daten lassen demnach unterschiedliche Schwerpunktsetzungen zu.

5. Ergebnisse

Eine detaillierte Evaluation des Übersetzungsprozesses tritt in diesem Beitrag in den Hintergrund. Nachfolgend werden v. a. die Einstellungen der Studenten gegenüber dem Einsatz von KI-Lösungen im Untertitelungsprozess vorgestellt (5.1). Sie werden, wo dies als sinnvoll erachtet wird, um empirische Daten aus den Bildschirmaufzeichnungen ergänzt. Die ca. 26 Stunden Filmmaterial

[11] Zum Nutzen von Selbstreportverfahren in der AVT-Ausbildung und AVT-Forschung vgl. Agnetta (2025b).

[12] Zwei Teilnehmer aus Gruppe A, sechs aus Gruppe B haben Reports abgegeben; diese sind in Deutsch (6), Französisch (1) und Spanisch (1) abgefasst.

werden in diesem Rahmen nicht detailliert besprochen, wohl aber dazu benutzt, den zeitlichen Aufwand bei der Untertitelung mit und ohne durchgehende Zuhilfenahme von KI-Systemen einzuschätzen (5.2). Einige Beobachtungen zu den Grenzen und der Replizierbarkeit des Experiments werden in Abschnitt 5.3 dargelegt.

5.1 Zur Einstellung gegenüber dem KI-basierten Untertiteln

Die Teilnehmer am Experiment und insbesondere jene, die in der Gruppe B waren, äußern sich weniger optimistisch als die befragten Untertitler in der Studie von Karakanta et al., die resümieren: „automatic subtitling has potential and its benefits are already recognised by the users" (2022, S. 262) oder „[o]ur findings suggest a neutral to positive experience" (ibid., S. 267)[13]. Die Ergebnisse des hier beschriebenen Experiments bestätigen vielmehr die eher negative bis neutrale Einstellung, die bereits Koponen et al. (2020) bei professionellen Untertitlern beobachtet haben. Die Studenten scheuten in den aufgezeichneten Gruppendiskussionen nicht davor zurück, die Erfahrung als „Horror" oder als „Achterbahn der Gefühle" zu bezeichnen. Dementsprechend fiel das Ergebnis auf die Frage hin, ob in Zukunft KI-Lösungen wie die in *Subtitle Edit* implementierten weiter benutzt werden, pauschal negativ aus. Obwohl (oder vielleicht auch gerade weil) die Studenten seit ca. zwei Jahren auch in anderen Kursen regelmäßig mit dem Output und dem Post-Editing maschineller Übersetzungen konfrontiert werden und sie in dieser Hinsicht also schon zwangsläufig eine gewisse Kompetenz haben, dominieren Vorbehalte gegenüber der Implementierung (semi-)automatischer Prozesse in ihren Arbeitsalltag.

Dies ist insofern verblüffend, als laut Karakanta et al. (2022, S. 268) ja gerade jüngere Untertitler als technikaffin gelten und die Bereitschaft mitbringen, mit automatisierten Lösungen für bestimmte Teilschritte des Untertitelns zu arbeiten. Eine solche Technikaffinität ist, wie die Arbeit in digitalen Umgebungen sowie die Zuhilfenahme von einzelnen Webanwendungen (Web-Recherche, Wörterbücher, Synonymlexika, Fachtexte und Fachenzyklopädien, Übersetzungskorpora, Übersetzungstools wie *Reverso* und

---

[13] Ähnlich äußern sich auch Kirov/Malamin (2022, S. 6–7, 12), die die Einstellung von bulgarischen Übersetzern gegenüber dem Gebrauch maschineller Übersetzungssysteme erforschen.

DeepL) zeigen, zweifelsohne gegeben. Dass sich das Tätigkeitsprofil laut Georgakopoulou/Bywood (2014) dauerhaft vom Untertitler zum „subtitle post-editor“ verschieben soll, dürfte zwar gegenwärtig noch eine Vorstellung sein, die von Untertitlern nicht gerade wohlwollend aufgenommen ist. Einige Versuchspersonen stellen in ihren Notizen aber explizit in Aussicht, in Zukunft mit KI-Lösungen arbeiten zu wollen, wenn diese bessere Ergebnisse liefern (EN-DE_B_05, FR-DE_A_01). Der Vollständigkeit halber sei erwähnt, dass in den Gruppendiskussionen auf die Frage hin, was denn jetzt schon Maschinen besser könnten als Humanübersetzer, eventuelle Rechtschreib- und Grammatikchecks genannt wurden. In allen anderen Bereichen ist, zumindest der Einschätzung der Studenten nach zu urteilen, beim Untertiteln allerdings noch nicht von „human parity“ (Hassan et al. 2018) oder gar einer Überholung professioneller Humanübersetzer („outperform[ing] professional translators“, Popel et al. 2020, S. 11) auszugehen.

Bei der Auswahl der zu untertitelnden Videoausschnitte wurde, wie oben erwähnt, darauf geachtet, dass diese eine gute Audioqualität und wenig Geräusche aufwiesen und sich die Sprecher in einer Standardvarietät äußerten. Und dennoch überwog in Bezug auf die Ergebnisse der ASR ein negativer Unterton[14]: In ihren Notizen machen die Versuchspersonen teils pauschale (EN-DE_B_03: „sehr schlecht umgesetzt“), teils eingeschränkt gültige Bemerkungen (EN-DE_B_01: „stellenweise relativ schlecht“, FR-DE_B_01: „ich musste quasi den ganzen Text neu schreiben“). EN-DE_B_03 evaluiert sowohl das Transkript als auch die Übersetzung als „überhaupt nicht hilfreich“, denn sie machen „wenig bis gar keinen Sinn“. EN-DE_B_05 bringt die interessante Bemerkung ein, dass er ein automatisch erstelltes Transkript vor allem dann konsultieren würde, wenn der Sprecher im Original nicht richtig zu verstehen war. Wo der Sprecher problemlos zu verstehen ist, bestünde kein Anlass für eine Speech-To-Text-Transkription.

Die Gruppendiskussion im Kurs zeigte, dass die Fehleranfälligkeit des ASR-Systems vor allem folgende Phänomene betraf: Eigennamen, Oralitäts- und

[14] Einige der Versuchsteilnehmer betonen explizit, dass ihre (in dieser Studie notwendigerweise nur bruchstückhaft wiedergegeben) Aussagen womöglich nur in Bezug auf den ihnen vorliegenden Videoausschnitt als Repräsentant eines sehr informationsintensiven Genres Gültigkeit reklamieren und in anderen Kontexten anders ausfallen können.

Hesitationsmarker, undeutliche Sprache und Sprecherwechsel. Zudem würde nach diesem ersten automatisierten Schritt eine Transkription vorliegen, die hinsichtlich der Interpunktion sowie Groß- und Kleinschreibung fehlerhaft ist. Diese Fehler wurden zum Teil durch die maschinelle Übersetzung weitergetragen, zum Teil aber auch ausgemerzt (bspw. der Großteil der Groß- und Kleinschreibungsfehler in den deutschen Zieltexten). In letztgenanntem Fall kann davon ausgegangen werden, dass die Referenztexte, mit denen das von *Subtitle Edit* mitgenutzte Large Language Model (LLM) trainiert wurde, in dieser Hinsicht fehlerfrei waren. Den genauen Umgang mit solchen Fehlern im Rahmen des Untertitelungsprozesses muss einer detaillierten Auswertung der Bildschirmaufzeichnungen überlassen bleiben.

Auch das maschinelle Spotting und Splitting werden durchweg negativ bewertet. Grund dafür ist zumeist wieder der Aufwand einer Bewertung und „ständigen Korrektur" (DE-ES_B_01) des maschinellen Outputs oder einer kompletten Neuabfassung eines „Großteils" der Untertitel (EN-DE_B_01). Konkreter werden die Teilnehmer, die auf die Ungenauigkeit (EN-DE_B_03), die mangelnde Synchronität zum Gesprochenen (EN-DE_B_05, DE-ES_B_01) oder den mangelnden Abstand von mindestens 2 freien *frames* zwischen zwei Untertiteln (vgl. Díaz-Cintas/Remeal 2021, S. 114) (EN-DE_B_03) hinweisen. Die meisten Teilnehmer merkten an, dass die maschinell gespotteten Untertitel nur eingeschränkt verwertbar seien, da sie häufig schlichtweg zu lang seien (EN-DE_B_01, EN-DE_B_05) und bei Korrektur der Segmentierung den zulässigen CPS-Wert überschreiten (EN-DE_B_03). In ihren Notizen dokumentiert FR-DE_A_01 im direkten Vergleich zu einer vorangegangenen Untertitelungsarbeit mit KI-Lösungen (EN-DE_B_03), dass das Spotting eigener Übersetzungslösungen „viel schneller und unkomplizierter" war als die Korrektur des automatisch gespotteten Texts. Dass sich die Notizen einiger Teilnehmer bezüglich des Spotting teilweise widersprechen (FR-DE_B_01: „präzise", „oft stimmte das Spotting nicht", „teilweise falsch bzw. unpräzise"), ist aber ein Hinweis darauf, dass die Spottingqualität nicht immer die gleiche und womöglich auch sprachenpaarabhängig ist (vgl. ibid.). Einige der Reports beinhalten Hinweise darauf, dass untertitelungsspezifische Anforderungen beim ‚herkömmlichen' Übersetzen ohne KI automatisch, ja manchmal unterbewusst schon beim Spotting und beim Übersetzen berücksichtigt werden (EN-DE_B_03, FR-DE_A_01) und nicht erst beim Kürzen nach vollendeter Übersetzung: Ein Student kommt zum Ergebnis: „[E]s war mühsam, alle

UT erst anpassen zu müssen, anstatt sie wie sonst einfach direkt passend zu erstellen“ (EN-DE_B_05). Ein Teilnehmer, der Untertitelungsaufträge in beiden Gruppen bearbeitet hat, zieht den direkten Vergleich und merkt an, dass bei der reinen Humanübersetzung „Spotting & Korrektur des Spotting viel schneller & unkomplizierter“ abliefen als beim ersten Versuch mit automatischem STT und MT (FR-DE_A_01).

In der Gruppendiskussion wurde das maschinelle Splitting als ‚großes Problem‘ beschrieben: Es wird bemängelt, dass die Maschine „Sätze völlig willkürlich unterteilt“ (EN-DE_B_01, DE-ES_B_01); das bedeutet, dass sich falsche Umbrüche finden, die sich nicht nach den Sinneinheiten richten (EN-DE_B_03, EN-DE_B_05). Der Blick auf die abgespeicherten STT-Fassungen gibt den Studenten Recht: Zusammengehörige Satzglieder – etwa Artikel und Substantiv, Hilfsverb und Verb, Adjektive und Substantive – finden sich willkürlich auf die zweizeiligen oder nacheinander eingeblendeten Untertitel aufgeteilt. Die Untertitelgrenzen fallen selten mit den Satzgrenzen zusammen und gehen sogar – dies ist laut den meisten Untertitelungsrichtlinien explizit verboten – über Bildschnitte.

Übersetzen und Post-Editing sind zu Recht als zwei unterschiedliche Tätigkeiten charakterisiert worden, deren Ausgangslage eine ganz andere ist: Zwar gibt es bei beiden Operationen einen Prätext, doch ist beim Post-Editing von vornherein klar, dass große Teile des gegebenen Textes erhalten werden müssen, um Effizienz zu reklamieren. Nur auf diese Weise hat diese Modalität überhaupt ihre Daseinsberechtigung. Den gegebenen Text, d. h. in diesem Fall: den Output von SST und MT, erachten die Studenten nun in den meisten Fällen als einen, der der Abfassung idiomatischer und genrespezifischer Untertitel eher im Weg steht. Dem Urteil eines Versuchsteilnehmers zufolge bot sich ihm „direkt nach der Text-to-speech-Konvertierung und Auto-Translation ein sehr verwirrendes Bild“, denn „oft hat das Programm den gesprochenen Text nicht richtig erkannt und falsch transkribiert und damit auch falsch übersetzt“ (EN-DE_B_05; ähnlich auch DE-ES_B_01), womit Folge- bzw. Kaskadenfehler explizit angesprochen sind. Und auch bei einem weiteren Studenten stellte sich nach anfänglicher Überraschung, wie rasch die maschinelle Übersetzung vonstattenging, eine „schnelle Ernüchterung“ (EN-DE_B_01) ein. In der Gruppendiskussion wurde auch die mangelnde Text-Bild-Kohärenz erwähnt, die sich einstellt, wenn das MT-System ein richtig erkanntes, aber mehrdeutiges Lexem nicht kontextsensibel übersetzt.

Nicht nur eine allgemeine Verwirrung angesichts eines fertigen, zunächst als funktionierend anmutenden Text wird beschrieben, sondern auch die limitierende Wirkung, die dieser meistens allzu wörtlich übersetzte Text (EN-DE_B_05) auf die Kreativität des Untertitlers ausüben kann. Es wird gleich mehrfach auf den in der Literatur beschriebenen Effekt des *priming* eingegangen (vgl. bspw. Orel Kos 2024). EN-DE_B_03 gesteht ein: „[A]utomatische Übersetzung schränkt mich in meiner übersetzerischen Freiheit und Kreativität etwas ein; man fixiert sich zu sehr auf den Stil, die Satzstruktur und die Ausdrücke, die in der automatisch generierten Übersetzung vorkommen". Ein weiterer Teilnehmer äußert sich ähnlich. Er ist überzeugt, „dass eine automatisch generierte Version [ihn] ziemlich in [seiner] Kreativität & künstlerischen Übersetzungsfähigkeit einschränkt; ohne KI hat man keine Textvorlage & denkt bei besonders schwierigen Stellen oftmals über den Tellerrand hinaus, um eine gute Lösung zu finden" (FR-DE_A_01). KI-generierte Übersetzungen, so schlecht und/oder gut sie auch sein mögen, werden hier gemeinhin als Faktor beschrieben, der die virtuelle Fülle an Übersetzungslösungen radikal einschränkt. So empfindet EN-DE_B_03 den Einsatz automatischer Übersetzungen beim Untertiteln mehr als „Hindernis" denn als „Hilfestellung". DE-ES_B_01 attestiert der Maschine zwar gewisse Vorzüge („muy rápido", „fácil y accesible", „bastante buenos resultados"[15]) bringt aber eine menschliche Metapher an, wenn er ein gewisses Misstrauen für angebracht hält („se necesita mirarlo bien y no confiar"[16]). Der Versuchsteilnehmer legt hier eine Sensibilität an den Tag, die gerade bei jungen *digital natives* nicht pauschal vorausgesetzt werden kann – zumindest Orel Kos (2024, S. 198-199, 202, 204–205) zufolge, die in ihrem Untertitelungskurs beobachtet hat, dass post-editierende Studenten maschinelle Übersetzungen tendenziell übernehmen und damit vergleichsweise häufiger fehlerhafte Untertitel produzieren als die, die von Grund auf selbst übersetzen. Fertig vorliegende, nur vordergründig plausible KI-generierte Übersetzungen führen manchmal zu dem oben erwähnten Übervertrauen (*overreliance*) in das maschinell erzeugte Output, das sich negativ auf den Übersetzungsprozess auswirkt. Hier wird auf eine wichtige Tatsache abgezielt,

[15] Zu Deutsch: „sehr schnell", „leicht und zugänglich", „hinreichend gute Ergebnisse".

[16] Zu Deutsch: „Man muss sie [sc. die Übersetzung] sich genau anschauen und darf ihr nicht allzu sehr trauen".

die beim Post-Editing maschinell übersetzter Texte nie vergessen werden darf: Das Vorliegen eines solchen Textes entbindet den Übersetzer, hier: den Untertitler, nicht von der Aufgabe, den Originaltext zu lesen und verstehend zu durchdringen. Der für gewöhnlich als zweiteilig beschriebene Prozess der Humanübersetzung (a. Verstehen und b. Zieltextproduktion) wird beim Post-Editing nicht um eine Komponente reduziert, sondern bleibt zweiphasig (a. Verstehen UND b. Zieltextrevision). Dies vergessen oder unterschlagen Akteure, die auf dem AVT-Markt Post-Editionen geringer vergüten möchten als Übersetzungen (vgl. Agnetta 2025a, S. 18). Es ist Aufgabe einer informierten AVT-Didaktik, Studenten für diese Umstände zu sensibilisieren. Der menschliche Akteur und seine beim Übersetzen stets notwendigen hermeneutischen Fähigkeiten des ganzheitlichen Verständnisses und der Aktivierung des eigenen Erfahrungsschatzes darf nicht aus den Augen gelassen werden (vgl. Liang 2022, S. 2) – auch nicht beim (qualitativ hochwertigen) Untertiteln. In Übereinstimmung hiermit resümiert EN-DE_B_05 erleichtert in seinem Report: „Insgesamt eine interessante Erfahrung, aber sie hat mir auch deutlich gezeigt, wie wichtig eine menschliche Instanz in der AVÜ immer noch ist (die automatisch erstellten Untertitel hätte man niemals so lassen können)“.

5.2 Zum zeitlichen Aufwand

Der Einsatz von KI-Lösungen wird dann breite Anwendung erfahren, wenn diese dazu beitragen, einen ungewollt hohen Aufwand zu minimieren. Wo sie den Aufwand nicht reduzieren, sondern vielleicht sogar noch erhöhen, werden sie schwerlich zum Einsatz kommen. Ausschlaggebend ist hierbei die Meinung der Endnutzer. Karakanta et al. (2022, S. 261) bestätigen: „Altogether, these technologies come with the promise of reducing the human effort in the subtitling process, but, to date, automatic subtitling has still to be put to test by the actual users“. Solche Bemerkungen betreffen nicht nur den zeitlichen Aufwand, der nachfolgend im Zentrum stehen soll, sondern auch den schwer messbaren kognitiven Aufwand und eine allgemeine Kosten-Nutzen-Kalkulation.

Eine Aufwandsminimierung kann entweder nur einen der oben genannten Schritte des Untertitelns oder aber global den ganzen Untertitelungsauftrag betreffen. Wenn eine bestimmte Phase des Untertitelungsprozesses durch eine KI-Lösung empfindlich verkürzt wird, dann findet diese höchstwahrscheinlich

Eingang in die digitale Arbeitsumgebung des Untertitlers. Beispiele hierfür sind die Grammatikkorrektur, Überprüfung untertitelungsspezifischer Anforderungen etc. In der Gruppendiskussion wurde allerdings immer wieder geäußert, dass KI-Lösungen wenig nutzen, wenn sie nicht den globalen Aufwand des Untertitelns reduzieren. Die vorherrschend negative Meinung zu ASR, STT und MT rührt daher, dass alle Studenten aus der Gruppe B das Gefühl hatten, ohne KI-Lösungen insgesamt schneller zu sein.

Wir fokussieren nachfolgend auf den zeitlichen Aufwand, d. h. auf die Bearbeitungszeit, die für die Abwicklung des reinen Untertitelungsvorgangs benötigt wurde. Die Dauer etwaiger Vorbereitungsschritte wie das notwendige Herunterladen und Installieren der Software (in beiden Gruppen) sowie das Herunterladen der verwendeten Sprachmodelle (Gruppe B) wurde nicht mitberücksichtigt. Bei den Videos des gleichen Genres und mit vergleichbarer Informationsdichte schien uns die Untertitelungsgeschwindigkeit folgendermaßen am besten repräsentiert: Ausgehend von der Länge der zu untertitelnden Videos (d_{DE} = 73 Sek., d_{EN} = 68 Sek., d_{ES} = 87 Sek., d_{FR} = 116 Sek., d_{IT} = 107 Sek.) und der für ihre vollständige Untertitelung benötigten absoluten Bearbeitungszeit (t_a), wurde für jeden Teilnehmer die relative Bearbeitungszeit berechnet, in der dieser eine Filmminute untertitelt hat (t_r). Die absolute Bearbeitungszeit (t_a) bezieht sich auf die Gesamtlänge der Bildschirmaufnahmen, und zwar vom Beginn der eigenständigen Untertitelungsarbeit (Gruppe A) bzw. dem Beginn der ASR (Gruppe B) bis zur Abspeicherung des fertigen Projekts. Es wurden alle Schritte mitberücksichtigt, welche die Teilnehmer beider Gruppen als notwendig erachteten, um ein publizierbares Endprodukt abzugeben: eine eventuelle Transkription, das Zwischen-Editing des maschinellen Outputs sowie etwaige (Online-)Recherchen.

Um eventuelle Korrelationen zwischen Bearbeitungszeit und Untertitelungserfahrung nachweisen zu können, wurde außerdem auch erhoben, wie viele Untertitelungskurse die einzelnen Teilnehmer bereits im Rahmen ihres bisherigen Studiums (SUB) und wie viele sie in der jeweils interessierenden Sprachkombination (SUB_X) absolviert haben oder im Begriff waren zu absolvieren. Ein vollständig absolvierter Untertitelungskurs entspricht während des Semesters etwa 14 x 90 Minuten Präsenz-Zeit und ca. noch einmal genauso viel Zeit, die die Studenten mit Untertitelungsaufträgen beschäftigt sind.

Wir kamen nun zu folgender Einschätzung des zeitlichen Bearbeitungsaufwands in Gruppe A (s. Tabelle 2) und B (s. Tabelle 3):

Tabelle 2: Absolute, relative Bearbeitungszeiten und Untertitelungserfahrung in Gruppe A

		Absolute Bearbeitungszeit (in Sekunden) (t_a/d)	**Relative Bearbeitungszeit (in Minuten) (t_r/d = 60 Sek.)**	**Bemerkungen**
1	**DE-EN_A_01**	2030	27,81	**[SUB: 3, SUB_{EN}: 2]** Kein Transkript
2	**EN-DE_A_01**	2900	42,65	**[SUB: 1, SUB_{EN}: 1]** Kein Transkript
3	**EN-DE_A_02 = ES-DE_B_02**	2903	42,69	**[SUB: 2, SUB_{EN}: 1]** Kein Transkript
4	**EN-DE_A_03**	4315	63,46	**[SUB: 2, SUB_{EN}: 2]** Kein Transkript
5	**ES-DE_A_01**	3575	41,09	**[SUB: 1, SUB_{ES}: 1]** Mit Transkript, dessen Erstellung aber nicht aufgezeichnet wurde
6	**FR-DE_A_01 = EN-DE_B_03**	3215	27,72	**[SUB: 3, SUBFR: 1]** Kein Transkript
7	**DE-FR_A_01**	3228	44,22	**[SUB: 1, SUB_{FR}: 1]** Transkript von Youtube konsultiert. In Worddatei übersetzt, dann in AegiSub eingefügt und dort angepasst
8	**DE-IT_A_01**	3517	48,18	**[SUB: 1, SUBIT: 1]** Kein Transkript
9	**IT-DE_A_01**	3043	28,44	**[SUB: 2, SUBIT: 2]** Kein Transkript
			Ø 40,69	**- Ø SUB: 1,78** **- Ø SUB_x: 1,30**

Tabelle 3: Absolute, relative Bearbeitungszeiten und Untertitelungserfahrung in Gruppe B

		Absolute Bearbeitungszeit (in Sekunden) (t_a/d)	Relative Bearbeitungszeit (in Minuten) (t_r/d = 60 Sek.)	Bemerkungen
1	DE-EN_B_01	1894	25,95	[SUB: 2, SUB_{EN}: 1]
2	EN-DE_B_01	3921	57,66	[SUB: 1, SUB_{EN}: 1]
3	EN-DE_B_02	2464	36,24	[SUB: 2, SUB_{EN}: 2]
4	EN-DE_B_03 = FR-DE_A_01	3830	56,32	[SUB: 3, SUB_{EN}: 2]
5	EN-DE_B_04	6315	92,87	[SUB: 2, SUB_{EN}: 2]
6	EN-DE_B_05	5488	80,71	[SUB: 2, SUB_{EN}: 2]
7	DE-ES_B_01	1115	15,27	[SUB: 2, SUB_{ES}: 2]
8	ES-DE_B_01	10545	121,21	[SUB: 2, SUB_{ES}: 2] Hat Zwischenedition vorgenommen
9	ES-DE_B_02 = EN-DE_A_02	3345	38,45	[SUB: 2, SUB_{ES}: 1]
10	ES-DE_B_03	13008	149,52	[SUB: 2 / SUB_{ES}: 2]
11	FR-DE_B_01	8759	75,51	[SUB: 1 / SUB_{FR}: 1] Hat Zwischenedition vorgenommen
12	IT-DE_B_01	3796	35,48	[SUB: 4, SUB_{IT}: 2]
13	DE-FR_B_01			[SUB: 2, SUB_{FR}: 2]
			Ø 65,34	**Durchschnitt** **- Ø SUB: 2,25** **- Ø SUBx: 1,83**

In unserem Experiment ist in zeitlicher Hinsicht keine Effizienzsteigerung durch den durchgängigen Einsatz von KI-Lösungen für die Spracherkennung und die Übersetzung zu verzeichnen. Im Gegenteil: Die Teilnehmer in Gruppe B benötigten mit durchschnittlichen 65,34 Minuten Bearbeitungszeit pro zu untertitelnder Filmminute 61 % mehr Zeit als die in Gruppe A ($Øt_r$ = 40,69 Min.). Dies lässt sich nicht auf die Untertitelungserfahrung der Teilnehmer zurückführen, ist doch sowohl die durchschnittliche sprachenpaarunabhängige wie sprachenpaarabhängige Untertitelungserfahrung

(SUB = 2,25 und SUB_x = 1,83 Semesterkurse) in Gruppe B sogar höher als in Gruppe A (SUB = 1,78 und SUB_X = 1,30 Semesterkurse).

In Gruppe A haben sieben von neun Versuchspersonen kein Transkript des Originals, sondern direkt nach dem Hörverstehen zielsprachige Untertitel erstellt. DE-FR_A_01 hat punktuell das automatische Transkript auf der Video-Plattform Youtube konsultiert; ES-DE_A_01 hat zwar ein Transkript erstellt, dessen Abfassung allerdings nicht aufgezeichnet. Beide Versuchsteilnehmer liegen mit 41,09 und 44,22 Minuten relative Bearbeitungszeit über dem Durchschnitt von 40,69 Minuten. Auch ein Versuchsteilnehmer aus der Gruppe B (FR-DE_B_01) hat interessehalber eine manuelle Transkription des Videoausschnitts (d_{FR}= 116 Sekunden) vorgenommen und eigenständig die Zeit gemessen (t_{mT} = 25 Minuten; auf 60 Filmsekunden genormt: ~13 Minuten). Insgesamt scheint sich für die von Grund auf Untertitelnden eine vollständige Transkription des Videos nicht zu lohnen. Bei schwer verständlichen Textpassagen wird allerdings maschinell generierter STT-Output (auf anderen Plattformen) konsultiert.

Aus der Gruppe B haben zwei Studenten (ES-DE_B_01, FR-DE_B_01) von zwölf eigenständig ein Zwischen-Editing vorgenommen, d. h. sie haben das Output des ASR zuerst verbessert und gespottet, bevor sie die maschinelle Übersetzung gestartet haben. Bezüglich der relativen Bearbeitungszeit besetzen sie mit deutlich überdurchschnittlichen Werten allerdings den drittletzten und vorletzten Platz. Nur ein Student (ebenfalls aus der Gruppe B: ES-DE_B_03) hat mehr Zeit für den Untertitelungsauftrag benötigt als sie. Die Vermutung der beiden Studenten, durch eine zwischengelagerte Qualitätsprüfung ließe sich das Post-Editing der maschinellen Übersetzung schneller abwickeln, hat sich nicht bewahrheitet. Im Zuge des studentischen Experiments stellt sich die Zwischenkontrolle der maschinell erstellten Transkription damit nicht als effizienter heraus.

Für Aussagen zum Aufwand beim Untertiteln mit und ohne KI stellt sich die zweimalige Teilnahme zweier Studenten am Experiment in unterschiedlichen Gruppen als besonders erkenntnisreich heraus. Laut ihrem Selbstreport kommt einer dieser Versuchsteilnehmer zu folgendem Ergebnis: Das Untertiteln von der Pike auf ist die „wesentlich einfachere und weniger zeitaufwändige Prozedur als die andere Variante mit KI“ (FR-DE_A_01). Dieses Urteil bestätigen die entsprechenden Bildschirmaufnahmen, benötigte doch der Versuchsteilnehmer im Durchlauf mit KI-Lösungen 56,32

Minuten, im Durchlauf ohne KI nur 27,72 Minuten für die Untertitelung einer Filmminute. Ein Teilnehmer aktivierte seine eigene Untertitelungserfahrung aus den letzten Semestern und resümiert: „[D]as Post-Editing nimmt mehr Zeit in Anspruch, als es eine rein humane Arbeit insgesamt tun würde; ich glaube nicht, dass ich für eine ‚normale' Untertitelung eine Stunde gebraucht hätte" (EN-DE_B_03; ähnlich: EN-DE_B_05).

5.3 Zu den Grenzen und der Replizierbarkeit des Experiments

Der hier beschriebene Versuch weist folgende Grenzen auf: Obwohl die studentischen Teilnehmer eine relativ homogene Gruppe bilden, gilt hier, wie für andere Studien auf dem Gebiet (vgl. Karakanta et al. 2022; Koponen et al. 2020), dass die Fokussierung auf 22 Studenten eine geringe Repräsentativität und damit keine Übertragung der Ergebnisse auf die allgemeine Untertitlerpopulation – wohl aber auf andere Gruppen mit ähnlichen Merkmalen (Studenten in der Ausbildung) – zulässt. Trotzdem gab es selbst bei dieser relativ homogenen Gruppe an Versuchsteilnehmern Variablen, die in einem strengen Versuchsaufbau konstant gehalten werden müssten, zum Beispiel:

(a) die Erfahrung mit dem spezifischen Übersetzungstool: ES-DE_A_01 empfindet es in seinem Report als erwähnenswert, dass er zum ersten Mal mit *Subtitle Edit* gearbeitet hat und dass einige zeitliche Verzögerungen dadurch entstanden, dass er sich in dieser neuen Arbeitsumgebung zurechtfinden musste (bspw. Wie zeigt das Programm an, wenn man die untertitelungsspezifischen Vorgaben wie die Zeichenzahl pro Zeile oder die CPS überschreitet?);
(b) der Bekanntheitsgrad des zu untertitelnden Videos: DE-EN_B_01 war der zu untertitelnde Videoausschnitt schon bekannt, weswegen er wahrscheinlich mit 25,95 Minuten relativer Bearbeitungszeit deutlich unter dem Durchschnitt (65,34 Minuten) liegt.

Eine weitere Begrenzung unseres Versuchsaufbaus besteht in der Auswahl des (einen!) Untertitelungs-Programms *Subtitle Edit*. Es handelt sich dabei nicht einmal um die in der Praxis meistverwendete Software (im deutschsprachigen Raum ist dies wohl das kostenpflichtige *EZTitles*). Allerdings ist zu sagen, dass hier unsere Studie solche ergänzen kann, die auf andere Programme fokussieren (bspw. *Matesub* in Karakanta et al. 2022). Das hier in den Vordergrund gerückte Programm ist als intuitiv und nutzerfreundlich einzustufen und ist dazu noch kostenlos. Da die meisten Studenten, die an dem Experiment teilgenommen haben, regelmäßig mit diesem Programm arbeiten, ist nicht von negativen Auswirkungen einer Unkenntnis der Software auf die Bewertung der maschinellen Untertitelung auszugehen.

In Folgeuntersuchungen müssten einzelne Faktoren stärker in den Fokus gerückt werden. Zum Beispiel müsste die Abhängigkeit der Einstellungen angehender Untertitler zum Einsatz maschineller Lösungen von dem Sprachenpaar, mit dem sie arbeiten, erforscht werden. In diesem Artikel wurde summarisch auf die am Innsbrucker Institut für Translationswissenschaft gelehrten Sprachen eingegangen (außer Russisch). Folgeuntersuchungen könnten getrennt nach Sprachenpaar vorgehen, um Rückschlüsse auf die Akzeptanz dieser Technologien in Kontexten zu ziehen, in denen entweder *high-* oder *low-resource-languages* involviert sind. So könnten auch besonders zeitaufwändige Korrekturen maschinengenerierter Texte womöglich auf sprachspezifische Herausforderungen zurückgeführt und durch entsprechendes Training der KI ausgemerzt werden.

Auch die Abhängigkeit des maschinellen Outputs vom Genre des audiovisuellen Materials müsste im Rahmen einer größeren und vergleichenden Studie näher betrachtet werden. Handfeste, aber noch auf breiterer Datenbasis zu überprüfende Hypothesen sind, dass MT bei ungescripteten (im Vergleich zu gescripteten) Formaten besser performt (Etchegoyhen et al. 2014, S. 50) und dass alltagssprachliche Sitcoms bessere MT-Ergebnisse erwarten lassen als Dokumentationen (Matusov/Wilken/Georgakopoulou 2019, S. 87). Letztgenanntem widerspricht die von Karakanta et al. (2022, S. 267) geäußerte Vermutung, die automatische Untertitelung würde im dokumentarischen Bereich besser funktionieren und daher eher angenommen werden als in Unterhaltungsgenres. Dies ließ sich im Rahmen dieser Studie aber nicht bestätigen. Im Gegenteil: Die im dokumentarischen Genre häufig erforderlichen Rücksichtnahmen auf Inserts und Bauchbinden, die hohe Informationsdichte und Fachsprachlichkeit, sind Herausforderungen, die je nach Fachgebiet und Textsorte von Mensch und Maschine unterschiedlich gemeistert werden.

6. Fazit und Ausblick

In der vorliegenden Studie rückten die Erfahrungen von angehenden Untertitlern beim Einsatz von KI-Lösungen im Untertitelungsprozess in den Fokus. Ausgangspunkt bildete ein Experiment, in dem Studenten mithilfe des Untertitelungsprogramms *Subtitle Edit* die Post-Edition vollständig automatisch generierter Untertitel durchführen und bewerten sollten. Als Kontrollgruppe dienten Studenten, die das gleiche Ausgangsmaterial von Grund auf selbst und ohne durchgängige Zuhilfenahme von KI-Tools untertiteln sollten. Die Ergebnisse dieses Versuchs zeigen, dass der Einsatz von KI-Lösungen wie der automatischen Spracherkennung und maschinellen Übersetzung mit einem erheblichen Aufwand verbunden ist, insbesondere im Hinblick auf die Bearbeitungsdauer. Ähnlich wie bei Koponen et al. (2020a), aber anders als bei Karakanta et al. (2022: passim), überwog bei den 22 Versuchsteilnehmern eine eher negative und nur bezüglich einzelner Funktionen positiv ausfallende Einschätzung des Einsatzes von automatisierten Untertitelungslösungen im Rahmen des eigenen Untertitelungsprozesses.

Insbesondere die als mangelhaft beurteilte Qualität des maschinellen Outputs (vor allem hinsichtlich des Spotting, des Splitting und von Kaskadenfehlern), der Priming-Effekt bei der maschinell erzeugten Übersetzung und der erhebliche zeitliche Aufwand fallen bei der Ablehnung von KI-Lösungen im interlingualen Untertitelungskurs ins Gewicht. Der konsequente Einsatz von KI-Lösungen führte in diesem Untertitelungssetting tatsächlich nicht, wie dies von Kunden auf dem AVT-Markt behauptet bzw. stillschweigend vorausgesetzt und von MT-Forschern für andere Textsorten belegt wird (vgl. Läubli et al 2019, S. 270), zu einer Zeitersparnis. Tatsächlich benötigten die Teilnehmer der Gruppe B, die die KI-Tools einsetzten, im Durchschnitt mehr Zeit für die Erledigung ihrer Untertitelungsaufgaben als die Teilnehmer der Gruppe A, die von Grund auf untertitelten. Dies deutet darauf hin, dass KI-Lösungen (ASR, STT, MT) noch nicht effizient genug sind, um ihren Einsatz in zeitgenössischen professionellen Untertitelungs-Workflows zu rechtfertigen, insbesondere für diejenigen, die Wert auf Geschwindigkeit und Genauigkeit legen. Möglicherweise ist dies aber auch ein Indiz für eine fehlende Post-Editing-Kompetenz bei den Studenten selbst. Die Teilnehmer äußerten überdies Bedenken hinsichtlich der Auswirkungen von KI-generierten Ergebnissen auf ihren kreativen Prozess. Die von MT-Systemen gelieferten wörtlichen und manchmal kontextuell unpassenden Übersetzungen wurden als einschränkend empfunden, da sie oft eine umfangreiche Nachbearbeitung erfordern, die die potenziellen Vorteile der Automatisierung zunichtemacht. Da das Output durchgängiger KI-Lösungen für die Untertitelung prinzipiell noch bearbeitungswürdig erscheint, ist eine grundsätzliche und vollständige Bewältigung der Untertitelungsaufgabe mit ihrer Hilfe also (noch) nicht erwünscht, die Arbeit mit ihnen wird mit einer Effizienzminderung in Verbindung gebracht. Wohl aber wird eine punktuelle externe Zuhilfenahme solcher KI-Tools gerne in Anspruch genommen.

Es besteht eindeutig ein Bedarf an weiterer Forschung zum Thema, insbesondere an groß angelegten, vergleichenden Studien, die den Einfluss von Genre und Sprachenpaar auf die Wirksamkeit von KI-Tools bei der Untertitelung untersuchen. Solche Studien könnten genauere Erkenntnisse darüber liefern, in welchen Kontexten KI am effektivsten in den Untertitelungsworkflow integriert werden kann. Damit KI-Tools in größerem Umfang in der professionellen Untertitelung eingesetzt werden können, muss ein größerer Schwerpunkt auf die Schulung von Untertitlern gelegt werden, damit sie diese Tools effektiv nutzen können. Darüber hinaus ist es für die Akzeptanz von KI-Lösungen entscheidend, sie so zu integrieren, dass sie den kreativen Prozess des Untertitlers ergänzen und nicht behindern.

Wie die Phänomene des Übervertrauens in und die Tendenz zur Beeinflussung durch maschinelle Übersetzungssysteme (*overreliance* und *priming*) zeigen, ist der Nutzen einer (Teil-)Automatisierung unmittelbar von Kompetenzen im Umgang mit diesen Technologien abhängig. Die Erarbeitung und Einübung eines einschlägigen Kompetenzensets, auf das man summarisch mit den Begriffen der „Machine Translation Literacy“ (Bowker/Buitrago Ciro 2019, S. 87 *et passim*) oder der „Artificial Intelligence Literacy“ (Krüger 2023 und Krüger in diesem Band) verweisen könnte, ist Sache einer (forschungsgeleiteten) Translationsdidaktik. Trotz der eher negativen Einstellungen der Studenten gegenüber dem Einsatz bestimmter KI-Lösungen im Untertitelungsprozess war die prinzipielle Akzeptanz des in diesem Aufsatz beschriebenen freiwilligen Experiments überwältigend. In den Gruppendiskussionen wurde die Durchführung desselbigen als wertvolle Erfahrung eingestuft. Mit der praktischen Erfahrung und dem Dialog zum Einsatz dieser Technologien ist ein (weiterer) Schritt auf dem Weg zu einer KI-Kompetenz unternommen worden, die zuallererst darin besteht, gewissenhaft evaluieren zu können, ob und wann sich gegenwärtig der Einsatz von KI-Lösungen im Übersetzungsprozess lohnt.

In dem hier beschriebenen Versuch ging es hauptsächlich um die praktischen Aspekte des Einsatzes von KI in Untertitelungsprojekten. Bei alledem dürfen allerdings ethische Dimensionen nicht ins Hintertreffen geraten (vgl. Agnetta 2025a): Auf dem AVT-Arbeitsmarkt stößt der Einsatz von KI, sowohl in Form von NMT als auch von LLMs, deswegen an seine Grenze, weil noch unklar ist, wie sich diese Instrumente in ein nachhaltiges Konzept überführen lassen, das Autoren- und Übersetzerrechte im Auge behält und damit den Menschen weiterhin, wieder oder überhaupt erst in den Fokus der Aufmerksamkeit rückt.

Quellenverzeichnis

Agnetta, Marco (2025a): „Zu Einschätzung und Akzeptanz von KI-Technologien in der AVT-Branche: Die Perspektive der Verbände". *Lebende Sprachen* 70/1, S. 1–28 [ahead of print].

Agnetta, Marco (2025b): „Das Logbuch als Form der translationsbezogenen Reflexion in der AVT-Ausbildung und AVT-Forschung, dargestellt am Beispiel der Lieduntertitelung". In: Schmidhofer, Astrid / Recio Ariza, María Ángeles (Hrsg.): *Zukunftsperspektiven der Translationswissenschaft. Ausgewählte Beiträge der Translata IV.* Innsbruck: IUP, S. 175–213.

Agnetta, Marco (2025, i. Dr.): „Investigating students' attitude toward the use of AI in interlingual subtitling process". In: Yahiaoui, Rashid (Hrsg.): *Transl-AI-tion 2.0. Embracing the AI revolution*. Berlin et al.: Peter Lang.

AVTE-MT (2021): *Machine translation manifesto*, abgerufen am 12.12.2024 auf https://avteurope.org/.

Bowker, Lynne / Buitrago Ciro, Jairo (2019): *Machine translation and global research: Towards improved machine translation literacy in the scholarly community*. Leeds: Emerald Publishing Limited. https://doi.org/10.1108/9781787567214.

Bywood, Lindsay / Etchegoyhen, Thierry / Georgakopoulou, Panayota (2017): „Embracing the threat: Machine translation as a solution for subtitling". *Perspectives. Studies in Translation Theory and Practice* 25, S. 492–508. https://doi.org/10.1080/0907676X.2017.1291695.

Defrancq, Bart / Fantinuoli, Claudio (2020): „Automatic speech recognition in the booth: Assessment of system performance, interpreters' performances and interactions in the context of numbers". *Target* 33(1), S. 73–102. https://doi.org/10.1075/target.19166.def.

Díaz-Cintas, Jorge / Remael, Aline (2021): *Subtitling. Concepts and practices*. London et al.: Routledge.

Etchegoyhen, Thierry / Bywood, Lindsay / Fishel, Mark / Georgakopoulou, Panayota / Jiang, Jie / van Loenhout, Gerard / del Pozo, Arantza / Sepesy Maučec, Mirjam / Turner, Anja / Volk, Martin (2014): „Machine translation for subtitling: a large-scale Evaluation“. *LREC 2014 Proceedings*, S. 46–53, abgerufen am 06.02.2025 auf http://www.lrec-conf.org/proceedings/lrec2014/pdf/463_Paper.pdf.

Georgakopoulou, Panayota (2019): „Technologization of audiovisual translation“. In: Pérez-González, Luis (Hrsg.): *The Routledge Handbook of audiovisual translation*. London: Routledge, S. 516–539.

Georgakopoulou, Panayota / Bywood, Lindsay (2014): „MT in subtitling and the rising profile of the post-editor“. *MultiLingual* 25(1), S. 24–28, abgerufen am 06.02.2025 auf https://multilingual.com/articles/mt-in-subtitling-and-the-rising-profile-of-the-post-editor/.

Granell, Ximo / Chaume, Frederic (2023): „Audiovisual translation, translators, and technology: From automation pipe-dream to human–machine convergence“. *Linguistica Antverpiensia, New Series: Themes in Translation Studies* 22, S. 20–40.

Hassan, Hany / Aue, Anthony / Chen, Chang / Chowdhary, Vishal / Clark, Jonathan / Federmann, Christian / Huang, Xuedong / Junczys-Dowmunt, Marcin / Lewis, William / Li, Mu / Liu, Shujie / Liu, Tie-Yan / Luo, Renqian / Menezes, Arul / Qin, Tao / Seide, Frank / Tan, Xu / Tian, Fei / Wu, Lijun / Wu, Shuangzhi / Xia, Yingce / Zhang, Dongdong / Zhang, Zhirui / Zhou, Ming (2018): „Achieving human parity on automatic Chinese to English news Translation“. retrieved 06.02.2025 from https://arxiv.org/abs/1803.05567.

Jaki, Sylvia / Bolz, Maren / Röther, Sophie (2024): „KI-Technologien in der Audiovisuellen Translation. Umfrageergebnisse aus der deutschen Translationsindustrie“. *trans-kom* 17(2), 320–342.

Jakobson, Roman (1959/1974): „Linguistische Aspekte der Übersetzung“. In: Jakobson, Roman (Hrsg.): *Form und Sinn*. München: Wilhelm Fink Verlag, S. 154–161.

Karakanta, Alina (2022): „Experimental research in automatic subtitling: At the crossroads between machine translation and audiovisual translation“. *Translation Spaces* 11(1), S. 89–112. http://doi.org/10.1075/ts.21021.kar.

Karakanta, Alina / Bentivogli, Luisa / Cettolo, Mauro / Negri, Matteo / Turchi, Marco (2022): „Post-editing in automatic subtitling: A subtitlers’ perspective". In: Moniz, Helena/Macken, Lieve/Rufener, Andrew/ Barrault, Loïc/ Costa-jussà, Marta R./ Declercq, Christophe/Koponen, Maarit/Kemp, Ellie/Pilos, Spyridon/Forcada, Mikel L./Scarton, Carolina/ Van den Bogaert, Joachim/Daems, Joke/Tezcan, Arda/ Vanroy, Bram/Fonteyne, Margot (Hrsg.): *Proceedings of the 23rd Annual Conference of the European Association for Machine Translation*, S. 261–270, abgerufen am 06.02.2025 auf https://aclanthology.org/2022.eamt-1.29/.

Kirov, Vassil / Malamin, Bagryan (2022): „Are translators afraid of artificial intelligence?" *Societies* 12(70), S. 1–14. https://doi.org/10.3390/soc12020070.

Koponen, Maarit / Sulubacak, Umut / Vitikainen, Kaisa / Tiedemann, Jörg (2020): „MT for subtitling: Investigating professional translators' user experience and feedback". *Proceedings of 1st Workshop on Post-Editing in Modern-Day Translation*, S. 79–92, abgerufen am 06.02.2025 auf https://aclanthology.org/2020.amta-pemdt.6.pdf.

Krüger, Ralph (2023): „Artificial intelligence literacy for the language industry – with particular emphasis on recent large language models such as GPT-4". *Lebende Sprachen* 68(2), S. 283–330. https://doi.org/10.1515/les-2023-0024.

Läubli, Samuel / Amrhein, Chantal / Düggelin, Patrick / Gonzalez, Beatriz / Zwahlen, Alena / Volk, Martin (2019): „Post-editing productivity with neural machine translation: an empirical assessment of speed and quality in the banking and finance domain" In: Forcada, Mikel/Way, Andy/Haddow, Barry/Sennrich, Rico (Hrsg): *Proceedings of Machine Translation Summit XVII*, S. 267–272, abgerufen am 06.02.2025 auf https://aclanthology.org/W19-6626.pdf.

Liang, Lisi (2022): „Illuminating humanist nature in teaching translation and interpreting studies: Devising an online customisable AI-driven subtitling course". *Humanities and Social Sciences Communications* 9, S. 1–10. https://doi.org/10.1057/s41599-022-01397-w.

Matusov, Evgeny / Wilken, Patrick / Georgakopoulou, Panayota (2019): „Customizing neural machine translation for subtitling". In: Bojar, Ondřej / Chatterjee, Rajen / Federmann, Christian / Fishel, Mark / Graham, Yvette / Haddow, Barry / Huck, Matthias / Jimeno Yepes, Antonio / Koehn, Philipp / Martins, André / Monz, Christof / Negri, Matteo / Névéol, Aurélie / Neves, Mariana / Post, Matt / Turchi, Marco / Verspoor, Karin (Hrsg.): *Proceedings of the Fourth Conference on Machine Translation*. Vol. 1: *Research Papers*, S. 82–93.

Melero, Maite / Oliver, Antoni / Badia, Toni (2006): „Automatic multilingual subtitling in the eTITLE Project“. In: *Proceedings of ASLIB Translating and the Computer 28*, London, November 2006, S. 1–18 (abgerufen am 06.02.2025 auf https://aclanthology.org/2006.tc-1.10.pdf.

Mjölsnes, Ettore (2022): *Der stumme Text. Eine Kritik der maschinellen Übersetzung.* Küsnacht: Digiboo.

Müller, Mathias / Volk, Martin (2013): „Statistical machine translation of subtitles: From OpenSubtitles to TED“. In: Gurevych, Iryna / Biemann, Chris / Zesch, Torsten (Hrsg.): *Language processing and knowledge in the web.* Heidelberg et al.: Springer, S. 132–138.

Nikolic, Kristijan / Bywood, Lindsay (2021): „Audiovisual translation: The road ahead“. *Journal of Audiovisual Translation* 4/1, S. 50–70. https://doi.org/10.47476/jat.v4i1.2021.156

Nitzke, Jean / Hansen-Schirra, Silvia (2021): *A short guide to post-editing (= Translation and Multilingual Natural Language Processing, Bd. 16).* Berlin: Language Science Press. https://doi.org/10.5281/zenodo.5646896.

Orel Kos, Silvana (2024): „Introduction of Machine Translation into Audiovisual Translation Teaching“. *ELOPE. English Language Overseas Perspectives and Enquiries* 21/1: *English Studies at the Dawn of the 21st Century*, S. 185–208.

Popel, Martin / Tomkova, Marketa / Tomek, Jakub / Kaiser, Łukasz / Uszkoreit, Jakob / Bojar, Ondřej / Žabokrtský, Zdeněk (2020): „Transforming machine translation: A Deep Learning system reaches news translation quality comparable to human professionals“. *Nature Communications* 11, S. 1–15. https://doi.org/10.1038/ s41467-020-18073-9.

Prandi, Bianca (2015): „The use of CAI tools in interpreters' training: A pilot study“. In: *Proceedings of the 37th Conference Translating and the Computer. Translating and the Computer*, London: AsLing, S. 48–57, abgerufen am 06.02.2025 auf https://aclanthology.org/2015.tc-1.8.

Prandi, Bianca (2023): *Computer-assisted simultaneous interpreting: A cognitive-experimental study on terminology.* Berlin: Language Science Press. https://doi.org/10.5281/zenodo.7143056.

Rokeby, David (o. J.): *CulturAll*, abgerufen am 06.02.2025 auf http://www.davidrokeby.com/Culturall2/contents.html.

Sousa, Sheila C. M. de / Aziz, Wilker / Specia, Lucia (2011): „Assessing the post-editing effort for automatic and semi-automatic translations of DVD subtitles“. *Recent Advances in Natural Language Processing Conference*, Hissar, Bulgaria, S. 97–103, abgerufen am 06.02.2025 auf https://aclanthology.org/R11-1014.pdf.

Volk, Martin / Sennrich, Rico / Hardmeier, Christian / Tidström, Frida (2010): „Machine translation of TV subtitles for large scale production“. In: Zhechev, Ventsislav (Hrsg.): *Proceedings of the Second Joint EM+/CNGL Workshop "Bringing MT to the User: Research on Integrating MT in the Translation Industry (JEC'10)*, S. 53–62, abgerufen am 06.02.2025 auf https://aclanthology.org/2010.jec-1.7.pdf.

Terminologie vor den Herausforderungen und Chancen von KI*

Rossella Resi
Universität Innsbruck

Christian Lang
Kaleidoscope GmbH

ABSTRACT
The aim of this chapter is to emphasise the important role of terminology in translator training and to illustrate how it is now more than ever an important basis for the training of translators, interpreters and language experts. This is particularly due to its close connection with technological developments in language processing and artificial intelligence. On the one hand, the chapter shows how AI can speed up terminology work, for example through term extraction, clustering and the creation of definitions, and how this can be implemented in teaching. On the other hand, it is argued that students should be taught how terminology can contribute to improving AI results. A central point of consideration remains the importance of teaching evaluation skills. If terminology teaching is integrated into the translation studies degree programme in a forward-looking way, it will open up new career opportunities for students who are already equipped with language and translation skills.

Keywords: terminology teaching, terminology processes, term extraction, natural language processing, terminology competences, LLM, AI tools

1. Einführung

Studiengänge im Bereich der Fachübersetzung gehören zu den ersten, in denen Terminologielehre und deren Anwendung im Terminologiemanagement gelehrt wurden. Ab den späten 1970er Jahren erscheinen in der Literatur zunehmend Diskussionen über Lehrpläne für die Terminologievermittlung im Kontext der Fachübersetzung (Übersicht in Korkas und Rogers 2010). Einer der frühesten Terminologiekurse wurde von Wüster (1975) an der Universität Wien angeboten. Ein weiterer früher Kurs fand an der Universität Saarbrücken statt. In der frankophonen Welt wurden ab den 1970er Jahren ebenfalls Terminologiekurse für Übersetzungsstudierende eingeführt. Die

---

* Der vorliegende Artikel ist das Ergebnis der Zusammenarbeit der beiden Autor:innen. Rossella Resi hat die Abschnitte 1, 2, 3, 4.1, 5 verfasst; Christian Lang die Abschnitte 4.2 und 4.3.

Bedeutung der Terminologielehre in der translatorischen Ausbildung wurde früh erkannt („FIT History"; Hönig 1995; Sandrini 1997) und dementsprechend in die Studiengänge eingebaut. Heute bieten alle translatorischen Ausbildungen Terminologielehre mit unterschiedlichen Schwerpunkten an.

Zum Tätigkeitsspektrum traditionell ausgebildeter Translator:innen wurde angesichts des sich verändernden Arbeitsmarkts auch die Notwendigkeit erkannt, diese auf das Berufsbild der Terminolog:innen vorzubereiten, das allerdings noch relativ unbekannt war und teilweise immer noch ist. Um dieser Aufgabe gerecht zu werden, bedurfte es schon damals neben der Vermittlung von Grundkenntnissen der Terminologielehre auch der Einarbeitung in, der Zeit entsprechend, moderne, rechnergestützte Terminologieverwaltungssysteme.

Der Aufschwung der Terminologie als Wissenschaft und Praxis ist mit dem Aufkommen der Informatik verbunden (Magris et al. 2001), da die Verwaltung und Aktualisierung von Terminologiebeständen auf Papier sehr mühsam war und oft als ineffizient empfunden wurde. Die technologische Entwicklung muss dementsprechend auch in der Ausbildung widergespiegelt werden, sodass Kompetenzen im Umgang mit den verfügbaren Softwareprodukten vermittelt werden. „Terminologieunterricht" wird in einer früheren DIN-Norm definiert als der „Unterricht, der Wissen und Fähigkeiten im Bereich der Terminologielehre und deren Anwendung in der Terminologiearbeit vermittelt" (DIN 2342 1992 Abschnitt 5). In der DIN-Norm 2342:1992 wird also die duale Natur des Terminologieunterrichts hervorgehoben.

Die Terminologiepraxis entwickelt sich weiterhin parallel zur Anwendung neuer Technologien, wobei derzeit vielversprechende Fortschritte und Herausforderungen aus dem Bereich der Künstlichen Intelligenz (KI), insbesondere von Large Language Models (LLM)-basierten KI-Tools zu erwarten sind. Während die Integration neuer Terminologielehre über die Allgemeine Terminologielehre (Wüster 1975) hinaus problemlos möglich ist, da dies zur natürlichen Entwicklung von Theorien gehört, auf welche die akademische Welt vorbereitet ist, stellt die Geschwindigkeit der technologischen Entwicklung eine große Herausforderung dar (He 2021).

Wie zuvor mit der Einführung von Technologien wie Computer-Assisted Translation (CAT)-Tools, Translation Memorys (TMs) und jüngst neuronaler maschineller Übersetzung (NMT) für die translatorische Ausbildung allgemein, wird auch der aktuelle technologische Fortschritt in der

Sprachverarbeitung und KI einen tiefgreifenden Eingriff in den Lehraufbau der translatorischen Ausbildung einschließlich der Terminologielehre bedingen. Es ist abzusehen, dass die zukünftigen Anforderungen sowohl an die Studierenden als auch an die Lehrenden davon stark beeinflusst sein werden, da sich bereits heute die Erwartung an das Kompetenzspektrum von Lehrenden und Ausgebildeten verändert hat (Müller 2023).

Im sich rasant ändernden Verhältnis zwischen menschlichem Eingriff und maschineller Leistung in den verschiedenen terminologischen Prozessen auf dem Arbeitsmarkt könnte sich die Vermittlung der derzeit gültigen Technologiekompetenzen für den zukünftigen Arbeitsmarkt als unzureichend erweisen. Da die erforderlichen Kompetenzen für den Zukunftsmarkt nur begrenzt vorhersehbar sind, ist es wichtig, auf langfristige, flexible und nachhaltige Kompetenzen abzuzielen.

Um die Chancen und Herausforderungen dieser Entwicklung zu schildern, wird in diesem Abschnitt zunächst darauf eingegangen, auf welche mit den neuen Technologien verbundenen Aspekte Terminologiestudierende heute und in der Zukunft vorbereitet werden sollen. In Abschnitt 2 soll ein kurzer Überblick zur Terminologie zu KI selbst gegeben werden, um die Unschärfe des Begriffs „KI" etwas zu durchleuchten, was auch in Form von Terminologiearbeit im Unterricht thematisiert werden kann. In Abschnitt 3 wird ein Überblick über die Berufsbilder für Terminolog:innen im heutigen Szenario und im Hinblick auf die laufenden Veränderungen gegeben, was als Grundlage für den Einsatz von KI-gestützten Systemen und LLMs in der Lehre dienen kann. Dabei werden die Gefahren und Potentiale dieser Technologien für Studierende in den unterschiedlichen terminologischen Prozessen aufgezeigt (Abschnitt 4). Ein besonderer Fokus liegt auf der Terminologieextraktion (Abschnitt 4.1), der Begriffsorientierung und der Extraktion von Beziehungen zwischen Begriffen, was für den Ontologieaufbau (Abschnitt 4.2) sowie die Verfassung von Definitionen und die Terminologierecherche (Abschnitt 4.3) hilfreich ist. In Abschnitt 5 wird umgekehrt untersucht, wie Terminologiekompetenzen für Translator:innen zur Entwicklung und effizienten Nutzung von KI eingesetzt werden können. Der Fokus liegt hier auf *terminology enforcement* (Abschnitt 5.1). Abschließend werden wesentliche Merkmale zukunftsorientierter und vor allem nachhaltiger Lehrkonzepte für die Terminologieausbildung zusammengefasst und Berufsmöglichkeiten für Studierende mit terminologischen Kompetenzen dargestellt (Abschnitt 6).

2. Terminologie zu KI

Im Zuge der rasanten Entwicklung von KI haben sich in allen Sprachen zahlreiche Begriffe und Bezeichnungen in diesem Bereich entwickelt. Diese Neologismen werden jedoch nicht von allen Personen, einschließlich Studierenden, einheitlich verstanden. Dies liegt nicht nur an mangelndem Wissen, sondern auch daran, dass die Geschwindigkeit und Verbreitung dieser Begriffe zu undefinierten Begriffsgrenzen und zur Überlappung von Definitionen geführt haben. Selbst der Begriff *Künstliche Intelligenz* ist sehr unscharf, da er als Oberbegriff für verschiedene Arten von Künstlicher Intelligenz verwendet wird, die sich stark voneinander unterscheiden. Die Begriffe *machine learning* (maschinelles Lernen) und *KI* werden oft von Studierenden synonym verwendet, obwohl es sich bei einem nur um einen Unterbereich des Feldes *Künstliche Intelligenz* handelt. Auch *deep learning* wird oft synonym mit *machine learning* genutzt. Wie oft in der täglichen Nutzung von Terminologie, werden Unterbegriffe und Oberbegriffe nicht klar auseinandergehalten.

Machine learning analysiert auf Basis von mathematischen Prinzipien bestehendes Material, um zukünftige Präferenzen vorherzusagen und personalisierte Ergebnisse vorzuschlagen (ISO/IEC 22989:2022 Eintrag 3.3.5). *Deep learning* ist eine spezielle Art von *machine learning* (ISO/IEC 22989:2022 Eintrag 3.4.4). Im Bereich Terminologie und Übersetzung kann *machine learning* verwendet werden, um Übersetzungsvorschläge durch die Analyse von strukturiertem Material (z. B. Glossare in Excel-Tabellen) zu verbessern, etwa durch verschiedene statistische Ansätze. Wenn Terminologie aus Bestandsdaten wie terminologisch einheitlich übersetzten Texten gelernt werden soll, werden meistens tief vernetzte neuronale Ansätze genutzt und deshalb wird eher von *deep learning* gesprochen. Die neuronalen Netze identifizieren Terminologiemuster und bieten Übersetzungen, die diese Muster enthalten. Im Gegensatz dazu können KI-Systeme (die oft auf neuronalen Netzen basieren) (ISO/IEC 22989:2022 Eintrag 3.1.4) auf spezifische Übersetzungsanfragen antworten, indem sie die in der Anweisung (*prompt*: noch nicht erfasst in ISO/IEC 22989) enthaltenen Kriterien berücksichtigen und entsprechend darauf reagieren.

Interessant in neuen Fachgebieten ist die Terminologisierung von schon vorhandenen Benennungen wie *context* (noch nicht erfasst in ISO/IEC 22989), die im Bereich der KI eine ganz andere Bedeutung annimmt und sich entweder auf die Gesamtheit des Textes bezieht, der für die Generierung der nächsten Textpassage eines KI-Modells mitgegeben wird (also *prompts* und *retrieved context*) oder nur den *context* der durch *retrieval-augmented generation (RAG)*-Methoden dem *prompt* hinzugefügt wird. Besonders für Studierende der Translationswissenschaft, die sich mit dem traditionellen Begriff *Kontext* auseinandersetzen, kann die Polysemie dieser Benennung verwirrend sein.

Neue, nicht fleckendeckend standardisierte Domänen wie KI bieten ein optimales Feld für Terminologieübungen. Studierende können dabei die Terminologie von KI-Branchen in den studierten Sprachen in Bezug auf Neologismen oder Anglizismen untersuchen, in Datenbanken systematisieren und bei der Begriffsanalyse gleichzeitig auch ihre Kenntnisse in diesem Fachgebiet vertiefen. Es soll dadurch vermittelt werden, dass Terminologie eine notwendige Grundlage für technische Standardisierung darstellt und dass sie gemeinsame Bezugsrahmen unter den involvierten Personen und über Disziplinen hinweg schafft. Terminologien in unterschiedlichen Sprachen spiegeln auch unterschiedliche technologische Kulturen wieder und offenbaren durch ihre Übereinstimmungen und Abweichungen das Vorhandensein von Benennungs- und Begriffslücken. Kulturelle Kompetenzen sind hier erforderlich.

Mit der Terminologie zu KI kann auch die unterschiedliche Einstellung von Sprachen und Kulturen gegenüber der Akzeptanz von Anglizismen thematisiert werden. Dabei kann auf verschiedene Faktoren in der Neologismenbildung wie Schnelligkeit, Flüchtigkeit der Begriffe, morphologische Möglichkeiten, mediale Verbreitung, Sprachenpolitik usw. hingewiesen werden.

Die Bedeutung der Terminologie geht also weit über die Vorteile beim Übersetzen hinaus, translatorische Kompetenzen sind aber bei mehrsprachiger Terminologiearbeit von Vorteil, insbesondere wenn es darum geht, Divergenzen und Inkonsistenzen zwischen Sprachen zu identifizieren und diese als Ansatzpunkte für Kooperation und Zusammenarbeit zu nutzen.

3. Kompetenzen und Berufsbilder für Terminolog:innen

Terminologieausbildungen werden heute sowohl in akademischen als auch in nicht-akademischen Umgebungen angeboten. Sie werden von Universitätsprofessor:innen und Fachleuten als Ergänzungskurse sowie als vollständige Studiengänge unterrichtet. Dies verdeutlicht, dass Terminologie zunehmend als eigenständige Wissenschaft anerkannt wird. Darüber hinaus zeigt es, dass die Terminologiewissenschaft eine umfassende Disziplin darstellt, deren Anwendungsbereich über den traditionellen Beruf des Fachübersetzers hinausgeht (Drewer et al. 2018; RaDT 2020; TerminOrgs 2016). Die Terminologielehre wird unterstützend als Bestandteil von Ausbildungen in Fachbereichen wie Jura oder Medizin unterrichtet. In diesen Bereichen liegt der Fokus auf der Sachkompetenz in den entsprechenden Fachgebieten und der monolingualen Terminologie. Zu diesen universellen Kompetenzen zählen grundlegende Kenntnisse der Terminologiewissenschaft, die Beherrschung terminologischer Arbeitsmethoden sowie Fähigkeiten im Projekt- und Prozessmanagement der Terminologie (Prieto Ramos 2024; RaDT 2020).

Das Bündnis mit der Translationswissenschaft bleibt jedoch unauflöslich. Terminologie liefert grundlegende Inhalte für die Ausbildung von Fachübersetzer:innen (PACTE 2011; Schmitz 2020). Gleichzeitig sind übersetzungswissenschaftliche Kompetenzen und sprachwissenschaftliche Perspektiven unverzichtbar für die Terminologieverwaltung, auch über den traditionellen Beruf der Fachübersetzer:innen hinaus (Drewer et al. 2018; RaDT 2020; TerminOrgs 2016). In der translatorischen Ausbildung wird neben dem Umgang mit mehrsprachiger Terminologie, Fachsprachenkompetenzen, Recherchefähigkeiten und dem kritischen Umgang mit Quellen auch die Beziehung zwischen Theorie und Praxis hervorgehoben. Die Beherrschung von Tools zur Terminologieverwaltung und -kontrolle sowie zur Beschleunigung von Terminologieprozessen hat immer eine zentrale Rolle für den Zugang zum Arbeitsmarkt gespielt (von Auger 1979 bis Prieto Ramos 2024). Übungen zur praktischen Terminologiearbeit am Rechner mit geeigneten Terminologieverwaltungswerkzeugen wie z. B. Tests zur automatischen Terminologieextraktion oder Generierung von Listen sind zunehmend Bestandteil translatorischer Ausbildungsgänge geworden.

Zu den Berufen, die mit diesen Schnittstellenkompetenzen verbunden sind, zählen: TDB-Expert:in in Unternehmen, Normungsorganisationen oder der Sprachindustrie, Content Manager:in, Product Manager:in, Expert:in für Corporate Identity, Qualitätsverantwortliche:r, Sprachplaner:in und Redakteur:in für technische Dokumentation. Diese Liste wird sich angesichts der neuen Entwicklungen im Bereich der KI und im spezifischen der LLM erweitern.

4. KI-Tools in den Prozessen der Terminologiearbeit

Die Einbeziehung von Personen mit translatorischen und terminologischen Kompetenzen rund um den Einsatz von KI erscheint zunächst weniger eindeutig. Ältere Methoden der maschinellen Übersetzung, wie Regelbasierte MT (RBMT), erforderten die Bereitstellung von (computer-)linguistischen Regeln, vorbearbeiteten und bereinigten Datenbanken mit zusätzlichen Attributen, manuell gesetzten Relationen zwischen den Übersetzungseinheiten oder sonstigem kodiertem Wissen, was unter anderem sprachwissenschaftliche und translatorische Kompetenzen voraussetzte (Meyer/Eck/Skuce 1997). Bereits mit Statistischer Maschineller Übersetzung (SMT), aber besonders mit NMT, wurde das Einbeziehen solcher Regeln oder Datenbanken optional, aber auch technisch nicht mehr ohne weiteres möglich. Abgesehen von der Bereitstellung kohärenter Terminologie als Trainingsdaten in Form von Translation Memorys, Paralleltexten oder Termbanken und dem Post-Editing (PE) der terminologischen Kohärenz, scheint es ansonsten keinen klaren Einbezug dieser Fachleute in den verschiedenen Prozessen der maschinellen Übersetzung selbst zu geben. Andererseits war bis vor kurzem generell die Meinung in der Öffentlichkeit vertreten, dass die Maschine nur für begrenzte, kompilative terminologische Aufgaben unterstützend sein konnte. Mit KI, d. h. generativen Sprachmodellen, können nun auch komplexere terminologische Tätigkeiten von der Maschine übernommen bzw. unterstützt werden, was die „Bedrohung" eines Ersatzes der translatorischen und terminologischen Kompetenzen erneut vor Augen führt. Dies mag auch dadurch gefördert sein, dass laut den Erkenntnissen von Computerlinguist:innen in der Regel weder KI-Modelle noch Menschen dazu in der Lage sind, maschinell generierte Leistungen von Humanleistungen mit hoher Sicherheit zu unterscheiden (Calvo-Ferrer 2023; Woodrum 2024). Somit verbreitet sich in der Öffentlichkeit die Idee, dass mit den rezenten Fortschritten in der KI durch LLMs die translatorischen bzw. terminologischen Kompetenzen nicht mehr notwendig seien.

Dabei zeigen z. B. Evaluierungen von LLMs für die Nutzung als MT-Tools, dass *state-of-the-art* Sprachmodelle wie GPT-4 in den meisten Auswertungen nicht besser (aber in der Regel auch nicht viel schlechter) abschneiden als vergleichbar kleine und effiziente NMT-Modelle (Lionbridge 2021; Woodrum 2024). Maschinelle Übersetzung gilt im Allgemeinen nicht als gelöstes Problem und erfordert für produktive Übersetzungsaufträge oft humane Nacharbeit in Form von *machine translation post editing* (MTPE) oder Neuübersetzung. Auch hier muss allerdings beachtet werden, dass diese Ergebnisse stark von der Art der Evaluierung, z. B. automatische Metriken wie Post-Edit Error Rate, BLEU (Papineni et al 2002) oder COMET (Rei et al. 2020) vs. Humanevaluierung durch Personen mit translatorischen Kompetenzen, den verwendeten Testdaten (Sprachrichtung, Fachgebiet, Textsorte etc.) sowie, im Falle von LLMs, den *prompts* und Hyperparametern abhängen. In Bezug auf terminologische Aufgaben können KI-Tools und insbesondere LLMs tatsächlich viele neue Aufgaben erledigen, die mit bestehenden Technologien bis dato nicht möglich waren. Allerdings zeigen erste Untersuchungen der Tools für z. B. die Generierung von terminologischen Definitionen, dass für Anwendungszwecke, bei denen eine hohe Zuverlässigkeit der Daten notwendig ist, von Terminolog:innen und Expert:innen gepflegte Ressourcen nicht gänzlich durch KI-Tools ersetzt werden können (San Martín 2024).

Der allgemeine Tenor, dass sich KI-Systeme wie NMT und LLMs verbessern und dem menschlichen Output näherkommen, wird also auch in der Literatur gezeigt. Allerdings sind die Systeme nicht unfehlbar, und menschliche Intervention ist, gerade was terminologische Genauigkeit und Kohärenz beim Output der Systeme angeht, nach wie vor unumgänglich. Es ist also weiterhin eine ausgeklügelte Vorbereitung und eine kontinuierliche Bewertung durch Expert:innen erforderlich. Der spezialisierte Umgang mit den Tools sowie die Einschätzung und Evaluierung der Ergebnisse aller terminologischen Vorgänge sind zu Schlüsselaufgaben geworden, auf die Studierende vorbereitet werden müssen. Marktanalysen der Sprachindustrie unterstützen nach wie vor diese Notwendigkeit (Luckin et al. 2022), und betonen sogar, dass die Nachfrage nach ausgebildeten Sprachexpert:innen in der Branche weiter wächst (Sun 2021).

Vor diesem Hintergrund wird in den folgenden Abschnitten erörtert, wie Studierende in Terminologiekursen zukunftsweisend ausgebildet werden können. Dabei wird insbesondere der Umgang mit neuen KI-Tools und die Entwicklung der damit verbundenen Kompetenzen untersucht. Es muss jedoch sichergestellt werden, dass diese Schritte, ob toolgestützt oder nicht, niemals strikt voneinander getrennt sind und dass Terminologie vielmehr ein fortlaufender, einheitlicher Prozess ist, der eine ganzheitliche Übersicht erfordert, die nur menschliche Terminolog:innen leisten können. Der Fokus auf die Technologie darf nicht von den übergeordneten terminologischen

Zielen ablenken, die stets als Teil des theoretischen Wissens und als Grundsatz für die Praxis im Blick behalten werden sollen. Hinzu kommt, dass die Studierenden auch für die mit der Nutzung von KI verbundenen ethischen Fragen und Datenschutzprobleme sensibilisiert werden sollen, auf die in diesem Beitrag nur begrenzt eingegangen wird. Diese Aspekte würden einer ausführlichen und eigenständigen Betrachtung bedürfen.

4.1 Automatische Termextraktion (ATE)

Eine der zeitintensivsten und herausforderndsten Aktivitäten im Aufbau und in der Pflege der Terminologie ist das Sammeln von Benennungen und Begriffen aus verschiedenen Quellen sowie das begriffsorientierte Gruppieren von synonymen Benennungen zu einzelnen Begriffen. Automatische Termextraktion soll dabei helfen, die Aufwände dieser Aufgabe zu reduzieren und Teile der Terminologiegewinnung zu automatisieren. Das Ziel von Automatischer Termextraktion (ATE) ist es, eine Liste potentiell relevanter Termini aus einem oder mehreren Dokumenten oder einem ganzen Textkorpus zu erstellen, idealerweise in der Grundform (*lemma*); dabei gilt es, die Anzahl der unbrauchbaren Kandidaten (*noise*) niedrig zu halten, aber auch sicherzustellen, dass tatsächliche Termini nicht von der Extraktion ausgeschlossen werden (*silence*). Gemessen wird die Leistung von ATE-Systemen in der Regel in *precision* (hohe Precision = niedrige *noise*) und *recall* (hohe *recall* = niedrige *silence*) oder das harmonische Mittel dieser Werte, genannt *F1-score*. Da statistische Systeme die Kandidaten oft nach einem *score* sortieren und oft nicht bekannt ist, welche Termini im Korpus überhaupt vorkommen, werden in vielen Studien nur die besten k Kandidaten (*top-k*) auf die Treffergenauigkeit evaluiert, d. h. man limitiert die Auswertung auf den *Precision@top-k*-Wert.

ATE ist dabei keineswegs eine neue Disziplin. So beschreiben Kageura und Umino 1996 in einem der ersten Reviews zu ATE bereits Ansätze, die bis ins Jahr 1957 zurückreichen (Kageura/Umino 1996). Bis zum Durchbruch von neuronalen Netzwerken waren hauptsächlich zwei dominierende Ansätze in der Wissenschaft und in verschiedenen kommerziellen sowie frei erhältlichen Termextraktions-Tools üblich: statistische und regelbasierte Ansätze. Regelbasierte Ansätze nutzen verschiedene von Computerlinguist:innen geschriebene Regeln und NLP-Ansätze, wie Tokenisierung, Lemmatisierung, Stemming, Chunking und POS-Tagging, um Kandidaten zu identifizieren, die für Termini typischen linguistischen Konstrukten folgen: So sind Termini z. B. meist Nomen oder Komposita, Adjektiv-Nomen-Verbindungen (z. B. „maschinelle Übersetzung“ oder „schwarzes Loch“), haben eine spezielle Schreibweise (z. B. Akronyme wie ISO oder NATO) oder finden sich in speziellen Kontexten wieder (z. B. Die Terminologielehre ist die Wissenschaft von Begriffen…). Diese Regeln sind teilweise natürlich sprachabhängig und auch sehr aufwändig zu erstellen und zu warten. Außerdem ist es schwierig, Unregelmäßigkeiten in der Sprache damit erfolgreich abzufangen.

Aufgrund der genannten Herausforderungen mit regelbasierten Ansätzen wurden verschiedene statistische Ansätze für die Termextraktion entwickelt. Auch statistische Ansätze basieren dabei auf gewissen Hypothesen darüber, was *termhood*[1] ausmacht (Kageura/Umino 1996), nutzen aber anstelle von Regeln statistische Ansätze. So wird mit Methoden wie TF-IDF (*term frequency inverse document frequency*) (Salton/Wong/Yang 1975) das *termhood* innerhalb eines Textkorpus berechnet oder mit *weirdness* (Ahmad/Gillam/Tostevin 1999) das Vorkommen von Termini innerhalb von domänenspezifischen Texten mit allgemeinen Texten verglichen, um das *termhood* eines Worts oder einer Phrase einer bestimmten Domäne zu bestimmen. Mit *C-Value* (Frantzi/Ananiadou/Mima 2000) werden zusätzlich auch sogenannte *nested terms* berücksichtigt, also Termini, die selbst andere Termini (Komposita oder Mehrwortbenennungen) beinhalten und somit die sogenannte *unithood*[2] (Kageura/Umino 1996).

Oft werden regelbasierte und statistische Ansätze miteinander kombiniert und bilden so einen „hybriden“ Ansatz, der meist aus einer Pipeline besteht, in der zuerst der Text regelbasiert vorbearbeitet wird und dann regelbasierte und statistische Kandidaten erhoben werden, die dann nochmal durch verschiedene statistische oder andere Methode „geranked“ werden (Astrakhantsev 2016). Automatische Termextraktion gilt allerdings selbst mit hybriden Methoden nicht als gelöst: Die *precision* solcher Methoden bewegt sich selbst bei großen Korpora und Einschränkung auf die besten 500-1000 Kandidaten unter 80 % (Astrakhantsev 2016), oder gar nur zwischen 20-30 %, wenn man die Evaluierung auf alle vorgeschlagenen Kandidaten

---

1 *Termhood* ist die Fähigkeit eines Indexterms, den Begriff in einem Dokument zu repräsentieren

2 *Unithood* bezeichnet Indexterme als syntagmatische linguistische Einheiten

ausweitet, mit einem meist ebenso niedrigen *recall* (Bakaric/Babic/Matetic 2021; Lang et al. 2021). Auch funktionieren die meisten Methoden nur bei großen Dokumenten oder Korpora mit zufriedenstellenden Ergebnissen, da es ansonsten kaum zu relevanten Statistiken kommen kann. Dennoch basiert die Mehrheit der kommerziell und frei verfügbaren Software für Termextraktion auf diesen Methoden.

4.1.1 ATE in der Terminologielehre

Die Voraussetzungen für regel- und statistikbasierte ATE stellen für die Terminologielehre, insbesondere in der translatorischen Ausbildung, eine Herausforderung dar. Zwar bieten viele CAT-Tools eine ATE-Funktion (z. B. MemoQ, PhraseTMS, Wordfast, XTM) oder können diese per Plugin hinzufügen (z. B. projectTermExtract für RWS Trados Studio). Allerdings lässt sich der Output der Extraktion oft nur schwer im Unterricht verwerten, da die Grundlagen für eine gute Extraktion beim Umfang von üblichen Übungsprojekten, besonders in der translatorischen Ausbildung, meist nicht gegeben werden können, und die Konfiguration der ATE-Komponente dieser Tools meist nicht genug Granularität zur Verbesserung der Ergebnisse erlaubt. Um Übungen mit solchen Tools mit besseren Ergebnissen zu gestalten, müssten die optimalen Voraussetzungen für diese Tools geschaffen werden:

- domänenspezifische Korpora in Form von einsprachigen Texten oder mehrsprachigen Paralleltexten (in manchen Tools auch TMs);
- eine bereits gut gepflegte und domänenspezifische Termbank, die allerdings auch noch Lücken beinhaltet, die mit der Extraktion gefüllt werden können;
- domänenfremde bzw. allgemeinsprachliche Vergleichskorpora.

Welche dieser Datensätze genutzt werden können und wie diese genutzt werden, ist von Tool zu Tool unterschiedlich, und der Zugriff auf die Tools und Datensätze müsste Studierenden über die Studiendauer hinweg gewährleistet werden. Für das Verständnis der historischen und künftigen Entwicklung dieser Tools ist nichtsdestotrotz relevant, diese sprachabhängigen und statistikbasierten Regeln sowie ihre Grenzen aus translatorischer Sicht zu thematisieren.

Eine interessante Alternative zur Nutzung von ATE-Komponenten in CAT-Tools ist das Nutzen von dedizierter Termextraktionssoftware in der Terminologielehre. Diese Tools erlauben in der Regel mehr Kontrolle über die statistischen und regelbasierten Parameter als Termextraktionskomponenten in CAT-Tools und binden Studierende nicht an ein bestimmtes Übersetzungstool. Es gibt eine Vielzahl von frei verfügbaren Programmen, die für die Extraktion herangezogen werden können[3]. Allerdings sind viele dieser Tools, wie z. B. ATR4S (Astrakhantsev 2016), vergleichsweise aufwändig zu installieren und besitzen keine oder eine sehr limitierte grafische Benutzeroberfläche (GUI). TermSuite (TermSuite 3.0.10) scheint unter den uns bekannten Applikationen die benutzerfreundlichste GUI zu haben und schneidet bei der Extraktion vergleichbar mit bezahlter regel- und statistikbasierter ATE-Software ab (Bakaric/Babic/Matetic 2021). Wie zuvor, benötigen auch diese Tools einen größeren Textkorpus, um aussagekräftige Statistiken zu berechnen und so Termini besser extrahieren zu können. In der Installationsanleitung von TermSuite wird deshalb auch ein Korpus verlinkt, das leider zum Zeitpunkt des Verfassens dieses Beitrags nicht mehr verfügbar ist. Die Installation und Instandhaltung solcher Tools sind demnach eine weitere Herausforderung für Studierende.

Hersteller von kostenpflichtiger Software wie Sketch Engine (Kilgariff et al. 2004) sind sich dieser Herausforderung bewusst, weshalb die Entwickler:innen von SketchEngine mit OneClickTerms eine verhältnismäßig einfach zu nutzende Lösung entwickelt haben, die selbst ohne große eigene Datensätze gute Ergebnisse liefern kann. Sketch Engine ist eigentlich ein Korpusabfragesystem und hat dementsprechend eine riesige Menge an Dokumenten, auf die es für die Termextraktion mit statistischen Ansätzen, wie z. B *weirdness*, zugreifen kann. Zusätzlich wird Sketch Engine als Webapplikation angeboten und ist in vielen Universitäten für Studierende mit Grundfunktionen kostenlos nutzbar. Insbesondere in Hinsicht auf die translatorische Ausbildung ist auch die bilinguale ATE-Funktion von OneClickTerms interessant. Sketch Engine bietet sich demnach als gute Lösung für die Termextraktion in der Lehre an, basiert aber auch weiterhin

---

[3] Eine unvollständige Auflistung findet sich im Annex I.

auf den „klassischen“ hybriden Methoden (Blahuš et al. 2023). Das bedeutet, dass auch mit OneClickTerms viele Termini nicht gefunden werden bzw. viele der gelieferten Kandidaten mitunter gar keine Termini sind, besonders wenn man etwas tiefer in der Ergebnisliste gräbt.

4.1.2 ATE und KI

Mit dem Aufkommen von neuronalen Modellen, die in einer Vielzahl von NLP-Aufgaben *state-of-the-art* Ergebnisse erzielen (Vaswani et al. 2017), werden neuronale (oder auch *deep learning*) und auch andere *machine learning*-basierte Ansätze verstärkt auf deren Verwendung für ATE untersucht (DiNunzio/Marchesin/Silvello 2023; Tran et al. 2023). Die Ergebnisse der meisten neuronalen Ansätze überflügeln die Ergebnisse der meisten nicht-neuronalen und besonders traditionellen „hybriden“ Ansätze in den aktuellen Studien (Lang et al. 2021; Tran et al. 2023) und werden teilweise bereits in kommerziellen Produkten verwendet.

Tatsächlich basieren die neuronalen Ansätze meist auf Sprachmodellen der Transformer-Architektur, also auf einer ähnlichen Architektur wie die GPT-Modelle von OpenAI, die wiederum hinter Tools wie ChatGPT stecken. Folglich gibt es auch schon eine Vielzahl von Sprachexpert:innen, Übersetzer:innen und Terminolog:innen, die LLM-basierte generative KI-Tools wie ChatGPT für die Termextraktion heranziehen (Giguere 2023; Rütten 2023; Winter 2024). Dieser Ansatz birgt, im Vergleich zu den für Termextraktion trainierten bzw. fine-getunten Ansätzen, einige Vorteile, besonders in der Terminologielehre und für Studierende, nämlich eine Niederschwelligkeit, die Expert:innentools nur selten bieten:

- Die Modelle müssen nicht auf die Aufgabe der Termextraktion fine-getuned werden.
- Der Output dieser Tools kann über *prompting* (also Anweisungen in natürlicher Sprache) ad-hoc angepasst werden.
- Das Einlesen der Daten erfordert keine besondere Vorbereitung; der zu analysierende Text muss nur in das Tool kopiert werden.

Einen qualitativen Vergleich zwischen *state-of-the-art* Modellen für Termextraktion in der Forschung und Termextraktion via LLM-basierte generative KI-Tools scheint es zum Zeitpunkt des Schreibens dieses Artikels noch nicht zu geben, aber einige der Limitierungen generativer KI liegen auf der Hand bzw. werden in allen oben zitierten Berichten auch erwähnt:

- Diese Tools sind per Design nicht deterministisch; die Antworten sind bei gleicher Eingabe immer etwas unterschiedlich[4], d. h. für den gleichen Text und *prompt* werden, je nach Anlauf, unterschiedliche Termini extrahiert.
- Extraktionsergebnisse sind nicht immer so wie im *prompt* definiert (z. B. werden Wörter mitunter nicht auf die Grundform heruntergebrochen).
- Extraktionsergebnisse können Halluzinationen (schlüssig wirkende, aber faktisch nicht korrekte oder fundierte Ausgaben) beinhalten; es werden z. B. Termini „extrahiert", die gar nicht im Text vorkommen.
- Große Korpora oder Dokumente können mitunter nicht analysiert werden (Längenbeschränkung für Inputs bei LLMs; diese wird aber stetig erhöht).
- Bestandsdaten können nur schwer bereitgestellt werden; bestehende Termbanken, Translation Memorys oder Vergleichskorpora können von diesen Tools (noch) nicht berücksichtigt werden.

Der allgemeine Tenor bleibt natürlich, dass die Tools großes Potential bieten; entsprechend eignen sich diese Tools auch für die Terminologielehre, da sie zum einen hilfreich für die Terminologieextraktion sein können und zum anderen interessant für die Forschung sind, da es noch ein zu geringes Literaturaufkommen dazu gibt, wie die Tools am besten zu nutzen sind und an welchen Aufgaben die Tools scheitern. Aus den ersten gesammelten Erfahrungen und bisherigen Berichten ist davon auszugehen, dass die

[4] Das Verhalten ist teilweise beabsichtigt (wirkt menschlicher), teilweise ein Nebenprodukt der Rechenvorgänge in LLMs und des Samplings der Wahrscheinlichkeiten des nächsten Worts (Tokens). Über sogenannte „Hyperparameter" des Modells kann das Verhalten gesteuert werden: „Temperature" (steuert die Wahrscheinlichkeitsverteilung), „Top P" oder „Top K" (definiert den Pool an wahrscheinlichsten Fortführungen) und „Seed" (beeinflusst die zufällige Auswahl des nächsten Tokens aus dem zuvor bestimmten Pool). Diese Parameter sind nur in den Entwicklungsumgebungen der KI-Anbieter oder bei „open weights" bzw. „open source"-Implementierungen von KI-Tools verfügbar (OpenAI 2024a).

generativen KI-Tools zwar teilweise bessere Ergebnisse erzielen als traditionelle hybride oder statistische Ansätze (Giguere 2023), aber wo sich die Leistung der Modelle quantitativ und qualitativ im Vergleich zu aktuellen *state-of-the-art* Ansätzen in der Termextraktionsforschung einreiht, ist momentan wegen der fehlenden Forschungslage, aber auch aufgrund der sich ständig ändernden Modelllandschaft, schwer zu erörtern.

Wie einleitend erwähnt, sind die Ergebnisse der neuronalen Ansätze in den rezenten Studien den traditionellen Ansätzen weitgehend überlegen; so sind die besten Ergebnisse für ATE-Datensätze wie ACTER (Rigouts/Ayla/Lefever 2020) mit einem *F1-score* um 60 % wesentlich höher als die *F1-scores* um die 27-30 % von traditionellen Ansätzen (Lang et al. 2021). Wie Di Nunzio, Marchesin und Silvello (2023) schreiben, zeigen diese Ergebnisse allerdings auch, dass selbst mit neuronalen Methoden nach wie vor die Nachbearbeitung durch Terminologie-Expert:innen notwendig ist. Umso wichtiger ist es also, dass Studierende lernen, mit den Ausgaben der verschiedenen Terminologieextraktionssoftwares umzugehen bzw. dass diese mehr als nur Termini extrahieren und so Terminologiestudierende wie auch professionell tätige Terminolog:innen bei der Ausarbeitung der Terminologie aus der initialen Liste unterstützen.

4.2 Clustering und Relationsextraktion

Wie im vorangehenden Unterabschnitt erwähnt, ist das Ergebnis von ATE in der Regel eine Liste von Termini, die keine oder nur sehr wenig Zusatzinfos zur Bildung von Begriffen (Konzepten) mitgibt. Das Ausarbeiten einer begriffsorientierten Terminologie auf Basis dieser Liste ist somit ein weiterer zeitintensiver Schritt für Studierende und Terminolog:innen. Begriffsorientierte Termbanken bieten auch in der Industrie unterschiedliche Vorteile im Vergleich zu reinen Glossaren, darunter auch die Möglichkeit, die Ambiguität der Sprache (z. B. Homographe und Synonyme) angebracht abdecken zu können. Der Aufwand, aus einer Termextraktion zu einer begriffsorientierten Termbank zu kommen, schließt eine einfache Termextraktion in der Praxis allerdings oft aus.

Die skandinavische Firma Fodina bietet mit ihrem Produkt TermCatch (Fodina 2024) eine Termextraktionssoftware an, die neben der allgemeinen Termextraktion auch eine Clustering-Logik zum Zusammenführen von Synonymen zu „Begriffskandidaten“ besitzt. Hierzu nutzt TermCatch bereits neuronale Ansätze für die Termextraktion auf Englisch, Deutsch und Schwedisch und kann in einem zweiten Schritt über weitere nicht genauer spezifizierte *machine learning*-Ansätze und „*synonym*-Nachweise“[5], die Termini aus der Liste *clustern*, d. h. zu einem Begriffskandidaten zusammenführen. Neben der automatisierten Zusammenführung der Termini zu Begriffskandidaten extrahiert TermCatch auch viele zusätzliche Informationen zum jeweiligen Terminus wie z. B. die Kontextsätze, die ermittelte Wortart (Nomen, Adjektiv, Verb etc.), ob es sich um einen allgemeinen Term (COMMON TERM), einen domänenspezifischen Term (SPECIFIC TERM) oder sonstige besondere Arten von Termini (z. B. PRODUCT NAME, ACRONYM) handelt. Zusätzlich lassen sich terminologische Bestandsdaten über Excelimporte und Termbankanbindungen (Acrolinx und Kalcium Quickterm) einbinden. Das Tool wird explizit als „Expertentool für Terminolog:innen“ vermarktet und soll es Terminolog:innen erleichtern, die automatischen Ergebnisse schneller und effizienter auszuarbeiten. Für einen vollen Überblick über das Tool empfiehlt sich der Artikel zum Tool aus der Fachzeitschrift für Terminologie *Edition* 2(23) (Trembczyk/Lang 2023). Derzeit besteht das Hindernis darin, dass Universitäten keinen Zugang zu dieser Software haben, um sie Studierenden zu zeigen und zur Übung bereitzustellen. Es wäre empfehlenswert, dass solche Tools den Universitäten zur Verfügung gestellt würden.

Terminologiedatenbanken sind in der Regel Sammlungen von Begriffen in einer oder mehreren Domänen oder einem oder mehreren Fachgebieten; dabei werden die Begriffe in Termbanken nur selten in Bezug zueinander gesetzt. Zwar bieten verschiedene Terminologieverwaltungstools und -standards die Möglichkeit, „Referenzen“ in den Einträgen zu hinterlegen (z. B. <ref> und <xref>-Elemente in *TBX* oder die Term- und Conceptlinks in *MultiTerm*), aber nur wenige Systeme erlauben die Erstellung von relationalen Begriffsnetzen, sogenannten *concept maps* oder *knowledge graphs*. Einige Tools ermöglichen das Erstellen solcher Graphen, allerdings ist die Erstellung noch großteils manuell und zwischen den verschiedenen Systemen nicht genormt. In *Kalcium Quickterm* (Kaleidoscope GmbH n.d.) lassen sich *concept maps* auf Basis der bestehenden Terminologie oder ad hoc angelegter Termkandidaten

---

5 Vermutlich Sprach-Datenbanken wie WordNet (https://wordnet.princeton.edu/), GermaNet/EuroWordNet (https://archive.illc.uva.nl//EuroWordNet/), selbstgeschriebene Regeln und weitere relationale Nachweise.

in einem visuellen Editor erstellen, auch wenn noch keine Relationen zwischen den Einträgen im System gesetzt wurden. Die Relationen zwischen den Beziehungen können dabei frei definiert werden, und die im System als *concept maps* bezeichneten Graphen können sowohl für die Navigation und die normierende Terminologiearbeit verwendet werden als auch im RDF/OWL-Format exportiert werden. Beim Produkt Coreon MKS (Coreon 2024) der gleichnamigen Firma Coreon ist die Anlage einer Relation für das Erstellen eines Begriffs in der Termbank sogar verpflichtend. Dabei sind die Relationen von der Software fix vorgegeben. So wird sichergestellt, dass die Graphen automatisch aus den vergebenen Relationen erstellt werden können, allerdings folgen die Relationen in Coreon MKS keinem bestimmten Standard, sondern wurden auf Basis der Anforderungen der Kund:innen gewählt. Coreon MKS bietet allerdings einen SPARQL-Endpoint an, um die relationalen Daten im Stile des RDF-Standards aus dem *knowledge graph* abzufragen. Ähnlich funktioniert das auch in der Taxonomie-Software der Semantic Web Company PoolParty (PoolParty 2024), welche die Datenbank auf dem SKOS-Standard aufbaut und somit für die Anlage von Einträgen immer eine Relation erfordert. Auch diese Software bietet einen Endpunkt für SPARQL-Queries sowie einen RDF-Export der gespeicherten Graph-Daten an. Wenngleich diese Austauschformate und Suchsprachen also durchaus wichtig sind, sollte es ausreichen, wenn Terminologiestudierende darüber Bescheid wissen und sich vielmehr mit dem Aufbau von *concept maps* und Ontologien, sei es über die Verbindung von Einträgen oder in visuellen Editoren, auseinandersetzen. Die Erstellung der Austauschformate oder die Durchsuchbarkeit der Ontologien wird bereits großteils durch die erwähnten Softwarelösungen abstrahiert und zugänglich gemacht, sodass Projektübungen, die das Erstellen von *concept maps* in spezifischen Domänen beinhalten, ermöglicht werden. Dadurch wird von den Studierenden gefordert, die Grundsätze der Terminologie in praxisnahen Kontexten anzuwenden.

Das automatische Erstellen von relationalen Begriffssystemen ist allerdings nach wie vor eine noch ungelöste Aufgabe, die auch dank der Neuerungen im Bereich von KI in der Forschung in letzter Zeit einen Aufwind erfahren hat. So stellte die Arbeitsgruppe unter Gromann eine Methode (Text2TCS) vor, mit der nach einer Termextraktion aus natürlichem Text ein Begriffssystem vollautomatisch mit Hilfe von verschiedenen neuronalen Sprachmodellen erstellt werden kann (Gromann et al. 2023). Wenngleich die Ergebnisse für größere Begriffssysteme nicht optimal waren, zeigte dieser Ansatz bereits das Potential von vortrainierten Sprachmodellen bei der Extraktion bzw. Erkennung von Begriffsbeziehungen. Verschiedene aktuelle Berichte zeigen auch, dass LLM-basierte Tools in der Lage sind, einfache Begriffssysteme auf Basis von spezifischen Anweisungen über *prompts* zu erstellen und teilweise sogar zu visualisieren (Winter 2024). Allerdings erwähnen die Berichte auch, dass obgleich die Ergebnisse mit Tools wie ChatGPT auf den ersten Blick beeindruckend sind, der Output zu oberflächlich und fehlerbehaftet ist, um tatsächlich praktisch einsetzbar zu sein (Reynolds 2023).

Reynolds von Epimorphics, einem Linked Data-Unternehmen, argumentiert, dass hier durchaus Potential für die Hilfe bei der Ausbildung besteht, indem der Output von solchen Modellen von Studierenden kritisch hinterfragt werden und ausgebessert werden muss, damit diese unter Anleitung von Lehrenden typische Modellierungsfehler erkennen und selbst Modellierungstaktiken erlernen können (Reynolds 2023). Auch hier bietet sich für die Terminologielehre also das Ausprobieren dieser neuen Technologie an, um Studierenden Modellierungskonzepte zu erklären und Beispiele zu generieren, die mitunter von den Studierenden ausgebessert und ausgearbeitet werden können. Es ist abzusehen, dass diese Modelle wesentlich bessere Outputs generieren könnten, wenn sie explizit für den Use-Case von Relationsextraktion oder Ontologieerstellung trainiert bzw. fine-getuned werden. Allerdings werden voraussichtlich auch solche Modelle nach wie vor Fehler machen, die nur von Expert:innen erkannt und korrigiert werden können, weshalb diese Fähigkeit weiterhin gefragt sein wird.

4.3 Definition und Recherche mit Hilfe von KI

Im Bereich der Terminologiearbeit hat sich traditionell der Einsatz von Technologien zur automatischen Befüllung bestimmter Felder in einer Terminologiedatenbank etabliert. Diese Automatisierung betraf jedoch selten die Definitionen, da diese als zu komplex und kontextabhängig galten, um sie zuverlässig automatisch generieren zu können. Bei der Erstellung von Definitionen müssen Terminolog:innen aus dem semantischen Potential eines Begriffs die relevanten Informationen auswählen. Diese Auswahl erfolgt unter Berücksichtigung der arbeitsspezifischen Ontologie, und insbesondere den Eigenschaften von Nachbarbegriffen, sowie Ober- und Unterbegriffen, um auf Vergleichbarkeit von Inhaltsdefinitionen zu setzen (Drewer/Schmitz 2017).

Zusätzlich richtet sich die Auswahl der Informationen nach den Bedürfnissen der User:innen und Eigenschaften der Datenbank. Präzision, Eindeutigkeit, Verständlichkeit und Nicht-Verbosität gelten als wesentliche Eigenschaften terminologischer Definitionen, was ihre Erstellung insgesamt zu einer zeitaufwändigen Aufgabe macht. Mit den Fortschritten in der KI, insbesondere im Bereich der generativen KI, wird nun verstärkt getestet, inwieweit auch Definitionen automatisiert erstellt werden können. Es wird davon ausgegangen, dass vortrainierte LLMs auf einen breiten Wissensfundus über die Gewichtungen im neuronalen Netzwerk zurückgreifen können, um auf Basis von speziellen *prompts,* die Benennung und relevante Zusatzinformationen (z. B. Fachgebiet, Synonyme oder Beispielsätze) beinhalten, terminologische Daten wie Definitionen, die den wissenschaftlichen Standards entsprechen (ISO 704:2022), generieren können. Umgekehrt können strukturierte und vergleichbare Definitionen als Ausgangspunkt für die automatische Erstellung von Ontologien dienen, wie schon von Congree Language Technologies GmbH für Daimler getestet wurde (Traub/Theurer 2022).

4.3.1 Prompting

In der Ausbildungsumgebung können Studierende laufend Versuche durchführen, indem sie anhand der terminologischen Grundsätze für die Verfassung von Definitionen die generative KI mit genauen Anweisungen dazu bringen, konsistente und fundierte terminologische Definitionen zu erstellen. Die Art und Weise, wie die Frage oder der Befehl formuliert wird, beeinflusst die Antwort des Modells, so dass die Aufforderungen besondere Schlüsseleigenschaften innehaben sollen (OpenAI 2024b), von denen hier einige aufgeführt werden:

- *Prompts* müssen klare Anfragen stellen. Klarheit wird unter anderem dadurch gewährleistet, dass die Arbeitsschritte explizit und komplexe Schritte in deutlichen Unterschritten ausformuliert werden.
- *Prompts* müssen strukturiert sein. Die richtige Anwendung von Konventionen mit bestimmten Bezugselementen wie XML-Tags oder (einfachen bis dreifachen) Anführungszeichen erleichtert es wiederum dem Modell, die Metasprache vom Inhalt zu unterscheiden.
- Wenn vertrauenswürdige Informationen als Teil der Eingabe bereitgestellt werden, kann das Modell angewiesen werden, diese Informationen als

Hilfe für die Antwortgenerierung zu verwenden. Die Mitgabe von relevanter Information erlaubt es dem Modell, fachspezifische oder aktuelle Informationen bei der Generierung von Texten zu berücksichtigen. Somit wird die Gefahr von Halluzinationen minimiert (vgl. auch Abschnitt 4.3.2).
- In *prompt*-Anleitungen wird oft empfohlen, dem Modell anzuweisen, eine bestimmte Rolle zu spielen. Mit dieser Strategie lässt sich der Textstil in eine grobe Richtung steuern, insbesondere wenn der *prompt* als *system message* mitgegeben wird.

Die Ergebnisse können im Unterricht in Gruppen validiert werden, um durch die Berücksichtigung von gemeinsamen Überlegungen neue verfeinerte Anweisungen zu verfassen und Ergebnisse kontinuierlich zu verbessern. Die Fähigkeit, eine unmissverständliche „Kommunikation" mit dem Modell zu etablieren, unterscheidet ausgebildete Terminolog:innen von Lai:innen, genauso wie die Fähigkeit, Ergebnisse kritisch zu hinterfragen und bei Bedarf auszubessern. Die Etablierung erfolgreicher Anweisungsmodelle und standardisierter Bedingungen ermöglicht es Studierenden auch, eine eigene App zur Bearbeitung von terminologischen Definitionen in ihrem Forschungsbereich zu entwickeln. Auf diese Weise können alle Änderungen und Verbesserungen dokumentiert und für zukünftige Referenzen genutzt werden.

Trotz guter Vorbereitungsphase und durchdachtem *prompting* besteht immer die Gefahr von faktischen, logischen und sprachlichen Fehlern, wie den schon genannten Halluzinationen, dem Bias (Modelle tendieren z. B. zu einem spezifischen politischen Spektrum oder diskriminierenden Aussagen) und der allgemeinen (von Herstellern gewollten) Unvorhersehbarkeit der Modelle, die mitunter auch zu logischen Fehlern aufgrund des fehlenden Weltwissens der Modelle führen kann (Borji 2023). Deshalb ist eine nachträgliche Überprüfung durch mit Terminologie vertraute Personen erforderlich, was San Martín als *post-editing terminography* bezeichnet (2024). Schwächen wurden auch bei der Differenzierung und Zusammenführung von Bedeutungen erkannt, so dass genaue terminologische Anweisungen und kontextuelle Informationen erforderlich sind, um eine Abgrenzung zu den lexikographischen Definitionen zu erkennen (Jakubíček/Rundell 2023). Die Quellen, aus denen generative KI die einzelnen Informationen nimmt, sind nicht ins Detail bekannt und es ist auch nicht nachvollziehbar, aus welcher Wissensquelle ein Modell bei der Generierung die Informationen, insbesondere ohne RAG-Vorgänge (vgl. 4.3.2) bezieht. Im Allgemeinen sind nur die Trainingsdaten für bestimmte „Grundmodelle" [*foundation models*] bekannt, aber mit diesem Wissen lassen sich gewisse Outputs auch erklären. So ist zu beobachten, dass Modelle eine Tendenz zu lexikographischen Definitionen haben. Dieses Verhalten lässt sich bei Tools wie ChatGPT mitunter damit erklären, dass z. B. das Grundmodell für ChatGPT, GPT-3, bei jeder Trainingsepoche den gesamten Inhalt der Wikipedia-Daten 3,4 mal gesehen hat, während der größte Teil der Trainingsdaten, der allgemein aus Webtexten besteht (CommonCrawl), lediglich 0,44 mal gesehen wurde (Brown et al. 2020). Selbst wenn man Modelle über *prompting* dazu bringt, terminologische Definitionen so zu schreiben, wie das gewünscht ist, so bleibt der Nachteil, dass entweder gar keine oder ungenaue, inkorrekte oder gar inexistente Quellen angeben werden. Dabei ist korrekte Quellenangabe das Fundament von korpusbasierten Wissenschaften wie der Terminologie. Obwohl Technologien historisch gesehen eine bedeutende Unterstützung für die Korpuszusammensetzung, Korpussuche und Textrecherche in puncto Geschwindigkeit dargestellt haben, mangelt es den neuesten Technologien noch an der Transparenz, die für die Terminologiewissenschaft in der Informationssammlung von zentraler Bedeutung ist. Die Überbrückung dieser Kluft und der Umgang mit Informationsnachweisen sind im Rahmen der bewussten und ethischen Nutzung von KI-Tools in der Ausbildung von großer Bedeutung. So muss auch auf die ethischen und rechtlichen Fragen hingewiesen werden, die sich, vor allem für die professionelle Anwendung, aus dem Modelltraining mit urheberrechtlich geschützten Materialien ergeben (Lee et al. 2023; Lucchi 2023). Im gleichen Zuge muss verstärkt Gewicht auf Rückverfolgbarkeit und Nachweis der Informationen bei wissenschaftlicher Arbeit gelegt werden. All dies spielt eine wichtige Rolle, um die KI-Kompetenz (*AI literacy*) von Studierenden auszubilden und zu fördern.

4.3.2 Semantische Suche und RAG

Wie im vorangehenden Abschnitt beschrieben, können KI-Tools durchaus für das Schreiben von Definitionen genutzt werden. Dabei können diese neuen Technologien nicht nur für End-to-End-Use-Cases wie das

Generieren von Definitionen, sondern auch bei der allgemeinen Recherche für Terminologiearbeit herangezogen werden. Es gibt bereits einige kommerzielle Plattformen, die, teilweise kostenfrei[6], die sogenannte *semantische Suche* mit Antworten durch generative KI anbieten. Dazu zählen Plattformen wie *Perplexity.ai*, *Microsoft Bing Co-Pilot* und verstärkt auch *Google*, die das Web mit der zuvor erwähnten semantischen Suche durchforsten und Suchenden darauf basierend direkte Antworten bieten können. Besonders interessant sind allerdings Tools wie *Consensus.app*, die die Suche auf vertrauenswürdige Dokumente wie peer-reviewed Paper einschränken. Der Einbezug einer Suche in zuverlässigen bzw. aktuellen Dokumenten und dem Internet dient dazu, dem erwähnten Defizit moderner generativer KI, also dass die Wissensbasis der Modelle unklar und nicht nachvollziehbar ist, und damit auch den sogenannten Halluzinationen entgegenzuwirken. Auch soll damit der Wissensstand von KI-Modellen auf Stand gebracht werden können, ohne ein neues Modell trainieren zu müssen. KI-Modelle sind grundsätzlich auf das Wissen in den Trainingsdaten und somit auf den Wissensstand zu einem gewissen Zeitpunkt in der Vergangenheit beschränkt. Forschung zu generativer KI und auch Anbieter von Tools, die auf generativer KI basieren, versuchen diese Lücken über verschiedene Ansätze, die unter den Sammelbegriff *retrieval augmented generation* (RAG) fallen, zu schließen. Das Grundkonzept von RAG ist es, den *prompt* der Nutzer:innen automatisch mit relevanten Informationen anzureichern. Dies geschieht durch eine Suche in, idealerweise, zuverlässigen Quellen, z. B. firmeneigenen Dokumenten, Datenbanken, Knowledge-Graphs. Das Modell kann sich dann auf diese Informationen für die Generierung der Antwort stützen. Ein weiterer Vorteil dieses Ansatzes ist, dass man durch den Vorgang der Suche ermitteln kann, auf welche Quellen sich das Modell schlussendlich in der Antwort bezieht. Allerdings bleiben diese Referenzen selbst in Produkten, die sich auf die nachweisbaren Antworten mit LLMs spezialisieren, wie z. B. *Perplexity.ai*, meistens eher vage. Das liegt unter anderem an einem der prominentesten Ansätze für RAG: die *semantische Suche* über *embeddings*.

---

6 Datenschutz ist allerdings wie bei allen Suchmaschinen immer genau zu untersuchen und abzuwägen.

Die Grundlage von semantischer Suche, wie diese üblicherweise bei RAG eingesetzt wird, sind wieder Sprachmodelle. Allerdings nicht generative Sprachmodelle (d. h. *decoder*-Modelle) sondern sogenannte *embedding*-Modelle oder (*encoder*-Modelle), die z. B. eine Repräsentation eines Worts, eines Satzes oder Absatzes, aber auch eines ganzen Dokuments in einem mehrdimensionalen Vektor (*embedding*) speichern können (OpenAI 2024c). Dieser Vektor bzw. dieses *embedding* beinhaltet in abstrakter Form eine Darstellung der Bedeutung des Textes auf Basis aller darin vorkommenden Wörter und deren bidirektionalen Kontexts (d. h. alles, was vor, und alles, was nach jedem Wort steht, was wiederum bedeutet, dass die einzelnen Termini im Text sehr wohl eine Rolle für das Ergebnis des *embeddings* haben werden). Nun können z. B. die Anfragen an das generative Modell mit den gespeicherten *embeddings* der Quelltexte verglichen werden, und die Texte, die der Anfrage am ähnlichsten sind, dem generativen Modell als Kontext mitgegeben werden. Dabei wird meistens nur der Winkel der Vektoren als Maßeinheit für die semantische Ähnlichkeit herangezogen (*cosine similarity*). Diese Art der Suche ist per definitionem „unscharf", d. h. die Ergebnisse der Suche sind mitunter gar nicht relevant für die Anfrage. Modelle müssen also aus den durch die semantische Suche teils arbiträr mitgegebenen Textstücken (*chunks*) die relevante Information extrahieren. Wenn das generative Modell nichts Relevantes im Kontext „findet", kann es nach wie vor zu Halluzinationen und faktisch inkorrekten Antworten kommen. Zusätzlich problematisch hierbei ist, dass mitunter die „zitierte" Information der Antwort gar nicht in der Quelle zu finden ist oder eine Quelle angegeben wird, die in der Antwort gar nicht zitiert wird.

Ein kritischer Blick ist also auf die Quellen genauso wie auf die Antwort der KI-Tools gefragt, und die Recherchekompetenz der Studierenden muss auf diese neue Art des Suchens vorbereitet werden, da diese Art von Wissens- bzw. Quellenbezug mit großer Wahrscheinlichkeit die allgemeine Interaktion der Nutzer:innen mit dem Web und anderen Wissensressourcen beeinflussen wird. Ein weiteres großes Potential, das auch für die Terminologielehre mit Blick auf Ontologien interessant ist, zeigt die Verwendung von *knowledge graphs* bei der Verbesserung der semantischen Suche bzw. von *RAG* (Blumauer 2024; Xu et al. 2024). Expertise im Erstellen von Begriffssystemen, vor allem im Hinblick auf diese neue Art von Recherchetools, birgt auch großes Potential für alternative Karrierepfade von Terminolog:innen.

5. Terminologiearbeit für die KI

Künstliche Intelligenz wird oft als Unterstützung für die Terminologiearbeit betrachtet, da sie große Textmengen analysieren und Begriffe effizient identifizieren kann. Allerdings gilt auch der umgekehrte Fall, denn Terminologiearbeit kann zur Verbesserung von KI-Systemen beitragen. Eine präzise und konsistente Terminologie hilft dabei, Trainingsdaten zu optimieren, maschinelle Übersetzungen zu verbessern und die semantische Genauigkeit von KI-Anwendungen zu erhöhen. In diesem Abschnitt wird anhand eines Beispiels dargestellt, wie diese Denkweise in der Lehre vertreten werden kann. Es wird darauf eingegangen, wie die Korrektur der terminologischen Kohärenz nach der Übersetzung bzw. während der maschinellen Übersetzung (*terminology enforcement*) erfolgen kann.

Die Entwicklung von Kompetenzen im Umgang mit CAT-Tools und Translation-Memory-Systemen (TM-Systemen) ist ein wesentlicher Bestandteil der Übersetzungsausbildung. Unabhängig von der verwendeten Software lernen die Studierenden den Umgang mit diesen Werkzeugen, da professionelle Fachübersetzungen ohne sie kaum noch möglich sind. Die Integration dieser Tools mit maschinellen Übersetzungssystemen ist bereits weit fortgeschritten und wird in Kursen translatorischer Ausbildung thematisiert. Allerdings gibt es noch erhebliches Verbesserungspotential bei der vollständigen Integration terminologiebezogener Funktionen, insbesondere bei der Nutzung von NMT und KI. In CAT-Tools hat sich Terminologiemanagement vorwiegend als Terminologierecherche, -verwaltung und -systematisierung vor der Übersetzung als auch zur Qualitätssicherung auf der Basis der erarbeiteten Datenbestände (Glossare, Termbanken usw.) nach der Übersetzung festgesetzt. Techniken, die sicherstellten, dass bestimmte vordefinierte Termini während dem Übersetzungsprozess maschinell forciert werden (*terminology enforcement*) ist in diesen Tools eher unüblich, da Translator:innen die Terminologie vor dem Übersetzungsauftrag vorbereiten bzw. vom Auftraggeber erhalten und während der Übersetzung berücksichtigen sollten. Hinweise zur bevorzugten Terminologie erhält man meistens über eine farbliche Codierung oder textuelle Hinweise durch die Terminologieerkennung der CAT-Tools.

Rezente Entwicklungen im Übersetzungsmarkt, wie die verstärkte Nutzung und Integration von NMT, die Rolle von Post-Editing und die Notwendigkeit, in alle Phasen der Dokumenterstellung eingreifen zu können

(z. B. um einen Text auf projektspezifische Stil- und Terminologievorgaben anzupassen), bedürfen eines neuen Denkansatzes, nämlich nicht nur maschinell zu übersetzen, sondern auch gleichzeitig oder in einem nachfolgenden Schritt die korrekte Terminologie automatisch einzufügen. Die Einbindung von Daten aus Termbanken ist eine gewünschte Eigenschaft von NMT, insbesondere in computergestützten Übersetzungsumgebungen. Allerdings ist das, was qualitativ erstrebenswert ist, technisch manchmal nicht leicht in den Systemen zu realisieren.

Im Laufe der Zeit und der technologischen Erfordernisse wurden verschiedene Ansätze hierfür vorgeschlagen, jedoch stehen zwei Hauptprobleme erfolgreichen Methoden im Weg: Zum einen werden von Terminolog:innen verwaltete Ressourcen oft nicht mit den Anforderungen von MT-Systemen konzipiert und formatiert (Yvon/Rauf 2020). Zum anderen ist der Grad der gewünschten terminologischen Kohärenz nicht immer einheitlich, so dass Überlegungen in Bezug auf Textsorte, Zielgruppe und Textfunktion notwendig sind. Diese Überlegungen erfordern Übersetzungskompetenzen und sollten im Unterricht thematisiert werden. Da Terminologiebestände bisher mehr für *content management* und Übersetzungszwecke und weniger für eine automatische Einbindung in Zieltexte optimiert sind, müssen Glossare für diese Zwecke bereinigt und angepasst werden. Im Gegensatz zu Terminologiedatenbanken sind Glossare für maschinelle Übersetzungen nicht begriffsbasiert und mehrsprachig, sondern benennungsorientiert, zweisprachig und sprachrichtungsspezifisch. Sie erfordern mitunter auch die Kodierung von morphologischen Informationen, Wortbildungsmustern oder einfach das Anführen aller morphologischen Varianten (Microsoft n.d.). Zu den möglichen Aufgaben für Studierende zu diesem Thema zählen beispielsweise das Identifizieren von für *terminology enforcement* relevanten Zusatzinformationen.

Zum anderen ist das Ergebnis der *terminology enforcement* ein Kompromiss zwischen der Durchsetzung spezifischer terminologischer Entscheidungen und der möglichst minimalen Änderung des textuellen Nahkontexts. Diese hängen stark von den strukturellen und lexikalischen Unterschieden der betroffenen Sprachkombination ab. Es lässt sich hieraus ableiten, dass *terminology enforcement* nicht nur ein Ergebnis von computergestützten Aufgaben ist, sondern auch sprachwissenschaftliche und translatorische Überlegungen erfordert.

Im Unterricht können daher die Herausforderungen und potentiellen Vorteile des *terminology enforcement* in den jeweiligen Sprachen und mit verschiedenen Methoden thematisiert werden. Dabei sollte die Frage gestellt werden, in welchen Szenarien eine automatische Integration von Terminologie vorteilhaft ist, welche Kompromisse dabei zu berücksichtigen sind und welche Ergebnisse in den jeweiligen Sprachen und Methoden erwartet werden können. Die Bewertung der Methoden sollte nicht nur die terminologische Genauigkeit, sondern auch die natürliche Einbettung der Zieltermini in den Zieltext umfassen. Eine Reihe von Leitfragen zur Qualitätsbewertung kann vorbereitet werden. Ausgehend von bekannten Übersetzungssystemen, die erste Versuche mit der Integration dieser KI-Komponente unternommen haben, bis hin zu ausgeklügelten NMT-Methoden können Studierende die Ergebnisse bewerten und Überlegungen anstellen.

Bei TM-Systemen wie PhraseTMS handelt es sich beim *terminology enforcement*-Funktion um eine reine Ersetzung von Benennungen im Zielsegment durch Glossareinträge. Durch das automatische Ersetzen entstehen aber viele Grammatikfehler, die unter anderem mit dem Unterschied im Genus zwischen der ersetzten und neuen Benennung zu tun haben. So wird beispielsweise eine Benennung wie *Blindstock* möglicherweise automatisch durch die von einer Firma standardisierte Benennung *Blindzarge* ersetzt, jedoch ohne die notwendige Anpassung des umgebenden Textes und des Genus, was zu inkorrekten oder missverständlichen Formulierungen führen kann. Größere Abweichungen entstehen bei Verben, die auch immer in ihrer Grundform eingefügt werden.

Andere Methoden, die direkt in den Zieltext eingreifen, wie der *placeholder approach* (Crego et al. 2016) oder die *alignment* Methode (Dinu et al. 2019) liefern bessere Ergebnisse, weisen aber immer noch Grenzen mit flektierenden Sprachen auf. Unterschiede in Bezug auf Genauigkeit hängen von der Menge an vergebenen Einschränkungen im Datensatz ab. Generell weisen sie immer noch eine niedrige Qualität auf, weil sie der Einhaltung von terminologischen Vorgaben Vorrang geben. Wenn Einträge für Substantive aber nicht für die abgeleiteten Adjektive in den Datenbestand aufgenommen werden, können durch die automatische Ableitung falsche Inferenzen entstehen. Somit kann es bei einer Montage mithilfe einer Blindzarge die Benennung *Blindzargemontage* inferiert und forciert werden, wenn die Benennung *zweistufige Montage* nicht eindeutig in den Datenbestand aufgenommen wird.

Mit NMT wurde auch die Vorgehensweise von *terminology enforcement* auf den Kopf gestellt, da diese Modelle nicht mehr auf regelbasierten oder statistischen „Wörterbüchern" wie noch RBMT oder SMT basieren und somit die Beeinflussung der Übersetzung selbst schwierig ist. Verschiedene Methoden, die während der Übersetzung integriert werden, wie die *constrained decoding method* (Chatterjee et al. 2017; Hasler et al. 2018; Hokamp/Liu 2017) liefern zwar flüssigere Texte als die zuvor beschriebene Ersetzungslogik, sind aber technisch gesehen nicht trivial umzusetzen: So müssen die korrekten morphologischen Varianten dem NMT-Modell mitgegeben werden, was wiederum zu einem erhöhten Rechen- und damit Zeitaufwand beim Generieren der Übersetzungen führt (Exel et al. 2020; Post/Vilar 2018).

Ein anderer interessanter Ansatz für das *terminology enforcement* ist auch die *target lemma annotation*-Methode (TLA). Hierbei lernt das Modell, Texte morphologisch korrekt und mit der korrekten Terminologie zu übersetzen, wobei die Zieltermini im Ausgangstext neben den entsprechenden Ausgangstermini als *lemma* annotiert werden. Das Modell lernt also durch den Trainingsprozess nicht nur, die annotierten Termini zu nutzen, sondern auch, wie es die Termini flektieren oder deklinieren muss, damit diese im Dekodierungsschritt (also in der Übersetzung) morphologisch korrekt eingesetzt werden (Bergmanis/Pinnis 2021; Exel et al. 2020). Ein weiterer Weg des *terminology enforcements* ist es, die gewünschte Terminologie mithilfe von Trainingsdaten beizubringen (Ailem/Liu/Qader 2021). Voraussetzung für das Tuning von Terminologie mittels Trainingsdaten sind damit nicht zwangsläufig gut durchdachte Terminologielisten, sondern einheitliches und sauber aufbereitetes Trainingsmaterial. Die ausbildungstechnischen Nachteile dieser Methoden bestehen darin, dass ein tiefgehendes Wissen zur computergestützten Sprachverarbeitung gebraucht wird, um diese Trainingsdaten herzustellen, ein maßgeschneidertes NMT-Modell benötigt wird, das mit solchen „annotierten" Ausgangstexten umgehen kann, und natürlich ein Tool oder Skript notwendig ist, das die Ausgangstexte vor der Übersetzung mit der gewünschten Terminologie annotieren kann. Es ist davon auszugehen, dass NMT-Anbieter wie DeepL mit einer ähnlichen Methode die *morphosyntaktisch* korrekte Ersetzung von Termini umgesetzt hat (DeepL 2025).

Dennoch kann die Bereinigung von *translation memorys* interessante Einblicke in die Tätigkeiten von MT-Engines geben und damit Studierende auch auf diese Laufbahn vorbereiten. Da *translation memorys* als relativ kleine und durchschaubare domänenspezifische Bestandsdaten betrachtet werden können, ist eine erste Bereinigung mit den Quality Assurance Funktionen von TM-Systemen eine Aufgabe, mit der Studierende mit der Bedeutung von bereinigten Daten vertraut werden können. Das Beheben von terminologischer Unstimmigkeit, die terminologische Filterung, sowie, viel breiter gesehen, das Löschen von Formatierungstags, das Löschen von älteren Übersetzungen gleicher Segmente, die Prüfung von Segmentlängen im Vergleich zum Ausgangstext usw. gehören zum Bereinigungsaufwand mittels TM-Systeme.

Ein ausbildungstechnischer Nachteil ist, dass es bei generativer KI und auch bei NMT schwierig ist, Einblicke in die tatsächlichen Vorgehensweisen zu erhalten, und es somit nicht einfach ist, die Ursachen für Terminologiefehler zu erkennen und direkt zu korrigieren.

Allerdings werden Versuche mit *terminology enforcement* durch generative KI für Nicht-Computerlinguist:innen viel zugänglicher, da dies durch *prompting* bewerkstelligt werden kann. Hier sind einerseits Kenntnisse in der Gestaltung und Formulierung der Anweisungen notwendig (Abschnitt 4.3.1), damit sie von einem generativen KI-Modell interpretiert und verstanden werden können. Andererseits müssen für die Forcierung von Terminologie kohärente und relevante Bestandsdaten (*context*) ausgewählt und, wo nötig, vorbereitet werden. Manche Tools für die Terminologieprüfung, die KI-Funktionen integrieren, wie z. B. *Kalcium Checkterm*, erlauben es den Terminolog:innen, die *prompts* für die Ersetzung von Terminologie selbst zu hinterlegen und so zu optimieren, dass grammatikalisch korrekte Ersetzungen in verschiedenen Sprachen möglich werden. Eine Gelegenheit wäre also, mit Hersteller:innen zusammenzuarbeiten, um gemeinsam mit Studierenden wertvolle Erfahrungen zur optimalen Formulierung von *prompts* für diese Aufgabe in verschiedenen Sprachen zu finden.

Zu den weiteren möglichen Aufgaben im Unterricht zählen auch die Anwendung eines oder mehrerer Modelle mit unterschiedlichen Sprachkombinationen, um zu verstehen, wie *terminology enforcement* in der Praxis funktioniert, sowie das Vergleichen von Ergebnissen sowohl in Bezug auf die verwendete Methode als auch in Bezug auf die Zielsprache und die Rentabilität dieser Funktion. Die Vorbereitung und Konfiguration von automatisierten Systemen kann viel menschliche Arbeitszeit erfordern und deshalb derzeit im Verhältnis zum geringen möglichen

Verbesserungsgrad einen hohen Aufwand darstellen. Hinzu kommt, dass Terminologiekohärenz viel mehr bedeutet als die schlichte (und trotzdem immer noch nicht so einfach umsetzbare) Benutzung von richtigen Benennungen für einen bestimmten Begriff. Und bei der Erkennung der Schwächen dieser Systeme sollte die Gelegenheit nicht verpasst werden, die Komplexität der terminologischen Überlegungen zu vermitteln. Es kann mit den Studierenden diskutiert werden, wie die relativen Kosten und Erträge in verschiedenen Kontexten unterschiedlich ausfallen können und ob ältere Methoden wie die semi-automatische Beseitigung von durch die *quality assurance*-Funktion von TM-Systemen erkannten Fehlern noch kostengünstigere Alternativen darstellen. Leitfragen zur Qualitätseinschätzung können vorgelegt werden.

6. Schlussfolgerung: artificial intelligence must know terms

In diesem Beitrag wurden drei wesentliche Aspekte der terminologischen Ausbildung hervorgehoben, die im Ausdruck *artificial intelligence must know terms* prägnant zusammengefasst werden:

- Studierende sollen in der Lage sein zu evaluieren, wann KI bei der Terminologiearbeit hilfreich eingesetzt werden kann, und zu erkennen, wo die Grenzen in Terminologieprozessen liegen bzw. welche Gefahren das blinde Vertrauen in moderne KI-Tools birgt.
- Studierende sollen Strategien kennenlernen, die KI terminologisch korrekt und zuverlässig arbeiten zu lassen und zu diesem Zweck der KI Terminologie und terminologierelevantes Wissen effizient mitzugeben.
- Studierende sollen die Bedeutung einer korrekten und einheitlichen Terminologie (zu KI) verstehen und damit exemplarisch die Gefahren von Unklarheit und Mehrdeutigkeit erkennen.

Inwieweit Terminolog:innen und Translator:innen in die neuen technologischen Entwicklungen involviert sein wollen, sollte ihrer eigenen Entscheidung überlassen werden. Die Universität sollte jedoch den Auszubildenden die Mittel in die Hand geben, um diese Entscheidung bewusst treffen zu können.

Es wäre wünschenswert, wenn Informatikingenieur:innen und Translator: innen bei der anspruchsvollen Aufgabe, diese neue technologische Welt weiterzuentwickeln, zusammenwirken. Dies erfordert, dass Erstere über sprachwissenschaftliche Kenntnisse verfügen und Letztere ausreichende technologische Kompetenzen besitzen, um Erstere zu unterstützen. Ein konstruktiver Dialog zwischen beiden Gruppen darf nicht dem Zufall überlassen werden, wenn z. B. ausgebildete Translator:innen eine Leidenschaft für computertechnische Aspekte zufällig entwickeln oder umgekehrt. Es soll gezielt daran gearbeitet werden, Leute auszubilden, die sowohl die Unvorhersehbarkeit und Fluidität der Sprache als auch die Potentiale der technologischen Entwicklung berücksichtigen können. Nur so können beide Branchen davon profitieren.

Die Vermittlung der notwendigen technologischen Kompetenzen für Translator:innen findet aus historischen und methodologischen Gründen in Terminologiekursen einen fruchtbaren Boden. Wie bereits gesehen, sind die Anwendungsszenarien und -möglichkeiten der KI in der Terminologieausbildung zahlreich. Es wäre wünschenswert, der Terminologie in der translatorischen Ausbildung mehr Raum zu geben und diesen Raum auch für die Entwicklung zukunftsweisender Terminologiekompetenzen zu nutzen. Zu den zentralen Kompetenzen der Gegenwart und Zukunft zählen vor allem auch die rasche Anpassbarkeit an neue Technologien, sowie die Einschätzungs- und Evaluierungskompetenz solcher Neuerungen.

Die Evaluierungskompetenz bezieht sich auf die Fähigkeit, die Rentabilität eigener Tools zu beurteilen. Das Verhältnis zwischen Qualitätsverbesserung und Investitionen von Ressourcen (z. B. Zeitaufwand) in der Vorbereitungsphase ist entscheidend, da das Hauptziel von KI schlechthin in der Prozessbeschleunigung liegt. Qualität kann jedoch nur mit einer guten Evaluierungskompetenz richtig eingeschätzt werden. Diese Kompetenz umfasst die Fähigkeit, die Ergebnisse mit teils automatisierten Prozessen, aber auch aus fachlicher Sicht zu beurteilen.

Die in diesem Beitrag beschriebenen Kompetenzen, die Studierende durch den Umgang mit KI-Tools in den Prozessen der Terminologiearbeit erwerben, eröffnen neue berufliche Möglichkeiten, die über das bereits breite Spektrum hinausgehen, das terminologische Kenntnisse bisher geboten haben. Zu diesen Berufen zählen: Knowledge Engineer, Language Data and AI-Lead, Linguistic Quality Manager, Machine Translation Expert und System Terminologist.

Quellenverzeichnis

Ahmad, Khurshid / Gillam, Lee / Tostevin, Lena (1999): „University of Surrey participation in TREC 8: Weirdness indexing for logical document extrapolation and retrieval (WILDER)“. In: *The Eighth Text REtrieval Conference (TREC 8)*, abgerufen am 03.05.2025 auf https://trec.nist.gov/pubs/trec8/t8_proceedings.html.

Ailem, Melissa / Liu, Jinghsu / Qader, Raheel (2021): „Encouraging neural machine translation to satisfy terminology constraints“, abgerufen am 03.05.2025 auf https://arxiv.org/abs/2106.03730. https://doi.org/10.48550/ARXIV.2106.03730.

Astrakhantsev, Nikita (2016): „ATR4S: Toolkit with state-of-the-art automatic terms recognition methods in Scala“, abgerufen am 03.05.2025 auf https://arxiv.org/abs/1611.07804. https://doi.org/10.48550/ARXIV.1611.07804.

Auger, Pierre (1979): „Les transferts des techniques“. *Tiers-Monde* 20(78), S. 317–321. https://doi.org/10.3406/tiers.1979.5832.

Bakaric, Marija Brkic / Babic, Nikola / Matetic, Maja (2021): „Application-based evaluation of automatic terminology extraction“. *International Journal of Advanced Computer Science and Applications: IJACSA* 12(1), S. 18–27. https://doi.org/10.14569/ijacsa.2021.0120103

Bergmanis, Toms / Pinnis, Marcis (2021): „Facilitating terminology translation with target lemma annotations“. In: Merlo, Paola / Tiedemann, Jorg / Tsarfaty, Reut (Hrsg.): *Proceedings of the 16th Conference of the European Chapter of the Association for Computational Linguistics: Main volume*, S. 3105–3111, Association for Computational Linguistics, abgerufen am 03.05.2025 auf https://aclanthology.org/volumes/2021.eacl-main/.

Blahuš, Marek / Cukr, Michal / Jakubíček, Miloš / Kovář, Vojtěch / Suchomel, Vít (2023): „Development of evidence-based grammars for terminology extraction in OneClick Terms“. In: *Electronic lexicography in the 21st century. Proceedings of the eLex 2023 conference*, abgerufen am 03.05.2025 auf https://elex.link/ojs/index.php/elex/issue/view/elex2023 S. 650–662.

Blumauer, Andreas (2024): „The seven cases for knowledge graph integration in a RAG architecture“, abgerufen am 28.07.2024 auf https://www.linkedin.com/pulse/seven-cases-knowledge-graph-integration-rag-andreas-blumauer-vjjbf.

Borji, Ali (2023): „A categorical archive of ChatGPT failures", abgerufen am 03.05.2025 auf https://arxiv.org/abs/2302.03494. https://doi.org/10.48550/arXiv.2302.03494.

Brown, Tom B. / Mann, Benjamin / Ryder, Nick / Subbiah, Melanie / Kaplan, Jared / Dhariwal, Prafulla / Neelakantan, Arvind / Shyam, Pranav / Sastry, Girish / Askell, Amanda / Agarwal, Sandhini /, Herbert-Voss, Ariel / Krueger, Gretchen / Henighan, Tom / Child, Rewon / Ramesh, Aditya / Ziegler, Daniel M / Wu, Jeffrey / Winter, Clemens / Hesse, Christopher / Chen, Mark / Sigler, Eric / Litwin, Mateusz / Gray, Scott / Chess, Benjamin / Clark, Jack / Berner, Christopher / McCandlish, Sam / Radford, Alec / Sutskever, Ilya / Amodei, Dario (2020): „Language models are few-shot learners", abgerufen am 03.05.2025 auf https://arxiv.org/abs/2005.14165. https://doi.org/10.48550/arXiv.2005.14165.

Calvo-Ferrer, José Ramón (2023): „Can you tell the difference? A study of human vs machine-translated subtitles". *Perspectives* 32(6), S. 1–18. https://doi.org/10.1080/0907676x.2023.2268149.

Chatterjee, Rajen / Negri, Matteo / Turchi, Marco / Federico, Marcello / Specia, Lucia / Blain, Frédéric. (2017): „Guiding neural machine translation decoding with external knowledge". In: In: Bojar, Ondřej / Buck, Christian / Chatterjee, Rajen / Federmann, Christian / Graham, Yvette / Haddow, Barry / Huck, Matthias / Jimeno Yepes, Antonio / Koehn, Philipp /Kreutzer, Julia (Hrsg.): *Proceedings of the Second Conference on Machine Translation*, Copenhagen: Association for Computational Linguistics, S. 157–168.

Coreon (2024): „Coreon: Multilingual knowledge system", abgerufen am 31.07.2024 auf https://coreon.com/product/.

Crego, Josep / Kim, Jungi / Klein, Guillaume / Rebollo, Anabel / Yang, Kathy / Senellart, Jean / Akhanov, Egor / Brunelle, Patrice / Coquard, Aurelien / Deng, Yongchao / Enoue, Satoshi / Geiss, Chiyo / Johanson, Joshua / Khalsa, Ardas / Khiari, Raoum / Ko, Byeongil / Kobus, Catherine / Lorieux, Jean /Martins, Leidiana / Zordan, Peter (2016): „Systran's pure neural machine translation systems", abgerufen am 03.05.2025 auf https://arxiv.org/abs/1610.05540. https://doi.org/10.48550/ARXIV.1610.05540.

DeepL (2025). Einheitliche Übersetzungen mit Glossaren, abgerufen am 01.03.2025 auf https://www.deepl.com/de/features/glossary.

Di Nunzio, Giorgio Maria / Marchesin, Stefano / Silvello, Gianmaria (2023): „A systematic review of Automatic Term Extraction: What happened in 2022?“ *Digital Scholarship in the Humanities* 38(Supplement_1), i41–i47. https://doi.org/10.1093/llc/fqad030.

DIN 2342 (1992): „Vocabulary of Terminology – basic concepts“ (zurückgezogen).

Dinu, Georgiana / Mathur, Prashant / Federico, Marcello / Al-Onaizan, Yaser (2019): „Training neural machine translation to apply terminology constraints“. In: Korhonen, Anna / Traum, David / Márquez, Lluís (Hrsg.): *Proceedings of the 57th Annual Meeting of the Association for Computational Linguistics*, S. 3063–3068, abgerufen am 03.05.2025 auf https://aclanthology.org/volumes/P19-1/al.

Drewer, Petra / Schmitz, Klaus-Dirk (2017): „Grundlagen der Terminologiewissenschaft“. In: Drewer, Petra / Schmitz, Klaus-Dirk (Hrsg.): *Terminologiemanagement*. Berlin/Heidelberg: Springer, S. 5–22. https://doi.org/10.1007/978-3-662-53315-4_2.

Drewer, Petra / Pulitano, Donatella / Winter, Tom (2018): „Professional profiles in and around terminology management“. *Proceedings of the 9th EAFT-Summit*, S. 63-77, abgerufen am 03.05.2025 auf https://files.eaft-aet.net/textos/EAFT%20SUMMIT%202018_Proceedings.pdf.

Exel, Miriam / Buschbeck, Bianka / Brandt, Lauritz / Doneva, Simona (2020): „Terminology-constrained neural machine translation at SAP“. In: Martins, André / Moniz, Helena / Fumega, Sara/ Martins, Bruno / Batista, Fernando / Coheur, Luisa / Parra, Carla / Trancoso, Isabel / Turchi, Marco / Bisazza, Arianna / Moorkens, Joss/ Guerberof, Ana / Nurminen, Mary / Marg, Lena / Forcada, Mikel L. (Hrsg.): *Proceedings of the 22nd Annual Conference of the European Association for Machine Translation*, S. 271–280, abgerufen am 03.05.2025 auf https://aclanthology.org/2020.eamt-1.pdf.

„FIT History“, abgerufen am 29.07.2024 auf https://en.fit-ift.org/history/.

Fodina (2024): *TermCatch*, abgerufen am 30.07.2024 auf https://fodina.se/termcatch/.

Frantzi, Katerina / Ananiadou, Sophia / Mima, Hideki (2000): „Automatic recognition of multi-word terms:. the C-value/NC-value method“. *International Journal on Digital Libraries* 3(2), S. 115–130. https://doi.org/10.1007/s007999900023.

Giguere, Julie (2023): „Leveraging large language models to extract terminology". In: Lázaro Gutiérrez, Raquel / Pareja, Antonio /Mitkov, Rusian (Hrsg.): *Proceedings of the First Workshop on NLP Tools and Resources for Translation and Interpreting Applications*, S. 57–60, abgerufen am 03.05.2025 auf https://aclanthology.org/2023.nlp4tia-1.9.

Gromann, Dagmar / Wachowiak, Lennart / Lang, Christian / Heinisch, Barbara (2023): „Extracting Terminological Concept Systems from Natural Language Text". In: Rehm, Georg (Hrsg.): *European Language Grid: A language technology platform for multilingual Europe*. Cham: Springer, S. 289–294.

Hasler, Eva / de Gispert, Adrià / Iglesias, Gonzalo / Byrne, Bill (2018): „Neural machine translation decoding with terminology constraints". In: Walker, Marilyn / Ji, Heng / Stent, Amanda (Hrsg.): *Proceedings of the 2018 Conference of the North American Chapter of the Association for Computational Linguistics: Human Language Technologies, Volume 2 (Short Papers)*, S. 506–512, abgerufen am 03.05.2025 auf https://aclanthology.org/volumes/N18-2/.

He, Ying (2021): „Challenges and countermeasures of translation teaching in the era of artificial intelligence". *Journal of Physics: Conference Series 1881* 2, 022086. https://doi.org/10.1088/1742-6596/1881/2/022086.

Hokamp, Chris / Liu, Qun (2017): „Lexically constrained decoding for sequence generation using grid beam search". In: Barzilay, Regina / Kann, Min-Yen (Hrsg.): *Proceedings of the 55th Annual Meeting of the Association for Computational Linguistics, Volume 1 (Long Papers)*, S. 1535–1546, abgerufen am 03.05.2025 auf https://aclanthology.org/volumes/P17-1/.

Hönig, Hans G. (1995): *Konstruktives Übersetzen.* Tübingen: Stauffenburg.

ISO 704:2022 Terminology work – Principles and methods.

ISO/IEC 22989:2022 Information technology – Artificial intelligence – Artificial intelligence concepts and terminology.

Jakubíček, Miloš / Rundell, Michael (2023): „The end of lexicography? Can ChatGPT outperform current tools for post-editing lexicography?" In: Medvev, Marek / Mechura, Michal / Tiberius, Carole / Kosem, Iztok / Kallas, Jelena / Jakubiček, Miloš / Krek, Simon (Hrsg.): *Electroniclexicography in the 21st Century (eLex 2023) Proceedings of the eLex 2023 Conference*, S. 518–533, abgerufen am 03.05.2025 auf https://elex.link/ojs/index.php/elex/issue/view/elex2023.

Kageura, Kyo / Umino, Bin (1996): „Methods of automatic term recognition: A review". *Terminology* 3(2), S. 259–289.

Kaleidoscope GmbH. (n.d.). Kalcium Quickterm, abgerufen am 31.07.2024 auf https://kaleidoscope.at/produkte/quickterm/.

Kilgarriff, Adam / Rychlý, Pavel / Smrž, Pavel / Tugwell, David (2004): „The Sketch Engine". In: *Proceedings of the 11th EURALEX International Congress*, S.105-116, abgerufen am 29.07.2024, auf https://euralex.org/publications/the-sketch-engine/.

Korkas, Vassilis / Rogers, Margaret (2010): „An old pedagogical dilemma in a new field: How much terminological theory do we need for practice?" In Thelen, Marcel / Steurs, Frieda (Hrsg.): *Terminology in Everyday Life*. Amsterdam/Philadelphia: John Benjamins, S. 123–36. https://doi.org/10.1075/tlrp.13.09kor.

Lang, Christian / Wachowiak, Lennart / Heinisch, Barbara / Gromann, Dagmar (2021): "Transforming term extraction: Transformer-based approaches to multilingual term extraction across domains." In: Zong, Chengqing / Xia, Fei / Li, Wenjie / Navigli, Roberto (Hrsg.): *Findings of the Association for Computational Linguistics: ACL-IJCNLP*, S. 3607–3620, abgerufen am 03.05.2025 auf https://aclanthology.org/volumes/2021.findings-acl/. https://doi.org/10.18653/v1/2021.findings-acl.316.

Lee, Jooyoung / Le, Thai / Chen, Jinghui / Lee, Dongwon (2023): „Do Language Models Plagiarize?" In: Ding, Ying / Tang, Jie / Sequeda, Juan / Aroyo, Lora / Castillo, Carlos / Houben, Gert-Jan (Hrsg.): *Proceedings of the ACM Web Conference 2023*, S. 3637–3647, abgerufen am 03.05.2025 auf https://dl.acm.org/doi/proceedings/10.1145/3543507. https://doi.org/10.1145/3543507.3583199.

Lionbridge MT Tracker: Analyse von MT-Engines (06.08.2021), abgerufen am 31.07.2024 auf https://www.lionbridge.com/de/machine-translation/mt-tracker/.

Lucchi, Nicola (2023): „ChatGPT: A case study on copyright challenges for generative artificial intelligence systems". *European Journal of Risk Regulation* 15(3), S. 602–624. https://doi.org/10.1017/err.2023.59.

Luckin, Rosemary / Cukurova, Mutlu / Kent, Carmel / Du Boulay, Benedict (2022): „Empowering educators to be AI-ready". *Computers and Education: Artificial Intelligence* 3, S. 100076. https://doi.org/10.1016/j.caeai.2022.100076.

Magris, Marella / Musacchio, Maria Teresa / Rega, Lorenza / Scarpa, Federica (2001): *Manuale di terminologia*. Mailand: Hoepli.

Meyer, Ingrid / Eck, Karen / Skuce, Douglas (1997): „Systematic concept analysis within a knowledge-based approach to terminology". In: Wright, Ellen Sue / Budin, Gerhard (Hrsg.): *Handbook of Terminology Management*. Amsterdam/Philadelphia: John Benjamins, S. 98–118. https://doi.org/10.1075/z.htm1.14mey.

Microsoft. (n.d.). Neural dictionary – Azure AI Translator – Azure AI services, abgerufen am 06.05.2025 auf https://learn.microsoft.com/en-us/azure/ai-services/translator/text-translation/how-to/use-neural-dictionary.

Müller, Madu-Silvia (2023): *Vorbereitung auf eine KI zentrierte Zukunft: Eine Untersuchung aktueller Ausbildungsmethoden*. MA-Arbeit, Universität Innsbruck.

OneClickterms, abgerufen am 29.07.2024 auf https://terms.sketchengine.eu/.

OpenAI (2024a): „Reproducible Outputs", abgerufen am 28.07.2024 auf https://platform.openai.com/docs/advanced-usage.

OpenAI. (2024b): „Prompt engineering", abgerufen am 29.07.2024 auf https://platform.openai.com/docs/guides/prompt-engineering.

OpenAI (2024c): „Embeddings", abgerufen am 29.07.2024 auf https://platform.openai.com/docs/guides/embeddings.

PACTE (2011): „Results of the validation of the PACTE Translation Competence Model: Translation problems and translation competence". In: Alvstad, Cecilia/Hild, Adelina/Tiselius, Elisabet (Hrsg.): *Methods and strategies of process research: Integrative approaches in translation studies*. Amsterdam/Philadelphia: John Benjamins, S. 317–343.

Papineni, Kishore / Roukos, Salim / Ward, Todd / Zhu, Wei.-Jing (2002): „Bleu: A method for automatic evaluation of machine translation". In: Isabelle, Pierre / Charniak, Eugene / Lin, Dekang (Hrsg.): *Proceedings of the 40th Annual Meeting on Association for Computational Linguistics (ACL '02)*, S. 311–318, abgerufen am 03.05.2025 auf https://aclanthology.org/volumes/P02-1/. https://doi.org/10.3115/1073083.1073135.

Post, Matt / Vilar, David (2018): „Fast lexically constrained decoding with dynamic beam allocation for neural machine translation". In: Walker, Marilyn / Ji, Heng / Stent, Amanda (Hrsg.): *Proceedings of the 2018 Conference of the North American Chapter of the Association for*

Computational Linguistics: Human Language Technologies, Volume 1 (Long Papers), S. 1314–1324, abgerufen am 03.05.2025, auf https://aclanthology.org/volumes/N18-1/.

PoolParty (2024): „PoolParty Ontology Management", abgerufen am 31.07.2024 auf https://www.poolparty.biz/ontology-management.

Prieto Ramos, Fernando (2024): „Revisiting translator competence in the age of artificial intelligence: The case of legal and institutional translation". *The Interpreter and Translator Trainer* 18(2), S. 148–173. https://doi.org/10.1080/1750399X.2024.2344942.

RaDT (2020): „Berufsprofil 2.0 Terminologe/Terminologin". Rat für Deutschsprachige Terminologie, abgerufen an 03.05.2025 auf https://www.buerob3.de/wp-content/uploads/2020/06/RaDT_Berufsprofil-2-0.pdf.

Rei, Ricardo / Stewart, Craig / Farinha, Ana C. / Lavie, Alon (2020): „COMET: A neural framework for MT evaluation". In: Webber, Bonnie / Cohn, Trevor / He, Yulan / Liu, Yang (Hrsg.): *Proceedings of the 2020 Conference on Empirical Methods in Natural Language Processing (EMNLP)*, S. 2685–2702, abgerufen am 03.05.2025 auf https://aclanthology.org/2020.emnlp-main.213.pdf.

Reynolds, Dave (2023): „Writing ontologies with ChatGPT", abgerufen am 29.07.2024 auf https://www.epimorphics.com/writing-ontologies-with-chatgpt/.

Rigouts Terryn / Ayla, Hoste Veronique / Lefever, Els (2020): „In no uncertain terms: A dataset for monolingual and multilingual automatic term extraction from comparable corpora". *Language Resources and Evaluation* 54(2), S. 385–418. https://doi.org/10.1007/s10579-019-09453-9.

Rütten, Anja (2023): „How to tell ChatGPT to extract terminology from parallel texts in different languages", abgerufen am 27.04.2024 auf https://blog.sprachmanagement.net/chatgpt-termextraction/.

Salton, Gerald / Wong, Andrew / Yang, Chungshu (1975): „A vector space model for automatic indexing". *Communications of the ACM* 18(11), S. 613–620. https://doi.org/10.1145/361219.361220

Sandrini, Peter (1997): „Terminologieausbildung im Curriculum für Sprachmittler". In: Fleischmann, Eberhard / Kutz, Wladimir / Schmitt, Peter A. (Hrsg.): *Translationsdidaktik: Grundfragen der Übersetzungswissenschaft*. Tübingen: Gunter Narr, S. 497–507.

San Martín, Antonio (2024): „What generative artificial intelligence means for terminological definitions“, abgerufen am 03.05.2025 auf https://arxiv.org/abs/2402.16139. https://doi.org/10.48550/arXiv.2402.16139.

Schmitz, Klaus-Dirk (2020): *Terminology work Best Practices 2.0*. Köln: Deutscher Terminologie-Tag e.V.

Sun, Qiaoke (2021): „Research on cultivating professionals for language service industry in the era of big data“. In: *Proceedings of the 2nd International Conference on Information Science and Education (ICISE-IE)*, S. 927–930, abgerufen am 03.05.2025 auf https://ieeexplore.ieee.org/xpl/conhome/9741749/proceeding. https://doi.org/10.1109/ICISE-IE53922.2021.00212.

Text2TCS (2021), abgerufen am 03.05.2025 auf https://live.european-language-grid.eu/catalogue/tool-service/8122.

TermOrgs (2016): „Terminology Starter Guide“, abgerufen am 29.07.2024 auf https://www.terminorgs.net/downloads/TerminOrgs_StarterGuide_V2.pdf.

TermSuite, abgerufen am 29.07.2024 auf https://termsuite.github.io/.

Tran, Hanh Thi Hong / Martinc, Matej / Caporusso, Jaya / Doucet, Antoine / Pollak, Senya (2023): „The recent advances in automatic term extraction: A survey“, abgerufen am 03.05.2025 auf https://arxiv.org/abs/2301.06767.

Traub, Julia / Theurer, Stefan (2022): „Wie man aus einem ‚Benennungswust‘ unternehmensweit und übergreifende Terminologiearbeit macht“. Vortrag auf der Tekom Jahrestagung in Stuttgart, 8.–10. November 2022.

Trembczyk, M. / Lang, Christian (2023): „KI-gestützte Termextraktion in der modernen Terminologiearbei“. *edition – Fachzeitschrift für Terminologie* 2/23, S. 23–30.

Vaswani, Aashish / Shazeer, Noam / Parmar, Niki / Uszkoreit, Jakob / Jones, Llion / Gomez, Aidan N. /Kaiser, Lukasz / Polosukhin, Illia (2017): „Attention is all you need“, abgerufen am 03.05.2025 auf https://arxiv.org/abs/1706.03762. https://doi.org/10.48550/ARXIV.1706.03762.

Winter, Tom (2024): „Terminologiearbeit und generative KI (am Beispiel von ChatGPT) – Prognose einer glücklichen Ehe“ (DTT-Webinar), abgerufen am 28.07.2024 auf http://dttev.org/aktuelles-terminologie-erleben/40-aktuelles-2024/260-dtt-webinar-terminologiearbeit-und-chatgpt-2024.html.

Woodrum, Charles (2024): „ChatGPT and language translation: A small case study evaluating English–Mandarin translation". In: Degen, Helmut / Ntoa, Stavroula (Hrsg.): *Artificial Intelligence in HCI*, S. 147–157. Cham: Springer Nature Switzerland.

Wüster, Eugen (1975): „Die Ausbildung in Terminologie und terminologischer Lexikographie". *Lebende Sprachen* 20(2), S. 33–38.

Xu, Zhentao / Cruz, Mark Jerome / Guevara, Matthew / Wang, Tie / Deshpande, Manasi / Wang, Xiaofeng / Li, Zheng (2024): „Retrieval-augmented generation with knowledge graphs for customer service question answering", abgerufen am 03.05.2025 auf https://arxiv.org/abs/2404.17723. https://doi.org/10.1145/3626772.3661370.

Yvon, François / Rauf, Sadaf Abdul (2020): „Utilisation de ressources lexicales et terminologiques en traduction neuronale". Technical report, LIMSICNRS, abgerufen am 03.05.2025 auf https://hal.science/hal-02895535v2.

Annex I Kostenlose Software für Terminologieextraktion

AntConc (Client GUI): https://www.laurenceanthony.net/software/antconc/

ATR4S (Client CLI): https://github.com/ispras/atr4s

OneClickTerms (Web GUI)*: https://terms.sketchengine.eu/

Rainbow (Client GUI): https://okapiframework.org/wiki/index.php/Rainbow

Termine (Client/Web GUI): https://www.nactem.ac.uk/software/termine/

Termsuite (Client GUI): https://termsuite.github.io/

Text2TCS (Web GUI): https://live.european-language-grid.eu/catalogue/tool-service/8122

* Limitierte Funktionalität in der kostenlosen Version

Assessing the impact of artificial intelligence on translation project management competences: an exploratory study

Irene Fuentes-Pérez
Universidad de Alcalá

Cristina Plaza-Lara
Universidad de Málaga

ABSTRACT
The advent of generative artificial intelligence (GenAI) is significantly transforming the landscape of translation project management (TPM), presenting both challenges and opportunities for professionals in this field. In response to this evolving scenario, this chapter proposes an empirical study based on interviews with practising Spanish-speaking project managers (PMs) to elucidate the multifaceted impact of artificial intelligence (AI) on the competences of translation PMs. The participants, representing diverse professional backgrounds and organisational contexts, provided insights into their use of AI tools, levels of AI adoption, and training approaches. Using semi-structured interviews, the data gathered have been analysed qualitatively with ATLAS.ti for content analysis purposes, revealing how AI technologies are reshaping daily practices and necessitating new competences in areas such as workflow optimisation, decision-making, and technical proficiency. The findings highlight the dynamic nature of competences in TPM and underscore the need for continuous learning and adaptation to meet the demands of a rapidly evolving industry. By identifying essential AI-related competences and offering guidance for adapting training programmes for future professionals, this study contributes to a deeper understanding of how AI integration is redefining the role of PMs within translation studies and practice.

Keywords: artificial intelligence, translation project management, competences, interview-based study

1. Introduction

Since translation studies developed into an academic discipline in its own right in the second half of the past century (see Hurtado Albir 2011, pp. 124–125), the areas of interest and research of this discipline have diversified significantly, encompassing a wide range of practical approaches and new profiles within the translation and interpreting (TI) industry. Over the past two decades, globalisation and the surge of digital convergence have impacted this field, leading to a period of transformation (Drugan 2013; Risku et al. 2013). As a result, as observed by Plaza-Lara, scholars in the field have turned their attention to exploring and defining the evolving professional roles associated with translators and interpreters (2018a, p. 511), such as that of the translation project manager (PM). While this professional profile has been present in the TI industry since the early 1990s when the first translation agencies were established worldwide, "it has been largely overlooked as an object of scholarly inquiry and critical pedagogical reflection in the field of translation studies" (Dunne/Dunne 2011, p. 6). However, since its inception, the landscape of translation project management (TPM) has evolved significantly, as PMs have had to adapt to new technologies and services that have directly impacted their daily operations and required skills and competences. This situation has been made even more challenging by the irruption of artificial intelligence (AI), and more recently generative artificial intelligence (GenAI), which is once again transforming the role of PMs and, consequently, their competences.

The primary objective of this study is to examine how AI impacts the competences required in TPM. To achieve this aim, the study explores how AI technologies are influencing PMs' daily practices and identifies the AI-driven tools and platforms currently employed by these professionals to enhance efficiency and ensure quality in translation projects. Through semi-structured interviews with experienced Spanish-speaking TPM professionals, this exploratory research aims to define the essential AI-related abilities required for future professionals and offer guidance for adapting training programmes for upcoming TI graduates. Therefore, the main research question that guides this study is: How is AI shaping the competences required in TPM?

To address this, the theoretical framework will outline the competences necessary for effective TPM. The methodological framework will describe the data collection process, including details on the sample, transcription, and coding procedures. Finally, the contribution will present the results and discuss the findings based on the interview data to draw conclusions.

2. Theoretical framework

While there has been considerable research on translator competences, the competences of translation PMs have received comparatively little scholarly attention. In order to answer the research question of the present study, it is deemed necessary to define a TPM competence framework as a starting point, so that the impact of AI on these competences can be assessed. This study will bring to the fore the dynamic nature of competences and the need to contextualise them (Calvo Encinas 2006; Kelly 2005). As explained by Calvo Encinas, the relationship between professional profiles and competences must be understood as a form of "cyclical conception" (2009, p. 150), in which society and job market serve as a guide to refine competences, thus avoiding the universality and exhaustiveness of any competence model (Calvo Encinas 2009, p. 62).

As far as the authors are aware, the first (and so far, only) comprehensive competence model for translation PMs is the one proposed by Plaza-Lara (2022). After a thorough literature review on TPM and the competences of translators and PMs (see Plaza-Lara 2018a, 2018b), this researcher conducted five empirical studies (Plaza-Lara 2018a, 2018b, 2020b, 2020a, 2022), using a multi-methodological approach that included surveys to PMs and other translation professionals, analysis of a corpus of job advertisements, and analysis of both translation curricula in Spanish universities and the European Master's in Translation (EMT) programmes. By drawing on multiple data sources from both industry and academia – specifically project management and translation – this approach allowed her to operationalise the different components of TPM competences.

Based on the translation competence model proposed by the PACTE research group (Hurtado Albir 2017), Plaza-Lara (2022) presented her provisional model of competences for translation PMs (Figure 1), which confirms that these professionals must be competent in both disciplines, namely translation and project management. But what about AI? How does this breakthrough technology affect the competences of those managing projects in the translation industry? The paradigm shift introduced by AI calls for a thorough reconsideration of the competences required for translation PMs, bearing in mind the "cyclical conception" of competences to which Calvo Encinas refers (2009, p. 150). In order to address this research inquiry, as mentioned in the introduction and methodology sections, five semi-structured interviews with experienced practitioners in the field of TPM were carried out.

Although the empirical study here presented is informed by the competences included in Figure 1, the interview structure does not strictly adhere to the competence framework proposed by Plaza-Lara (2022). This decision was made to simplify the interview process and prevent an extensive list of competences from overwhelming or disengaging participants. Professional PMs do not necessarily need to be aware of the terminology used in the academic field regarding the description of their competences. In contrast, they do have a thorough knowledge of the workflow applied in project management. This explains why the main section of the interview is based on the tasks and processes in TPM and not on competences (see section 3 and appendix 1).

Knowledge of Translation sub-competence	Strategic sub-competence	Instrumental sub-competence
Budgeting Invoicing Issuing purchase orders Writing productivity and profit reports Meeting and negotiating with clients and vendors Attracting new customers Preparation and supervision of instructions, reference material, etc. Query and feedback management Knowledge of standards and regulations in the industry Industry and market knowledge	Teamwork Management of human resources Time management Problem solving Multitasking Analysis skills Management of quality, costs and deadlines Project coordination from start to finish	Computer-assisted translation Localisation tools Project management software Research skills Corpus creation/management Terminology extraction/use of termbases Management of different file formats Machine translation Natural language processing Speech recognition
Bilingual sub-competence	Psycho-physiological components	Extralinguistic sub-competence
Knowledge of at least one foreign language (preferably English, for communication purposes) Translation Review Quality assurance Proficiency in the industry's professional jargon	Communication skills Ability to work under pressure Organisation skills Attention to detail Motivation Autonomy Interpersonal skills Proactive and positive attitude Ability to adapt to different situations Leadership skills Responsibility Ability to listen Open-mindedness Empathy Assertiveness	Analysis of text specialisations Analysis of cultural implications in texts Cultural components of international communication

Figure 1: Competence model for TPM proposed by Plaza-Lara (2022, p. 216).

3. Methodology

This study presents data obtained from individual interviews with five PMs from the industry. As mentioned earlier, the findings will contribute to understanding the impact of AI in TPM. In contextualising this research,

Grotjahn's framework (1987, pp. 59–60) proved particularly valuable. This framework classifies research paradigms in applied linguistics and distinguishes between quantitative and qualitative approaches based on three key variables: the research method, the type of data, and the type of data analysis. According to his classification, this study aligns with paradigm 7, owing to its non-experimental design and reliance on qualitative data for interpretative analysis.

3.1 Participant selection process

During June and July 2024, a brief survey was developed to reach out to PMs who might be interested in participating in this research. This survey only included three questions: a) Are you currently working as a PM? b) Do you use AI services in your work? c) Would you be interested in participating in an interview for a TPM study?

The survey was distributed through the researchers' LinkedIn networks, employing "non-probability sampling" (Hernández Sampieri/Fernández Collado/Baptista Lucio 2014, p. 175; Mellinger/Hanson 2016, p. 12; Sharma 2017, p. 750), specifically convenience sampling (Mellinger/Hanson 2016, p. 12). The survey was written in Spanish, given that most of the researchers' contacts in the TI industry on this social network were Spanish speakers. By the end of the survey period, eight responses were received. However, when contacting the PMs for interview participation, the number decreased from eight to five: one participant did not meet the requirements to participate in the study, another participant did not respond to e-mails, and a third participant ultimately decided not to take part in the project.

Prior to the interviews, an information sheet for participants, including an informed consent form, was prepared and sent to each participant. This ensured that they had all the necessary information and could raise any relevant questions before the interviews took place. All five participants reviewed, signed, and returned the consent forms before the confirmed date of their interview.

The interview questions were sent to three TI professionals for review and validation, and their feedback was incorporated into the final version of the interview protocol before implementation. In September 2024, all five online interviews were conducted using the collaborative platform Microsoft Teams. Each interview lasted an average of 30 minutes, resulting in a total of 153 minutes and 26 seconds of recorded material. The interviews were conducted individually, following a semi-structured format (see appendix 1).

3.2 Sample

The following inclusion criteria were established for the selection of interviewees: participants had to be working as PMs, either as employees or self-employed, and they had to use AI services in their daily work as PMs.

The final sample comprises three women and two men currently working in the TPM industry. As can be seen in Table 1, a total of five participants were interviewed individually in September 2024. Although small and not representative of the population, this sample can be considered a good starting point for identifying emerging patterns and challenges in the TPM industry while acknowledging the need for larger-scale studies in the future.

Table 1: Breakdown of participants interviewed

Code	Position	Nationality	Years in the TPM industry	Company size
P01	CEO + PM	Spain	Over 35	<20 employees
P02	PM + translator	Spain	14	<20 employees
P03	VM + PM	Spain	8	<20 employees
P04	PM	Colombia	3	>250 employees
P05	PM	Argentina	10	>250 employees

The participants have diverse professional backgrounds, with experience in the TPM industry ranging from 3 to over 35 years. The sample includes professionals from different Spanish-speaking countries (Argentina, Colombia and Spain), all holding PM positions. Although two participants (P04 and P05) work exclusively as PMs, the majority of interviewees also take on additional roles. Specifically, one participant (P01) combines CEO and TPM responsibilities with over three decades of industry experience, while others combine TPM with translation (P02) or vendor management (VM) duties (P03).

Additionally, the sample represents two distinct organisational contexts: small companies with fewer than 20 employees (P01, P02, and P03) and large enterprises with over 250 employees (P04 and P05). When assessing both individual AI literacy and organisational AI implementation levels, participants were presented with a four-tier classification framework adapted from GenAI adoption patterns, originally used by the Project Management Institute (PMI 2024, p. 7) in a survey carried out with over 500 PMs (see Figure 2). This framework categorises AI adoption and implementation levels into distinct groups: *explorers* (in the early stages of exploring and experimenting with GenAI); *adapters* (embracing GenAI to a moderate extent); *innovators* (making significant strides in adopting GenAI); and *trailblazers* (at the forefront of GenAI adoption).

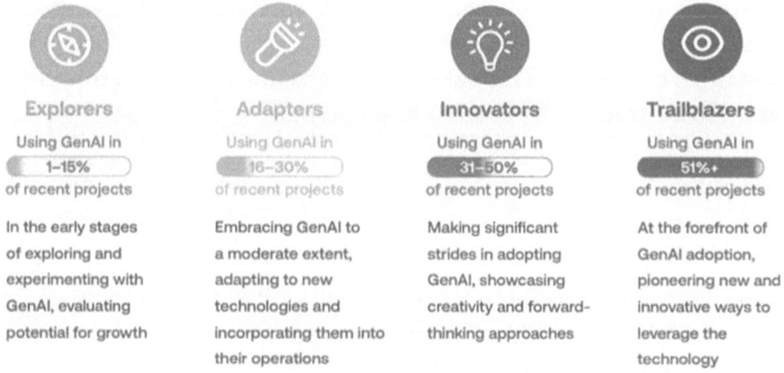

Figure 2: Project professional GenAI adoption levels (PMI 2024, p. 7).

None of the five participants identified as being at the *explorer* level, which suggests a sample group with relatively mature AI engagement. P01 self-identified between *adapter* and *innovator* levels in personal knowledge, while their company demonstrated stronger AI implementation at the *innovator* level. P02 showed consistent alignment between individual knowledge and organisational implementation, both at the *adapter* level. P03 stated that their personal AI knowledge was at the *adapter* level, while their company demonstrated more advanced implementation, straddling between *innovator* and *trailblazer* levels. P04's individual knowledge reached the *innovator* level, while their company's implementation bridged *adapter* and *innovator* categories. P05 showed the highest overall AI engagement, with both personal knowledge and company implementation ranging between *innovator* and *trailblazer* levels.

Lastly, participants' AI training backgrounds revealed diverse approaches to skills development, ranging from formal certifications to self-directed learning. The AI training patterns can be categorised into the following approaches:

Formal education and certifications:

- P02 is currently pursuing a master's degree in Natural Language Processing, complemented by self-paced learning through online platforms.
- P05 is a Project Management Professional (PMP®), a globally recognised certification issued by the PMI that validates expertise in project management principles, methodologies, and best practices. P05 has obtained several professional certifications, including two from PMI and specialised training in Prompt Engineering.

Self-directed learning:

- P01 describes an informal, collaborative learning environment within their company, where knowledge is shared internally among employees without formal training structures.
- P04 has adopted a purely self-taught approach, investing personal time and resources in introductory courses through paid learning platforms.

Upcoming training:

- P03 represents a case of planned, targeted training, specifically focused on practical tools like GitHub Copilot[1], an AI editor, indicating a strategic approach to AI skill development aligned with specific business needs.

This distribution of training approaches appears to correlate with organisational contexts: participants from larger organisations (P04 and P05) show more structured and credential-focused learning paths, while those from smaller companies (P01–P03) tend toward more flexible, needs-based learning approaches. Notably, regardless of the training format, all participants

[1] https://github.com/features/copilot (retrieved on 07/05/2025)

demonstrated active engagement in continuous learning about AI technologies, although through varying channels and with different levels of formality.

3.3 Interview structure

The interview is articulated around three different sections. Section 1 focuses on the participant profile, gathering information such as their years of experience as a PM, the approximate number of employees in their company, their level of knowledge regarding AI, the extent of AI implementation within their company, and whether they have received any specific training in AI.

The main section of the interview, section 2, focuses on tools and processes, exploring what AI tools the participant utilises in their role as a PM and for which specific tasks these tools are applied. The tasks of this section were organised in three groups according to the standard ISO 17100 (ISO 2015): administrative, technical and linguistic tasks, and it was also supported by slides to facilitate discussion.

Finally, section 3 addresses opinions and perceptions, prompting participants to share their thoughts on how AI might impact TPM and, consequently, the competences required of PMs. Additionally, this section seeks to uncover their expectations regarding the integration of AI in TPM, and the challenges it may pose to future PMs.

3.4 Transcription and coding

The interviews conducted via Microsoft Teams were recorded for transcription purposes. Following the completion of all five interviews, the transcription process was carried out using Notta.ai[2], a transcription and voice recognition tool that uses AI to convert spoken audio into written text. The software's AI-powered transcription feature was employed to generate preliminary transcripts, and it was followed by thorough verification and correction by both researchers. To ensure confidentiality, all transcriptions were anonymised, removing interviewees' names. Instead, a consistent participant/interviewer structure was used across all five transcriptions.

[2] https://www.notta.ai/en (retrieved on 07/05/2025)

The coding process was conducted using the qualitative data analysis tool ATLAS.ti[3], following a structured approach based on predetermined conceptual categories designed to address the initial research question. The researchers developed a comprehensive coding scheme organised around four main theoretical constructs based on the structure of the interview: sample; tools; processes/competences; and opinion (see Table 2). This systematic categorisation, initially designed prior to the interviews, allowed for a detailed analysis of the qualitative data while maintaining consistency across all interviews. During the coding process, one sub-theme within the "Opinion" category was adjusted: "AI as a helpful resource" was added, as most participants highlighted benefits of AI that did not fit into the original categories.

Table 2: List of codes used for the coding process

	Code
Sample	Years of experience
	Company size
	AI adoption and implementation – individual
	AI adoption and implementation – company
	AI training
Tools	Tools – Automation
	Tools – GenAI
Processes/Competences	Bilingual sub-competence
	Translation knowledge sub-competence
	Strategic sub-competence
	Extralinguistic sub-competence
	Instrumental sub-competence
	Psycho-physiological components
Opinion	AI expectations in TPM
	AI challenges in TPM
	AI issues/threats in the industry
	AI as a helpful resource

[3] https://atlasti.com/ (retrieved on 07/05/2025)

4. Analysis of results

The translation industry has long been at the forefront of AI adoption, primarily through translation management systems (TMSs) that have enabled significant task automation. While these traditional AI applications have become foundational tools in the sector, the recent emergence of GenAI by the end of 2022 (van der Veer/Bostoen 2024), exemplified by tools like ChatGPT[4], has initiated a new wave of transformation in work processes across multiple industries, including the TI sector. Our study examined both established AI automation tools and emerging GenAI applications in TPM workflows. Across participants, a combination of traditional TMSs alongside emerging GenAI applications such as large language models (LLMs), plugins, and application programme interfaces (APIs) was observed.

Several participants highlighted the long-standing use of TMSs for TPM, such as Plunet[5] and XTRF[6]. P01, for example, reported that implementing Plunet resulted in PMs saving approximately 40 % of their workload through automation. They emphasised the reliability of these systems, a sentiment echoed by P03, who detailed how their API integration with XTRF and SDL Trados[7] streamlined translation tasks. In their words, "you upload the prepared file, specify the client and language combination, and the system creates a translation package automatically," reducing manual workload and freeing up time for more complex tasks. Similarly, P05 mentioned integrating Plunet with the computer-assisted translation (CAT) tool MemoQ[8], further speeding up the process.

Regarding GenAI, its use varies across participants. While P02 frequently employs ChatGPT for daily tasks, stating that it is "part of [their] everyday work," P05 prefers using Claude 3.5 Sonnet[9], a LLM that allows the creation and sharing of artefacts such as automated reports and graphics. As a matter of fact, P05 expressed a preference for Claude 3.5 Sonnet over ChatGPT due to its functionalities. While GenAI tools are increasingly integrated into

---

4 https://chatgpt.com/ (retrieved on 07/05/2025)
5 https://www.plunet.com/en/ (retrieved on 07/05/2025)
6 https://xtm.cloud/xtrf/ (retrieved on 07/05/2025)
7 https://www.trados.com/product/studio/ (retrieved on 07/05/2025)
8 https://www.memoq.com/ (retrieved on 07/05/2025)
9 https://www.anthropic.com/claude/sonnet (retrieved on 07/05/2025)

their workflows, their use is mostly experimental or for specific tasks like generating marketing posts (P03) or correcting e-mails (P04).

Although some PMs or their companies are experimenting with LLMs, they have not yet fully integrated them into professional workflows. In this regard, P01 mentioned, "[w]e are researching [LLMs], but we don't use them professionally yet." This cautious approach suggests a wait-and-see attitude toward these new technologies, even when companies acknowledge their potential.

A recurring theme among participants was the integration of AI-driven plugins and APIs to optimise project management. P02 and P03 emphasised their reliance on Trados plugins, with P03 highlighting the convenience of automatically creating project folders in Outlook based on e-mail content. P05 also praised MemoQ Adaptive Generative Translation (AGT)[10], an AI plugin that integrates seamlessly with MemoQ's interface, although they acknowledged that it still lags behind some competitors in functionality. These tools are used to automate routine tasks, thereby enhancing efficiency in project workflows. However, there was less enthusiasm about AI-driven chatbots or virtual assistants. P03 explained that while their company had considered adding a chatbot for client interaction, it had not yet been implemented. Similarly, P01 had worked on projects involving chatbots but noted that such tools were not part of their company's internal operations.

As explained above, the main section of the interview was articulated around the different tasks in which AI could be implemented depending on their nature: administrative, technical and linguistic tasks. The analysis of the participants' answers, based on the procedural knowledge they hold of the entire translation workflow, has allowed the authors to identify observable behaviours (Hurtado Albir 2019, p. 63) that shape competences and therefore to draw conclusions about how AI impacts on the competences of PMs. Consequently, the presentation of results for this group of questions will be structured around the competences of translation PMs presented by Plaza-Lara (2022) in her provisional model (Figure 1).

A technological breakthrough such as that introduced by AI has had its most significant impact on the instrumental sub-competence. This sub-competence, as defined by PACTE (1998), includes the ability to use various

10 https://www.memoq.com/products/memoq-agt (retrieved on 07/05/2025)

resources effectively in translation work and to navigate professional contexts. Among others, it encompasses procedural knowledge related to the use of documentation resources, information and communication tools applied to translation. As already reported, according to the questions concerning the tools, automation tools such as TMSs are widely established in the industry. In contrast, GenAI is posing new challenges that demand swift adaptation from professionals. The interviewees' answers proved that they are aware of the enormous potential of GenAI to carry out tasks other than translating or generating content. However, it must be noticed that only P04 and P05 mentioned GenAI tools beyond the most widely known options (namely, LLMs such as ChatGPT, Copilot[11], Gemini[12], etc.), despite the fact that since 2023 the market has been flooded with technology solutions coming from outside the industry (Akhulkova 2023). The main tasks within the instrumental sub-competence for which three of the participants admitted using LLMs are terminology management, file preparation and desktop publishing (DTP). Two of them also added web crawling and writing Excel formulas. However, they acknowledged that the final output does not always meet expectations, largely because of the critical role of effective prompt formulation – a factor emphasised as a challenge by all interviewees – as well as the need to know which GenAI tool is best suited for each specific task.

The influence of AI on various sub-competences of PMs is largely tied to their use of AI tools, which falls under the instrumental sub-competence. However, the interviewees' responses provide important insights that have significant implications for the other sub-competences as well. These findings shed light on how AI affects the broader skill set of translation PMs beyond just their technical abilities. Regarding the strategic sub-competence, all interviewees stated that for project coordination from start to finish, they rely on TMSs, and the different automation features offered by these resources (workflow management, use of templates, management of costs and deadlines, etc.). However, P02, P04 and P05 reported having tested GenAI tools for time, risk and human resources management. With regard to time management, P02 acknowledged that in the case of complex projects, ChatGPT has proved useful for planning steps and deadlines, providing all project data

11 https://copilot.microsoft.com/ (retrieved on 07/05/2025)
12 https://gemini.google.com/app (retrieved on 07/05/2025)

are entered. P05 has used the same tool for human resources management. After providing the tool with the vendors' blind CVs, a prompt was entered into the AI tool to obtain feedback on their suitability for a specific project. Risk management was mentioned by P04, who simply acknowledged to be testing it, as in those cases AI requires a vast amount of information. This data dependency of AI was mentioned as a challenge by all interviewees, which could also lead to confidentiality issues in those cases in which open AI systems are used.

As far as the knowledge of translation sub-competence is concerned, once again TMSs are at the forefront in project workflows according to the answers received in the interviews. Administrative tasks such as budgeting, invoicing, issuing purchase orders or generating reports are completely automated by these systems. In the case of reports, P01 and P03 acknowledged that the final result provided by the tool does not always meet the company expectations and they have to manually process the data obtained. In no case is GenAI used for that purpose. Nonetheless, again three participants confirmed they are employing GenAI for tasks such as meeting summaries and note taking, query management and feasibility studies. Tools for taking notes and summarising meetings were considered very useful by two interviewees. Even P04 admitted having used this kind of resource for translating meetings in which the language variant was difficult to understand. Another participant also recognised that GenAI tools could be useful to obtain possible answers to the queries received for a project, before they are confirmed on the client side. Finally, P05 acknowledged to have tested GenAI for a feasibility study in a very specific project in which the client had proposed their own workflow. P05 compared the client's existing workflow with the one their team suggested, analysing costs and turnaround times for both. In this sense, GenAI proved particularly useful in generating visual representations, such as charts, to illustrate how quickly the client could recover their investment.

With regard to the bilingual sub-competence, P01, P02 and P03 referred to quality assurance tasks, for which they mainly used software such as ApSIC Xbench[13], a tool designed to assist in quality assurance processes, which is based on predefined rules or databases and not on AI. P02 also referenced

---

[13] https://www.xbench.net/ (retrieved on 07/05/2025)

Stilus[14], an AI-based proofreading and grammar-checking tool designed for Spanish texts tool. In contrast, P03 noted that when using ChatGPT for this purpose, the tool output is not always reliable, pointing out that its quality varies and occasionally produces hallucinations. Another key use case emphasised during the interviews is the application of GenAI to produce linguistic alternatives for a given text, mentioned by all five participants. In this sense, two interviewees also reported to have employed it for copywriting or transcreation purposes. Especially important for PMs, according to four of the five interviewees, seems to be the use of GenAI tools for writing e-mails and modifying the register and tone of these messages, particularly when they write them in a language other than their mother tongue. Finally, P04 stated to have used ChatGPT to confirm the source language and even to carry out a content analysis to find out the field of specialisation to which the text belongs. In this last task, the extralinguistic sub-competence comes into play.

The preceding analysis suggests that AI directly influences the psycho-physiological aspects of translation PMs, defined as "the ability to use all kinds of psychomotor, cognitive and attitudinal resources" (PACTE 1998, p. 102), especially when it comes to soft skills (see Fuentes-Pérez 2023). As stated in relation to the bilingual sub-competence, communication skills, and more specifically PMs' writing abilities, are reinforced through the use of AI tools. Moreover, the need to explore and learn autonomously new features and tools and integrate them into the project workflow requires a proactive attitude and an open-minded approach toward the use of this technology. In this sense, self-learning and creativity skills could be added to the list of soft skills.

5. Discussion and conclusions

The insights gathered in this study allow us to conclude that while AI has long been part of TPM through task automation, the advent of GenAI is introducing substantial shifts within the industry. As evidenced in our findings, GenAI is gradually being incorporated into various project management tasks, but it still poses significant challenges for the PMs interviewed, and its full integration into the workflow remains a distant prospect. Despite a

[14] https://www.mystilus.com/ (retrieved on 07/05/2025)

generally positive attitude toward GenAI, most interviewees currently view it as an assistant tool rather than a central driver of project processes. All participants highlighted the crucial role of human expertise in the workflow to critically assess the GenAI output and determine its suitability for specific project requirements. This finding only reinforces the argument that PMs must possess solid competences in translation and project management.

In line with the above-mentioned idea, there is indeed a dual trajectory in AI adoption within TPM: the established presence of traditional AI through TMSs and the emerging influence of GenAI tools. While TMSs have proven their value in automation, the integration of GenAI presents a more complex picture. Despite the availability of certain tools in the market, their adoption remains largely experimental, and they are primarily used for specific tasks such as marketing content generation or e-mail correction. This cautious approach extends to LLMs, where companies acknowledge their potential but have not yet fully integrated them into professional workflows. The implementation of AI-driven plugins and APIs, particularly in established tools in the TI industry, represents a middle ground, offering practical automation benefits while maintaining familiar workflows. However, more advanced AI applications, such as chatbots for client interaction, remain largely unexplored, suggesting that the industry is carefully evaluating the balance between innovation and operational reliability.

As concerns our research question, it is notable that the instrumental sub-competence is the most impacted by the integration of GenAI. Effective use of GenAI in TPM requires not only selecting the most appropriate GenAI tools for each specific purpose, but also generating precise prompts to perform specific tasks. These two components may diminish in importance in the future if the project management tools used by translation companies begin to incorporate GenAI features that streamline the PMs' tasks. But for the time being, the impact of GenAI on other sub-competences such as the strategic or knowledge of translation competences depends entirely on the selection of GenAI tools and the generation of effective prompts. Likewise, data dependency of AI raises concerns regarding corporate privacy, particularly when proprietary systems are not employed. Finally, it should be noted that GenAI appears to be achieving more consistent results in tasks related to the bilingual sub-competence, though the latter remains a secondary focus for PMs in many organisations.

Several limitations of this study should be acknowledged. First, the sample size, while providing valuable insights, could be expanded in future research to capture a broader range of perspectives and practices. Second, the study's participants were all Spanish-speaking PMs, with three from Spain, one from Colombia, and one from Argentina. This limited geographical and linguistic scope may not fully represent the global project management landscape. Future research could benefit from including participants from a more diverse range of countries and language backgrounds to provide a more comprehensive perspective on AI implementation in TPM across different markets. Third, given the recent emergence of many AI tools, particularly GenAI, this study represents an early snapshot of their implementation in TPM; future longitudinal studies could better track the evolution and impact of AI applications in coming years. Finally, the wide variety of available AI tools poses challenges for smaller companies without dedicated technological departments, potentially limiting their ability to fully develop and implement these solutions.

There is no doubt that the landscape of TPM stands at a pivotal moment of transformation. Looking ahead, the integration of AI in TPM appears to be following a dual path: the continued refinement of established TMS solutions alongside the gradual incorporation of emerging GenAI capabilities. This evolution suggests that future PMs will need to develop increasingly sophisticated technological competences while maintaining their crucial role in critical assessment and decision-making. As the field continues to evolve, it seems that the ability to effectively balance human expertise with AI capabilities will likely become a defining characteristic of successful TPM.

Acknowledgements

The authors would like to express their sincere gratitude to Juanjo Arevalillo Doval, Martín Novillo and all the interviewees for their invaluable insights and expertise on the TPM landscape during the interview process.

We would also like to extend our appreciation to our colleagues who assisted in validating the interview protocols prior to their implementation. Their contributions have significantly enhanced the quality and depth of this research.

This paper has been partially carried out in the framework of the research project "App para entrenar en posedición de traducción automática neuronal mediante la gamificación en entornos profesionales" (GAMETRAPP; ref. TED2021-129789B-I00), funded by MCIN/AEI/10.13039/501100011033 and the European Union "NextGenerationEU/PRTR"; and "Register Variation in Machine Translation: A Multidimensional Analysis of a Corpus from the Third Social Sector" (PID2024-157849OB-I00), funded by MICIU/ AEI/10.13039/501100011033/FEDER, European Union.

This work was supported by a predoctoral research fellowship (ref. PIPF-2022/PH-HUM-26244) from the Community of Madrid and the University of Alcalá.

Bibliography

Akhulkova, Yulia (2023): *Nimdzi language technology atlas*, retrieved on 17/10/2024 from https://www.nimdzi.com/language-technology-atlas/.

Calvo Encinas, Elisa (2006): "Orientación profesional para futuros licenciados de traducción e interpretación: estrategias centradas en las necesidades del estudiantado." In: Bravo Utrera, Sonia / García López, Rosario (Eds.): *Estudios de traducción: problemas y perspectivas*. Las Palmas de Gran Canaria: Servicio de Publicaciones Universidad de Las Palmas de Gran Canaria, pp. 633–648.

Calvo Encinas, Elisa (2009): *Análisis curricular de los estudios de traducción e interpretación en España: perspectiva del estudiantado.* Ph.D. thesis, Universidad de Granada, retrieved on 20/08/2024 from https://digibug.ugr.es/handle/10481/3488.

Drugan, Joanna (2013): *Quality in professional translation: Assessment and improvement.* London: Bloomsbury.

Dunne, Keiran J. / Dunne, Elena S. (Eds.) (2011): *Translation and localization project management: The art of the possible*. Amsterdam / Philadelphia: John Benjamins, pp. 1–16. https:/doi.org/10.1075/ata.xvi.

Fuentes-Pérez, Irene (2023): *Top 5 soft skills for translation project managers*, retrieved on 29/10/2024 from https://www.gala-global.org/knowledge-center/professional-development/articles/top-5-soft-skills-translation-project-managers.

Grotjahn, Rüdiger (1987): "On the methodological basis of introspective methods." In: Faerch, Claus / Kasper, Gabriele (Eds.): *Introspection in second language research*. Bristol: Multilingual Matters, pp. 54–81.

Hernández Sampieri, Roberto / Fernández Collado, Carlos / Baptista Lucio, Pilar (2014): *Metodología de la investigación*. Mexico et al.: McGraw Hill Education.

Hurtado Albir, Amparo (2017) (Ed.): *Researching translation competence by PACTE group*. Amsterdam / Philadelphia: John Benjamins.

Hurtado Albir, Amparo (2011): *Traducción y traductología: Introducción a la traductología*. Madrid: Cátedra.

Hurtado Albir, Amparo (2019): "La investigación en didáctica de la traducción. Evolución, enfoques y perspectivas." In: Tolosa Igualada, Miguel / Echeverri, Álvaro (Eds.) *Porque algo tiene que cambiar. La formación de traductores e intérpretes: presente & futuro / Because something should change: Present & future training of translators and interpreters. MonTI* 11, pp. 47–76. https:/doi.org/10.6035/MonTI.2019.11.2.

ISO (International Organization for Standardization) (2015): *ISO 17100: Translation services – Requirements for translation services*. Geneva: ISO.

Kelly, Dorothy (2005): *A handbook for translator trainers*. London: St. Jerome.

Mellinger, Christopher / Hanson, Thomas (2016): *Quantitative research methods in translation and interpreting studies*. London: Routledge.

PACTE (1998): "Acquiring translation competence: Hypotheses and methodological problems of a research project." In: Beeby, Allison / Ensinger, Doris / Presas, Marisa (Eds.): *Investigating translation: Selected papers from the 4th international congress on translation*. Amsterdam / Philadelphia: John Benjamins, pp. 99–106.

Plaza-Lara, Cristina (2018a): "Las competencias del gestor de proyectos de traducción: análisis de un corpus de anuncios de trabajo." *Meta* 63(2), pp. 510–531. https:/doi.org/10.7202/1055150ar.

Plaza-Lara, Cristina (2018b): "Project management: Defining competences for translator training." In: Bogucki, Łukasz / Pietrzak, Paulina / Kornacki, Michał (Eds.): *Understanding translator education*. Berlin: Peter Lang, pp. 193–210.

Plaza-Lara, Cristina (2020a): "Competencias en traducción del gestor de proyectos: análisis desde la perspectiva de los traductores." *Sendebar* 31, pp. 133–157. https:/doi.org/10.30827/sendebar.v31i0.11301.

Plaza-Lara, Cristina (2020b): "Las competencias de los gestores de proyectos de traducción: un estudio basado en encuesta." *Hermēneus. Revista de Traducción e Interpretación* 22, pp. 311–335. https:/doi.org/10.24197/her.22.2020.311-335.

Plaza-Lara, Cristina (2022): "Competences of translation project managers from the academic perspective: Analysis of EMT programmes." *The Interpreter and Translator Trainer* 16(2), pp. 203–223. https:/doi.org/10.1080/1750399X.2021.1987085.

PMI (2024): *First movers' advantage. The immediate benefits of adopting generative AI for project management*, retrieved on 28/10/2024 from https://www.pmi.org/-/media/pmi/documents/public/pdf/learning/thought-leadership/genai-adoption-report.pdf?rev=95e95d270aae4ac1bd18a2f20dd7a699.

Risku, Hannah / Rossmanith, Nicole / Reichelt, Andreas / Zenk, Lukas (2013): "Translation in the network economy: A follow-up study." In: Way, Catherine / Vandepitte, Sonia / Meylaerts, Reine / Bartłomiejczyk, Magdalena (Eds.): *Tracks and treks in translation studies*. Amsterdam / Philadelphia: John Benjamins, pp. 29–48. https:/doi.org/10.1075/btl.108.02ris.

Sharma, Gaganpreet (2017): "Pros and cons of different sampling techniques." *International Journal of Applied Research* 3(7), pp. 749–775, retrieved on 29/10/2024 from https://www.allresearchjournal.com/archives/2017/vol3issue7/PartK/3-7-69-542.pdf.

van der Veer, Anouk / Bostoen, Friso (2024): *Two views on regulating competition in generative AI*, retrieved on 20/10/2024 from https://www.networklawreview.org/veer-bostoen-generative-ai/.

Appendix 1: Semi-structured interview

Section 1: Background information

How many years of experience do you have as a PM?

What is the approximate number of employees in your company/the company you work for?

How would you define your level of knowledge in AI?

How would you define the degree of AI implementation in your company/ the company you work for?

Have you received specific training in AI?

Section 2: Tools and processes

Which AI tools/systems do you use in your practice as a PM? How frequently do you use them?

For which of the following tasks do you use AI tools/systems? (Administrative tasks, technical tasks, and linguistic tasks)

Do you find these tools useful for your work, or do you not always get the expected response? What limitations do you think AI tools have in TPM?

Section 3: opinion

How do you think AI will affect TPM and, consequently, PMs' competences?

What expectations do you have regarding the application of AI to TPM?

End of interview

Would you like to add any additional comments to the issues discussed in the interview?

Interpreting in the age of AI: a new curriculum adapting training to future market demands

Bianca Prandi
Università di Bologna

Ira Torresi
Università di Bologna

Nicoletta Spinolo
Università di Bologna

ABSTRACT
The rapid evolution and diffusion of technologies, particularly supportive AI-based tools for interpreters, coupled with the appearance of new language services (such as live subtitling), calls for a similar innovation in interpreter education. To prepare interpreting graduates for this dynamic landscape, education must innovate not only by teaching the use of these technologies but also by cultivating long-term adaptability to rapidly changing technologies and workflows. These reflections inspired the development of the new *Interpreting and Technologies for Communication* (InTeCo) curriculum at the University of Bologna's Master's in Interpreting programme. Starting from the academic year 2024/25, InTeCo is offered alongside the "traditional" *Conference Interpreting* track. Courses are largely delivered remotely combining synchronous and asynchronous methods. This chapter explores the motivations and objectives behind the InTeCo curriculum, which is firmly rooted in constructivist and experiential learning approaches. The teaching methods employed are illustrated using one of the courses as a paradigmatic example. Finally, the chapter discusses future steps in assessing course effectiveness through an action-research approach with the initial student cohorts. With this contribution, we aim to spark reflection on the necessary evolution in interpreter education and the technological competence required to navigate an increasingly dynamic professional landscape.

Keywords: interpreter training, artificial intelligence, interpreting technologies, constructivism, action research

1. Introduction: motivation for the new curriculum

Technological developments, particularly those generated by artificial intelligence (AI) in terms of written and oral text translation, speech synthesis, speech-to-text technology, etc., can be frightening for interlingual communication professionals. As a matter of fact, a recent report by Slator.com (Txabarriaga 2024) highlights how many interpreters and translators have seen a decline in demand for 'traditional' interpreting and translation services in recent times.

However, according to the same survey, there are increasing demands for 'less traditional' services, and these seem to be mostly related to using and contributing to the development of AI-based technologies for translation.

In this scenario, it falls onto academic institutions to supplement their educational offer for graduates to be as ready as possible for the professional demands that the translation industry will present to them (Rodríguez Melchor/Horváth/Ferguson 2020), and which may evolve and change multiple times in the future. This is far from being an easy task: change is happening so rapidly that it is difficult for both the research community and the academic community at large to keep up in a relevant and research-informed way.

The aim of this chapter is to present an effort made in this direction at the Department of Interpreting and Translation (DIT) of the University of Bologna (Forlì), which has implemented a new curriculum called "Interpreting and Technologies for Communication" (InTeCo) in its MA programme in Interpreting.

At the DIT, potential employers of freshly graduated interpreters (e.g., interpreting/language service agencies, EU DG SCIC and DG LINC) and professional associations are surveyed regularly by the quality assurance team of the MA in Interpreting to continuously monitor job market demands (most recently, in early 2022 and late 2023; next consultation with stakeholders to be held in 2026). Being skilled in interpreting technologies has always featured prominently among employers' requirements after the COVID pandemic. While interpreting technologies were already part and parcel of the MA's syllabus, which had been revised starting from academic year 2020/21, they were largely targeted as distance conference interpreting and computer-assisted interpreting (CAI) tools. Such proactive inclusions in the syllabus were deemed sufficient to cater for the kind of technological competence outlined by survey respondents in 2022, which focused mainly on distance interpreting. In 2023, however, respondents highlighted that interpreting technologies had become absolutely necessary for the profession, even when the job is done in presence rather than online. Some respondents mentioned AI and machine interpreting[1] as

1 We are aware that using the term "machine interpreting" to define the translation of speech performed by a machine is not without its implications (Pöchhacker 2024). We use it as an overarching concept, as opposed to "human interpreting."

examples of such technologies. Unfortunately, the current syllabus simply did not have room (i.e., timetable openings, and physical classrooms) to accommodate any further addition. The same applied to other desiderata mentioned by survey respondents, such as interpreting classes in more languages than the five traditionally offered in combination with Italian (English, French, Spanish, German and Russian). Some respondents suggested that we add non-European languages, most prominently, Chinese – a recurrent request from DIT's very own BA graduates, where Chinese is taught as a B language, as well as being one of the languages of tuition in our sister programme in Specialised Translation. Some others suggested expanding the language pools to "all" EU languages, again an impractical option given that, among other constraints, the conference interpreting syllabus must comply with the European Master's in Conference Interpreting (EMCI) core curriculum standards and therefore offer a high number of interpreting hours per language taught.

All such requests on one side, and constraints on the other side, demanded for an additional curriculum to be set up – one that would centre the MA's teaching around interpreting technologies, with a syllabus aimed at developing a set of skills rather than focusing on language pairs, ensuring adaptability to each student's very own language pool. Ideally, such a curriculum would accommodate the needs of native speakers or bilinguals of languages other than English or Italian (the curricular languages). The skills and techniques acquired during the MA would be applied independently by the student rather than through dedicated language (and direction)-based training, while all students would receive individual feedback by teachers and tutors.

This programme was designed to be taught mainly at a distance, with a first on-site semester and three online and mostly asynchronous ones to favour the inclusion of international and working students who need flexible timetables to adjust to different time zones or working hours. Although successfully following an interpreting programme might be particularly challenging for a working student, the InTeCo curriculum can be an opportunity for practising language professionals wishing to upgrade their skills and expertise for the changing market, as well as for other professionals wishing to expand their skills. The annual intake of this curriculum is 15 students, who are accepted into the programme after an admission test.

We will begin by laying out the theoretical underpinnings on which the curriculum design is based (section 2) and move on to describe teaching methods and activities by presenting one module in the course as a paradigmatic example (section 3). Section 4 explores possible ways of assessing and improving the curriculum's effectiveness following an action-research approach, while section 5 presents some concluding remarks.

2. Theoretical framework

As Amato and Mack (2022, p. 457) point out,

> there is a longstanding distinction between interpreter training, which focuses on skill development and problem-solving, and interpreter education, which underpins practice-orientation with the acquisition of academic knowledge and an ability to theorise.

Education entails both the acquisition of episteme (knowledge) and the development of phronesis, i.e., practical wisdom (Haro-Soler/Kiraly 2019, p. 257). In devising a new curriculum centred around interpreting technologies, our aim is to provide students with the ability to extrapolate from their learning experience and the individual learning activities they engage in, so that they may become critical users of interpreting technologies (and maybe even developers or decision-makers).

Amato and Mack (2022, p. 459) conceptualise interpreting as a "complex cognitive activity performed as situated practice in a social context." To successfully practice this ever-evolving profession, interpreters must constantly react and adapt to the social context in which it is embedded.

As we see it, achieving this educational objective requires conceiving interpreting competence as *emerging* from the students' learning processes and interaction with their teachers and peers. The pedagogical epistemology underlying the development of the InTeCo curriculum is therefore a socio-constructivist/emergentist one (Haro-Soler/Kiraly 2019) which places emphasis on experiential learning (Kiraly 2000). The essential tenet of Kiraly's (2000, 2019) social constructivism lies in a view of competence as arising gradually thanks to the influence of the educational environmental factors in which the student is immersed and is therefore compatible with situated views of cognition (Spinolo/Muñoz Martín 2022, p. 193). We do not envision our students completing their studies with a pre-packaged set of skills and competences, but rather as individuals who will have developed their own understanding of relevant theories, the strategies most suited to their personal objectives and interests, and an ability to theorise on their own working processes, progressively moving from the state of novices who need to be introduced to the profession to that of competent individuals ready to navigate the professional job market in an autonomous way. In other words, the curriculum is heavily student-centred and promotes trainee individuality (Setton/Dawrant 2016b), thanks to a certain curricular flexibility that allows for adaptation to the individual background. While achieving immersion and situatedness in a distance education setting is challenging, it should be considered that working from home is currently a (share of) reality for many interpreters; furthermore, an effort is made to assign tasks that are as close to real-life ones as possible.

Having established the epistemological approach guiding our curriculum development and educational strategies, it was necessary to define what should be taught in an interpreting curriculum centred around technology.

The curriculum covers all key areas of interpreting technologies, with a focus on technology-supported and technology-mediated interpreting, as well as introductions to technology-automated interpreting and hybrid modes of interpreting (e.g., Braun 2019). In addition, students familiarise with recent technological developments, for instance by addressing the role of generative AI for the interpreter's workflow (e.g., Fantinuoli 2023).

Turning to models of interpreting competence was useful only to a limited extent, as the technological sub-competence does not appear prominently in the ones currently available (e.g., Albl-Mikasa 2012, 2013; Kutz 2010; Pöchhacker 2001). This is likely due to the fact that such sub-competence emerged with more prominence in later years. Technology is nonetheless mentioned in the EMCI core curriculum, which lists "*conference preparation techniques such as terminology, information retrieval and other uses of information technology*"[2] as elements of interpreting practice to be taught to students. Here, technologies are referred to in general terms.

---

[2] https://www.emcinterpreting.org/emci/core-curriculum (retrieved on 20/07/2024)

There is a lack of specification of which technologies interpreters should be proficient users of, and which competences are needed to achieve this objective. In their *Trainer's Guide* to conference interpreting, Setton and Dawrant (2016b, pp. 575–577) discuss technologies as part of interpreters' ancillary competences. In the *Complete Course* (Setton/Dawrant 2016a), they emphasise that trainees should be prepared for distance interpreting (p.36) and learn to use technology in their preparation, but the role of technology still appears marginal, again probably due to the fact that breakthrough developments in interpreting technology have been particularly rapid in the more recent years.

With the development of (AI-based) CAI tools, the diffusion of remote interpreting as a standard interpreting service, and the astonishing progress in speech translation technologies, it would be high time to feature technologies more prominently in interpreter competence models, potentially as an additional vortex developing along the other competences in Kiraly's (2019, p. 13) dynamic model of learning processes. One such proposal was recently put forward by Wang and Li (2022), who identified awareness of interpreting technology, skills and knowledge of interpreting technology, and learning of interpreting technology as the three core "processes" to be mastered when learning about technology in interpreting. The authors derived their proposal from the responses to a survey involving professional interpreters working between Chinese and English. While this approach helped them gain insight into interpreters' attitudes and experiences, it is representative of only one language combination and has not yet been tested in an educational setting. For these reasons, we deemed essential to consider additional research approaches in order to specify the skills needed to interact with such technologies. For instance, Frittella's (2024) dissertation aimed to develop research-based recommendations for CAI training following an instructional design approach. Empirical investigations into interpreter-computer interaction also informed the development of modules focused on technology (e.g., Chmiel/Spinolo 2022; Defrancq/Fantinuoli 2020; Defrancq/Snoeck/Fantinuoli 2024; Prandi 2023; Saeed et al. 2022).

Finally, our pilot curriculum was also guided by the practical experience gained by instructors teaching interpreting technologies over the years, as reported in Fantinuoli and Prandi (2018), who provide concrete suggestions on how to introduce interpreting students to different interpreting technologies. To further refine the curriculum, we plan to test less widely explored teaching strategies, such as those which will be discussed in the next section, to help us identify the areas which would require greater focus in the classroom and a more structured pedagogical intervention. This is another benefit of an emergent view of education, as it allows us to tailor our pedagogy to the students' needs, interests and personal profiles. In turn, we hope our work will contribute to enhance the modelling of interpreters' technological competence.

3. Curriculum design: teaching methods and activities

As described in section 2, the curriculum was designed following a constructivist approach.

Courses can be grouped into three main areas. The first includes methodological foundations in advanced dialogue interpreting, consecutive and simultaneous interpreting, and multimedia content creation, editing and transcreation (see Table 1 for a complete subject list). The second area includes interpreting practice-based courses, such as distance interpreting and a consecutive and simultaneous workshop between Italian and English. The third area focuses on language skills (applied linguistics and Italian language). All courses in the curriculum contribute to the development of students' interpreting competence, emerging progressively as they proceed along their learning journey. Technology features heavily in almost all courses (e.g., distance interpreting, multimedia content creation and editing) and receives closer attention in technology-centred courses.

Discussing all courses in the curriculum would go beyond the scope of the chapter. As our aim is to provide an example of situated experiential learning within a constructivist pedagogical framework, in this section we will focus on the module *Technology-Assisted Interpreting I*, which is taught in the first year as part of the courses belonging to the technological and theoretical-methodological area. The module is taught partly in face-to-face classes and partly online. In our discussion, we will focus on the asynchronous activities delivered through the University of Bologna's Moodle platform *Virtuale*, highlighting the potential and limitations of online teaching, which is a key feature of the curriculum.

Table 1: InTeCo curriculum overview

	Semester	Hours	Credits
First year			
Consecutive and dialogue interpreting Introduction to consecutive interpreting Dialogue interpreting, advanced	1	60	12
Technology-Assisted Interpreting I	1	40	8
Linguistics Linguistics for Italians Italian linguistics for interpreters Applied linguistics for interpreters or Linguistics for non-Italians Italian L2 for interpreters Applied linguistics for interpreters	1	60	12
Distance interpreting	2	40	8
Introduction to simultaneous interpreting	2	30	6
Multimedia content creation and editing	2	30	6
Electives	Any time over both years	Depending on exam(s) chosen	10
Second year			
Workshop – Interpreting between Italian and English	1	20	3
Technology-Assisted Interpreting II	1&2	60	12
Multimedia content transcreation Multimedia transcreation I Multimedia transcreation II	1&2	70	14
Internship	Any time over both years	150	6
Elective	Any time over both years	Depending on exam(s) chosen	5
Final examination (final project/dissertation) Self-training *Self-training course to be completed over both years*			15 3

The *Technology-Assisted Interpreting I* course focuses on technologies supporting interpreters in their work, particularly on CAI tools. Additional classes in the curriculum introduce students to other types of interpreting technologies, particularly those mediating the provision of interpreting services, such as solutions for distance interpreting. Online lessons and activities complement face-to-face hours of instruction. The online component of the module is composed of five learning units. Students engage with the introductory units (1–3) during self-directed learning sessions, attend face-to-face classes, and conclude the course with the final units of the online course (4–5).

The five units making up the online component of the course address the following topics:

1. Introduction to interpreting technologies (overview)
2. Ethical considerations around interpreting technologies
3. CAI tools (overview)
4. Assignment preparation with InterpretBank and AI functions
5. Large language models and generative AI for assignment preparation

Each of the five units comprises a video lecture, bibliographical suggestions for further study, a learning task and a self-evaluation questionnaire. Students are required to view the lectures and complete the learning tasks and the questionnaires before moving on to the next unit. This is essential for the course instructors to be able to monitor students' progress and compliance with the course objectives despite the limited direct engagement with students due to the online format.

In the course, students progress from general discussions around technology applied to interpreting (units 1 and 2), to a narrower focus on specific technologies, i.e., computer-assisted interpreting and generative AI. The video lectures are meant to introduce students to the topic in question, discussing relevant knowledge, theories, and research findings to foster reflection on the potential implications of technology use. An example is the discussion of the main drivers of technological change in unit 1 (Fantinuoli 2018). Unit 2 also focuses on promoting students' critical thinking by addressing the main ethical implications of interpreting technology use, both for support and for automation, as recently discussed for instance by Bowker (2020), Defrancq (2024), Horváth (2022) and Moorkens (2022). The unit introduces students to AI ethics (Coeckelbergh 2020) before focusing on issues specifically related to interpreting technologies, such as confidentiality in machine interpreting. The decision to introduce a dedicated unit on AI ethics in interpreting stems from recent discussions emphasising the importance of raising student awareness about technology use, enabling them to become competent voices as pertains legal and ethical issues, particularly in the areas where AI falls short compared to humans (Defrancq 2024). Unit 3 helps students to place CAI tools within the broader framework of interpreting technologies. In the first-year instantiation of the module, the focus is on assignment preparation, as students are still developing their interpreting technique. The more theory-centred instruction in units 1 and 2 is thus followed by two more hands-on units dedicated to assignment preparation, in particular terminology and knowledge management with and without AI support. In unit 4, students receive a hands-on introduction to InterpretBank (Fantinuoli 2016), one of the most popular CAI tools at the time of writing. Here, education meets training, enabling students to acquire the practical knowledge required to effectively explore and utilise CAI tools. Finally, unit 5 provides a detailed explanation of the inner workings of neural machine translation (NMT), focusing on neural networks, as these technologies are integrated in various CAI functions. It also provides an explanation of large language models (LLMs) and generative AI, which may also be used in the pre-assignment phase and are expected to be already familiar to students. In this unit, which is more technical than the previous ones, explanations are provided without mathematical complexity. Nonetheless, attention is paid to clarifying the technical jargon for trainee interpreters, so that they will feel empowered rather than overwhelmed when employing such solutions.

A core tenet of constructivist views of education lies in the active participation of students in co-constructing the learning experience (Dingfelder Stone 2019). The online component of the module is designed for self-directed study; therefore, it is crucial that the learning activities foster student engagement and facilitate interaction within groups. Different kinds of learning tasks were selected to promote students' autonomy in engaging with the content of the units: quizzes, forum discussions, collaborative Wiki creations, and submission-type assignments.

Quizzes, forums and collaborative projects are many-to-many techniques which have not fully been exploited in technology training (O'Brien/Rodríguez Vázquez 2020, p. 271). In particular, we decided to integrate forums and collaborative projects as learning activities in the course to assess their effectiveness and because we hoped they would boost students' elaboration of the materials addressed in the lectures. A quiz was included in unit 1 to test students' understanding of key factors addressing the uptake of technologies in interpreting and key concepts which would be relevant throughout their studies. We believed including a discussion forum in unit 2 would be an effective way to foster each students' participation in the joint reflection on the ethical implications of AI use in interpreting. This is promoted by requiring each student to carry out research work on a specific ethical issue, looking for real-world examples and sharing them with their peers before being able to see other people's contributions. Each student is further required to comment under at least one of their peers' posts, which is expected to bring up additional insights and promote students' collaborative learning experience.

In unit 3, students' further autonomous elaboration on the topic of interpreting technologies, cooperation and responsibility in their learning path is promoted with the joint creation of a Wiki, i.e., a central information hub (similar to a Wikipedia page). The main objective is to help them develop their research skills, as they are required to identify examples for each category of interpreting technologies identified, i.e., setting-oriented, process-oriented and automation technologies (e.g., Braun 2019). Students are provided with a list of relevant sources, but they are required to take their learning into their own hands by all contributing to the project. The Wiki is a small-scale example of project-based learning, which has proved particularly effective in translation and interpreting education (Dingfelder Stone 2019; Kiraly 2019).

The first assignment in unit 4, which requires students to submit a short glossary compiled following the trainer's instructions, is meant to help students consolidate what they learned in the lecture. The second assignment promotes their ability to use tools autonomously and solve problems. The lecture gives a detailed introduction to InterpretBank, but students are then asked to keep exploring the tool on their own and discover one additional feature which they found useful. They then present the feature to their peers in a forum, which is further expected to boost cooperation in the online classroom.

Finally, the assignment in unit 5 asks students to engage with ChatGPT in a creative way. The goal is to show them the importance of selecting the right prompt to achieve their goals. The activity does not concern interpreting directly and it is rather unorthodox: it asks students to try out 'prompt hacking,' getting ChatGPT to break its built-in limitations. The activity is closely related to the topics discussed in unit 2 and is expected to give students a taste of what might go wrong when AI is used in an unethical way.

Self-evaluation questionnaires are integrated at the end of each unit and serve as an additional reflection step before moving on to the following unit. Furthermore, they contain informative feedback directly provided by the students on their learning experience and expectations, which can be harnessed to improve the content, structure and teaching strategies of the course and for further tuning of the curriculum.

The final assessment of the course is not conducted through an exam, but by asking students to complete a set of assignments which make up an e-portfolio. The portfolio is a tool that helps students self-organise what they learned and focus on the aspects of the course which they deem most relevant. This is a further step to foster autonomy in their learning process. To submit the portfolio, students are required to hand in four assignments relating to the learning units:

1. An interpreting technology atlas (unit 1), which serves as an overview of the interpreting technologies most relevant to each student. For instance, they can focus on the tools available for their language combination.
2. An AI ethics checklist (unit 2), which is presented as a negotiation tool in a realistic interpreting assignment. The students are given the instructions that a potential client is asking their opinion on using human vs AI interpreting and they are consulted as experts in the field. They are asked to create an AI ethics checklist detailing the most relevant arguments concerning ethical issues related to interpreting technology.
3. A description of their ideal CAI tool (units 3–5), which is a small creative task helping students think outside the box, while also promoting their ability to select tools based on their goals and needs, rather than on the tools' affordances.

4. Two glossaries created on a topic of their choice (units 4–5). One glossary is created "manually," using InterpretBank as support but without resorting to automation. The other glossary is put together using the AI functions in InterpretBank as well as ChatGPT or another LLM. Students are then asked to reflect and report on the differences in the process and product of glossary building with and without AI support.

The teaching strategies and activities in the course were selected following the insights deriving from several years of adoption of a constructivist approach to interpreter education and previous reflections on training on technology-related aspects of interpreting (e.g., Spinolo/Muñoz Martín 2022). Testing their effectiveness is, however, paramount to further tune the pilot curriculum, as discussed in the next section.

4. Assessing course effectiveness: an action-research approach

The new InTeCo curriculum had its first run in the academic year 2024–2025. Developing a technology-focused interpreting curriculum necessitates evaluating the adequacy of learning objectives, the effectiveness of the chosen methodologies, and the teaching activities designed to enhance students' technological competence within the broader context of interpreting skills. With the goal of continuously refining the curriculum, particularly the classes dedicated to technology, and thus keeping the curriculum relevant and attractive to students in the years to come, we envisage the adoption of an action-research approach to test our teaching methods. In doing so, we agree with Kiraly (2000, p. 122) when he says that "[a]dopting the role of teacher as researcher is […] the key innovation in our field."

Action research can be defined as "a participatory approach to inquiry that couples action and reflection in the pursuit of practical solutions to issues of pressing concern within a community" (Nicodemus/Swabey 2015, p. 163). As Neves (2016, p. 239) notes, action research does not simply entail including practice in a (teaching) project. It is rather a systematic endeavour which requires applying established research methods, and which should have as a goal that of improving a certain situation, with a practical impact on the lives of people. Action research is considered a qualitative orientation to inquiry (Nicodemus/Swabey 2015, p. 158), and multiple methods may be used within this framework. Rather than a methodology, it is "an *orientation* to knowledge creation" (Bradbury 2015, p. 1).

Overall, action research is characterised by a series of cycles, each feeding on the results of the previous one. Each cycle requires the identification of the problem to address, the planning of the intervention, the collection of data to assess the problem, reflection on the findings and the revision of the plan of intervention until satisfactory outcomes are achieved (e.g., Mertler 2013).

While this approach to inquiry has not yet been used extensively in our field, it is recognised as a "unique approach with great potential for interpreting studies" (Pöchhacker 2011, p. 19), and a few studies have used it successfully to address interpreting education (e.g., Orozco-Jutorán 2024; Pavez 2021). This motivated us to include action research as an integral part of our curriculum development process.

As noted by Slatyer (2015, p. 5), action research may reflect different epistemologies, i.e., reflective practice and critical theory. For the purpose of our project, we are not concerned with deriving principles to guide interpreter education in the age of AI (critical theory). Rather, our objective is much more modest, but not less valuable, i.e., that of reflecting on our practice with the goal of helping our students construct the knowledge and develop the skills they need to effectively integrate technologies into their workflows, understand how and why they are developed and employed, and the impact they may have on their professional future as well as their broader socio-cultural impact.

As the pedagogical epistemology guiding our approach to interpreter education is a socio-constructivist one with emergentist traits (see section 3), it is only natural to select an approach to assessment that is in line with said epistemology. Action research, revolving around the inclusion of all players involved in the educational context, i.e., in our case, curriculum developers, teacher-researchers and students, is best positioned to help us to achieve our educational goals. In particular, students are not seen as the subjects to study, but rather as active researchers themselves, as it is their self-reflection on their learning processes, in addition to the teacher-researchers' reflection on their interventions, that is expected to raise the questions to address in the research and, possibly, identify desiderata and even solutions.

Given the novelty of the curriculum and the unique nature of the student cohort which involves multiple language combinations and backgrounds, an essential aspect in planning our action-research study will be considering the characteristics of the students involved. Overall, the aim of our inquiry is to study the students' reaction to the new curriculum and the impact of the envisaged teaching strategies on their learning processes.

In methodological terms, we plan to adopt feedback questionnaires from the first two cohorts of students and possibly to organise focus groups during the academic year 2025–2026 to help us reconceptualise the issues to investigate. The exact methodological choices will depend on the availability of the students involved, as most teaching is done online and asynchronously through self-learning activities on the *Virtuale* platform. The results of this first cycle of assessment, which may also involve collecting students' learning journals, will be our basis for refining the teaching activities in the module *Technology-Assisted Interpreting I* for the academic year 2026–2027. We also plan additional cycles of assessment, reflection and refinement of our updated teaching interventions, until we are satisfied that the interventions we designed can help us to achieve our educational objectives. Adopting an action-research approach is, however, not only in the interest of the developers of this curriculum and of those who will have to teach it. Students are also expected to benefit from an active inclusion in curriculum development. We hope this approach will boost their motivation to learn, support classroom integration despite the physical boundaries, and promote a reflective attitude toward their learning. Finally, since interpreting technologies have only recently been introduced more systematically into interpreting curricula (Prandi 2020), we hope that our research will provide insight and spark ideas on how we should approach the education of future interpreters and how including technologies in the curriculum, particularly AI-based ones, may impact the learners' experience.

5. Concluding remarks

Language professions and the types of services required of them are undergoing a period of epochal change, sparked by the dramatic development of technologies, especially AI. This makes it challenging for Higher Education Institutions to provide educational opportunities that can prepare their students to be the professionals of the future. In the face of this unpredictability of both the speed and the possibilities of new technologies for interlingual communication, a possible educational strategy may be to train students on foundational skills: flexibility, adaptive expertise in their use of technologies, and autonomy in their own training and evolution as professionals.

In this chapter, we have presented an initiative made in this direction at the University of Bologna (Forlì), where a new curriculum called Interpreting and Technologies for Communication (InTeCo) has been launched with the aim of bringing students closer to interpreting technologies and technologies for oral interlingual communication at large. This was done by designing a course that is primarily online based and self-paced, allowing students to take responsibility for their learning journey with the support and guidance of teachers and tutors and hopefully including working or adult students who need flexibility in their timetables.

This is a first step which is all but consolidated, as it has only just been launched; as a matter of fact, the aim is to fine-tune and improve it by observing its progress and effectiveness, with an action-research approach. We hope that this contribution can be useful to motivate other similar initiatives and be part of a broader dialogue toward a joint effort to accompany the transition of the language professions in the new era they are entering.

Note

This contribution has been conceived in all its parts by all authors, but sections 2, 3 and 4 were written by Prandi, sections 1 by Torresi, section 5 by Spinolo.

Bibliography

Albl-Mikasa, Michaela (2012): "The importance of being not too earnest: A process- and experience-based model of interpreter competence." In: Ahrens, Barbara / Albl-Mikasa, Michaela / Sasse, Claudia (Eds.): *Dolmetschqualität in Praxis, Lehre und Forschung. Festschrift für Sylvia Kalina*. Tübingen: Narr, pp. 59–92.

Albl-Mikasa, Michaela (2013): "Developing and cultivating expert interpreter competence." *The Interpreter's Newsletter* (18), pp. 17–34, retrieved on 10/11/2024 from http://hdl.handle.net/10077/9749.

Amato, Amalia / Mack, Gabriele (2022): "Interpreter education and training." In: Zanettin, Federico / Rundle, Christopher (Eds.): *The Routledge handbook of translation and methodology*. London: Routledge, pp. 457–475. https://doi.org/10.4324/9781315158945-32.

Bowker, Lynne (2020): "Translation technology and ethics." In: Koskinen, Kaisa / Pokorn, Nike K. (Eds.): *The Routledge handbook of translation and ethics*. London et al.: Routledge, pp. 262–278. https://doi.org/10.4324/9781003127970-20.

Bradbury, Hilary (ed.) (2015): *The Sage handbook of action research*. Los Angeles et al.: Sage. https://doi.org/10.4135/9781473921290.

Braun, Sabine (2019): "Technology and interpreting." In: O'Hagan, Minako (ed.): *The Routledge handbook of translation and technology*. London: Routledge, pp. 271–288. https://doi.org/10.4324/9781315311258-19.

Chmiel, Agnieszka / Spinolo, Nicoletta (2022): "Testing the impact of remote interpreting settings on interpreter experience and performance – methodological challenges inside the virtual booth." *Translation, Cognition & Behavior* 5(2), pp. 250–274. https://doi.org/https://doi.org/10.1075/tcb.00068.chm.

Coeckelbergh, Mark (2020): *AI ethics*. Cambridge: MIT Press. https://doi.org/10.7551/mitpress/12549.001.0001.

Defrancq, Bart (2024): "Conference interpreting in AI settings: New skills and ethical challenges." In: Massey, Gary / Ehrensberger-Dow, Maureen / Angelone, Erik (Eds.): *Handbook of the language industry: contexts, resources and profiles*. Berlin et al.: De Gruyter Mouton, pp. 473–488. https://doi.org/10.1515/9783110716047-021.

Defrancq, Bart/ Fantinuoli, Claudio (2020): "Automatic speech recognition in the booth: Assessment of system performance, interpreters' performances and interactions in the context of numbers." *Target* 33(1), pp. 73–102. https://doi.org/10.1075/target.19166.def.

Defrancq, Bart/ Snoeck, Helena / Fantinuoli, Claudio (2024): "Interpreters' performances and cognitive load in the context of a CAI tool." In: Deane-Cox, Sharon / Böser, Ursula / Winters, Marion (Eds.): *Translation, interpreting and technological change: Innovations in research, practice and training*. London: Bloomsbury Academic, pp. 38–58. https://doi.org/10.5040/9781350212978.0009.

Dingfelder Stone, Maren (2019): "Authenticity, autonomy and automation: Training conference interpreters." In: Kiraly, Donald / Massey, Gary (Eds.): *Towards authentic experiential learning in translator education*. Newcastle upon Tyne: Cambridge Scholars, pp. 172–189.

Fantinuoli, Claudio (2016): "InterpretBank. Redefining computer-assisted interpreting tools." In: Esteves-Ferreira, João / Macan, Juliet / Mitkov, Ruslan/Stefanov, Olaf-Michael (Eds.): *Proceedings of 38th Conference Translating and the Computer*. Geneva: Editions Tradulex, pp. 42–52, retrieved on 05/05/2025 from https://aclanthology.org/2016.tc-1.5/.

Fantinuoli, Claudio (2018): "Interpreting and technology: The upcoming technological turn." In: Fantinuoli, Claudio (Ed.): *Interpreting and technology*. Berlin: Language Science Press, pp. 1–12. https://doi.org/10.5281/zenodo.1493289.

Fantinuoli, Claudio (2023): "Towards AI-enhanced computer-assisted interpreting." In: Corpas Pastor, Gloria / Defrancq, Bart (Eds.): *Interpreting technologies – current and future trends*. Amsterdam: John Benjamins, pp. 46–71. https://doi.org/10.1075/ivitra.37.03fan.

Fantinuoli, Claudio / Prandi, Bianca (2018): "Teaching information and communication technologies: A proposal for the interpreting classroom." *trans-kom: Journal of Translation and Technical Communication Research* 11(2), pp. 162–182, retrieved on 10/07/2024 from http://www.trans-kom.eu/bd11nr02/trans-kom_11_02_02_Fantinuoli_Prandi_Teaching.20181220.pdf.

Frittella, Francesca Maria (2024): *Computer-assisted interpreting: Cognitive task analysis and evidence-informed instructional design recommendations*. Ph.D. thesis, University of Surrey. https://doi.org/10.15126/thesis.901410.

Haro-Soler, Maria Del Mar / Kiraly, Don (2019): "Exploring self-efficacy beliefs in symbiotic collaboration with students: An action research project." *The Interpreter and Translator Trainer* 13(3), pp. 255–270. https://doi.org/10.1080/1750399X.2019.1656405.

Horváth, Ildikó (2022): "AI in interpreting: Ethical considerations." *Across Languages and Cultures* 23(1), pp. 1–13. https://doi.org/10.1556/084.2022.00108.

Kiraly, Don (2000): *A social constructivist approach to translator education: Empowerment from theory to practice*. Manchester et al.: St. Jerome.

Kiraly, Don (2019): "Authentic project work and pedagogical epistemologies: A question of competing or complementary worldviews?" In: Kiraly, Don / Massey, Gary (Eds.): *Towards authentic experiential learning in translator education*. Newcastle upon Tyne: Cambridge Scholars, pp. 1–16.

Kutz, Wladimir (2010): *Dolmetschkompetenz: Was muss der Dolmetscher wissen und können?* München: European University Press.

Mertler, Craig A. (2013): *Action research: Improving schools and empowering educators*. Los Angeles: Sage Publications.

Moorkens, Joss (2022): "Ethics and machine translation." In: Kenny, Dorothy (Ed.): *Machine translation for everyone: Empowering users in the age of artificial intelligence*. Berlin: Language Science Press, pp. 121–140. https://doi.org/10.5281/zenodo. 6759984.

Neves, Josélia (2016): "Action research: So much to account for." *Target. International Journal of Translation Studies* 28(2), pp. 237–247. https://doi.org/10.1075/target.28.2.05nev.

Nicodemus, Brenda / Swabey, Laurie (2015): "Action research." In: Angelelli, Claudia V. / Baer, Brian James (Eds.): *Researching translation and interpreting*. London et al.: Routledge, pp. 157–167.

O'Brien, Sharon / Rodríguez Vázquez, Silvia (2020): "Translation and technology." In: Laviosa, Sara / González-Davies, Maria (Eds.): *The Routledge handbook of translation and education*. Oxon et al.: Routledge, pp. 264–277.

Orozco-Jutorán, Mariana (2024): "Didactic and assessment materials for court interpreting training: Action research." *Hermēneus. Revista de traducción e interpretación* 25, pp. 277–314. https://doi.org/10.24197/her.25.2023.277-314.

Pavez, Pedro (2021): "Dialogic education in the interpreting classroom: Action research for developing simultaneous interpreting quality assessment tools." *The Interpreter and Translator Trainer* 15(3), pp. 360–377. https://doi.org/10.1080/1750399X.2021.1906078.

Pöchhacker, Franz (2001): "Dolmetschen und translatorische Kompetenz." In: Kelletat, Andreas F. (Ed.): *Dolmetschen: Beiträge aus Forschung, Lehre und Praxis*. Bern: Peter Lang, pp. 19–37.

Pöchhacker, Franz (2011): "Researching interpreting: Approaches to inquiry." In: Nicodemus, Brenda / Swabey, Laurie (Eds.): *Advances in interpreting research: Inquiry in action*. Amsterdam: John Benjamins, pp. 5–26. https://doi.org/10.1075/btl.99.04poch.

Pöchhacker, Franz (2024): "Is machine interpreting interpreting?" *Translation Spaces*, pp. 1–21. https://doi.org/10.1075/ts.23028.poc.

Prandi, Bianca (2020): "The use of CAI tools in interpreter training: Where are we now and where do we go from here?" *inTRAlinea*, pp. 1–10, retrieved on 10/07/2024 from https://www.intralinea.org/specials/article/2512.

Prandi, Bianca (2023): *Computer-assisted simultaneous interpreting: A cognitive-experimental study on terminology*. Berlin: Language Science Press. https://doi.org/10.5281/zenodo.7143056.

Rodríguez Melchor, María Dolores / Horváth, Ildikó / Ferguson, Kate (2020): "Introduction." In: Rodríguez Melchor, María Dolores / Horváth, Ildikó / Ferguson, Kate (Eds.): *The role of technology in conference interpreter training*. Oxford: Peter Lang, pp. 1–4.

Saeed, Muhammad Ahmed / Rodríguez González, Eloy / Korybski, Tomasz / Davitti, Elena / Braun, Sabine (2022): "Connected yet distant: An experimental study into the visual needs of the interpreter in remote simultaneous interpreting." In: Kurosu, Masaaki (Ed.): *Human-computer interaction. User experience and behavior*. Cham: Springer International, pp. 214–232. https://doi.org/10.1007/978-3-031-05412-9_16.

Setton, Robin / Dawrant, Andrew (2016a): *Conference interpreting – a complete course*. Amsterdam: John Benjamins. https://doi.org/10.1075/btl.120.

Setton, Robin / Dawrant, Andrew (2016b): *Conference interpreting – a trainer's guide*. Amsterdam: John Benjamins. https://doi.org/10.1075/btl.121.

Slatyer, Helen (2015): "Action research." In: Pöchhacker, Franz (Ed.): *The Routledge encyclopaedia of interpreting studies*. London: Routledge, pp. 5–6.

Spinolo, Nicoletta / Muñoz Martín, Ricardo (2022): "Experiential learning for the remote interpreting classroom." In: Abels, Katja / Hansen-Schirra, Silvia / Oster, Katharina / Schaeffer, Moritz J. / Signer, Sarah / Wiedmann, Marcus (Eds.): *Re-thinking translator education*. Berlin: Frank & Timme GmbH, pp. 193–208. https://doi.org/10.57088/978-3-7329-9133-4_13.

Txabarriaga, Rocío (2024): *Slator. Over 50 % of freelance linguists have thought about changing career, Slator survey finds*, retrieved on 10/11/2024 from https://slator.com/50-of-freelance-linguists-have-thought-about-changing-career-slator-survey-finds/.

Wang, Huashu / Li, Zhi (2022): "Constructing a competence framework for interpreting technologies, and related educational insights: an empirical study." *The Interpreter and Translator Trainer* 16(3), pp. 367–390. https://doi.org/10.1080/1750399X.2022.2101850.

Future skills für die translationsorientierte Sprachlehre im Kontext von KI-Tools

Eva Seidl
Universität Graz

ABSTRACT
This article critically examines language learning and teaching in the context of translation and interpreting students' undergraduate years in higher education. Language educators must prepare these (mostly) young adults for a variety of possible future occupations in the translation and interpreting profession. Obviously, the impact of generative AI on the language industry and language service provision cannot be overestimated. Therefore, the article first explores the great number of changes, challenges, and opportunities of artificial intelligence in the realm of higher education. Particular emphasis is put on translation- and interpreting-oriented language learning and teaching (TILLT). With the aim of getting a better understanding of the enormous changes in today's world of work, the article aligns recent literature on the critical role of the human with research and practice of TILLT. Based on this first step, an existing model of future skills will then be adapted for translation-oriented language education in times of generative AI.

Keywords: future skills, TILLT, language learning and teaching research, higher education pedagogy

1. Einleitung

Dieser Beitrag thematisiert, wie sich der Einfluss neuer Technologien auf die Sprachausbildung von Studierenden im Rahmen einer akademischen Translationsausbildung auswirkt. Hochschullehrende, die im Bereich TILLT tätig sind, was für *Translation- and Interpreting-oriented Language Learning and Teaching* steht, sehen sich vor die Herausforderung gestellt, ihre Sprachlehre so zu gestalten, dass sie *zukunftstauglich* ist. Was genau darunter zu verstehen ist, wird im Folgenden speziell für den TILLT-Kontext erörtert. Angesichts der dynamischen und fast nicht zu überblickenden Entwicklung vor allem auf dem Gebiet der Künstlichen Intelligenz sind Lehrende genauso wie ihre Studierenden wieder Lernende und bewegen sich auf unbekanntem Terrain. Dies manifestiert sich beispielsweise darin, dass gegenwärtig Lehrende von Studierenden nicht als primäre Ansprechpersonen für den Kompetenzerwerb im Umgang mit KI-Tools angesehen werden (Bernstein et al. 2023, S. 5). Mithin gilt es, innezuhalten und sich darauf zu besinnen, was in der Hochschulbildungsforschung auch schon vor dem revolutionären Umbruch durch den Launch von ChatGPT im November 2022 als zukunftstauglich galt. Bernstein et al. (2023, S. 6) formulieren vier zentrale KI-harte Kompetenzen und Fähigkeiten, die unbedingt weiterhin von Menschen beherrscht werden sollen, nicht zuletzt um die Arbeit von KI-Systemen beurteilen zu können. Diese lauten (1) grundlegende technische Fähigkeiten, (2) Sozialisationsfähigkeiten, (3) kritisches Denken sowie (4) Handeln in Unsicherheit.

Besonders der letzte Aspekt, also die Fähigkeit, sich auch unter unsicheren kontextuellen Bedingungen handlungsfähig und wirkmächtig zu erleben, deckt sich mit kürzlich von Fürstenberg und Schumm Fauster (2024) vorgeschlagenen *transition skills*, welche im Rahmen von Hochschulbildung von eminenter Bedeutung sind. Beim Übergang von der sekundären zur tertiären Bildungsstufe, aber auch bei jenem von der Hochschule auf den Arbeitsmarkt hilft es jungen Erwachsenen, wenn sie über folgende Fähigkeiten verfügen bzw. diese an der Hochschule erwerben: (1) communication, collaboration and mediation, (2) creativity and critical thinking, (3) cultural intelligence, (4) self-leadership und (5) digital literacy. Dieser Fokus auf sogenannte Übergangsfähigkeiten hat drei zentrale Implikationen für die translationsorientierte Sprachlehre.

1.1 Enkulturation begleiten

Erstens sind TILLT-Lehrende in der Regel eine der ersten Ansprech- und oft auch Vertrauenspersonen von Erstsemester-Studierenden, da translationsorientierte Sprachkurse in den ersten Studiensemestern auf Bachelorniveau angeboten werden und expliziten übersetzungs- und dolmetschpraktischen Lehrveranstaltungen curricular zeitlich vorgelagert sind. Das bedeutet, dass Sprachlehrenden die verantwortungsvolle Aufgabe zukommt, Studierende beim Übertritt von der Sekundar- zur Tertiärstufe insofern zu unterstützen, als ihnen zu verdeutlichen ist, dass Universität nicht die Fortsetzung von Schule ist (Seidl 2013). Darüber hinaus sollte eine TILLT-Lehrenden-Identität vom Bewusstsein getragen sein, nicht nur Hochschulsozialisationsprozesse von Studienanfänger:innen zu begleiten, sondern ebenso eine Enkulturation in das gewählte Studienfach (Seidl 2023a).

1.2 Autonomie fördern

Zweitens bedeutet der oft von Unsicherheit geprägte Übergang von „teacher-directed school learning to self-directed university learning" (Fürstenberg/Schumm Fauster 2024, S. 3) für TILLT, dass in diesen Sprachkursen der Grundstein dafür gelegt werden muss, dass Translationsstudierende autonome Sprachlernende werden, zum Beispiel durch „self-assessment of the strengths and weaknesses in their language use, setting realistic language learning goals for themselves and planning measures to achieve these goals" (ibid., S. 15). In TILLT-Kursen sollten Studierende solide Sprach-, Text- und Kulturkompetenzen entwickeln, sich aber auch metakognitive Fähigkeiten und Selbstlernstrategien erarbeiten. Letztere erleichtern den Übergang von Sprach- zu Translationskursen, sind aber genauso für den Übergang von der universitären Lern- und Lebenswelt zur Welt der Berufstätigkeit als Hochschulabsolvent:innen von zentraler Bedeutung.

1.3 Zukunftsängste nehmen

Drittens, und das schließt direkt an die oft von Unsicherheit geprägte Phase der Arbeitssuche nach erfolgreichem Studienabschluss an, sollte sensibel mit möglichen Verunsicherungen und Zukunftsängsten von Studierenden umgegangen werden. Die Arbeitswelt im Bereich Übersetzen und Dolmetschen erfährt gerade massive Umwälzungen, die auch mit neu entstehenden translatorischen Berufsfeldern einhergehen (Massey/Ehrensberger-Dow/Angelone 2024). Was Studierende brauchen, ist Bestärkung, dass ihre an einem translationwissenschaftlichen Studiengang erworbenen Kompetenzen, Fähigkeiten und Fertigkeiten auch in Zukunft am Arbeitsmarkt gebraucht werden. Was etwa das technikgestützte und technikunterstützte Dolmetschen anbelangt, so hält Pöchhacker (2024, S. 44) fest, dass unter der Bedingung, dass Absolvent:innen auch über Versiertheit im Umgang mit neuen Technologien verfügen, die Zukunft des Dolmetschens „weiterhin sprach- und kultursensiblen Menschen mit Freude an der Ermöglichung und Vermittlung von zwischenmenschlicher Kommunikation [gehört]".

Zwischenmenschliche Kommunikation, Zusammenarbeit und Mediation stellen für Fürstenberg und Schumm Fauster (2024) wichtige Übergangsfähigkeiten dar. Als Sammelbegriff dafür könnte man die von Bernstein et al.

(2023) als KI-harte Kompetenz bezeichneten Sozialisationsfähigkeiten verstehen. Von genau diesen handeln die nächsten zwei Abschnitte.

2. Zur Rolle des Humanen in der Sprachlehre

Nach Fürstenberg und Schumm Fauster (2024, S. 28) ist der Englischunterricht im Lehramtsstudium „an ideal place for developing transition skills due to its focus on communication, culture and collaboration, which are also at the heart of the transition skills framework“. Umgelegt auf die akademische Sprachausbildung für angehende Translator:innen erscheint mir der Unterricht jeglicher Sprache im Kontext von TILLT als idealer Ort, um Übergangsfähigkeiten zu erwerben. Denn TILLT-Unterricht ist immer – ungeachtet der jeweils unterrichteten Sprache – auf Kommunikation, Kultur und Zusammenarbeit ausgerichtet. Wenn nun die verstärkte KI-Technologienutzung, einhergehend mit einer größeren Individualisierung des Lernens auch zu Vereinsamung, Vereinzelung und Fragmentierung von Studierendengruppen führen kann, so braucht es umso mehr die bewusste Förderung von Sozialisationsfähigkeiten wie „soziales Lernen, Einfühlungsvermögen, Resilienz und effektives Teamwork“ (Bernstein et al. 2023, S. 6). Die Hochschulbildungsforscherin Reinmann (2023) beschreibt eindrücklich, welche Auswirkungen vermehrte Mensch-Maschine-Interaktionen zulasten zwischenmenschlicher Interaktionen haben könnten.

> Ersetzt die Interaktion etwa mit generativer sprachbasierter KI mehr und mehr Austausch, Zusammenarbeit, gegenseitige Rückmeldung und Hilfestellung zwischen Personen, werden weniger menschliche Beziehungen praktiziert, die grundsätzlich wenig(er) kontrollierbar sind. Das wiederum könnte einen Effekt auf die Erwartung an Kommunikation haben und Empathie, Geduld und Kompromissbereitschaft schmälern (Reinmann 2023, S. 7).

Eine mögliche Erwartung an zwischenmenschliche Kommunikation könnte sein, dass sie so reibungslos und zuvorkommend vonstatten gehen sollte wie ein Chat-Verlauf mit einem Chatbot. Dessen vermeintlich permanente Verfügbarkeit, endlos scheinende Geduld und Bedachtheit darauf, stets ausgleichend zu agieren, um nur nicht anzuecken, könnte unrealistische Erwartungen an menschliches Kommunikationsverhalten wecken. Was die Rückmelde- und Feedbackstruktur von Sprachlerntechnologien betrifft, mit oft übertriebenem Lob für kleinste Lernfortschritte, so könnte eine Gewöhnung daran möglicherweise dazu führen, dass Studierende sich mit Feeback von Lehrenden oder Studienkolleg:innen schwer tun, das mitunter kritischer oder nüchterner kommuniziert wird. Auf hochschulisches Sprachenlernen bezogen ist auch kritisch zu hinterfragen, was es mit der intrinsischen Motivation von Studierenden macht, wenn sie an kontinuierliche, maschinengenerierte, motivationssteigernde Rückmeldungen gewöhnt sind. Erleben sie dann noch Freude am Akt des Sprachenlernens selbst, an Erkenntnis und besserem Verständnis einer Sprache nach erfolgter intellektueller Anstrengung, alleine oder im Austausch mit anderen Personen?

2.1 Freude am Sprachenlernen und -lehren

Diese Sprachlernfreude wird seit einiger Zeit verstärkt als *Foreign Language Learning Enjoyment* (FLLE) erforscht, mit dem Pedant dazu, das die Lehrendenseite in den Blick nimmt, also *Foreign Language Teaching Enjoyment* (FLTE) (Mierzwa 2019). Die Freude an der Sprachlehrtätigkeit steht seit dem Einzug von ChatGPT & Co. vor einer Bewährungsprobe und geht mit Fragen nach der Relevanz menschlicher Lehrpersonen und nach den Unterschieden zwischen menschlicher versus maschineller Sprachlehre einher. Gao (2024, S. 557) vermutet daher, „that the community of language teachers faces a crisis, as the rise of generative AI tools will lead to a worldwide diminishing of the scale of language education". Aktuell sinkende Studierendenzahlen an österreichischen translationswissenschaftlichen Instituten scheinen ihm Recht zu geben. Seiner Einschätzung nach wird sich in Zukunft auf Geduld und Durchhaltevermögen erfordernde Sprachlernprozesse nur einlassen, wer Expert:innenlevel anstrebt bzw. über intrinsische Motivation verfügt.

> Opportunities to learn languages will likely be reserved for those aiming for an expert level of proficiency and competence that enables them to outperform and manage machine translation and generative AI tools in language use; or those who are intrinsically motivated to learn languages (Gao 2024, S. 557).

Auf den im obigen Zitat erwähnten kompetenten Umgang mit KI-Generaten komme ich in Abschnitt 5 noch genauer zu sprechen. Im Hinblick auf die Rolle des Humanen in der Sprachlehre und die damit einhergehende Bedeutung der Sozialisationsfähigkeiten von Studierenden seien noch zwei zentrale Aspekte erwähnt, und zwar *digital disarray* und *embodied cognition*, zusammengefasst als fokussierte Aufmerksamkeit.

2.2 Fokussierte Aufmerksamkeit

Pegrum und Palalas (2021) zufolge hat seit der zunehmenden Technologisierung des Lehrens und Lernens, ausgelöst durch die Corona-Pandemie eine gewisse Konfusion zugenommen, bezeichnet als *digital dissaray*. Dieses Phänomen gliedern sie in drei Teile, nämlich (1) *digital distraction*, (2) *digital disorder* und (3) *digital disconnection*. Ersteres manifestiert sich in verringerter Konzentrationsfähigkeit durch ständige Ablenkungen in unserer technologisierten und mediatisierten Lebens-, Lern- und Arbeitswelt. Zweiteres beschreibt „the circulation of misinformation, disinformation and ‚fake news'" (Pegrum/Palalas 2021, S. 2), was durch die leichte Erstellung und Verbreitung KI-generierter oder manipulierter Audio- und Videodateien umso bedenklicher geworden ist. Dritteres zeigt sich schließlich als „lack of connection to the self and others" (ibid., S. 1), aber auch als „inability or unwillingness to engage effectively or constructively with difference" (ibid., 2), was während der Pandemie in einer Radikalisierung von Meinungen in sozialen Medien und im öffentlichen Diskurs deutlich wurde. Um in Bildungskontexten auf *digital dissaray* reagieren zu können, schlagen Pegrum und Palalas (2021) die Stärkung von *attentional literacy* von Lernenden vor.

Loviscach (2024) bezeichnet Aufmerksamkeitsregulation sogar als einzig wichtige *21st century skill*. Aufmerksamkeit steht auch im Fokus des Konzepts der *embodied cognition*, wie Witte (2021, S. 45) für den Erwerb von „intercultural situational attentiveness" im Sprachlernkontext ausführt[1]. „[A]ttentiveness to the sentient body's resonances with atmospheric fields of significant situations requires the whole body […] to be involved in the learning process, and not just cognition" (ibid., S. 35). Fokussierte Aufmerksamkeit, nicht nur im Sinne von Konzentrationsfähigkeit als Gegengewicht zur oben genannten *digital distraction*, sondern im Speziellen aufmerksames Wahrnehmen körperlicher Empfindungen beim Sprachenlernen birgt das Potenzial, die Empathiefähigkeit von Sprachlernenden zu steigern (ibid., S. 45). Nicht zuletzt

---

1 Für eine Darstellung, wie das Konzept der *embodied cognition* in TILLT zum Tragen kommen kann, siehe Seidl (2022).

aus diesem Grund fordert Gao (2024, S. 558) die Sprachlehr-/-lernforschung und -praxis auf, „language learning needs to be promoted as a fundamentally humanistic endeavor".

> Although generative AI tools may appear to be increasingly humanlike when interacting with us, our deep, intrinsic needs – such as a sense of belonging, identity aspirations, and desirable attributes associated with speaking languages other than our own (such as 'coolness', creativity, etc.) – cannot be satisfied by these tools. The value of language study lies in the human life journeys that language teachers undertake together with learners (Gao 2024, S. 558).

Sprachbezogene Studiengänge müssen sich daher um ein Selbstverständnis dessen bemühen, was den Wert und menschlichen Mehrwert ihrer – möglichst zukunftsrelevanten – Hochschulbildungsangebote in einer technologisierten, algorithmisierten Bildungslandschaft ausmacht. So auch translationswissenschaftliche Studiengänge, deren Sprachlehre im Fokus des folgenden Abschnitts steht.

3. Eine human-zentrierte translationsorientierte Sprachlehre

In zweierlei Hinsicht lassen sich im Kontext von KI-Tools zentrale Verbindungslinien zwischen der Sprachlehr-/-lernforschung und der Translationswissenschaft nachzeichnen: Sichtbarkeit und Interdisziplinarität.

3.1 Sichtbarkeit

Bei der ersten Verbindungslinie geht es um die für beide Disziplinen notwendige Sichtbarmachung ihres Werts und menschlichen Mehrwerts. So identifiziert Kern (2024, S. 516) für die Sprachlehre einen kritischen Wendepunkt und appelliert an die Wissenschaftsgemeinde, aber auch an Praktiker:innen, „we urgently need to articulate and communicate the value of language study [...], identify what technology offers that is positive for language education [...], and be clear about what technology cannot do". Er sieht es als Aufgabe von Sprachlehrenden, aufzuzeigen, wo die Schwächen generativer KI-Tools liegen, da Studierende sonst womöglich glauben, damit nicht konkurrieren zu können. Wenn sie denken, dass beispielsweise ChatGPT bessere Texte verfasst als sie selbst, „students will be demoralized, and the whole enterprise of studying a new language will seem pointless" (Kern 2024, S. 525). Dass das langwierige Unterfangen, sich in Zeiten von KI auf das gewissenhafte Lernen einer neuen Sprache einzulassen, alles andere als sinnlos ist, verdeutlicht Gao (2024, S. 561), indem er zusätzlich auf „nonlinguistic outcomes such as perseverance, adaptability, and creativity" verweist. Um all das bringen sich Studierende selbst, wenn sie eine allzu große Abhängigkeit von KI-Tools riskieren, einhergehend mit der „illusion of linguistic ability" (Kern 2024, S. 522). Eine persönliche Kommunikation mit seinem Kollegen an der Universität Berkeley, Ken Worthy, zitierend, argumentiert Kern (2024, S. 525) „students asking a machine to do tasks assigned to develop their intellectual skills and knowledge is like an athlete hiring someone to do their workout for them".

Genauso wenig wie Sprachtechnologien Translationsstudierenden die Aufgabe abnehmen, sich dem Sprachenlernen auch unabhängig von digitalen Hilfsmitteln, beispielsweise schlichtweg mit Stift und Papier, zu widmen, genauso wenig wird ihnen als Absolvent:innen erspart bleiben, potenziellen Auftraggeber:innen ihren Wert als akademisch gebildete Sprachdienstleister:innen bewusst zu machen. Die oben erwähnte Adaptabilität und Kreativität als nicht rein sprachbezogene Lernergebnisse von Sprachlehre betonen Massey, Huertas Barros und Katan (2023, S. 8) auch für die Translationslehre, wenn sie die Vorzüge von Humanübersetzer:innen unterstreichen, nämlich als „the added value that human translators can and do bring to bear as adaptive, creative, digitally literate experts". Hinsichtlich der notwendigen Sichtbarmachung des Werts und vor allem des menschlichen Mehrwerts professioneller Sprachdienstleister:innen mahnen Moorkens und Guerberof Arenas (2024), dies nicht auf die eigene Community zu beschränken.

> It is not within the translation and interpreting sector where we have to show the value added by language professionals, but further beyond. Real interdisciplinary work is needed, as AI is interdisciplinary by nature, and more visibility of the impact of the language professionals should reach the users of translation services (Moorkens/Guerberof Arenas 2024, S. 88).

Dies führt mich zur zweiten zentralen Verbindungslinie zwischen der Sprachlehr-/-lernforschung und der Translationswissenschaft, nämlich der erforderlichen Interdisziplinarität.

3.2 Interdisziplinarität

Moorkens und Guerberof Arenas (2024) argumentieren mit der der Künstlichen Intelligenz inhärenten Interdisziplinarität, die den Blick – und das Agieren – über den Tellerrand der eigenen Disziplin hinaus erforderlich macht. Für die translationsorientierte Sprachlehre mahnt Schmidhofer (2022, S. 278) interdisziplinäres Vorgehen ein, indem sich TILLT als „interdisciplinary field of enquiry" etabliert, „with firm links to other disciplines", um nicht auf der Stelle zu treten oder sich theoretisch, methodisch und praktisch im Kreis zu drehen. Um nun eine human-zentrierte translationsorientierte Sprachlehre zu propagieren, scheint mir der Begriff der *agency* ein zentraler Dreh- und Angelpunkt im Zusammenspiel der Disziplinen zu sein. Was beispielsweise Öner Bulut und Alimen (2023) für eine zeitgemäße Translationslehre fordern, kann gleichermaßen für TILLT eingemahnt werden. Translationsstudierende sollten demnach Unterstützung erfahren bei der Entwicklung von „self-efficacy beliefs and self-concept as *human* agents of the translation process who are capable of creating *human* added value" (Öner Bulut/Alimen 2023, S. 379, Hervorh. i. O.). Für TILLT müsste im obigen Zitat statt vom Translationsprozess schlicht vom Sprachlernprozess die Rede sein. Dieser sollte Studierenden ermöglichen, Vertrauen und Zutrauen in ihre Fähigkeiten zu erleben, unabhängig von der Verlockung bzw. Verfügbarkeit sprachtechnologischer Unterstützung. Das Menschliche in der aktuellen technikzentrierten Bildungslandschaft hervorhebend, konstatiert Kern (2024) mit Fokus auf die Sprachlehre wie folgt:

> What I believe we want to encourage is a genuine agency and autonomy that is born of an integration of language, culture, mind, and body. An integration that allows connection with other people, creative expression of new identities in multiple modalities, and critical remove from monolingual and monocultural perspectives (Kern 2024, S. 522).

Dieses Zitat liest sich wie eine Beschreibung einer gut gelungenen TILLT-Kurseinheit. Um Sprache, Kultur, Körper und Geist sowohl in TILLT als auch in der Translationslehre miteinander zu verbinden und damit kreativen Selbstausdruck von Studierenden zu fördern, schlagen Pagano/Ebner/Seidl (2025) – angelehnt an den Ansatz der *Positive Language Education* (PLE) (Mercer et al. 2018) – die Etablierung einer *Positive Translation Education* (PTE) vor. Eine solche human-zentrierte Translations- und Sprachdidaktik propagiert eine emotionsfokussierte Begegnung zwischen Lehrenden und Studierenden auf Augenhöhe, bestehend aus den vier Aspekten (1) Relevanz von Inhalten, (2) Vertrauen und Zutrauen, (3) Fürsorge und Wertschätzung sowie (4) Feedback. Wie sich nun die bisherigen Ausführungen in einem Future Skills-Modell für die translationsorientierte Sprachlehre niederschlagen können, welches einer von KI geprägten Lern-, Lebens- und Arbeitswelt gerecht wird, ist Gegenstand der folgenden Abschnitte.

4. Future Skills in der Kritik

Analog zu O'Briens (2022, S. 105, Hervorh. i. O.) Diktum, das besagt, „we need to embrace and claim technology as a *core component* of translation [...], even if our embrace needs to be sometimes critical and resistant", gilt es auch, kritisch mit Future Skills-Konzepten umzugehen. Im deutschsprachigen Hochschulraum dominiert den Diskurs Ehlers' (2021) kompetenztheoretischer Zugang zu sogenannten Future Skills, prominent gemacht durch die Zusammenarbeit mit dem Stifterverband und der Unternehmensberatung McKinsey[2]. Dies ist auch schon ein zentraler Kritikpunkt, nämlich die starke Einflussnahme von Politik und Wirtschaft auf die Hochschulbildung (Kalz/Reinmann 2024). Weiters wird bemängelt, dass es an wissenschaftlicher Fundierung fehlt und nicht klar ist, ob es sich bei Future Skills nun um Skills, also Fähigkeiten, oder um Kompetenzen handelt (ibid.).

Ehlers (2021, S. 359) spricht von „Kompetenzkonstrukte[n] mit besonderer inhaltlicher Profilierung", die auf „kognitiven, motivationalen, volitionalen sowie sozialen Ressourcen [basieren], wertebasiert [sind] [und] in einem Lernprozess angeeignet werden [können]" (ibid.). Insgesamt 17 einzelne Future Skills werden in subjektbezogene, objektbezogene und organisationsbezogene Fertigkeiten unterteilt. Die fehlende Trennschärfe zwischen Skills, Fähigkeiten, Fertigkeiten und Kompetenzen steht dabei genauso in der Kritik wie der überfachliche Ansatz, welcher einen fachwissenschaftlichen und fachspezifischen Zugang zu Zukunftskompetenzen von Hochschulabsolvent:innen vermissen lässt.

---

[2] https://nextskills.org

Für eine detaillierte Diskussion und eine literaturbasierte Kritik der Zukunftskompetenzen sei auf Kalz (2023) verwiesen, der neun Problemdimensionen und Forschungsbedarfe identifiziert. Darunter fallen etwa die Problematik der Erfassung und Messung von Zukunftskompetenzen, die fehlende Evidenz zu Effekten oder die unklare Beziehung zum Lerntransfer. Kalz (2023, S. 347) moniert zudem, dass beim derzeit herrschenden Hype um Future Skills keine Klarheit darüber besteht, ob es sich „um neue Lernziele, neue Lerninhalte oder neue didaktische Methoden oder einer (sic!) Kombination dieser Optionen" handelt. Für eine ausführliche Darstellung des aktuellen Diskurses bezüglich pro und contra Future Skills in der Hochschulbildung sei auf Ehlers et al. (2024) verwiesen.

5. Future Skills für TILLT revisited

Ehlers (2021, S. 360) unterscheidet Future Skills von Kompetenzen, die nicht explizit zukunftsorientiert sind anhand des Konzepts der Emergenz als Unterscheidungsdimension bzw. Trennlinie zwischen „aktuellen oder bisherigen Kompetenzanforderungen und solchen, die zukunftsrelevant sind". Demnach benötigen Handlungskontexte mit hochemergenten Entwicklungen zur Anforderungsbewältigung Future Skills im Sinne der Abgrenzung zu bisherigen, vertrauten, bekannten oder traditionellen Anforderungsbereichen (ibid.). Eine ähnliche Unterscheidung treffen Massey und Kiraly (2019), wenn sie zwischen *education* und *training* in der Translationsausbildung unterscheiden.

> We need education, which means acquiring a solid foundation in general, holistic competencies, skills and abilities, and then we need training in order to be able to use particular tools. Another way to frame this dichotomy might be to see training as preparation for iterative, routine tasks and education as preparation for solving problems that lie outside the box (Massey/Kiraly 2019, S. 21).

Eine derartige Unterscheidung zwischen *education* und *training* wird nicht immer konsequent verfolgt, wie die Argumentation von Moorkens und Guerberof Arenas (2024) zeigt. Was für mich nach erforderlicher *education* klingt, diskutieren sie unter dem Aspekt von *training* bezüglich der Verantwortungsübernahme von Translationsabsolvent:innen, „[who] do not become linguists, but rather move into a role within the language industry, rising to roles of power and influence" (Moorkens/Guerberof Arenas 2024, S. 89).

> The opportunity during training to highlight ethics and sustainability issues should be taken so that graduates have a basis to evaluate the repercussions of decisions during their career. Training not just in the use of technology, but also in understanding and communicating the underlying processes of technology should empower graduates and practitioners to advise on their appropriate (and inappropriate) uses, allowing them to fill expert roles relating to translation workflows (Moorkens/Guerberof Arenas 2024, S. 89).

Für die akademische Translationsausbildung ortet Way (2020, S. 181) schließlich ein Dilemma „between preparing whole, critical thinking citizens and providing professional training to meet industry demands". Fachspezifische Hochschuldidaktik, wie im Falle von TILLT, muss sich also die Frage stellen, welche Kompetenzen es sind, die Translationsabsolvent:innen brauchen, um als Sprachdienstleister:innen oder Entscheidungsträger:innen in der Sprachdienstleistungsbranche fachlich professionell und ethisch zu handeln. TILLT-Lehrende sind dabei gefordert, über ihren Beitrag als Sprachausbildner:innen innerhalb der Translationsausbildung nachzudenken. Ein Ergebnis eines solchen Nachdenkprozesses über eine zukunftsorientierte TILLT-Lehre ist ein 2023 vorgeschlagenes Future Skills-Modell, das der Kritik begegnen wollte, dass Future Skills zu wenig Fachbezug aufweisen, wenn sie fachübergreifend definiert werden (Seidl 2023b).

Im Folgenden wird dieses Modell adaptiert, um der zunehmenden Durchdringung der Lern- und Arbeitswelt durch Sprachtechnologien und generativer KI im Rahmen einer translationswissenschaftlichen Hochschulbildung gerecht zu werden, wobei der Fokus auf translationsorientiertem Lehren und Lernen von Sprachen liegt. Dabei werden Überlegungen von Ehlers, Lindner und Rauch (2024) einbezogen, die mit ihrem Kompetenzmodell AIComp ein Kompetenzstrukturmodell vorlegen, das Future Skills für eine von KI durchdrungene Lebens- und Arbeitswelt in drei Kompetenzbereiche gliedert: (1) arbeitsbezogene Kompetenzen, (2) persönliche Entwicklung und (3) soziales Umfeld und Organisation. Jeder Bereich umfasst mehrere Kompetenzfelder, „die für das Navigieren in einer KI-integrierten Realität erforderlich sind" (ibid., S. 7). Insgesamt definieren Ehlers, Lindner und Rauch (2024) folgende zwölf Kompetenzfelder des AIComp-Modells: (1) Aktivitäts- und Umsetzungskompetenz, (2) Systemdesignkompetenz,

(3) Kreative Problemlösekompetenz, (4) Kritische digitale Kompetenz, (5) Entscheidungskompetenz, (6) Selbstwirksamkeit, (7) Kritisches Denken, (8) Aktive Steuerungsfähigkeit, (9) Selbstbestimmtheit, (10) Ethische Kompetenz, (11) Kooperationskompetenz und (12) Kommunikationskompetenz.

Abbildung 1 ist eine Überarbeitung des speziell für TILLT zur Diskussion gestellten Future Skills-Modells (Seidl 2023b), mit der der Versuch unternommen wird, *transition skills* (Fürstenberg/Schumm Fauster 2024), Future Skills für eine von KI beeinflusste Lebens- und Arbeitswelt (Ehlers/Lindner/Rauch 2024), aber auch Überlegungen zu einer human-zentrierten Translations- und Sprachdidaktik im Sinne einer *Positive Translation Education* (PTE) (Pagano/Ebner/Seidl 2025) einzubeziehen.

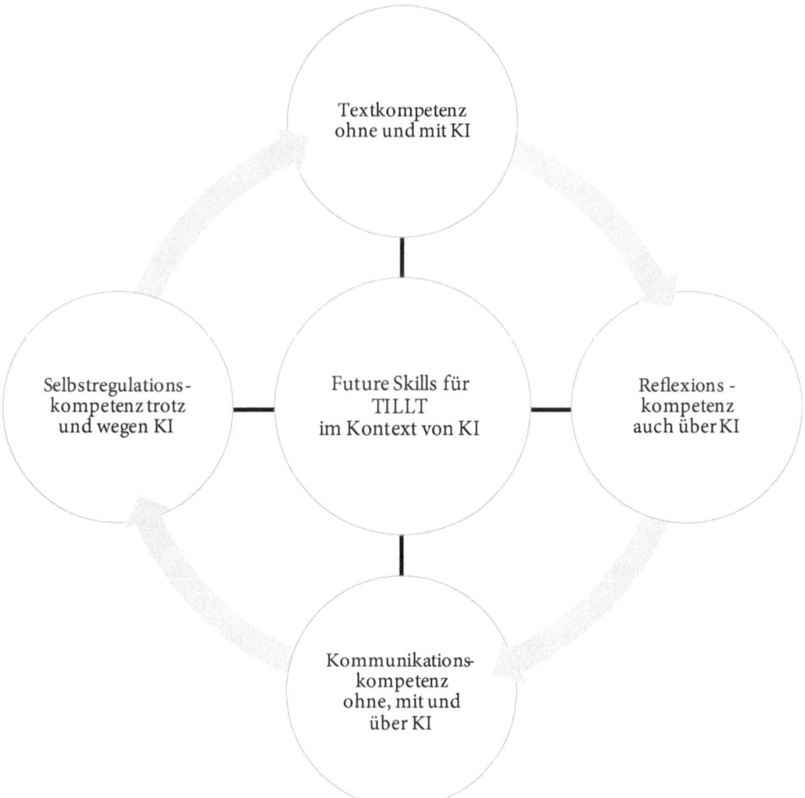

Abbildung 1: Future Skills für TILLT im Kontext von KI (eigene Darstellung).

Das Modell ist ausgehend von Textkompetenz im Uhrzeigersinn zu lesen, wobei die vier Komponenten miteinander in Beziehung stehen, was durch die Verbindungslinien zum Ausdruck kommen soll. Die Komponenten, die im Folgenden näher ausgeführt werden, lauten:

- Textkompetenz ohne und mit KI
- Reflexionskompetenz auch über KI
- Kommunikationskompetenz ohne, mit und über KI
- Selbstregulationskompetenz trotz und wegen KI

5.1 Textkompetenz ohne und mit KI

Texte, seien es mündliche, schriftliche oder multimodale zu rezipieren, zu paraphrasieren, zusammenzufassen, situations- und adressatengerecht selbst zu produzieren, zu redigieren oder zu editieren, ist ein zentraler Aspekt von TILLT. Zahlreiche Textkompetenzen, die in TILLT-Kursen erworben werden können, bilden eine unerlässliche Basis für darauf aufbauenden Translationsunterricht. Findet die Entwicklung solcher Kompetenzen nicht mehr ohne Nutzung von KI-Tools statt, riskiert man „the atrophy of human skills and agency and an increased dependency on the availability of AI and other technology“ (OECD 2023, S. 403). In Bezug auf Rezeption, Evaluation, Adaption oder Produktion von Texten sollten Studierende dahingehend sensibilisiert werden, dass diese Tätigkeiten, wenn sie unabhängig von Maschinen ausgeführt werden, eine tiefgehende und zeitintensive Beschäftigung mit Texten erfordern. Die Kulturtechniken KI-unabhängigen Lesens und Schreibens sollten als solche auch in Zukunft Wertschätzung erfahren, „to ensure that future generations can still enjoy activities that have been valued by human beings for centuries and which will help them value and continue human heritage and culture into the far future“ (ibid., S. 407).

Liegt der Fokus auf Textkompetenz im TILLT-Unterreicht, der meist in den ersten Studiensemestern stattfindet, zu sehr auf KI-Tools, bringt man Studierende darum, Fähigkeiten zu entwickeln, „that they will then be able to apply whatever slots [in the language industry] may exist 5, 10, 15 or 25 years from now“ (Mossop 2003, S. 20). Als derart zukunftsfähige Kompetenzen nennt Mossop (ibid.) solche, „which take a very long time to learn: text interpretation, composition of a coherent, readable and audience-tailored draft translation, research, and checking/correcting“. Auch wenn hier von

Übersetzungsentwürfen die Rede ist, auf die TILLT ja nicht abzielt, können Textaufgaben zum translationsorientierten Sprachenlernen so gestaltet sein, dass sie – in adaptierter Form – übersetzungs- oder dolmetschrelevant sind. Pym und Hao (2025) verfolgen einen solchen integrativen Ansatz, indem sie Lernaktivitäten vorschlagen, die den kritischen Umgang mit Sprachtechnologien fördern und passend sind „for *both* translator training and the language class, or they can be adapted". (S. 82-83, Hervorh. i. O.)

> The general classroom procedure is to start from unaided ("fully human") translation and only then move to the technologies, so that the student will explore how their current skills can be augmented rather than replaced. The risk in each case is that the student might short-circuit the process and decide to depend on the technology from the outset (Pym/Hao 2025, S. 83).

Um zu vermeiden, dass sich Studierende von Anfang an von der Verfügbarkeit und den Zugangsmöglichkeiten zu Technologien abhängig machen, brauchen sie Anstrengungsbereitschaft und Freude am eigenen, kritischen Denken.

5.2 Reflexionskompetenz auch über KI

Kritisches Denken wird in diesem Future Skills-Modell unter Reflexionskompetenz gefasst. Mit Fokus auf KI-Kompetenzen definieren Ehlers, Lindner und Rauch (2024, S. 39) etwa kritische digitale Kompetenz als Disposition, „die Eigenlogik von KI-Systemen im Hinblick auf ihre Nutzung von Daten sowie ihre Wirkung auf Organisationen und die Gesellschaft zu verstehen, zu analysieren und kritisch bewerten zu können". Zweifelsohne ist dies eine Kompetenz, die von Translationsabsolvent:innen erwartet wird. Eine interessante Verbindung zwischen kritischem Denken und Kreativität als für hochemergente Handlungskontexte erforderliche Future Skills zeigen Fürstenberg und Schumm Fauster (2024) im Kontext von *transition skills* auf.

> Critical thinking enables us to assess a situation, make judgements and draw conclusions; creativity allows us to find various novel solutions and strategies to deal with such challenges [posed by AI]. In this way, they complement each other in the form of **agile thinking**, which is helpful for navigating ambiguity and coping with uncertainty (Fürstenberg/Schumm Fauster 2024, S. 13, Hervorh. i. O.).

Wenn in TILLT agiles Denken durch gut durchdachte Sprachlehr- und -lernaktivitäten gefördert wird, können gleichzeitig die von Bernstein et al.

(2023, S. 6) formulierten sogenannten KI-harten Kompetenzen des kritischen Denkens und Handelns in Unsicherheit entwickelt werden. Dies erfordert allerdings, dass sich Studierende metakognitiv mit ihrem Sprachhandeln auseinandersetzen können und getroffene Entscheidungen auf Wort-, Satz- und Textebene reflektieren, begründen oder gar verteidigen können. So kann von ihnen verlangt werden, ihre Herangehensweise an Textarbeit zu dokumentieren und dadurch die verschiedenen Prozesse von Textrezeption oder -produktion für andere nachvollziehbar zu machen. Die Verwendung von KI-Tools kann so für Lehrende transparent gemacht werden. Angestoßen werden kann auf diese Weise aber auch eine Reflexion darüber, wie viel Zeitersparnis oder umgekehrt zeitlicher Mehraufwand sich durch die Nachbearbeitung von KI-Output tatsächlich ergibt.

Schließlich fällt unter diese auf TILLT bezogene Zukunftskompetenz auch noch die Verantwortung von Sprachlehrenden, bei der Themenwahl bewusst Inhalte zu wählen, die eine Reflexion über Sprache sowie über sprachliches und translatorisches Handeln anregen. Pagano, Ebner und Seidl (2025) nennen die Relevanz von Inhalten als einen von vier Aspekten einer *Positive Translation Education* (PTE). Erleben Studierende den mehrfachen Nutzen einer Aufgabenstellung, kann das ihre intrinsische Motivation fördern, da ihre nach diesem Prinzip didaktisierte Spracharbeit nicht nur Wissenszuwachs ermöglicht, sondern auch Erlebniswert bietet, persönliche Entfaltung zulässt und sozio-emotionale Kompetenzen fördert. Um Letztere geht es in der dritten Komponente des Modells.

5.3 Kommunikationskompetenz ohne, mit und über KI

Die oben angesprochene Fähigkeit agilen Denkens, welches Flexibilität und Adaptionsfähigkeit auszeichnet, korrespondiert mit der Veränderung von Arbeitsbedingungen in agilen und vernetzten statt streng hierarchisch strukturierten Organisationen. In von erforderlicher Anpassungsfähigkeit geprägten Arbeitskontexten besteht ein verstärkter Bedarf an einem Kommunikations- und Beziehungsmanagement in „beteiligungsorientierten Zielfindungsprozessen" (Ehlers 2021, S. 371). Um als Future Skill zu gelten, sollte Kommunikationskompetenz nach Ehlers (2021) über bisherige Kompetenzanforderungen hinausgehen. Für die Translationsausbildung ist dies insofern relevant, als Absolvent:innen sich stärker als bisher selbstbewusst am Arbeitsmarkt als Sprachexpert:innen präsentieren müssen, die über Planungs- und Beratungskompetenz für das Management von Translationsprojekten verfügen (Sandrini 2022). Dies impliziert, dass sie Arbeit- bzw. Auftraggeber:innen bezüglich des Einsatzes von Sprach- und Translationstechnologien beraten und Aufklärungsarbeit gegen simplifizierte Auffassungen von Translation leisten können.

Beteiligungsorientierte Zielfindung bedeutet aber auch, in vermehrt transdisziplinären und transkulturellen Teams für Verständlichkeit und Verständigung zu sorgen. Mindestens drei von Ehlers, Lindner und Rauch (2024) formulierte KI-bezogene Future Skills gilt es daher, bereits in TILLT-Kursen zu fördern: (1) Kommunikationskompetenz, (2) Kooperationskompetenz und (3) Entscheidungskompetenz. Über Kommunikationskompetenz im Bereich von KI zu verfügen, gilt für Ehlers, Lindner und Rauch (2024, S. 64) als „Schlüsselkomponente für Führung und Teamdynamik, insbesondere in interdisziplinären Umgebungen, in denen KI-Anwendungen diskutiert und entwickelt werden". Kooperationskompetenz wiederum bezeichnen sie als die Fähigkeit, in organisations-, abteilungs- oder kulturübergreifenden Transformationsprozessen KI-Projekte umzusetzen (ibid., S. 60).

> In einer Welt, in der KI immer mehr Entscheidungsprozesse beeinflusst, wird die Kooperationskompetenz immer wichtiger. Sie befähigt Menschen, nicht nur als Einzelkämpfer:innen, sondern als Teil eines größeren Ganzen zu agieren, das durch die gemeinsamen Anstrengungen aller Beteiligten gestärkt wird. Diese Kompetenz spiegelt die moderne Arbeitsrealität wider, in der Flexibilität, Anpassungsfähigkeit und lebenslanges Lernen Schlüsselkompetenzen für den beruflichen Erfolg darstellen (Ehlers/Lindner/Rauch 2024, S. 61).

Entscheidungskompetenz im Kontext von KI-Nutzung manifestiert sich schließlich in einem Zusammenspiel aus „praktischer Anwendung, emotionaler Bereitschaft und zukunftsorientierter Einschätzung" (ibid., S. 43). In diesem Bereich kompetente Personen verfügen über „das notwendige Wissen, die Fertigkeiten und inneren Haltungen, um bewusst Verantwortung für die durch KI unterstützten und/oder getroffenen Entscheidungen zu übernehmen" (ibid., S. 42). Die Aufzählung und Beschreibung der bisher genannten drei Teilaspekte von Future Skills für TILLT im Kontext von KI verdeutlichen die hohen Anforderungen an Studierende. Insofern scheint es nur folgerichtig, dass der vierte Teilaspekt ihre Selbstregulationskompetenz in den Blick nimmt.

5.4 Selbstregulationskompetenz trotz und wegen KI

Umwälzungen technologischer Art in translatorischen Berufsfeldern, geprägt von Beschleunigung sowie vermehrtem Produktivitäts- und Effizienzdruck (Baumgarten/Bourgadel 2023, S. 508) erfordern eine Sprachlehre, die Studierende auf eine Berufstätigkeit vorbereitet, die von Termin- und Leistungsdruck, hohen Qualitätsansprüchen und geforderter Präzision gekennzeichnet ist. Bereits in TILLT kann ein reflektierter Umgang mit den hohen Anforderungen, die das Berufsfeld mit sich bringt, eingeübt werden. Wenn KI-Tools suggerieren, dass Sprach- und Textarbeit per Mausklick in Sekundenschnelle erledigt werden kann, dann liegt es in der Verantwortung von TILLT-Lehrenden, vor allem Studienanfänger:innen bewusst zu machen, wie viel Zeit und Mühe es erfordert, technologieunabhängig tief in eine Sprache und ihre kulturellen Implikationen einzudringen. Ungeachtet der Verfügbarkeit und Verlockung von KI-Tools müssen Studierende lernen, hohe Qualitäts- und Leistungsansprüche an sich selbst zu stellen, denen sie – im Vertrauen, dies auch ohne Maschinen zu schaffen – trotz hohen Zeitdrucks gerecht werden. Qualität vor Geschwindigkeit, das sollte hier die Devise sein.

In der Mensch-Maschine-Interaktion können Gefühle wie Getriebenheit und Fremdbestimmtheit aufkommen. Daher sind Selbstbestimmtheit und Selbstregulationskompetenz trotz und wegen der Durchdringung von verschiedenen Lebensbereichen durch KI umso wichtiger. Als wichtige *transition skill* von der Hochschule in die Berufstätigkeit bezeichnen Fürstenberg und Schumm Fauster (2024, S. 15) folgerichtig *self-leadership*, die sie mit emotionaler Intelligenz in Verbindung bringen und mit der Reflexion darüber „what we do, why we do it and how we do it". In der Diktion von Ehlers, Lindner und Rauch (2024, S. 46) lässt sich Selbstregulationskompetenz als Selbstwirksamkeit, aktive Steuerungsfähigkeit und Selbstbestimmtheit beschreiben. Eine selbstwirksame Nutzung von KI baut auf „kontinuierliches Lernen als auch auf kritisches Verständnis und autonome[s] Handeln [auf]" (ibid.). Aktive Steuerungsfähigkeit versetzt Menschen in die Lage, „KI-Systeme effektiv zu ihrem Vorteil zu nutzen, ohne von diesen Systemen überwältigt oder fehlgeleitet zu werden" (ibid., S. 52). Mit KI selbstbestimmt zu handeln, impliziert, diese „kritisch zu reflektieren und sich der potenziellen Einflüsse bewusst [zu sein], die diese Technologien auf [die] Autonomie haben können" (ibid., S. 54). Für das hier diskutierte Future Skills-Modell ist von besonderer Bedeutung, dass Selbstbestimmtheit auch die Fähigkeit beinhaltet, „eigene Bedüfnisse und Grenzen zu erkennen und KI-Systeme entsprechend zu regulieren oder anzupassen, um eine selbstbestimmte Nutzung zu gewährleisten" (ibid., S. 55).

Für TILLT ergeben sich daraus mehrere Implikationen. Bei allem Streben nach Sprachperfektion und lebenslanger Weiterbildungsbereitschaft ist Selbstfürsorge eine genauso wichtige Zukunftskompetenz. Zunehmende Mensch-Maschine-Interaktionen machen es umso wichtiger, auf körperliche und mentale Gesundheit zu achten. Dies erfordert eine gute Balance zwischen hohem Arbeitsethos und selbstfürsorglichem Verhalten. Durch Fürsorge und Wertschätzung – ein zentrales Prinzip einer *Positive Translation Education* (PTE) (Pagano/Ebner/Seidl 2025) – kann Selbstregulationskompetenz trotz und wegen KI gefördert werden. TILLT-Lehrende können Studierenden dabei als Vorbild dienen, wie dem Humanen und dem zwischenmenschlichen Austausch in der heutigen Zeit hoher Wert beigemessen werden kann. Die oben erwähnten Reflexionsfragen über das Was, Warum und Wie des eigenen Tuns ermöglichen Manuti (2023) zufolge eine nachhaltige Translationskarriere, wenn die eigene translatorische Arbeit als für die Gesellschaft bedeutungsvoll wahrgenommen wird und vielfältige Anregungen für das eigene Leben damit verbunden sind. In TILLT-Kursen kann durch translationsorientierte Sprach- und Textarbeit diese Sinnhaftigkeit einer anstrengenden intellektuellen Beschäftigung bewusst gemacht werden.

6. Fazit und Ausblick

Ausgangspunkt dieses Beitrags war ein bestehendes Future Skills-Modell für TILLT, das angesichts der massiven Veränderungen in Hochschule, Lebens- und Arbeitswelt durch aktuelle Sprachtechnologien einer Adaption bedurfte. Nach einer Diskussion der Bedeutung des Humanen in der translationsorientierten Sprachlehre und einer kurzen Darstellung des Hochschuldiskurses um das umstrittene Konzept von Future Skills wurden solche für TILLT vorgeschlagen. Erweitert um die Perspektive darauf, wie KI-Systeme das Sprachenlernen von Translationsstudierenden beeinflussen können, wurden vier KI-bezogene Future Skills für TILLT vorgeschlagen: (1) Textkompetenz ohne und mit KI, (2) Reflexionskompetenz auch über KI, (3) Kommunikationskompetenz ohne, mit und über KI sowie (4) Selbstregulationskompetenz trotz und wegen KI. Doch nicht nur

Studierende sind dazu angehalten, sich mit Zukunftskompetenzen auseinanderzusetzen. Sprachlehrende, die fachsensibel und hochschuldidaktisch professionell auf technologieinduzierte Veränderungen und Verunsicherungen reagieren wollen, müssen sich immer wieder mit Fragen auseinandersetzen, die Ehlers et al. (2024) im Kontext von KI als umso bedeutsamer herausstreichen.

> *Warum* lehren wir? Welches Zukunftsversprechen gibt jede Hochschule vor dem Hintergrund ihrer eigenen Strategie und Mission über ihre Studiengänge in der Lehre? Welches Verständnis von Hochschulbildung liegt der Strategie zugrunde?
>
> *Was* lehren wir? Welches konkrete Kompetenz-Angebot stellen die Fächer gemeinsam mit überfachlich agierenden Einrichtungen für die Studierenden bereit, um den Herausforderungen der Gesellschaft zu begegnen?
>
> *Wie* lehren wir? Wie werden didaktische und methodische Zugänge zu Lernprozessen gegebenenfalls vor dem Hintergrund komplexer beziehungsweise hochemergenter und digitalisierter gesellschaftlicher Herausforderungen neu oder anders beantwortet? (Ehlers et al. 2024, S. 20-21, eigene Hervorh.)

Idealerweise gelingt es angesichts zahlreicher Veränderungen, Translationsstudierende dabei zu unterstützen, „[to] grasp the roles, responsibilities, values and ethical positions incumbent upon translators as key communicative actors in society" (Massey/Kiraly 2019, S. 27). Die beiden Translationswissenschafter kommen in ihren 2019 – also noch vor der Corona-Pandemie und vor dem Siegeszug von ChatGPT & Co. – geführten Überlegungen zur Zukunft der Translationsausbildung zu dem Schluss: „I find it just as thrilling and enjoyable, as enlightening and as much an invaluable learning experience as I did 40 years ago" (ibid., S. 27). Ganz ähnlich argumentiert Manuti (2023, S. 134), nämlich dass eine nachhaltige Karriere im Translationsberuf in post-pandemischen Zeiten idealerweise wie folgt aussieht: „[It] entails investing physical, mental, and psychological resources into it, searching for meaning, and pursuing happiness and well-being while engaged in this important sphere of life". Was könnte man sich Besseres wünschen für Translationsabsolvent:innen, die an der Hochschule auf eine Zukunft vorbereitet werden, die niemand vorhersehen kann? Ein Versuch, zukunftsrelevante Kompetenzen für die translationsorientierte Sprachlehre zu fassen, wurde mit dem hier zur Diskussion gestellten Future Skills-Modell unternommen.

Quellenverzeichnis

Baumgarten, Stefan / Bourgadel, Carole (2023): „Digitalisation, neo-Taylorism and translation in the 2020s". *Perspectives. Studies in Translation Theory and Practice* 32(3), S. 508–523. https://doi.org/10.1080/0907676X.2023.2285844

Bernstein, Abraham / Cordoba, Anaïc / Witt, Claudia / Siegers, Daniel / Wessels, Doris / Thouvenin, Florent / Hastings, Janna / Hatt, Jean-Michael / Buhmann, Joachim / Martinez Moreno, Judit / Schawinski, Kevin / Christen, Markus / Coors, Michael / Denner, Michael / Hunger, Patricik / von Thiessen, Raphael / Fabrikant, Sara / Friemel, Thomas / Neupert, Titus / Sachs, Uli (2023): „KI in Bildung, Forschung und Innovation". *DSI Strategy Lab 2023 – Positionspapier.* Digital Society Initiative Universität Zürich, abgerufen am 22.12.2024 auf https://www.dsi.uzh.ch/de/current/news/2024/strategy-lab-23-results.html.

Ehlers, Ulf-Daniel (2021): „Future Skills für die Welt von morgen: Das Future-Skills-Triple-Helix-Modell der Handlungsfähigkeit in emergenten Praxiskontexten". In: Hochschulforum Digitalisierung (Hrsg.): *Digitalisierung in Studium und Lehre gemeinsam gestalten. Innovative Formate, Strategien und Netzwerke*. Wiesbaden: Springer VS, S. 355–373.

Ehlers, Ulf-Daniel / Eigbrecht, Laura / Horstmann, Nina / Matthes, Wibke / Piesk, David / Rampelt, Florian (2024): „Future Skills für Hochschulen: Eine kritische Bestandsaufnahme. Vorveröffentlichung aus Future Skills lehren und lernen: Schlaglichter aus Hochschule, Schule und Weiterbildung". Stifterverband, abgerufen am 22.12.2024 auf https://www.stifterverband.org/sites/default/files/2024-06/future_skills_fuer_hochschulen_kritische_bestandsaufnahme_vorveroeffentlichung.pdf.

Ehlers, Ulf-Daniel / Lindner, Martin / Rauch, Emily (2024): „AIComp. Future Skills für eine von KI beeinflusste Lebens- und Arbeitswelt. Forschungsbericht 2: Empirische Konstruktion & Beschreibung des Kompetenzmodells AIComp". Karlsruhe, abgerufen am 22.12.2024 auf https://next-education.org/downloads/AIComp_Part_2_Kompetenzmodell_final.pdf.

Fürstenberg, Ulla / Schumm Fauster, Jennifer (2024): *Navigating tomorrow: transition skills for Higher Education.* Oxford: Oxford University Press, abgerufen am 21.12.2024 auf https://elt.oup.com/feature/global/expert/higher-ed?cc=de&selLanguage=en.

Gao, Xuesong (2024): „Language education in a brave new world: A dialectical imagination“. *The Modern Language Journal* 108, S. 556–562. https://doi.org/10.1111/modl.12930.

Kalz, Marco (2023): „Zurück in die Zukunft? Eine literaturbasierte Kritik der Zukunftskompetenzen“. *MedienPädagogik*, S. 332–352. https://doi.org/10.21240/mpaed/00/2023.11.19.X.

Kalz, Marco / Reinmann, Gabi (2024): „Erneuerung der Hochschule von außen nach innen oder umgekehrt? Kritische Diskussion und Alternativen zur Future Skills-Bewegung“. *Impact Free* 57, S. 1–10. https://gabi-reinmann.de/wp-content/uploads/2024/08/Impact_Free_57.pdf.

Kern, Richard (2024): „Twenty-first century technologies and language education: Charting a path forward“. *The Modern Language Journal* 108, S. 515–533. https://doi.org/10.1111/modl.12924.

Loviscach, Jörn (2024): „Aufmerksamkeitsregulation. Der einzige 21st Century Skill“. Lankau, Ralf (Hrsg.): *Die pädagogische Wende. Über die notwendige (Rück-)Besinnung auf das Unterrichten*. Weinheim: Beltz, S. 133–148.

Manuti, Amelia (2023): „Performance and well-being in changing work environments. Pursuing a sustainable career in translation in post-pandemic times“. In: Hubscher-Davidson, Séverine / Lehr, Caroline (Hrsg.): *The psychology of translation. An interdisciplinary approach*. London/New York: Routledge, S. 130–154.

Massey, Gary / Kiraly, Don (2019): „The future of translator education: A dialogue“. *Cultus* 12, S. 15–34, abgerufen am 21.12.2024 auf https://digitalcollection.zhaw.ch/handle/11475/19460.

Massey, Gary / Huertas Barros, Elsa / Katan, David (2023): „The human translator in the 2020s: An introduction“. In: Massey, Gary / Huertas Barros, Elsa / Katan, David (Hrsg.): *The human translator in the 2020s*. London/New York: Routledge.

Massey, Gary / Ehrensberger-Dow, Maureen / Angelone, Erik (Hrsg.) (2024): *Handbook of the Language Industry. Contexts, Resources and Profiles*. Berlin/Boston: De Gruyter Mouton.

Mercer, Sarah / MacIntyre, Peter D. / Gregersen, Tammy / Talbot, Kyle (2018): „Positive Language Education: Combining Positive Education and Language Education“. *Theory and Practice of Second Language Acquisition* 4(2), S. 11–31.

Mierzwa, Ewelina (2019): „Foreign language learning and teaching enjoyment: Teachers' perspectives". *Journal of Education Culture and Society* 10(2), S. 170–188. https://doi.org/10.15503/jecs20192.170.188.

Moorkens, Joss / Guerberof Arenas, Ana (2024): „Artificial intelligence, automation and the language industry". In: Massey, Gary / Ehrensberger-Dow, Maureen / Angelone, Erik (Hrsg.): *Handbook of the language industry. Contexts, resources and profiles*. Berlin/Bosten: De Gruyter Mouton, S. 71–97.

Mossop, Brian (2003): „What should be taught at translation school?". In: Pym, Anthony / Fallada, Carmina / Biau, José Ramón / Orenstein, Jill (Hrsg.): *Innovation and e-learning in translator training.* Tarragona: Intercultural Studies Group Universitat Rovira i Virgili, S. 20–22, abgerufen am 21.12.2024 auf https://www.intercultural.urv.cat/media/upload/domain_317/arxius/Innovation/innovation_index.pdf.

O'Brien, Sharon (2022): „The dark horse of translation?". In: Franco Aixelá, Javier / Olalla-Soler, Christian (Hrsg.): *50 years later. What have we learnt after Holmes (1972) and where are we now?* Las Palmas de Gran Canaria: ULPGC ediciones, S. 93–104. https://accedacris.ulpgc.es/bitstream/10553/124520/1/9788490424612.pdf.

OECD (2023): „Opportunities, guidelines and guardrails for effective and equitable use of AI in education". In: OECD Digital Education Outlook 2023 (Hrsg.): *Towards an effective digital education ecosystem*. Paris: OECD Publishing, S. 400–411. https://doi.org/10.1787/2b39e98b-en.

Öner Bulut, Senem / Alimen, Nilüfer (2023): „Translator education as a collaborative quest for insights into the re-positioning of the human translator (educator) in the age of machine translation: The results of a learning experiment". *The Interpreter and Translator Trainer* 17(3), S. 375–392. https://doi.org/10.1080/1750399X.2023.2237837.

Pagano, Delia / Ebner, Clara / Seidl, Eva (2025): „Emotionsfokussierte Translations- und Sprachdidaktik aus Lehrenden- und Studierendenperspektive". In: Schmidhofer, Astrid / Recio Ariza, María Ángeles (Hrsg.): *Zukunftsperspektiven in der Translationswissenschaft*. Innsbruck: Innsbruck University Press, S. 15–32.

Pegrum, Mark / Palalas, Agnieszka (2021): „Attentional literacy as a new literacy: Helping students deal with digital disarray". *Canadian Journal of Learning and Technology* 47(2), S. 1–18. https://doi.org/10.21432/cjlt28037.

Pöchhacker, Franz (2024): „Die Zukunft des Dolmetschens“. *Mitteilungsblatt UNIVERSITAS Austria* 3(2), S. 41–44.

Pym, Anthony / Hao, Yu (2025): *How to Augment Language Skills. Generative AI and Machine Translation in Language Learning and Translator Training.* London/New York: Routledge.

Reinmann, Gabi (2023): *Deskilling durch Künstliche Intelligenz? Potenzielle Kompetenzverluste als Herausforderung für die Hochschuldidaktik. Diskussionspapier Nr. 25.* Berlin: Hochschulforum Digitalisierung, abgerufen am 21.12.2024 auf https://hochschulforumdigitalisierung.de/sites/default/files/dateien/HFD_DP_25_Deskilling.pdf.

Sandrini, Peter (2022): „Die neuronale didaktische Herausforderung: Berufsbild und Kompetenzen im Wandel“. In: Hebenstreit, Gernot / Hofeneder, Philipp (Hrsg.): *Translation im Wandel: Gesellschaftliche, konzeptuelle und didaktische Perspektiven*. Berlin: Frank & Timme, S. 115–134.

Schmidhofer, Astrid (2022): „Translation and interpreting-oriented language learning and teaching (TILLT): Where do we stand?“ *Sendebar* 33, S. 264–283. https://doi.org/10.30827/sendebar.v33.23654.

Seidl, Eva (2013): „Universität ist nicht die Fortsetzung von Schule. Über die Schwierigkeiten von StudienanfängerInnen beim Übertritt von der Schule zur Hochschule und mögliche didaktische Implikationen“. In: Schwarz, Eveline / Stachl-Peier, Ursula (Hrsg.): *Das Spiel der Sprachen 3. Impulse zu einer Sprachdidaktik im tertiären Bildungsbereich und zur Translationsdidaktik*. Graz: Universität Graz, S. 10–38.

Seidl, Eva (2022): „Sozio-emotionales Lernen im Fokus hochschulischer Sprachlehre“. In: Pauschenwein, Jutta / Hernády, Birgit / Michelitsch, Linda (Hrsg.): *Wie beeinflussen Gefühle und Sprache den (Online-)Lernprozess? Tagungsband zum 21. E-Learning-Tag der FH JOANNEUM*. Graz: Verlag der FH JOANNEUM, S. 62–72.

Seidl, Eva (2023a): „Conceptualizing language teacher identity in translator and interpreter education“. In: Karpava, Sviatlana (Hrsg.): *Handbook of research on language teacher identity.* Hershey, PA: IGI Global, S. 64–80.

Seidl, Eva (2023b): „Zur Rolle von Future Skills in der translationsorientierten Sprachlehre“. *Neues Handbuch Hochschullehre* 112, K 3.6, S. 1–20, abgerufen am 21.12.2024 auf https://www.nhhl-bibliothek.de/de/handbuch/gliederung/#/Beitragsdetailansicht/300/3748/Zur-Rolle-von-Future-Skills-in-der-translationsorientierten-Sprachlehre.

Way, Catherine (2020): „Training and pedagogical implications“. In: Angelone, Erik / Ehrensberger-Dow, Maureen / Massey, Garry (Hrsg.): *The Bloomsbury companion to language industry studies*. London et al.: Bloomsbury Academic, S. 179–207.

Witte, Arnd (2021): „The sentient body and intercultural situational attentiveness“. In: Witte, Arnd / Harden, Theo (Hrsg.): *Rethinking intercultural competence: Theoretical challenges and practical issues*. Oxford et al.: Peter Lang, S. 19–48.

ChatGPT als Tutor und Korrekturwerkzeug in der translationsorientierten Sprachausbildung (TILLT)

Saverio Carpentieri
Universität Innsbruck

Natalie Mair
Universität Innsbruck

Astrid Schmidhofer
Universität Innsbruck[1]

ABSTRACT
The rapid emergence of AI technologies, including tools such as ChatGPT, presents both opportunities and challenges for education, particularly in language learning and translation-oriented training. This article examines the suitability of ChatGPT as a language tutor and correction tool for students learning Italian and Spanish in translation and interpreting contexts. Practical examples are used to demonstrate how ChatGPT can take on tutoring and correction roles to support learners to achieve their foreign language learning goals. Our study contrasts Italian and Spanish with German to address specific challenges faced by German speakers, filling a research gap, as most literature on language learning and teaching with large language models (LLMs) centres on learning English. Hence, this work contributes to a more diversified approach in language learning research by also examining non-English contexts. While ChatGPT offers opportunities to increase learner autonomy and classroom efficiency, its limitations underscore the essential role of human educators. The future of language education lies in a synergy between human instruction and AI technology, fostering balanced and effective learning environments.

Keywords: language learning, language competence, translation and interpreting, artificial intelligence, large language models, TILLT

1. Einleitung

Die breite Verfügbarkeit von KI-Technologien stellt den Bildungsbereich vor zahlreiche neue Fragen, eröffnet aber gleichzeitig auch ungekannte Perspektiven für das Lehren und Lernen. So werden neue Modellierungen von Bildungskompetenzen und der Einsatz solcher Tools im Unterricht

[1] Namen in alphabetischer Reihenfolge

erforscht, seit KI-Tools wie ChatGPT Ende 2022 in das breite öffentliche Interesse gerückt sind. Laupichler et al. (2022) betonen, dass interdisziplinäre Forschung zu diesem Thema zwar beginnt, jedoch das akademische Verständnis von KI-Kompetenzen noch sehr überschaubar ist. Die Eingliederung von KI-basierten Textgeneratoren wie ChatGPT in den Lehrbetrieb ist trotz ihres Potenzials für eine Vielzahl an Bereichen, von der Beurteilung bis hin zu Forschung und Lehre, an den Universitäten noch nicht sehr weit verbreitet. Luckin et al. (2022) argumentieren, dass sich viele Lehrende der bevorstehenden Auswirkungen von KI auf ihren Beruf noch nicht vollständig bewusst sind und dass interdisziplinäre Ansätze notwendig sind, um Lehrkräfte auf diese Veränderungen vorzubereiten. Ein inzwischen weit verbreiteter Ansatz in diese Richtung ist die Modellierung und spätere Vermittlung einer KI-Grundkompetenz, meist *AI literacy* genannt (vgl. Krüger in diesem Band sowie Ureel et al. in diesem Band).

Auch für den Sprachunterricht bieten KI-Tools – wir beziehen uns hier hauptsächlich auf Large Language Models (LLMs) und darunter vorrangig auf ChatGPT – großes Potenzial für die Entwicklung von neuen Lehr- und Lernmethoden, bringen jedoch auch Risiken mit sich. Ethische Probleme bei der Nutzung von LLMs in der Bildung und insbesondere bei Prüfungen sind schon an anderer Stelle ausführlich beschrieben worden (vgl. bspw. UNESCO 2023). Wir möchten in diesem Beitrag kritisch beleuchten, inwieweit ChatGPT für bestimmte Ziele in der translationsorientierten Sprachausbildung eingesetzt werden kann.

Das zielgerichtete Erlernen von Sprachen für späteres Übersetzen und Dolmetschen ist ein kleines Forschungsfeld der Translationswissenschaft, das sich seit den 1990er Jahren entwickelt hat (vgl. Cerezo Herrero/ Schmidhofer 2021). Die Ziele dieser Sprachausbildung werden innerhalb des Forschungsfeldes häufig in Anlehnung an die Übersetzungskompetenz (vgl. bspw. EMT 2022; Hurtado Albir 2017) definiert (vgl. bspw. Andreu et al. 2002; Schmidhofer/Ahmann 2015). Dazu gehören, unter vielen anderen, die Entwicklung hoher sprachlicher Präzision im Sprachgebrauch, die für Personen, die sich professionell mit Sprache beschäftigen, eine *conditio sine qua non* darstellt, sowie die Entwicklung der Lernendenautonomie, da ein Großteil der Sprachentwicklung aufgrund der geringen Anzahl an Kontaktstunden bei gleichzeitiger schneller Progression außerhalb des Unterrichts stattfinden muss. Dabei sind die beiden genannten Ziele nicht als komplett unabhängig voneinander zu betrachten.

In diesem Beitrag möchten wir anhand von praktischen Beispielen zeigen, inwieweit ChatGPT dabei helfen kann, diese Ziele zu erreichen, indem das Tool eine Tutorfunktion übernimmt und als Korrekturwerkzeug herangezogen wird. Die hier diskutierten Experimente wurden mit den Sprachen Italienisch und Spanisch in Kontrast zum Deutschen, also aus der Perspektive von deutschsprachigen Studierenden, durchgeführt. Diese Wahl liegt vor allem darin begründet, dass ein Großteil der einschlägigen Literatur zum Sprachenlernen mit LLMs auf Englisch und über das Erlernen des Englischen verfasst wurde. So möchten wir mit diesem Beitrag auch zu einer stärkeren Diversifizierung der Forschung in diesem Feld beitragen.

Der vorliegende Beitrag umfasst jeweils ein umfangreiches Kapitel zu jedem der beiden ausgewählten Aspekte. In Abschnitt 2 wird der Stand der Forschung zur Rolle von ChatGPT als Tutor beim Sprachenlernen dargelegt und danach mit praktischen Anwendungsbeispielen verglichen und ergänzt. Abschnitt 3 bildet den Stand der Forschung zu ChatGPT als Korrekturwerkzeug ab und wird ebenso durch praktische Anwendungsbeispiele vervollständigt. Am Ende des Beitrags ziehen wir ein Fazit zu den erhaltenen Ergebnissen.

2. ChatGPT als Tutor beim Sprachenlernen

Bevor wir uns der wissenschaftlichen Literatur zu diesem Thema widmen, möchten wir kurz zeigen, welche Einschätzung ChatGPT selbst zu seiner Eignung als Tutor beim Sprachenlernen äußert. Auf unsere Frage an ChatGPT 4[2] erhielten wir eine lange und ausführliche Antwort, in der sich der Chatbot für verschiedene Zusammenhänge des Sprachunterrichts als durchaus geeignet erklärt, u. a. in den Bereichen interaktive Konversation, Grammatik- und Vokabelübungen, Lese- und Schreibübungen und kulturelles Wissen. Gleichzeitig wird jedoch auch darauf hingewiesen, dass ChatGPT keine menschliche Lehrkraft ersetzen kann – insbesondere nicht bei der Aussprache oder bei kulturellen Nuancen –, jedoch eine wertvolle Ergänzung darstellt.

2.1 ChatGPT als Tutor: Stand der Forschung

Wenn wir von ChatGPT als möglichem Tutor beim Sprachenlernen sprechen, kann sich dies auf zahlreiche unterschiedliche Aspekte, angefangen von der Erstellung von Lernplänen über die Bereitstellung von Beispielen, Übungen

---

2 ChatGPT 4 am 07.07.2024

und Erklärungen bis hin zu personalisierter sprachlicher Interaktion beziehen (vgl. Kohnke/Moorhouse/Zou 2023; Xiao/Zhi 2023). Auch die in Punkt 3 beschriebene Funktion als Korrekturwerkzeug könnte man unter diesen Punkt subsumieren. Es gibt im Internet inzwischen unzählige Webseiten und Videos, die Möglichkeiten beschreiben, wie ChatGPT zum autonomen Sprachenlernen eingesetzt werden kann. Besonders häufig wird dabei die Möglichkeit genutzt, ChatGPT zur Textoptimierung einzusetzen, indem man den Chatbot Textbeispiele generieren lässt oder die Korrektheit von selbst produzierten Texten überprüfen lässt. Ebenso kann ChatGPT als Tutor personalisierte Vokabelübungen generieren, die auf das Sprachniveau des Lernenden abgestimmt sind. Neue Vokabeln werden in gezielte Kontexte eingebettet, um das Verständnis und die Merkfähigkeit zu fördern. Eine kritische Betrachtung zur Eignung des Outputs für autonomes Sprachenlernen ist jedoch (vor allem für Sprachen abseits des Englischen) überschaubar.

Trotz dieses unbestreitbaren Potenzials von ChatGPT (und ähnlichen Tools) für autonomes Lernen darf nicht vergessen werden, dass es der KI an emotionaler Intelligenz und an Selbstbewusstsein fehlt, wodurch Interaktionen zwischen Menschen und KI oft mechanisch ablaufen (Pavlik 2023). Die Fähigkeit von Lehrenden, emotionale Unterstützung zu bieten, ist entscheidend für die Motivation und das Engagement der Lernenden; dies ist eine Eigenschaft, die KI-Systeme bisher nicht nachbilden können. Systeme wie ChatGPT können zwar reaktiv auf Höflichkeitsfloskeln adäquat reagieren, doch nicht proaktiv motivationsfördernde Interaktionen schaffen. Das Problem besteht darin, dass die in diesem Kontext eingesetzten Systeme der Large Language Models größtenteils nach einem Nachahmungsprinzip arbeiten, das auf der Vorhersagbarkeit bestimmter Sequenzen beruht. In diesem Zusammenhang verwenden u. a. Bender et al. den Begriff „stochastic parrots“ (2021, S. 610). Damit ist gemeint, dass diese Modelle Informationen auf eine stochastische (zufällige) Weise wiederholen, basierend auf den riesigen Datenmengen, mit denen sie trainiert wurden, ohne wirkliches Verständnis der Bedeutung oder des Kontexts der Wörter, die sie generieren. Darüber hinaus können soziale Werte und Normen nicht effektiv in Zahlen übersetzt oder auf einfache Algorithmen reduziert werden (Felix 2020). Trotz zahlreicher Gegenargumente zu der Stellungnahme von Bender, bspw. von Arora (2023), und Verbesserungen durch ChatGPT 4, bleibt das zugrundeliegende Problem noch ungelöst. Hinzu kommt, dass diese Systeme ursprünglich für die englische Sprache programmiert wurden und bis dato die Tutorfunktion für andere Sprachen als Englisch nicht immer zuverlässig ist.

Dies möchten wir im Anschluss für die hier gewählten Fremdsprachen Italienisch und Spanisch, betrachtet aus der Perspektive des deutschsprachigen Lernenden, analysieren. Wir beschränken uns aus Platzgründen auf die Bereitstellung von Erklärungen zu sprachlichen Schwierigkeiten und Beispielen.

2.2 ChatGPT als Tutor: Anwendungsbeispiele

Beispiel 1: Grammatikalische Erklärungen: Niveau B1 (Spanisch)

Im folgenden Szenario findet ein Lernender eine unbekannte Verbform vor (*tuviese*) und bittet ChatGPT um eine Erklärung[3] mit folgendem Prompt: *Ich habe in einem Text die Form "tuviese" gefunden. Der Satz war "si tuviese que elegir, elegiría la primera". Ich verstehe diese Form nicht. Kannst du sie mir erklären?*

ChatGPT bietet folgende Antwort: "Tuviese" ist die Konjunktivform des Verbs "tener" in der dritten Person Singular der Vergangenheit. In diesem Fall wird sie im Hypothetischen verwendet, was oft in Sätzen mit "si" (wenn) vorkommt.

Der Satz "si tuviese que elegir, elegiría la primera" bedeutet "wenn ich wählen müsste, würde ich die erste wählen."

Hier ist die Struktur:

- *"si tuviese" drückt eine hypothetische Situation aus (wie "wenn ich hätte").*
- *"elegiría" ist die Bedingungsform (Konditional) und bedeutet "würde wählen".*

Es ist eine häufige Konstruktion im Spanischen, um über unwirkliche oder hypothetische Szenarien zu sprechen.

Kommentar: Die Erklärung ist geeignet, um ein Grundverständnis dieser Verbform zu erhalten. Auch die Anwendungskontexte sind korrekt dargestellt. Allerdings ist die grammatikalische Terminologie (*Konjunktiv*) irreführend; ebenso könnte es für den Lernenden unklar sein, dass *tuviese* einmal mit *müsste* und ein anderes Mal mit *hätte* übersetzt wird. Die Nachfrage nach

[3] ChatGPT 4.o am 19.10.2024

dem zweiten Punkt ist absolut unzureichend, da der Unterschied zwischen *tener* und *tener que* nicht erkannt wird:

"Tuviese" kann je nach Kontext unterschiedlich übersetzt werden. In diesem Fall:

- *"si tuviese" wird oft als "wenn ich hätte" übersetzt, weil es sich auf eine hypothetische Situation bezieht, in der man die Möglichkeit hat, etwas zu wählen oder zu haben.*
- *Die Bedeutung von "müsste" kommt von der impliziten Bedingung, dass, wenn man diese hypothetische Situation hätte, man dann eine Entscheidung treffen müsste.*

Die Übersetzung kann also variieren, je nachdem, wie man die Situation interpretiert. In diesem Kontext könnte man auch einfach "wenn ich wählen könnte" sagen, um die Bedeutung klarer zu machen.

Beispiel 2: Lexikalische Erklärungen: Niveau B2 (Spanisch)

Im folgenden Szenario möchte ein Lernender den Unterschied zwischen drei bedeutungsähnlichen spanischen Wörtern wissen: *hermoso*, *bello* und *bonito* und bittet ChatGPT mit folgendem Prompt um eine Erklärung[4]: *Was ist der Unterschied zwischen* bomito, hermoso *und* bello?

ChatGPT bietet folgende Antwort: *Die Wörter "bomito," "hermoso" und "bello" werden im Spanischen verwendet, um Schönheit oder Anziehung zu beschreiben, aber es gibt einige Unterschiede in ihrer Verwendung:*

1. ***Hermoso:***
   - *Bedeutet "schön" und wird oft für Menschen, Orte und Dinge verwendet. Es hat eine positive und etwas formelle Konnotation.*
   - *Beispiel: "Es una casa hermosa." (Es ist ein schönes Haus.)*
2. ***Bello:***
   - *Auch "schön," hat eine ähnliche Bedeutung wie "hermoso," wird aber oft in literarischen oder poetischen Kontexten verwendet. Es klingt eleganter und kann auch eine tiefere emotionale oder ästhetische Schönheit implizieren.*
   - *Beispiel: "El paisaje es bello." (Die Landschaft ist schön.)*

[4] ChatGPT 4.0 am 19.10.2024

3. ***Bomito:***
   - *Dieses Wort ist weniger gebräuchlich und bezieht sich oft auf etwas, das schön oder ansprechend ist, wird aber in vielen Regionen nicht verwendet. In einigen Kontexten kann es sich auf Tiere beziehen, besonders im Zusammenhang mit ihrer Schönheit.*

Kommentar: Die Erklärung ist geeignet, um grundlegende Unterschiede zwischen den ersten beiden Wörtern zu verstehen. Beim dritten Wort hat sich im Prompt ein Tippfehler eingeschlichen (es müsste *bonito* heißen). ChatGPT macht den Lernenden nicht auf den Fehler aufmerksam, sondern behandelt das falsch geschriebene Wort wie ein reales.

In anderen Bereichen, wie z. B. der schriftlichen Produktion oder der mündlichen Interaktion, erweisen sich die Tutoring-Möglichkeiten von ChatGPT als flexibler und wertvoller im Sprachlernkontext. ChatGPT kann die Interaktion zwischen den Lernenden erleichtern, indem es eine Konversationsplattform bereitstellt, die ihnen ermöglicht, auf natürliche Weise zusammenzuarbeiten. Im Bereich der Schreibproduktion haben wir zum Beispiel festgestellt, dass durch gezielte und spezifische Aufforderungen, bei denen Aufgaben, Arbeitsschritte, konkrete Ziele und Ausgabeformate genau definiert sind, interessante Ergebnisse erzielt werden können.

Beispiel 3: Schriftliche Produktion Italienisch (Niveau A2-B1)

Ein konkretes Beispiel eines Prompts, das wir dem Chatbot im Rahmen von Aktivitäten zur schriftlichen Produktion auf Italienisch gegeben haben, ist folgendes[5]: *Kannst du eine Stadtbeschreibung in italienischer Sprache mit den folgenden Inhalten anfertigen: Geographische Lage, Infrastruktur, charakteristische Stadtviertel, historische Gebäude, lokale Kultur, Traditionen, kulinarische Spezialitäten. Die Beschreibung sollte dem B1-Niveau entsprechen und maximal 250 Wörter enthalten.*

Kommentar: Zuerst haben wir ein Ergebnis erhalten, das noch nicht zufriedenstellend war, weil der Wortschatz im erstellten Text nicht dem Niveau B1 entsprach und einige Unzulänglichkeiten auf kultureller Ebene auftraten,

---

5 ChatGPT 3.5 am 11.04.2024

wie z. B. *La nostra città si trova nella regione del Nord Italia*, aber Norditalien nicht als Region definiert werden kann. Deshalb haben wir die Aufforderung verfeinert und einen Text erhalten, der für das geforderte Niveau geeignet ist und den Lernenden als Beispiel zur Verfügung gestellt werden kann.

Durch spezifische Prompts wurde der Chatbot dann ersucht, mögliche didaktische Aktivitäten anzubieten, um mit diesem Text im Unterricht weiterzuarbeiten. ChatGPT hat daraufhin mehrere Vorschläge unterbreitet, von Vokabelübungen bis Fragen zum Text, Diskussionen und Rechercheaufgaben, also vielfältige Möglichkeiten, verschiedene sprachliche Fähigkeiten zu fördern. Wie Al Ka'bi (2023) und Fariani, Junus und Santoso (2023) anmerken, kann ChatGPT in solchen Lernszenarien Bildungsinhalte an die individuellen Bedürfnisse, Interessen und Lernstile jedes einzelnen Lernenden anpassen und so maßgeschneiderte Lernmaterialien und Aktivitäten bieten.

3. ChatGPT als Korrekturwerkzeug beim Sprachenlernen

Bevor wir uns dem Stand der Forschung zu ChatGPT als Korrekturwerkzeug beim Sprachenlernen widmen, werfen wir einen Blick darauf, wie ChatGPT selbst seine Eignung einschätzt[6].

Wenn man ChatGPT fragt, ob es in der Lage sei, spezifische Fehler beispielsweise in Textproduktionen zu korrigieren, erklärt das System, dass es Fehler erkennen und auf diese hinweisen kann. Ebenso kann es Korrekturvorschläge anbieten, insbesondere bei Grammatik- oder Rechtschreibfehlern, welche die Lernenden gemacht haben, und es kann sie so bei der Verbesserung ihrer Schreibkompetenz unterstützen.

Ob diese Korrekturvorschläge und Erklärungen richtig und hilfreich sind, wird in den nächsten zwei Abschnitten erläutert.

3.1 ChatGPT als Korrekturwerkzeug beim Sprachenlernen: Stand der Forschung

Prinzipiell kann ChatGPT sowohl von Lehrenden als auch von Lernenden als Korrekturwerkzeug zum Erlernen von Fremdsprachen eingesetzt werden. Lehrende haben dabei den Vorteil, dass sie selbst über die notwendige

[6] ChatGPT 4 am 10.07.2024

sprachliche Kompetenz verfügen, um zu beurteilen, ob sich der Chatbot dafür eignet und wie viel Nachbearbeitung erforderlich ist. Der größte Vorteil eines solchen Einsatzes von ChatGPT ist die Effizienz und Zeitersparnis, die entsteht, wenn ChatGPT einen Teil der Korrekturarbeit übernimmt und gleichzeitig Empfehlungen zur Behebung von Lernlücken gibt (vgl. Akinwalere/Ivanov 2022). Dadurch werden Ressourcen bei Lehrenden frei, die in individuelle Betreuung investiert werden können (vgl. Chukwuere 2023; Restrepo/Reyes 2024). Lehman (2024) beschreibt verschiedene Übungen und Tests, die er mit ChatGPT durchgeführt hat. Besonders beeindruckt war Lehman von der Fähigkeit des Modells, Essays sowohl nach dem ACTFL *(American Council on the Teaching of Foreign Languages)* als auch nach dem Gemeinsamen Europäischen Referenzrahmen für Sprachen (GERS) zu bewerten. Ebenso betont Lehman, dass Lehrende ihre eigenen Bewertungsmaßstäbe in die Prompts einfließen lassen können, um sicherzustellen, dass ChatGPT die Texte nach den Standards der jeweiligen Lehrenden beurteilt. Lehman (2024) beschreibt eine Übung, bei der Lernende im ersten Schritt einen handgeschriebenen Aufsatz auf Deutsch ohne Hilfsmittel verfassen sollen. Wörter, die sie auf Deutsch nicht kannten, wurden in Großbuchstaben auf Englisch geschrieben. Im zweiten Schritt durften sie die englischen Wörter nachschlagen und den Aufsatz mit dem Computer verfassen. Im dritten Schritt ließen die Studierenden den Aufsatz von ChatGPT korrigieren. Alle drei Aufgaben wurden dann zur Bewertung an den Lehrenden abgegeben. Dieses Beispiel zeigt, wie ChatGPT dazu genutzt werden kann, die Schreibfähigkeiten der Lernenden zu verbessern und ihnen gleichzeitig zu zeigen, wo sie Fehler gemacht haben. Diese Übung kann auch für weitere Sprachen eingesetzt werden. Der Vorteil dieser Methode liegt in der Effizienz: Lehrende können größere Klassen effizienter unterrichten und die Lernenden erhalten schnelles Feedback durch den Einsatz von ChatGPT.

Jedoch bringt die Verfügbarkeit von ChatGPT auch die Schwierigkeit für Lehrende mit sich, dass es bei traditionellen Schreibaufgaben als Hausübung schwierig ist, herauszufinden, ob bzw. welche Hilfswerkzeuge die Lernenden genutzt haben und „it becomes every day more difficult to ascertain how much of that content is the pure work of the student with no outside help, and therefore a bigger waste of the instructor's time to try to police it" (Lehman 2024, S. 173), weshalb laut Lehman reine Schreibaufgaben ohne

Hilfswerkzeuge im Unterricht gemacht werden sollten. Aus unserer Sicht ist es sinnvoll, neue Arten von Schreibaufgaben mit Hilfswerkzeugen als Hausübung zu geben, damit die wertvolle Unterrichtszeit für den direkten Austausch zwischen Lehrenden und Lernenden genutzt werden kann.

Für Lernende wird als größter Vorteil genannt, dass sie jederzeit sofortiges Feedback zu ihren Texten oder Übungen erhalten, was den Lernprozess beschleunigen kann. Allerdings wird auch in fast allen einschlägigen Beiträgen auf die Grenzen von ChatGPT in diesem Bereich hingewiesen. So erkennt ChatGPT im Vergleich zu Lehrenden subtile sprachliche Nuancen nicht immer korrekt und kann nicht immer kreative Lösungen für komplexe Probleme bieten, was darauf zurückgeführt werden kann, dass ChatGPT auf statistischen Modellen basiert und dadurch Schwierigkeiten haben kann, den spezifischen Kontext eines Texts vollständig zu erfassen. Außerdem hängt die Qualität der Korrekturvorschläge stark von den Trainingsdaten ab, auf denen ChatGPT basiert, welche sich zwischen den einzelnen Sprachen sehr stark unterscheiden (Statistics of Common Crawl Monthly Archives). So berichtet der Sprachwissenschaftler Antonelli (2024) in einem Webinar mit dem Titel *Gli autori raccontano* von einem Beispiel einer in Italienisch formulierten Anfrage über die Möglichkeit der Korrektur von Fehlern im geschriebenen Italienisch. Dazu hat er ChatGPT danach gefragt und die Antwort lautete wörtlich: *quando si notano errori o imprecisioni nella lingua, è importante sollevarli* .... Hier enthält bereits die Antwort von ChatGPT einen gravierenden Lexikfehler, denn das Verb *sollevare* ist in diesem Kontext nicht korrekt. Stattdessen sollte ein Begriff wie *segnalare*, *sottolineare*, *evidenziare* verwendet werden. Antonelli erklärt, er habe später versucht, den Satz mit einem maschinellen Übersetzungssystem ins Englische übersetzen zu lassen, und sei zu folgendem Ergebnis gekommen: *When you find errors, it is important to raise them*. Eine der Bedeutungen des englischen Verbes *to raise* ist im Italienischen *sollevare*. Die KI übersetzt in diesem Fall einfach aus ihrer Hauptsprache. Der Fehler kann also nicht auf eine der sogenannten „Halluzinationen" von ChatGPT zurückgeführt werden, sondern auf ein strukturelles Problem, das auch Tavosanis in seinem Artikel „Valutare la qualità dei testi generati in lingua italiana" (2024) feststellt. Nur durch den Versuch, den Satz vom Englischen ins Italienische rückübersetzen zu lassen, kam er zu der korrekten Form: *Quando si notano errori, è importante segnalarli*.

Die oben genannten Grenzen von ChatGPT führen oft zu fehlerhaftem oder lückenhaftem Feedback (Akinwalere/Ivanov 2022). Dies zeigt sich auch in der Studie von Bok und Cho (2023), welche die Erfahrungen koreanischer EFL-Studenten mit ChatGPT als Korrekturwerkzeug untersuchten. Die Ergebnisse brachten eine positive Resonanz der Studierenden, die das Feedback von ChatGPT als hilfreich und vertrauenswürdig empfanden. Es wurden jedoch auch Herausforderungen festgestellt, wie das Fehlen von Fehlerbeschreibungen und die manchmal unverständlichen Rückmeldungen der KI. Ähnlich äußern sich Restrepo und Reyes (2024), die darauf hinweisen, dass ChatGPT dabei helfen kann, offensichtliche Fehler zu identifizieren, aber bei komplexeren sprachlichen Nuancen oder kontextabhängigen Fehlerkorrekturen weniger zuverlässig ist. Deshalb heben Restrepo und Reyes (2024) hervor, dass Lehrende bei fehlenden oder falschen Korrekturen eingreifen müssen.

Die Kommentare von ChatGPT erfolgen oft in einem autoritären Stil, was dazu führen kann, dass Lernende diese kritiklos als richtig erachten (Kohnke/Moorhouse/Zou 2023, S. 545). Die Anerkennung von Chatbots als Autorität in sprachlichen (und auch anderen) Fragen birgt die Gefahr einer zunehmenden Abhängigkeit von Technologie, was oftmals bedeutet, dass Lernende weniger selbstständig denken und ihre eigenen Fähigkeiten zur Fehlererkennung und -korrektur nicht einschätzen können und vernachlässigen (Akinwalere/Ivanov 2022; Chukwuere 2023).

3.2 ChatGPT als Korrekturwerkzeug beim Sprachenlernen: Anwendungsbeispiele

Im Anschluss führen wir wieder einige Beispiele in den gewählten Sprachkombinationen an, um die Eignung von ChatGPT als Korrekturwerkzeug zu überprüfen.

Beispiel 1: Korrektur von Dialogen Italienisch (Niveau B1)

Wir haben ChatGPT nach der sprachlichen Korrektheit von Satzsequenzen gefragt, deren Verwendung in einem niedrigen bis mittleren Register des Italienischen häufig, aber aus grammatikalischen Gründen falsch ist[7].

[7] ChatGPT 3.5 am 11.04.2024

Der Prompt lautete: *Puoi valutare la correttezza linguistica di questa sequenza*:

· *Che regalo fai a Lucrezia?*
· *Ci do un mazzo di fiori.*

ChatGPT antwortete folgendermaßen: *La frase che hai scritto è quasi corretta, ma ha un piccolo errore di coniugazione verbale. L'uso di "do" dovrebbe essere sostituito con "dò" per essere grammaticalmente corretto, perché il verbo "dare" richiede un accento sulla prima persona singolare presente indicativo. Quindi, la frase corretta sarebbe:*

"Che regalo fai a Lucrezia?
Ci dò un mazzo di fiori."

Kommentar: Die Antwort ist nicht korrekt, da die Verbform *do* im obigen Beispiel korrekt und ohne Akzent verwendet wird. Hingegen wird der gröbste Fehler, nämlich die falsche Verwendung des Personalpronomens *ci*, anstelle dessen *le* verwendet werden sollte, nicht erkannt. Dies erkennt ChatGPT jedoch bei einer späteren Nachfrage, ob es sich sicher sei.

Beispiel 2: Korrektur von Sätzen Italienisch (B2)

In diesem Fall wollten wir von ChatGPT wissen, ob der folgende Satz richtig ist[8]:

Al matrimonio c'erano una trentina di invitati. Questa frase è corretta?

Die Antwort von ChatGPT lautet:
Sì, la frase "Al matrimonio c'erano una trentina di invitati" è corretta. Utilizza una forma comune in italiano per indicare approssimativamente il numero di persone presenti, in questo caso circa trenta invitati. L'espressione "una trentina" è usata per quantità approssimative intorno al trenta, e l'uso del verbo "c'erano" è appropriato per indicare la presenza di persone in un evento passato come un matrimonio.

---

[8] Als Prompt wurde die gleiche Frage gestellt: *Puoi valutare la correttezza linguistica di questa sequenza?* (ChatGPT 3.5 am 11.04.2024).

Kommentar: In diesem Fall treten bei ChatGPT sogenannte Halluzinationen auf. Es erkennt das kritische Element im Satz, nämlich das Pluralverb mit dem kollektiven Singularsubjekt, das einen Pluralpartitiv enthält, nicht. Es handelt sich um das wichtigste Bedeutungselement, das im sogenannten „Neostandard" in dieser Form akzeptiert wird; diese Varietät des Italienischen wird hauptsächlich mündlich, aber auch schriftlich in Texten niedriger und mittlerer Formalität verwendet (Berruto 1987).

Beispiel 3: Korrektur eines Texts Spanisch (Niveau B2)

In diesem Fall baten wir ChatGPT, einen Text auf Spanisch zu verfassen und dabei das Sprachniveau und die typischen Fehler eines Lernenden nachzuahmen[9]. Der erste Prompt lautete: *Schreibe einen Text auf Spanisch, GERS-Niveau B2. Der Text soll typische Fehler auf diesem Niveau beinhalten. Textlänge ca. 250 Wörter.* Im Text kamen typische Fehler für das B2-Niveau, wie zum Beispiel die Verwendung von *era* statt *fue*, die überflüssige Verwendung von *yo* am Anfang eines Satzes, sowie kleinere Grammatik- und Ausdrucksfehler vor. Danach wurde der Aufsatz von ChatGPT verbessert. Dafür wurde folgender Prompt verwendet: *Ich habe folgenden Text auf Spanisch verfasst. Das Niveau ist GERS-Niveau B2. Verbessere den Text und erkläre die Fehler und Verbesserungsvorschläge.* Insgesamt wurden sechs Stellen verbessert.

Erklärungen zu den Fehlern und Verbesserungen:

1. *"yo viajé" → "viajé": Das "yo" ist überflüssig, da das Verb schon die Person angibt.*
2. *"me ayudaron" → "me ayudó": "La gente" ist ein kollektives Substantiv und erfordert das Verb in der Einzahl.*
3. *"me sorprendió era" → "me sorprendieron fue": Die Mehrzahl von "cosas" erfordert "sorprendieron". Außerdem passt "fue" besser als "era", weil es sich um ein abgeschlossenes Ereignis handelt.*
4. *"También, tuve" → "También tuve": Das Komma nach "también" ist nicht notwendig.*
5. *"di cuenta que" → "di cuenta de que": Das Verb "darse cuenta" wird immer mit "de que" verwendet.*
6. *"quería decir 'la carta' para el menú" → "quería decir 'el menú'": Der korrekte Begriff für die Speisekarte ist "el menú", nicht "la carta".*

---

[9] ChatGPT 4 am 12.07.2024

Kommentar: Fünf von sechs Erklärungen zu den Fehlern und Verbesserungen waren hilfreich. Eine Verbesserung und Erklärung (Nummer 6) war nicht korrekt und verwirrend. Die Übersetzung von *die Speisekarte* ins Spanische ist laut PONS *la carta (del menú)*. Das *Diccionario de la Lengua Española* definiert *la carta* als *En un restaurante o establecimiento análogo, lista de platos y bebidas que se pueden elegir. El menú* wird als Synonym aufgelistet.

4. Fazit

In diesem Text haben wir überprüft, inwieweit ChatGPT als Tutor und Korrekturwerkzeug für das Erlernen der Sprachen Italienisch und Spanisch aus der Perspektive eines deutschsprachigen Lernenden geeignet ist. Spanisch und Italienisch zählen zu den *high resource* Sprachen (Statistics of Common Crawl Monthly Archives), weshalb für diese beiden Sprachen (sowie auch für Deutsch) eine große Menge an Sprachdaten zur Verfügung steht, die jedoch bei Weitem nicht an jene des Englischen heranreichen. Ebenso darf nicht vergessen werden, dass ChatGPT nicht für das Erlernen von Fremdsprachen entwickelt wurde und in vielen Fällen keine geeigneten Antworten für die spezifischen Bedürfnisse von Sprachenlernenden bietet. Verstärkt wird dies durch die Variabilität der Antworten von ChatGPT zwischen unterschiedlichen Anfragen, aber auch in einer einzigen Interaktion mit unterschiedlichen Prompts.

Auf die Frage, ob ChatGPT eine Tutorfunktion im Fremdsprachenunterricht ausüben kann, ziehen wir aus den obigen Ausführungen folgende Schlüsse: KI in dieser Form ist ein neuer Ansatz, dessen Verwendung noch einige Zeit brauchen wird, um vollständig und sinnvoll in den Sprachunterricht integriert zu werden. Es ist jedoch klar, dass sich die Zukunft des Unterrichts zunehmend auf die Synergie zwischen menschlicher Interaktion und Technologie konzentrieren wird, wodurch sich die Dynamik zwischen Lehrenden und Lernenden verändern wird. Eine Zusammenarbeit zwischen KI-Chatbots und menschlichen Lehrkräften wird es diesen ermöglichen, ihren Unterricht effektiver zu gestalten und die Interaktion mit den Lernenden zu intensivieren. Die Ergebnisse einer Studie von Wang et al. (2022) deuten jedoch darauf hin, dass nicht alle Lernenden gleichermaßen von der Nutzung von KI beim Sprachenlernen profitieren. Insgesamt konnten viele ihren Lernfortschritt durch KI-gestütztes Lernen verbessern, aber einige hatten Schwierigkeiten, effektive Methoden zu finden, um mit der KI zu arbeiten. Wang et al. heben daher hervor, dass Lehrkräfte die Interaktion der Lernenden mit der KI unterstützen sollten, anstatt sie „einfach der KI zu überlassen" (S. 14). Die Kompetenz, Erfahrung und das Verständnis der Lehrenden sind somit unerlässlich, um sachkundige didaktische Entscheidungen treffen zu können.

Die obigen Beispiele haben gezeigt, dass die Erklärungen, die ChatGPT Lernenden bietet, auch auf niedrigem Niveau nicht an jene von Lehrkräften (oder guten Grammatiken und Wörterbüchern) heranreichen. Problematisch war dabei vor allem das Nichterkennen von inexistenten Wortformen sowie die oberflächlichen und lückenhaften Erklärungen, die bei Lernenden Verwirrung oder sogar das Erlernen von falschen Formen und Äquivalenzen nach sich ziehen können. Ebenso ist zu beachten, dass die Qualität der Antwort in vielen Fällen von der Formulierung des Prompts abhängig ist, weshalb Lernende für die Nutzung von ChatGPT als Tutor zuerst Bewusstsein für die Nutzung dieses Tools und die Formulierung von effektiven Prompts entwickeln müssen. Beides kann vor allem im schulischen Kontext nicht vorausgesetzt werden.

Bezüglich der Funktion von ChatGPT als Korrekturwerkzeug kann gesagt werden, dass KI-gestützte Werkzeuge in vielerlei Hinsicht die Arbeitslast von Lehrenden reduzieren oder sogar bestimmte Aufgaben übernehmen können, die traditionell von Lehrkräften ausgeführt werden. Es kann den Lehrprozess effizienter gestalten und den Lernenden wertvolle, sofortige Rückmeldungen geben. Doch wie die erwähnten Beispiele verdeutlichen, bleibt die menschliche Anleitung in verschiedenen Bereichen nach wie vor unverzichtbar. Denn unsere Versuche haben gezeigt, dass einfache Fehler (z. B. Konjugationsfehler) von ChatGPT normalerweise leicht erkannt und korrigiert werden; nicht immer so ist es jedoch bei Fehlern, die den Sprachgebrauch betreffen. Die Erklärungen, die ChatGPT liefert, sind nicht immer hundertprozentig verlässlich und teilweise weitschweifig.

Zusammenfassend kann festgehalten werden, dass ChatGPT im Fremdsprachenunterricht sowohl erhebliche Chancen als auch Herausforderungen bietet. Deshalb muss sichergestellt werden, dass die Technologie sinnvoll und ergänzend eingesetzt wird, um die Eigenständigkeit der Lernenden zu fördern und die menschliche Komponente nicht zu ersetzen. Eine ausgewogene Integration von Large Language Models wie ChatGPT und menschlichem Feedback scheint der Schlüssel zum Erfolg im modernen Fremdsprachenunterricht zu sein.

Quellenverzeichnis

Akinwalere, Susan Nwadinachi / Ventsislav Ivanov (2022): „Artificial intelligence in Higher Education: Challenges and opportunities". *Border Crossing* 12(1), S. 1–15. https://doi.org/10.33182/bc.v12i1.2015.

Al Ka'bi, Amin (2023): „Proposed artificial intelligence algorithm and deep learning techniques for development of higher education". *International Journal of Intelligent Networks 4*, S. 68–73.

Andreu Lucas, Maribel / Berenguer, Laura / Orero, Pilar / Ripoll, Odile (2002): „Competéncia traductora i ensenyament de llengues estrangeres". *Quaderns. Revista de traducció* 7, S. 155–165.

Antonelli, Giuseppe (2024, 13. März): „Dall'e-taliano all'IA-taliano". Podcast: *Gli autori raccontano, Mondadori Education*, abgerufen am 15.01.2025 auf https://www.mondadorieducation.it/webinar-e-eventi/appuntamenti/dalle-taliano-allia-taliano/.

Arora, Sanjeev (2023): „Are language models mere stochastic parrots? The SkillMix test says NO". PLI Blog, abgerufen am 15.01.2025 auf https://pli.princeton.edu/blog/2023/are-language-models-mere-stochastic-parrots-skillmix-test-says-no.

Bender, Emily / Gebru, Timnit / McMillan-Major, Angelina / Shmitchell, Shmargaret (2021): „On the dangers of stochastic parrots: Can language models be too big?" In *Proceedings of the 2021 ACM conference on fairness, accountability, and transparency (FAccT '21)*. New York: Association for Computing Machinery, S. 610–623. https://doi.org/10.1145/3442188.3445922.

Berruto, Gaetano (1987): *Sociolinguistica dell'italiano contemporaneo*. Firenze: La Nuova Italia Scientifica.

Bok, Eunim / Cho, Youngsang (2023): „Examining Korean EFL college students' experiences and perceptions of using ChatGPT as a writing revision tool". *STEM Journal* 24(4), S. 15–27. https://doi.org/10.16875/stem.2023.24.4.15.

Cerezo Herrero, Enrique / Schmidhofer, Astrid (2021): „25 years of research on language training in TI programmes: Taking stock and ways forward". In: Schmidhofer, Astrid / Cerezo Herrero, Enrique (Hrsg.): *Foreign Language Training in Translation and Interpreting Programmes*. Berlin: Peter Lang, S. 17–44.

Chukwuere, Joshua Ebere (2023): *The use of ChatGPT in higher education: The advantages and disadvantages*, abgerufen am 24.05.2024 auf https://arxiv.org/pdf/2403.19245.

EMT Board (2022): *European Master's in Translation: Competence Framework 2022*, abgerufen am 20.10.2024 auf https://commission.europa.eu/system/files/2022-11/emt_competence_fwk_2022_en.pdf.

Fariani, Rida Indah / Junus, Kasiyah / Santoso, Harry Budi (2023): „A systematic literature review on personalised learning in the higher education context". *Technology, Knowledge and Learning* 28(2), S. 449–476.

Felix, Catherine V. (2020): „The role of the teacher and AI in education". In: Sengupta, Enakshi. / Blessinger, Patrick / Makhanya, Mandla S. (Hrsg.): *International perspectives on the role of technology in humanizing Higher Education*. Leeds: Emerald Publishing Limited, S. 33–48. https://doi.org/10.1108/S2055-364120200000033003.

Hurtado Albir, Amparo (Hrsg.) (2017): *Researching translation competence by PACTE group*. Amsterdam / Philadelphia: John Benjamins.

Kohnke, Lucas / Moorhouse, Benjamin Luke / Zou, Di (2023): „ChatGPT for Language Teaching and Learning". *RELC Journal* 54(2), S. 537–550. https://10.1177/00336882231162868.

Laupichler, Matthias Carl / Aster, Alexandra / Schirch, Jana / Raupach, Tobias (2022): „Artificial intelligence literacy in higher and adult education: A scoping literature review". *Computers and education: Artificial intelligence, Volume 3, 100101*. https://doi.org/10.1016/j.caeai.2022.100101.

Lehman, Will (2024): „Chat(bot)ing up a storm: How AI is changing the game of foreign language teaching". In: Grieb, Margit / Lehman, Will / Clemmen, Yves-Antoine (Hrsg.): *World languages and cultures in the public sphere: Selected proceedings of the 25th Southeast Conference on Languages, Literatures, and Film*. Irvine: BrownWalker Press, S. 165–174.

Luckin, Rosemary / Cukurova, Mutlu / Kent, Carmel / Du Boulay, Benedict (2022): „Empowering educators to be AI-ready". *Computers and Education: Artificial Intelligence, Volume 3, 100776*. https://doi.org/10.1016/j.caeai.2022.100076.

Pavlik, John V. (2023): „Collaborating with ChatGPT: Considering the implications of generative artificial intelligence for journalism and media education". *Journalism & Mass Communication Educator* 78(1), S. 84–93. https://doi.org/10.1177/10776958221149577.

Restrepo, Juan Sebastian / Reyes, Nicole Andrea (2024): *ChatGPT as a peer correction tool for language learners*, abgerufen am 1.10.2024 auf https://www.colomboamericano.edu.co/wp-content/uploads/2024/05/Research-Impacts-2024_WEB.pdf#page=99.

Schmidhofer, Astrid / Ahmann, Heiko (2015): „Translationsrelevanter Fremdsprachenunterricht: Besonderheiten und Zielsetzungen". *Moderne Sprachen* 59(1), S. 49–70.

Statistics of Common Crawl Monthly Archives: *Distribution of Languages*, abgerufen am 01.11.2024 auf https://commoncrawl.github.io/cc-crawl-statistics/plots/languages.

Tavosanis, Mirko (2024): „Valutare la qualità dei testi generati in lingua italiana". *AI-Linguistica. Linguistic Studies on AI-Generated Texts and Discourses* 1(1). https://doi.org/10.62408/ai-ling.v1i1.14.

UNESCO (2023): *ChatGPT and Artificial Intelligence in Higher Education*, abgerufen am 24.05.2024 auf https://unesdoc.unesco.org/ark:/48223/pf0000385146.

Wang, Xinghua / Liu, Qian / Pang, Hui / Tan, Seng Chee / Lei, Jun / Wallace, Matthew P. / Li, Linlin (2022): „What matters in AI-supported learning: A study of human-AI interactions in language learning using cluster analysis and epistemic network analysis". *Computers and Education* 194. https://doi.org/10.1016/j.compedu.2022.104703.

Xiao, Yangyu / Zhi, Yuying (2023): „An exploratory study of EFL learners' use of ChatGPT for language learning tasks: Experience and perceptions". *Languages* 8(3): S. 212. https://10.3390/languages8030212.

Forum Translationswissenschaft

Herausgegeben von / Edited by Lew N. Zybatow, Alena Petrova, Astrid Schmidhofer und / and Michael Ustaszewski

Band 1 Lew N. Zybatow (Hrsg.): Translation zwischen Theorie und Praxis. Innsbrucker Ringvorle-sungen zur Translationswissenschaft I. 2002.

Band 2 Lew N. Zybatow (Hrsg.): Translation in der globalen Welt und neue Wege in der Sprach- und Übersetzerausbildung. Innsbrucker Ringvorlesungen zur Translationswissenschaft II. 2004.

Band 3 Lew N. Zybatow (Hrsg.): Translationswissenschaft im interdisziplinären Dialog. Innsbrucker Ringvorlesungen zur Translationswissenschaft III. 2005.

Band 4 Peter Sandrini (Hrsg.): *Fluctuat nec mergitur.* Translation und Gesellschaft. Festschrift für Annemarie Schmid zum 75. Geburtstag. 2005.

Band 5 Lew N. Zybatow (Hrsg.): Translatologie – neue Ideen und Ansätze. Innsbrucker Ringvorlesungen zur Translationswissenschaft IV. 2005.

Band 6 Lew N. Zybatow (Hrsg.): Kulturelle Vorstellungswelten in Metaphern. Metaphorische Stereotypen der deutschen und russichen Medien als Hypertext. 2006.

Band 7 Lew N. Zybatow (Hrsg.): Sprach(en)kontakt – Mehrsprachigkeit – Translation. Innsbrucker Ringvorlesungen zur Translationswissenschaft V. 60 Jahre Innsbrucker Institut für Translationswissenschaft. 2007.

Band 8 Wolfgang Pöckl (Hrsg.): Im Brennpunkt: Literaturübersetzung. 2008.

Band 9 Assumpta Camps / Lew N. Zybatow (eds.): Traducción e interculturalidad. Actas de la Conferencia Internacional „Traducción e Intercambio Cultural en la Época de la Globalización", mayo de 2006, Universidad de Barcelona. 2008.

Band 10 Assumpta Camps / Lew N. Zybatow (eds.): La traducción literaria en la época contemporánea. Actas de la Conferencia Internacional „Traducción e Intercambio Cultural en la Época de la Globalización", mayo de 2006, Universidad de Barcelona. 2008.

Band 11 Lew N. Zybatow (Hrsg.): Translation: Neue Entwicklungen in Theorie und Praxis. Summer-Trans-Lektionen zur Translationswissenschaft. IATI-Beiträge I. 2009.

Band 12 Lew N. Zybatow (Hrsg.): Translationswissenschaft – Stand und Perspektiven. Innsbrucker Ringvorlesungen zur Translationswissenschaft VI. 2010.

Band 13 Saverio Carpentieri / Angelo Pagliardini / Barbara Tasser / Lew Zybatow (cur.): Italia e „Italie". Identità di un paese al plurale. 2010.

Band 14 Alexandra Vranceanu / Angelo Pagliardini (cur.): Migrazione e patologie dell'*humanitas* nella letteratura europea contemporanea. 2012.

Band 15 Lew N. Zybatow / Alena Petrova / Michael Ustaszewski (Hrsg./eds.): Translationswissenschaft interdisziplinär: Fragen der Theorie und Didaktik. Translation Studies: Interdisciplinary Issues in Theory and Didactics. Tagungsband der 1. Internationalen Konferenz TRANSLATA „Translationswissenschaft: gestern – heute – morgen", 12.-14. Mai 2011, Innsbruck. Proceedings of the 1st International Conference TRANSLATA "Translation & Interpreting Research: yesterday – today – tomorrow", May 12-14, 2011, Innsbruck. 2012.

Band 16 Lew N. Zybatow / Alena Petrova / Michael Ustaszewski (Hrsg./eds.): Translationswissenschaft: alte und neue Arten der Translation in Theorie und Praxis. Translation Studies: Old and New Types of Translation in Theory and Practice. Tagungsband der 1. Internationalen Konferenz TRANSLATA „Translationswissenschaft: gestern – heute – morgen", 12.-14. Mai 2011, Innsbruck. Proceedings of the 1st International Conference TRANSLATA "Translation & Interpreting Research: yesterday – today – tomorrow", May 12-14, 2011, Innsbruck. 2012.

Band 17 Lew N. Zybatow / Michael Ustaszewski (Hrsg.): Translationswissenschaftlicher Nachwuchs forscht. IATI-Beiträge II. 2012.

Band 18 Lew N. Zybatow / Michael Ustaszewski (Hrsg.): Bausteine translatorischer Kompetenz *oder* Was macht Übersetzer und Dolmetscher zu Profis? Innsbrucker Ringvorlesungen zur Translationswissenschaft VII. 2014.

Band 19 Lew N. Zybatow / Andy Stauder / Michael Ustaszewski (eds.): Translation Studies and Translation Practice: Proceedings of the 2nd International TRANSLATA Conference, 2014. Part 1. 2017.

Band 20 Lew N. Zybatow / Andy Stauder / Michael Ustaszewski (eds.): Translation Studies and Translation Practice: Proceedings of the 2nd International TRANSLATA Conference, 2014. Part 2. 2017.

Band 21 Lew N. Zybatow / Alena Petrova / Andy Stauder / Michael Ustaszewski (Hrsg.): Übersetzen und Dolmetschen: Berufsbilder, Arbeitsfelder, Ausbildung. Ein- und Ausblicke in ein sich wandelndes Berufsfeld der Zukunft. 70 Jahre Innsbrucker Institut für Translationswissenschaft. 2017.

Band 22 Lew N. Zybatow / Alena Petrova (Hrsg./eds.): Was ist und was soll Translationswissenschaft? Ausgewählte Beiträge der 3. Internationalen Konferenz zur Translationswissenschaft TRANSLATA III (Innsbruck 2017). Unter Mitarbeit von Lisa Lanthaler und Robert Lukenda / Redefining and Refocusing Translation and Interpreting Studies. Selected Papers from the 3rd International Conference on Translation and Interpreting Studies TRANSLATA III (Innsbruck 2017). In collaboration with Lisa Lanthaler and Robert Lukenda. 2020.

Band 23 Astrid Schmidhofer / Enrique Cerezo Herrero (eds.): Foreign Language Training in Translation and Interpreting Programmes. 2021.

Band 24 Josep Marco / Isabel Tello (eds.): Towards an Empirical Verification of the Gravitational Pull Hypothesis. Evidence from the COVALT Corpus. 2024.

Band 25 Alena Petrova, Bianca Prandi & Astrid Schmidhofer (Hrsg./eds.): Der Einfluss neuer Technologien auf die Ausbildung von Translatoren / The Influence of New Technologies on Translator and Interpreter Education. 2026.

www.peterlang.com

www.ingramcontent.com/pod-product-compliance
Ingram Content Group UK Ltd.
Pitfield, Milton Keynes, MK11 3LW, UK
UKHW041825100926
8556IPUK00002B/22

9 783631 917756